Beginning gRPC with ASP.NET Core 6

Build Applications using ASP.NET Core Razor Pages, Angular, and Best Practices in .NET 6

T0225045

Anthony Giretti

Apress®

Beginning gRPC with ASP.NET Core 6: Build Applications using ASP.NET Core Razor Pages, Angular, and Best Practices in .NET 6

Anthony Giretti
La Salle, QC, Canada

ISBN-13 (pbk): 978-1-4842-8007-2
https://doi.org/10.1007/978-1-4842-8008-9

ISBN-13 (electronic): 978-1-4842-8008-9

Managing Director, Apress Media LLC: Welmoed Spahr
Acquisitions Editor: Joan Murray
Development Editor: Laura Berendson
Coordinating Editor: Jill Balzano
Copyeditor: Bill McManus

Cover image designed by Freepik (www.freepik.com)

Distributed to the book trade worldwide by Springer Science+Business Media LLC, 1 New York Plaza, Suite 4600, New York, NY 10004. Phone 1-800-SPRINGER, fax (201) 348-4505, email orders-ny@springer-sbm.com, or visit www.springeronline.com. Apress Media, LLC is a California LLC and the sole member (owner) is Springer Science + Business Media Finance Inc (SSBM Finance Inc). SSBM Finance Inc is a **Delaware** corporation.

For information on translations, please e-mail booktranslations@springernature.com; for reprint, paperback, or audio rights, please e-mail bookpermissions@springernature.com.

Apress titles may be purchased in bulk for academic, corporate, or promotional use. eBook versions and licenses are also available for most titles. For more information, reference our Print and eBook Bulk Sales web page at https://www.apress.com/bulk-sales.

Any source code or other supplementary material referenced by the author in this book is available to readers on GitHub via the book's product page at https://github.com/Apress/beg-grpc-w-asp.net-core-6.

Printed on acid-free paper

Table of Contents

About the Author

Anthony Giretti is a senior lead software developer at OneOcean in Montreal, Canada. He is a technical leader and four-time Microsoft MVP award recipient. Anthony specializes in web technologies (17 years' experience) and .NET. His expertise in technology and IT, and a heartfelt desire to share his knowledge, motivates him to dive into and embrace any web project, complex or otherwise, in order to help developers achieve their project goals. He invites challenges such as performance constraints, high availability, and optimization with open arms. He is a certified MCSD who is passionate about his craft and always game for learning new technologies.

About the Technical Reviewer

 **Fiodar Sazanavets** is an experienced full-stack lead software engineer who mainly works with the Microsoft software development stack. The main areas of his expertise include ASP.NET (Framework and Core), SQL Server, Azure, Docker, Internet of Things (IoT), microservices architecture, and various front-end technologies.

Fiodar has built his software engineering experience while working in a variety of industries, including water engineering, financial, retail, railway, and defense. He has played a leading role in various projects and, as well as building software, his duties have included performing architectural and design tasks. He has also performed a variety of technical duties on clients' sites, such as in-house software development and deployment of both software and IoT hardware.

Fiodar is passionate about teaching other people programming skills. He has published a number of programming courses on various online platforms. Fiodar regularly writes about software development on his personal website, https://scientificprogrammer.net. He has also published a number of articles on other websites.

Acknowledgments

The completion of this book could not have been possible without the participation and assistance of many people and I would like to express my special thanks to them.

First, thanks to Camille Viot, my boss, for accommodating me so that I could overcome this immense challenge.

Next, I would like to thank my friend Dave Brock (Madison, Wisconsin) for both his moral but technical support; he was a great help when I felt overwhelmed by the magnitude of the task. I also thank him for reviewing my chapters one by one—many thanks for his contribution! Thanks also to Damien Vande Kerckhove for his technical support, which allowed me to adjust the shot when I was not going in the right direction. He was also an essential asset for ensuring this book was able to see the light of day.

I also thank all my family for their unwavering support. Finally, I would like to thank a special member of my family that I unfortunately lost recently; he was there every night next to me when I was writing my lines. Thank you, Ulysse, you helped me so much and kept me company.

Introduction

Take a new technological turn with gRPC and ASP.NET Core while discovering .NET 6, the latest release of the Microsoft .NET platform, and C# 10.

gRPC has become more and more famous because of its performance compared to JSON/XML APIs. In this book, you'll discover how to develop ASP.NET Core APIs with the gRPC specification, and gRPC will no longer be mysterious to you.

After you discover how gRPC works, you'll learn how to use it to build high-performance web applications with the best development standards. You'll use gRPC with various ASP.NET Core 6 project types such as Razor Pages and minimal APIs. You'll also discover gRPC-web and the great mix it does with Angular 12.

For Windows Communication Foundation (WCF) developers, you will learn how to migrate from WCF to gRPC by comparing the similarities and differences between the two frameworks.

We'll also explore using gRPC and gRPC-web with OpenId Connect authentication and authorization to secure your applications.

Let's go!

PART I

Getting Started with .NET 6

CHAPTER 1

Welcome to Modern .NET

.NET is 20 years old, having been introduced in 2002 with the release of the .NET Framework, .NET 1. Since then, it has evolved with the needs of the computing industry to become even faster, lightweight, and cross-platform. As I write this book, we are at a crossroads, if you will, of the original .NET Framework and the newer .NET Core framework coming together under one new .NET. Microsoft has recently released .NET 5 and .NET 6 in November 2021, and with it, you can build powerful web applications with ASP.NET Core 6.

For those of you who are already .NET developers, feel free to skip this chapter. For the rest of you, this chapter is designed to give you just enough history and background to provide some foundation for your learning moving forward. We'll cover the following topics:

- A brief history of .NET

- Modern .NET, a unified platform

- .NET schedule and what it means

- How to explore .NET 6

- Recap of C# 9 and introduction to C# 10

A Brief History of .NET

A .NET application is developed for and runs in one or more implementations of .NET. Implementations include the *.NET Framework, .NET Core, Mono*, .NET 5 and now *.NET 6*. There is an API specification common to several implementations of .NET, called *.NET Standard*. This section introduces these concepts.

© Anthony Giretti 2022
A. Giretti, *Beginning gRPC with ASP.NET Core 6*, https://doi.org/10.1007/978-1-4842-8008-9_1

.NET Framework

Since Microsoft's release of .NET 1, there have been nine releases of the .NET Framework, with seven of them released with a new version of Visual Studio. Two of these releases, .NET Framework 2.0 and .NET Framework 4.0, have upgraded the *Common Language Runtime (CLR)*, which runs .NET applications. When the CLR version is the same, new versions of the .NET Framework replace older versions. .NET Framework 4.8 is the latest version of the .NET Framework. Table 1-1 shows .NET Framework releases from .NET 1 to .NET 4.8.

Table 1-1. *All .NET Framework Versions Released*

Version	Release Date	Visual Studio Version
1.0 (major version)	2/13/2002	VS.NET
1.1 (minor version)	4/24/2003	VS.NET 2003
2.0 (major version)	11/7/2005	VS 2005
3.0 (major version)	11/6/2006	VS 2005
3.5 (major version)	11/19/2007	VS 2008
4.0 (major version)	4/12/2010	VS 2010
4.5 (major version)	8/15/2012	VS 2012
4.5.1 (minor version)	10/17/2013	VS 2013
4.5.2 (minor version)	5/5/2014	VS 2015
4.6 (major version)	7/20/2015	VS 2015
4.6.1 (minor version)	11/30/2015	VS 2015
4.6.2 (minor version)	8/2/2016	VS 2017
4.7 (major version)	4/5/2017	VS 2017
4.7.1 (minor version)	10/17/2017	VS 2017
4.7.2 (minor version)	4/30/2018	VS 2017
4.8 (major version)	4/18/2019	VS 2019

The .NET Framework was designed to develop Windows-only applications, as Windows is heavily reliant on the .NET Framework. Its successor, .NET Core, changed that by becoming open source software and providing cross-platform support.

.NET Core

In June 2016, Microsoft announced the .NET Core project, an open source, cross-platform successor with compatibility for Windows, macOS, and Linux. Since then, Microsoft has released two significant versions, .NET Core 2.0 and .NET Core 3.0, both of which have minor releases associated with them. .NET Core 3.1 is the latest version of .NET Core and will be supported until December 2022. Table 1-2 shows the .NET Core releases since 2016.

Table 1-2. *All .NET Core Versions Released*

Version	Release Date	Visual Studio Version
.NET Core 1.0 (major version)	6/27/2016	VS 2015
.NET Core 1.1 (minor version)	11/16/2016	VS 2017
.NET Core 2 (major version)	8/14/2017	VS 2017
.NET Core 2.1 (minor version)	5/30/2018	VS 2017
.NET Core 2.2 (minor version)	12/4/2018	VS 2019
.NET Core 3.0 (major version)	9/23/2019	VS 2019
.NET Core 3.1 (minor version)	12/3/2019	VS 2019

In addition to .NET Core and .NET Framework, Microsoft also maintains the *Mono* project, an open source implementation of Microsoft's .NET Framework. Launched in 2004 to allow developers to create cross-platform applications easily, it's based on the *European Computer Manufacturers Association (ECMA)* standards for C# and the CLR.

Note   ECMA is a European nonprofit organization responsible for defining IT standards, both for hardware and software (programming languages), ECMAScript being the most famous standard developed by this organization. ECMA is also known for having developed the *Near Field Communication (NFC)* standard.

When it comes to API surface area, .NET Core 3 is not as robust as .NET Framework 4.8, a mature platform with a 15-year head start. However, Microsoft has added about 50,000 .NET APIs to the .NET Core platform to date. To continue closing this gap, Microsoft has built on the efforts made with .NET Core and taken the best of Mono to create a unique platform that you can use for all your .NET programs: .NET 5 and so on with .NET 6.

Microsoft has named this new version simply *.NET 5* (and then .NET 6) so as not to confuse developers, because it's *not* the successor to .NET Framework 4.8.

.NET Standard

In 2011, Microsoft released the *Portable Class Libraries (PCL)*, which are binaries that are compatible with many frameworks. PCLs were a significant improvement because they were supported by several runtimes such as Mono, *Universal Windows Platform (UWP)*, and .NET. In the meantime, it was hard to find information on what APIs were available or not. To help with this confusion, .NET Standard was born.

.NET Standard is a bunch of APIs implemented by the *Base Class Library (BCL)*. It's a specification of .NET APIs that proposes a unified set of contracts that you can compile in your compatible projects. These contracts are implemented in several .NET implementations. Various .NET implementations target specific versions of .NET Standard. Table 1-3 shows the minimum implementation versions that support each .NET Standard version.

Table 1-3. *All .Net Standard Versions Supported by .NET Implementations*

.NET Standard Versions	1.0	1.1	1.2	1.3	1.4	1.5	1.6	2.0	2.1
.NET Core	1.0	1.0	1.0	1.0	1.0	1.0	1.0	3.0	3.1
.NET Framework	4.5	4.5	4.5.1	4.6	4.6.1	4.6.1	4.6.1	4.6.1	N/A
Mono	4.6	4.6	4.6	4.6	4.6	4.6	4.6	5.4	6.4
Xamarin.iOS	10.0	10.0	10.0	10.0	10.0	10.0	10.0	10.14	12.16
Xamarin.Mac	3.0	3.0	3.0	3.0	3.0	3.0	3.0	3.8	5.16
Xamarin.Android	7.0	7.0	7.0	7.0	7.0	7.0	7.0	8.0	10.0
UWP	10.0	10.0	10.0	10.0	10.0	10.0.x	10.0.x	10.0.x	N/A
Unity	2018.1	2018.1	2018.1	2018.1	2018.1	2018.1	2018.1	2018.1	N/A

.NET 6 implements .NET Standard 2.1 (and earlier), which is not deprecated, but .NET 6 (unified across platforms) is the new Microsoft implementation of .NET to share code between .NET projects.

Modern .NET: A Unified Platform

Released in November 2020, .NET 5 is the next major evolution of .NET after .NET Core. The later has been followed by .NET 6 released in November 2022. You can now create various applications with the same runtime, allowing uniformity in the execution behaviors of your .NET applications, all with a homogeneous development experience (single code base). Therefore, code in your applications and your project files will look similar regardless of the type of your project. To make all this possible, .NET 5 & NET 6 combines the best of .NET Core and Mono. Figure 1-1 shows the unified ecosystem of .NET 5. In November 2021, .NET 6 has came and offers everything that has been brought by .NET 5 plus huge features like *Multi-platform App UI (MAUI)* and *ahead-of-time (AOT)* compilation.

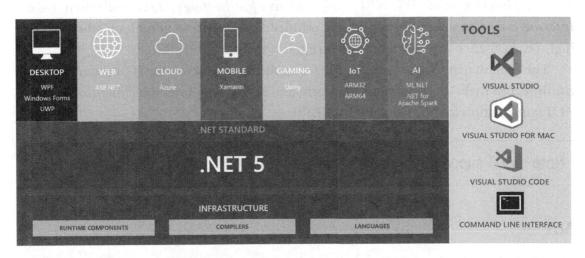

Figure 1-1. .NET 5/6 unified ecosystem (source: Microsoft)

Note   .NET 5 was released after this diagram was released. Since then, Microsoft pushed the launch of Xamarin in the .NET unified platform to .NET 6.

Mono and CoreCLR

We'll discuss two different development experiences with .NET: .NET with Mono and .NET with CoreCLR.

Differences and Commonalities

Mono is the cross-platform implementation of .NET. It started as an open source alternative to the .NET Framework and made the transition to targeting mobile devices like iOS and Android much easier. Mono is the runtime used to run Xamarin. Mono allows developers to run .NET applications cross-platform (even older game consoles such as PlayStation 3 and Xbox 360) and provides powerful development tools for Linux. *Core Common Language Runtime (CoreCLR)* is the runtime used as part of .NET Core.

.NET Core and Mono have a lot of similarities but also many differences. As a developer, you have the capability to select the desired development experience you want while making the switch from one to the other as straightforward as possible.

JIT

Since the beginning of .NET, .NET was based on a *just-in-time (JIT)* compiler to translate *Intermediate Language (IL)* code into optimized code. Microsoft built an efficient, high-performance runtime that made programming easy and efficient.

The default experience for most .NET 6 applications will use the JIT-based CoreCLR runtime, but there are exceptions: Xamarin and Blazor WebAssembly. Microsoft delivers *AOT* compilation for both projects in .NET 6.

Note   AOT support has been planned for .NET 5 but finally postponed to .NET 6.

AOT

The Mono compiler is an AOT compiler that allows you to compile native code that can be executed everywhere. The Blazor project uses Mono AOT compilation since .NET 6. However, AOT compilation is required for Xamarin (Android/iOS) and gaming consoles (Unity). AOT compilation is mostly intended for applications that need a quick start and a small footprint.

The Best of Both Worlds

Microsoft will invest effort in improving throughput and reliability in CoreCLR while working further to improve bootability and memory consumption with the Mono AOT compiler.

Since the effort is not identical in these aspects, this doesn't mean that the investment in others will be different. For example, the diagnostic capabilities must be the same on .NET 6 for all kinds of diagnostics.

Finally, all .NET 6 applications will also build with the *.NET command-line interface (.NET CLI)*, providing developers the same command-line tools.

.NET Schedule and What It Means

.NET 6 will be *supported in the long term (LTS release),* unlike .NET 5, which is why many companies have waited for .NET 6 instead of jumping on .NET 5. Only even-numbered versions will be supported in the long term. Finally, Microsoft plans to release no (or few) minor versions, and instead intends to release a major version of .NET once a year. Figure 1-2 shows Microsoft's .NET release cadence.

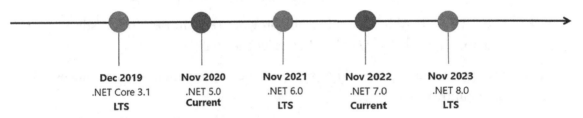

Figure 1-2.   .NET release cadence (source: Microsoft)

To stay informed about upcoming releases, support information, and .NET release schedules, visit the Microsoft page ".NET and .NET Core Support Policy": `https://dotnet.microsoft.com/platform/support/policy/dotnet-core`.

How to Explore .NET 6

While this chapter aims to introduce you to .NET 6, this book will not cover this framework in detail. The primary focus of this book is to help you learn how to begin using gRPC and ASP.NET Core 6. However, I will list some notable improvements made since .NET Core 3.1 and explain why they are so good, then show you how to install .NET 6 so you can take full advantage. Because .NET 5 is a lightweight version of .NET 6, I will recap what .NET 5 introduced so that you understand why .NET 6 and its improvements make it a modern .NET platform.

.NET 5 and 6 Improvements

Before .NET 5, Microsoft was responsible for maintaining about 100 repositories between ASP.NET Core, .NET Core, and Entity Framework Core—making things quite difficult. Microsoft has significantly simplified this by offering three consolidated repositories; if you want to find out more about .NET 6 (or even contribute to the open source projects), you can visit the following repositories, which will make it easier for you to understand what's going on and what you can do if you want to contribute:

- The runtime, which combines the previous repositories dotnet/corefx, dotnet/coreclr, and dotnet/core-setup (`https://github.com/dotnet/runtime`)

- ASP.NET Core, which combines several repositories from the ASP.NET organization (`https://github.com/dotnet/aspnetcore`)

- The .NET SDK, which combines the previous repositories dotnet/sdk and dotnet/cli (`https://github.com/dotnet/sdk`)

In terms of performance, .NET 5 has several huge improvements, which makes .NET 6 (and 5) significantly faster:

- Much more efficient machine code generated by the JIT compiler. While I can't list them all here, the following is the GitHub repository if you want to know more: `https://github.com/dotnet/runtime`

- Many improvements to the garbage collector (GC).

- Improved HTTP/1.1 and HTTP/2 performance.

- Improved performance of extensions on strings (two to five times faster).

- Performance improvement for ARM64-type processors.

- Reduction in the size of container images such as Docker.

The list of other improvements is too extensive to include here. However, you can check out the interesting links on Microsoft's blog detailing their announcements as the previews were released: `https://devblogs.microsoft.com/dotnet/`.

Regarding .NET 6 specifically, here is what it offers:

- Support of HTTP/3, which offers development opportunities in the web world

- Unification of Xamarin through MAUI, which provides a unified .NET experience across many devices

- AOT compilation in MAUI and Blazor, which makes applications faster because the code is not compiled at the first application execution (which can cause slowness)

- Hot reload, which allows you to modify your code without restarting your app, making the development experience faster

Get Started with .NET 6

Now let's take a quick tour of .NET. Before we get started, you will want to set up your environment. If you haven't already done so, go ahead and download Visual Studio 2022 from here: `https://visualstudio.microsoft.com/vs/`. The latter included all what you need to get started, even the .NET 6 SDK.

Now that you have your environment set up, let's begin by looking at the templates you can use in Visual Studio 2022. Figure 1-3 shows the main Visual Studio project creation window with all available project types.

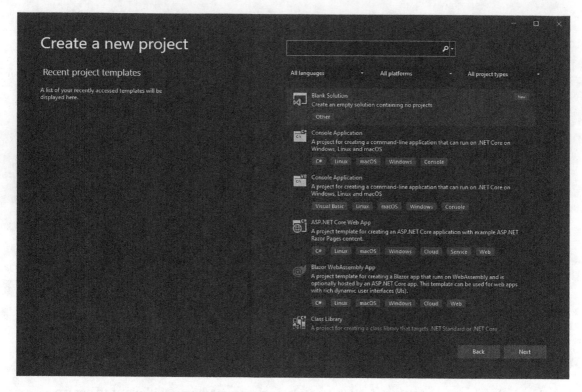

Figure 1-3. *Visual Studio 2022 main project creation window*

Visual Studio 2022 introduced a great context menu to choose the language, the project type, and the platform you want to use for your new project, as shown in Figure 1-4.

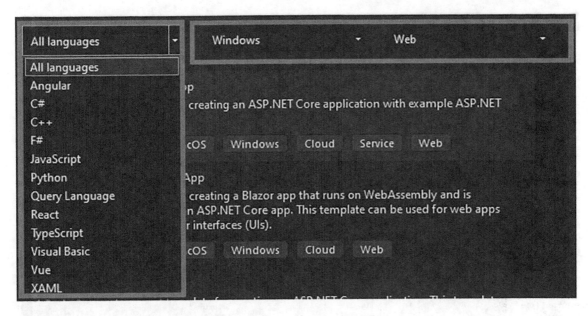

Figure 1-4. *Visual Studio's 2022 context menu*

If you prefer, you can also use the .NET CLI to get the same information by opening a terminal window and entering the following:

```
dotnet new --list
```

The output of this command is shown in Figure 1-5.

```
Admin: C:\WINDOWS\system32 - PowerShell 5.1 (52272)                                    —    □    ✕
C:\WINDOWS\system32> dotnet new --list
These templates matched your input:


Template Name                                Short Name          Language      Tags
-------------------------------------------  ------------------  ----------    -----------------------------------
ASP.NET Core Empty                           web                 [C#],F#       Web/Empty
ASP.NET Core gRPC Service                    grpc                [C#]          Web/gRPC
ASP.NET Core Web API                         webapi              [C#],F#       Web/WebAPI
ASP.NET Core Web App                         webapp,razor        [C#]          Web/MVC/Razor Pages
ASP.NET Core Web App (Model-View-Controller) mvc                 [C#],F#       Web/MVC
ASP.NET Core with Angular                    angular             [C#]          Web/MVC/SPA
ASP.NET Core with React.js                   react               [C#]          Web/MVC/SPA
ASP.NET Core with React.js and Redux         reactredux          [C#]          Web/MVC/SPA
Blazor Server App                            blazorserver        [C#]          Web/Blazor
Blazor WebAssembly App                       blazorwasm          [C#]          Web/Blazor/WebAssembly/PWA
Class Library                                classlib            [C#],F#,VB    Common/Library
Console Application                          console             [C#],F#,VB    Common/Console
dotnet gitignore file                        gitignore                         Config
Dotnet local tool manifest file              tool-manifest                     Config
EditorConfig file                            editorconfig                      Config
global.json file                             globaljson                        Config
MSTest Test Project                          mstest              [C#],F#,VB    Test/MSTest
MVC ViewImports                              viewimports         [C#]          Web/ASP.NET
MVC ViewStart                                viewstart           [C#]          Web/ASP.NET
NuGet Config                                 nugetconfig                       Config
NUnit 3 Test Item                            nunit-test          [C#],F#,VB    Test/NUnit
NUnit 3 Test Project                         nunit               [C#],F#,VB    Test/NUnit
Protocol Buffer File                         proto                             Web/gRPC
Razor Class Library                          razorclasslib       [C#]          Web/Razor/Library/Razor Class Library
Razor Component                              razorcomponent      [C#]          Web/ASP.NET
Razor Page                                   page                [C#]          Web/ASP.NET
Solution File                                sln                               Solution
Web Config                                   webconfig                         Config
Windows Forms App                            winforms            [C#],VB       Common/WinForms
Windows Forms Class Library                  winformslib         [C#],VB       Common/WinForms
Windows Forms Control Library                winformscontrollib  [C#],VB       Common/WinForms
Worker Service                               worker              [C#],F#       Common/Worker/Web
WPF Application                              wpf                 [C#],VB       Common/WPF
WPF Class library                            wpflib              [C#],VB       Common/WPF
WPF Custom Control Library                    wpfcustomcontrollib [C#],VB       Common/WPF
WPF User Control Library                      wpfusercontrollib   [C#],VB       Common/WPF
xUnit Test Project                           xunit               [C#],F#,VB    Test/xUnit

C:\WINDOWS\system32>
```

Figure 1-5. *All available project types and languages from the command line*

Personally, I like both ways to create a project. Both are simple. Let's now create a new project named **MyMVCApp**, where -o allows to specify the project name (and its folder name), which uses an ASP.NET MVC template with the command as seen here:

```
dotnet new mvc -o MyMVCApp
```

The command output is shown in Figure 1-6.

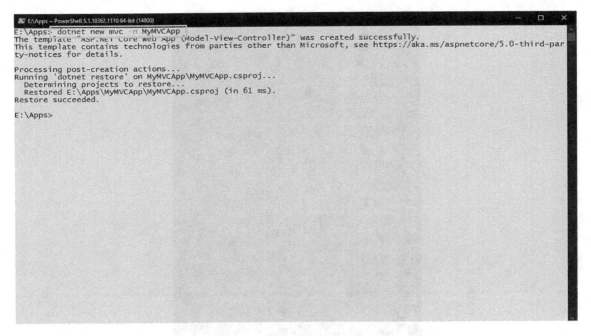

Figure 1-6. *The output generated after creating a new project with the .NET CLI*

To confirm your project is set up to use .NET 6, you can build it by running the following command:

```
dotnet build
```

Or, if you want to build and run your project, you can use the following command:

```
dotnet run
```

You can integrate the new Windows Terminal with Visual Studio. To enable it in Visual Studio 2022, click the View menu and choose Terminal, as shown in Figure 1-7.

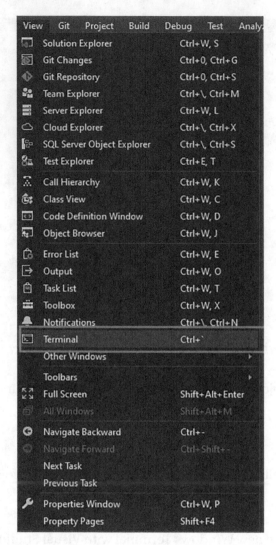

Figure 1-7. *Enabling the new Windows Terminal in Visual Studio 2022*

Once completed, the terminal window appears in the bottom panel. Then, you'll be able to run any command you want—such as PowerShell, Git, and CLI commands, as shown in Figure 1-8.

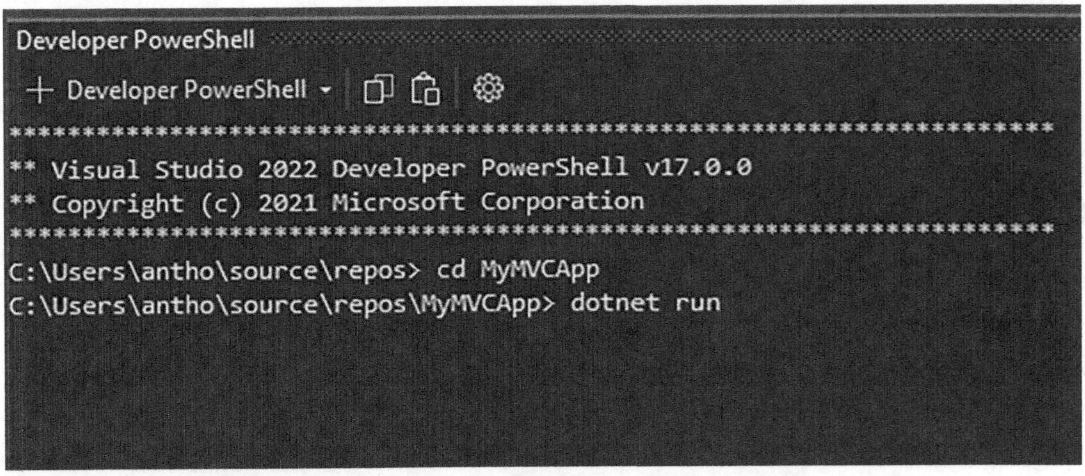

```
Developer PowerShell
+  Developer PowerShell  ▾    ⧉  ⧉    ⚙
*********************************************************************
** Visual Studio 2022 Developer PowerShell v17.0.0
** Copyright (c) 2021 Microsoft Corporation
*********************************************************************
C:\Users\antho\source\repos> cd MyMVCApp
C:\Users\antho\source\repos\MyMVCApp> dotnet run
```

Figure 1-8. *Running a command in the terminal window*

It's is my favorite feature because I don't need to open a new window on my computer. I don't know about you, but I find it a bit annoying to deal with multiple windows. On Visual Studio, no problem! The Terminal is integrated into the existing menu, positioned by default at the bottom of the menu, and you can easily drag it and drop it elsewhere!

Recap of C# 9 and Introduction to C# 10

We can't discuss the C# language without mentioning the latest updates with C# 9 and C# 10. Although this isn't a C# programming book, I'll help you discover the new features because most of my examples use C# 9 and C# 10 features. Going into detail about each version of C# is beyond the scope of this book, so I strongly recommend that you visit this web page that describes all the C# versions and their main features: `https://docs.microsoft.com/en-us/dotnet/csharp/whats-new/csharp-version-history`.

Recap of C# 9

Here are the most important improvements introduced in C# 9:

- Init-only properties

- Records

- Improved pattern matching

17

- Improved target typing

- Covariant returns

- Static anonymous functions

Init-Only Properties

C# 9 introduced an init accessor, a variant of the set accessor. This accessor allows
properties to be assigned once during object initialization. If you apply this accessor to
all the properties of your object, it makes the object immutable. If you try to reassign a
property initialized with this accessor, the compiler will warn you of an error. Listing 1-1
shows an example of a Product class with its immutable CategoryId property; this code
could be created in any C# project.

Listing 1-1. Product Class with CategoryId Property and Its init Accessor

```
using System;
namespace CSharp9Demo.Models
{
    public class Product
    {
        public string Name { get; set; }
        public int CategoryId { get; init; }
    }
}
```

Records

C# 9 added a new record keyword. A record makes it possible to create an immutable
reference type object (either with the init accessor or a primary constructor) and give it
a value type object for comparison. Listing 1-2 shows an immutable record with init-
only properties, and Listing 1-3 shows an immutable record with a primary constructor.

Listing 1-2. Immutable Product Record with `init`-Only Properties

```
using System;
namespace CSharp9Demo.Models
{
    public record Product
    {
        string Name { get; init; }
        int CategoryId { get; init; }
    }
}
```

Listing 1-3. Immutable Product Record with a Primary Constructor

```
using System;

namespace CSharp9Demo.Models
{
    public record Product(string Name, int CategoryId);
}
```

Suppose you want to create a new object from another object because the new object requires all but one of the same property values. Unfortunately, your existing object is immutable. The with keyword fixes that. It allows you to create an object from another object and specify which properties to change; Listing 1-4 shows an example of the usage of the with keyword.

Listing 1-4. Example of the Use of the with Keyword

```
var product = new Product
        {
            Name = "VideoGame",
            CategoryId = 1
        };

var newProduct = product with { CategoryId = 2 };
```

Interestingly, the record keyword makes the virtual Equals method overridden and allows value-based comparison between records. On that point, it behaves as a *struct*, but it's not. Records may be appreciated for that possibility. Listing 1-5 shows an example of a comparison between two records.

Listing 1-5. Records Comparison

```
var product = new Product
{
    Name = "VideoGame",
    CategoryId = 1
}

var anotherProduct = new Product
{
    Name = "VideoGame",
    CategoryId = 1
};

product.Equals(anotherProduct); // returns true
```

I love that feature, and I try to use the record keyword as much as I can. I often use it on *Data Transfert Object (DTO)* to carry data between layers because they must not mutate, and I can enforce immutability easily

Improved Pattern Matching

First introduced with C# 6, pattern matching has evolved. C# 8, released in 2019, brought many pattern-matching improvements. Miguel Bernard has an excellent article on the C# 8 improvements: https://blog.miguelbernard.com/pattern-matching-in-csharp/. If you want a primer on the C# 8 features, check out his great series here: https://blog.miguelbernard.com/csharp-8-0-new-features/.

C# 9 allows you to use relational patterns, enabling the usage of <, >, <=, and >=, and allows you to use logical operators such as and, or, and not—and the great thing is they can be combined!

Listing 1-6 shows a tax selector depending on the CategoryId property of a Product object.

Listing 1-6. Tax Selector Using C# 9 Improved Pattern Matching

```csharp
using System;

namespace CSharp9Demo
{
    class Program
    {
        static void Main(string[] args)
        {
            var product = new Product { Name = "Food", CategoryId = 4 };
            GetTax(product); // Returns 5
        }

        // Relational pattern combined with logical patterns
        private static int GetTax(Product p) => p.CategoryId switch
        {
            0 or 1 => 0,
            > 1 and < 5 => 5,
            > 20 => 15,
            _ => 10
        };
    }

    public class Product
    {
        public string Name { get; set; }
        public int CategoryId { get; set; }
    }
}
```

The not pattern is also making an appearance—you'll see the not logical operator can also be used in an if statement (it also works with a ternary statement). Listing 1-7 shows a discount selector based on an object type, ElectronicProduct, which is a Product child object.

Listing 1-7. Discount Selector Using the not Pattern

```
using System;

namespace CSharp9Demo
{
    class Program
    {
        static void Main(string[] args)
        {
            var product = new Product { Name = "Food", CategoryId = 4 };
            GetDiscount(product); // Returns 25
            GetDiscountTernary(product); // Returns 25
        }

        // Not pattern
        private static int GetDiscount (Product p)
        {
            if (p is not ElectronicProduct)
                return 25;

            return 0;
        }

        private static int GetDiscountTernary (Product p) => p is not
        ElectronicProduct ? 25 : 0;
    }

    public class Product
    {
        public string Name { get; set; }
        public int CategoryId { get; set; }
    }

    public class ElectronicProduct : Product
    {
    }
}
```

Improved Target Typing

With C# 9, Microsoft improved target typing: "In C# 9.0 some expressions that weren't previously target typed become able to be guided by their context" (https://devblogs. microsoft.com/dotnet/welcome-to-c-9-0/#improved-target-typing).

You can now infer the object type you are instantiating, meaning you don't have to write the object type on the right side of the new keyword. You can't combine it with the var keyword, but you can combine it with a conditional statement. In other words, you can't infer types on both sides of the equal sign.

Listing 1-8 shows an omitted type on instantiating Book and Headset classes and comparing them with a conditional operator (not allowed before C# 9). Both examples use Product as a base type.

Listing 1-8. Omitted Type and Conditional Operator Usage on Book and Headset Objects

```
namespace CSharp9Demo
{
    class Program
    {
        static void Main(string[] args)
        {
            Book aBook = new ("gRPC", 1);
            Headset headset = new ("Logitech", 2);
            Product anotherProduct = aBook ?? headset;
        }
    }

    public class Product
    {
        private string _name;
        private int _categoryId;

        public Product(string name, int categoryId)
        {
            _name = name;
```

```
            _categoryId = categoryId;
        }
    }
}

    public class Book : Product
    {
    }

    public class Headset : Product
    {
    }
}
```

Covariant Returns

One of the most underrated features of C# 9 is covariant returns. Usually, in C#, when you inherit from a class, you can override a method if it is declared abstract or virtual, but you can't change the return type of this method. C# 9 allows you to do this. In addition to overriding a virtual or abstract method, you can now return a covariant type of the initial type declared in the parent class.

Listing 1-9 shows a covariant return usage on the Book class, inheriting from the Product abstract class. The abstract Order method that returns a ProductOrder object can be overridden within the Book class by returning a BookOrder object that inherits from the ProductOrder class.

Listing 1-9. Covariant Return Usage on Order Method of the Book Class

```
public abstract class Product
{
    protected string Name { get; }
    protected int Id { get; }

    protected Product(string name, int id)
    {
        Name = name;
        Id = id;
    }
```

```csharp
    public abstract ProductOrder Order(int quantity);
}

public class Book : Product
{
    public string ISBN { get; }

    public Book(string name, int categoryId, string Isbn) : base(name,
    categoryId)
    {
        ISBN = Isbn;
    }

    public override BookOrder Order(int quantity) => new BookOrder {
    Quantity = quantity, Product = this };
}

public class ProductOrder
{
    public int Quantity { get; set; }
}

public class BookOrder : ProductOrder
{
    public Book Product { get; set; }
}
```

Static Anonymous Functions

In C# 9, Microsoft introduced an important improvement to anonymous functions by allowing the static modifier on them, bringing us static anonymous functions! Why? Because allocation matters! The Microsoft DevBlogs article "Dissecting the local functions in C# 7" explains as follows why lambdas bring a cost (https://devblogs. microsoft.com/premier-developer/dissecting-the-local-functions-in-c-7/):

"If you ever work on a performance critical application, then you know that anonymous methods are not cheap:

- Overhead of a delegate invocation (very small, but it does exist).

- 2 heap allocations if a lambda captures local variable or argument of enclosing method (one for closure instance and another one for a delegate itself).

- 1 heap allocation if a lambda captures an enclosing instance state (just a delegate allocation).

- 0 heap allocations only if a lambda does not capture anything or captures a static state."

Listing 1-10 shows the contextual private property _text captured by the anonymous function, which can cause unintended allocation consequences.

Listing 1-10. Example of Unintended Memory Allocation on the Contextual _text Variable

```
using System;

namespace CSharp9Demo
{
    class Program
    {
        private string _text = "{0} is a beautiful product !";
        static void Main()
        {
            PromoteProduct(product => string.Format(this._text, "Surface
            book 3"));
        }

        private void PromoteProduct(Func<string, string> func)
        {
            Console.WriteLine(func(country));
        }
    }
}
```

C# 9 fixed that. Listing 1-11 shows the fix achieved by applying the `const` keyword on the _text variable and by adding the `static` keyword to the lambda expression.

Listing 1-11. Example of the Unintended Memory Allocation Fix on the Contextual _text Variable

```csharp
using System;

namespace CSharp9Demo
{
    class Program
    {
        private const string _text = "{0} is a beautiful product !";
        static void Main()
        {
            PromoteProduct(static product => string.Format(this._text,
            "Surface book 3"));
        }

        private void PromoteProduct(Func<string, string> func)
        {
            Console.WriteLine(func(country));
        }
    }
}
```

Top-Level Programs

C# 9 introduced a fun and practical feature: top-level programs. A top-level program is the simplest way to write a program on its top level. Concretely in your .NET 5+ applications, you'll be able to write a lighter `Program.cs` file. This feature allows you to remove all enclosing declarations (`namespace` declaration, `Program` class declaration, `Main` method declaration).

Everything works the same (accessing arguments, making async calls, declaring local functions, etc.). Listing 1-12 shows a lighter `Program.cs` file in ASP.NET Core 5 where the application namespace is named `CountryService.Web`.

Listing 1-12. Top-Level Programs in ASP.NET Core 5

```
using CountryService.Web;
using Microsoft.AspNetCore.Hosting;
using Microsoft.Extensions.Hosting;

CreateHostBuilder(args).Build().Run();

static IHostBuilder CreateHostBuilder(string[] args) =>
Host.CreateDefaultBuilder(args)
    .ConfigureWebHostDefaults(webBuilder =>
    {
        webBuilder.UseStartup<Startup>();
    });
```

Before ASP.NET Core 5, you would have written your `Program.cs` file as shown in Listing 1-13.

Listing 1-13. `Program.cs` File Before ASP.NET Core 5

```
using Microsoft.AspNetCore.Hosting;
using Microsoft.Extensions.Hosting;

namespace CountryService.Web
{
    public class Program
    {
        public static void Main(string[] args)
        {
            CreateHostBuilder(args).Build().Run();
        }

        public static IHostBuilder CreateHostBuilder(string[] args) =>
            Host.CreateDefaultBuilder(args)
                .ConfigureWebHostDefaults(webBuilder =>
                {
                    webBuilder.UseStartup<Startup>();
                });
    }
}
```

In C# 10, this feature has been improved so that the `Startup.cs` file is no longer helpful for the `Program.cs` file is sufficient on its own, and I'll show you that in the next section.

Introduction to C# 10

C# 10 is the major new version of C # shipped with .NET 6, and following on from C# 9, it brings remarkable changes, not to say a real breakthrough in coding .NET applications. C# 10 includes the following most important features:

- Global usings

- File-scoped namespaces

- Record struct

- Improved top-level program

Global Usings

C# 10 brings an attractive feature that will simplify and lighten your C# files: global usings. What is a global using? It's simply a manner to declare once a `using` statement in a single C# project. In this way, you can create a single file and declare globally all the needed `using` statements for your project. This simplifies your code greatly, and you no longer need to repeat the `using` statement across files. To declare a `using` statement as global, you have to write it like this:

```
global using AssemblyToImport;
```

For example, it could give the following as shown on Listing 1-14 if you decide to declare all usings in a single file. I prefer to name it `GlobalUsings.cs`, which is meaningful, and you'll find this convention in several chapters in this book.

Listing 1-14. Declaring All Necessary Usings in the Same File

```
global using System;
global using System.Threading.Tasks;
global using System.IO;
global using System.IO.Compression;
global using System.Collections.Generic;
```

```
global using System.Linq;
global using Microsoft.Data.SqlClient;
global using Microsoft.EntityFrameworkCore;
global using Microsoft.Extensions.Logging;
global using Microsoft.AspNetCore.Hosting;
global using Microsoft.AspNetCore.Builder;
global using Microsoft.AspNetCore.Http;
global using Microsoft.Extensions.DependencyInjection;
global using Microsoft.Extensions.Configuration;
```

Convenient, isn't it?

File-Scoped Namespaces

Still, to continue with the simplification of the code, I suggest you discover another feature of C# 10 that you will often review in this book: file-scoped namespaces. Namespaces declared in a file (without braces, but whose instruction ends with a semicolon) will apply to all elements declared in the same file. It's practical, and it lightens the code. However, there is a limitation: only one namespace can be declared in the file. I love this new feature of C# 10, and I'm sure you'll love it too. Listing 1-15 shows a sample of a file-scoped namespace. The CountryModel class is defined in another file.

Listing 1-15. Example of a File-Scoped Namespace

```
namespace CountryService.gRPC.Mappers;

public static class CountryReplyMapper
{
    public static CountryReply ToReply(this CountryModel country)
    {
        if (country is null)
            return null;

        var countryReply = new CountryReply
        {
            Id = country.Id,
            Name = country.Name,
            Description = country.Description,
```

```
        Anthem = country.Anthem,
        CapitalCity = country.CapitalCity,
        FlagUri = country.FlagUri
    };
    countryReply.Languages.AddRange(country.Languages);

    return countryReply;
    }
}
```

Combined with the global usings feature, file-scoped namespaces results in much more readable C# files.

Record struct

In .NET 5 and C# 9, the record keyword is applied only to classes. Starting with .NET 6 and C# 10, the record keyword can be applied to a struct. To avoid confusing the two, declare a record applied to a class as public record class MyClass and declare a record applied to a struct as public record struct MyStruct. If you omit the class or the struct keyword, it will behave as a record class by default. Record struct works like a record class (with-expressions, equality comparison), except it's a struct and not a class, and positional records work differently: positional records on a struct *don't make the record immutable* as a record class. Because it's a struct, you have to set the readonly keyword to make the *record struct* immutable. The major fact with record struct is that reading/writing performance is higher than a regular struct. Interesting too!

Summary

In this chapter, you were given a primer on modern .NET. You learned about its origins and why Microsoft made some of the developer choices that it did. You were also given a quick primer on C# 10 and even a recap of C# 9, whose features often appear in this book. The next chapter briefly introduces ASP.NET Core 6, which runs on .NET 6.

CHAPTER 2

Introducing ASP.NET Core 6

Microsoft released its first ASP.NET framework in 2002 with ASP.NET Webform. The years that followed were rich in developments such as ASP.NET MVC, ASP.NET WebAPI, and SignalR. The framework evolved a little too quickly with new functionalities without changing its core, more precisely the assembly named *System.Web*. Very quickly, new challenges appeared, such as performance, the possibility of running ASP.NET on servers other than IIS, increasing the framework's affinity with the cloud to significantly facilitate its deployment, and greatly improving its configuration by making it more flexible. ASP.NET Core is born! ASP.NET Core is even designed to support containerization such as *Docker*.

ASP.NET Core is a complete overhaul of the trendy ASP.NET framework and allows you to develop four types of applications:

- Web apps

- Web APIs

- Remote Procedure Call (RPC) apps

- Real-time apps

At the time of writing, ASP.NET Core 6 (delivered with .NET 6) is the latest version. This chapter introduces you to ASP.NET Core 6, as we'll use it throughout this book. Note that ASP.NET Core 6 no longer supports ASP.NET WebForms and Windows Communication Foundation (WCF).

In this chapter, I'll teach you ASP.NET Core fundamentals and the following application types:

- ASP.NET Core fundamentals

- ASP.NET Core Web API (web API)

© Anthony Giretti 2022
A. Giretti, *Beginning gRPC with ASP.NET Core 6*, https://doi.org/10.1007/978-1-4842-8008-9_2

- ASP.NET Core MVC (web app)

- ASP.NET Core Razor Pages (web app)

- ASP.NET Core Blazor (web app)

- ASP.NET Core SignalR (real-time app)

- ASP.NET Core gRPC (Remote Procedure Call app)

- ASP.NET Core minimal APIs (web API)

ASP.NET Core Fundamentals

Before diving into ASP.NET Core, let's talk about the fundamentals. Once you know the fundamentals of ASP.NET Core, you can use this knowledge to build any web application you'd like, including gRPC.

For an ASP.NET Core application, the entry point of the application is the Program. cs file, an example of which is shown in Listing 2-1. In this file, you start creating your application by instantiating a *WebApplicationBuilder* with the static method WebApplication.CreateBuilder. The *WebApplicationBuilder* allows customization by adding the desired components (configuration) and activating them (activations).

Listing 2-1. Example of Program.cs File

```
var builder = WebApplication.CreateBuilder(args);
var app = builder.Build();

app.MapGet("/", () => "Hello World!");

app.Run();
```

Note   This is the default Program.cs file generated from the ASP.NET Core 6 template. It implements the C# 9 top-level programs feature (introduced in Chapter 1). The same remark applies to using statements, and the default ASP.NET Core 6 template uses the C# 10 global usings feature (also introduced in Chapter 1).

The Program.cs file has two distinct parts:

- **Services configuration**: Includes the type of application, third-party libraries, authentication, authorization, and the registration of services with dependency injection.

- **Services activation**: Defines the ASP.NET Core middleware pipeline. Middleware is a component that, once assembled (in a particular order) into an application, can handle requests and responses and perform operations before and after the next component, as shown in Figure 2-1.

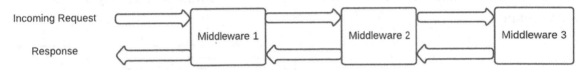

Figure 2-1. *The ASP.NET Core middleware pipeline*

Service configuration is implemented at the beginning of the file, *before* building the app with the builder.Build() method, and services activation occurs after the latter but *before* the app.Run() method, as shown in Listing 2-2, which is a sample of a configuration of an ASP.NET Core Razor Pages application.

Listing 2-2. Example of Configured Program.cs File

```
var builder = WebApplication.CreateBuilder(args);

// Services configuration
builder.Services.AddRazorPages();

var app = builder.Build();

// Services activation
if (!app.Environment.IsDevelopment())
{
    app.UseExceptionHandler("/Error");
    app.UseHsts();
}
```

```
app.UseHttpsRedirection();
app.UseStaticFiles();

app.UseRouting();

app.UseAuthorization();

app.MapRazorPages();

app.Run();
```

This discussion may still seem blurry to you; don't be concerned, because the rest of this section explains the architecture of ASP.NET Core, summarized in Figure 2-2, in more detail.

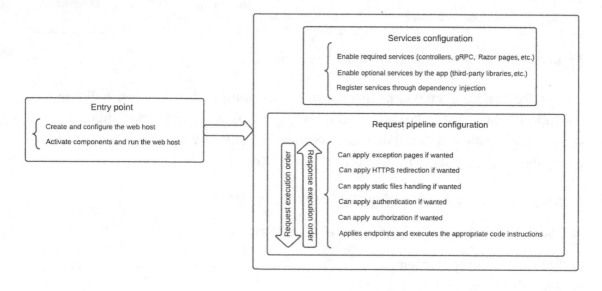

Program.cs

Figure 2-2. *ASP.NET Core architecture*

First, you must understand dependency injection since it's central to ASP.NET Core. *Dependency injection* is a technique that weakly couples objects and service classes with each other and their dependencies. Instead of directly instantiating services in methods through constructors or using statements, the class declares what dependencies it needs. In this book, we'll use services configured with their implemented interface. These interfaces will be injected into the constructors of the classes calling these services. This decoupling allows our code to be abstracted and also facilitates testability. Later in this book, we'll see how to easily test our code and take advantage of dependency injection. The service lifetime injected by dependencies is essential. Depending on the injected services, some need to be used once or several times for the Hypertext Transfer Protocol (HTTP) request context or even used only once for all users making an HTTP request to the server. ASP.NET Core supports three service lifetimes:

- **Transient**: A new instance of the service is created for each new incoming request. This means that on the same incoming HTTP request, the developer can deal with a new instance of the same service for each HTTP request.

- **Scoped**: The service is instantiated once per incoming request. This is the most commonly used lifetime. It guarantees the uniqueness of a service instance per user.

- **Singleton**: The service is instantiated once for the entire application's lifetime (as long as it is not restarted), and all users share this instance. In ASP.NET Core, Singleton lifetime is thread-safe (during object construction); ASP.NET Core manages it for you as long as you register your service correctly in the dependency injection container. However, if you need to modify a property, such as a `Dictionary`, you'll need to use a `ConcurrentDictionary` instead.

Listing 2-3 shows how to configure the three different lifetimes. Note that the parameter on the left is the interface and the parameter on the right is the concrete class which implements this interface. A compilation error will occur if the class doesn't implement the interface to be injected by dependency.

Listing 2-3. Configure Each Lifetime Type

```
var builder = WebApplication.CreateBuilder(args);

services.AddControllers();
services.AddSingleton<ISingletonService, SingletonService>();
services.AddScoped<IScopedService, ScopedService>();
services.AddTransient<ITransientService, TransientService>();

var app = builder.Build();
```

```
if (!app.Environment.IsDevelopment())
{
    app.UseExceptionHandler("/Error");
    app.UseHsts();
}

app.UseHttpsRedirection();
app.UseStaticFiles();

app.UseRouting();

app.UseAuthorization();

app.MapRazorPages();

app.Run();
```

Listing 2-4 shows how to inject services with an MVC controller.

Listing 2-4. Example of MVC Controller Where Services Are Injected by Constructor

```
public class DemoController : Controller
{
    private readonly ISingletonService _singletonService;
    private readonly IScopedService _scopedService;
    private readonly ITransientService _transientService;

    public DemoController(ISingletonService singletonService,
                          IScopedService scopedService,
                          ITransientService transientService)
    {
        _singletonService = singletonService;
        _scopedService = scopedService;
        _transientService = transientService;
    }
}
```

Depending on your needs, you might sometimes want to use a service as *Singleton*, *Scoped*, or *Transient*, but you must be aware of the scope hierarchy.

A *Scoped* service can directly access a *Singleton* service or *Transient* service, which can directly access a *Singleton* service. The opposite is impossible because any object with a longer life than another cannot access it directly. Figure 2-3 summarizes the scope hierarchy.

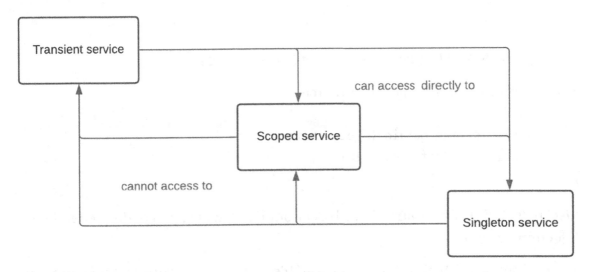

Figure 2-3. *The scope hierarchy*

ASP.NET Core provides a way to add extra configuration within your application that dependency injection can access to anywhere in the application. You can customize and store the additional configuration in an `appsettings.json` file. You can store settings here that differ by environment. For example, in development mode, the `appsettings. development.json` file can contain configuration specific to development mode. If a JSON key/value pair is present in both files, the more specific file (`appsettings. development.json`) will override the value presented in the main file for a given key. You can create an `Options` object to populate with your configuration—this is referred to as the *Options pattern*. Listing 2-5 shows an SMTP configuration in `appsettings.json` that maps the `SmtpConfiguration` object shown in Listing 2-6, then uses the dependency injection system as shown in Listing 2-7. Finally, the `IOptions<TOptions>` interface is injected in the `DemoController`, as shown in Listing 2-8.

Listing 2-5. SMTP Configuration in appsettings.json

```
{
  "SmtpConfiguration": {
    "Domain": "smtp.gmail.com",
    "Port": 465
  }
}
```

Listing 2-6. SMTP Configuration object in Program.cs

```
public record class SmtpConfiguration
{
    public string Domain { get; init; }
    public int Port { get; init; }
}
```

Listing 2-7. SmtpConfiguration Object Bound and Registered in the Dependency Injection System

```
var builder = WebApplication.CreateBuilder(args);    services.Configure<Smt
pConfiguration>(Configuration.GetSection("SmtpConfiguration"));
....
```

Listing 2-8. Injecting SmtpConfiguration Options into DemoController

```
public class DemoController : Controller
{
    private readonly SmtpConfiguration _smtpConfiguration;

    public DemoController(IOptions<SmtpConfiguration> smtpConfiguration
    Options)
    {
        _smtpConfiguration = smtpConfigurationOptions.Value;
    }
}
```

This is the simplest way to use options in ASP.NET Core. You can also leverage `IOptionsSnapshot<TOptions>` and `IOptionsMonitor<TOptions>`, depending on your needs. To learn more, read Microsoft's documentation: `https://docs.microsoft.com/ en-us/aspnet/core/fundamentals/configuration/options?view=aspnetcore-6.0`.

The last important option to mention is the possibility of setting up development mode in ASP.NET Core by configuration. What is development mode? It allows developers to configure a different behavior of the application (for example, set up connection strings that are encrypted in production but not encrypted in development mode). Another important feature is the ability to display more detailed information about the unhandled error that occurred. Because it's more detailed, developers *should not enable development mode* in production. To enable it, you need to set the `ASPNETCORE_ENVIRONMENT` environment variable to `Development` in the `launchSettings.json` file or within the project properties panel. Further in this book, you'll see a concrete example of using environment variables and encrypted connection strings. Listing 2-9 shows a `launchSettings.json` file configured for development mode with IIS and self-hosted mode.

Listing 2-9. Development Mode Enabled Within `lauchSettings.json` File

```
{
  "iisSettings": {
    "windowsAuthentication": false,
    "anonymousAuthentication": true,
    "iisExpress": {
      "applicationUrl": "http://localhost:57090",
      "sslPort": 44366
    }
  },
  "profiles": {
    "IIS Express": {
      "commandName": "IISExpress",
      "launchBrowser": true,
      "environmentVariables": {
        "ASPNETCORE_ENVIRONMENT": "Development"
      }
    },
```

```
    "MVCDemo": {
      "commandName": "Project",
      "dotnetRunMessages": "true",
      "launchBrowser": true,
      "applicationUrl": "https://localhost:5001;http://localhost:5000",
      "environmentVariables": {
        "ASPNETCORE_ENVIRONMENT": "Development"
      }
    }
  }
}
```

ASP.NET Core Web API

ASP.NET Core Web API allows you to...you guessed it...create web APIs.

A web API is an *application programming interface (API)* that is used in conjunction with HTTP. Currently, web APIs use the *Representational State Transfer (REST)* protocol, which associated with the *JavaScript Object Notation (JSON)* interchange format, and Extensible Markup Language (XML), though less commonly. APIs use HTTP features such as *Uniform Resource Identifiers (URIs)*.

Because Internet users access the Web using a wide variety of terminals and we want to provide data to browsers and more recent device applications in a fast and secure manner, we need a web API that is compatible with all access points. ASP.NET Core Web API is designed specifically to be an efficient framework for building web services that many users can use.

ASP.NET Core Web API follows the *Model-View-Controller (MVC)* pattern. In traditional web apps, the *V* (view) in MVC is the web page. With web APIs, it's a response in JSON, XML, or any other format. Figure 2-4 gives an overview of this pattern.

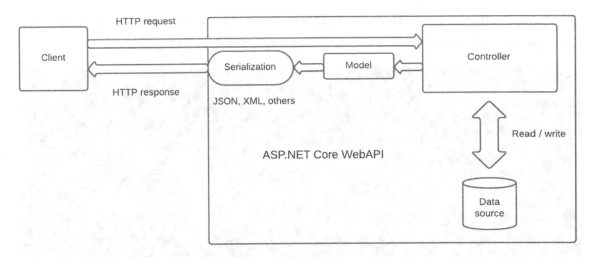

Figure 2-4. *ASP.NET Core Web API architecture*

Now, let's explore how to create a web API in Visual Studio 2022. As shown in Figure 2-5, select Web in the drop-down list to more easily find the project type you're looking for: ASP.NET Core Web API.

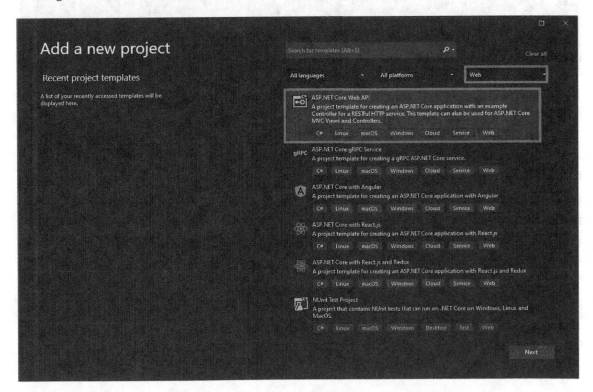

Figure 2-5. *How to find the project type: ASP.NET Core Web API*

Choose ASP.NET Core Web API, click Next, and then configure the project name, the location on your computer, and the solution name, as shown in Figure 2-6.

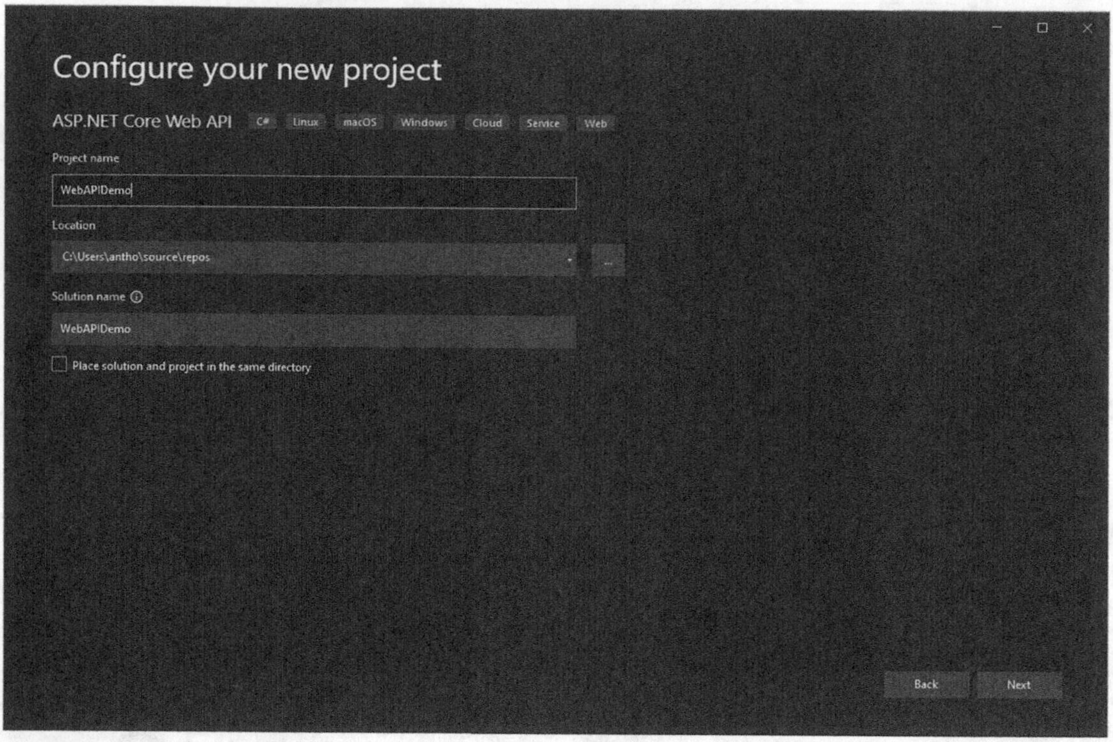

Figure 2-6. *How to create your new ASP.NET Core Web API project*

After that, you get the opportunity to select a variety of options to customize your application. As shown in Figure 2-7, you can choose the runtime to run your ASP.NET Core Web API, and I strongly suggest that you select the latest (.NET 6) in the Framework drop-down list; ASP.NET Core 6 can only be run by this framework. You can also set the authentication type (Windows, Microsoft identity Platform, or no authentication), configure for HTTPS, enable Docker, and enable OpenAPI support.

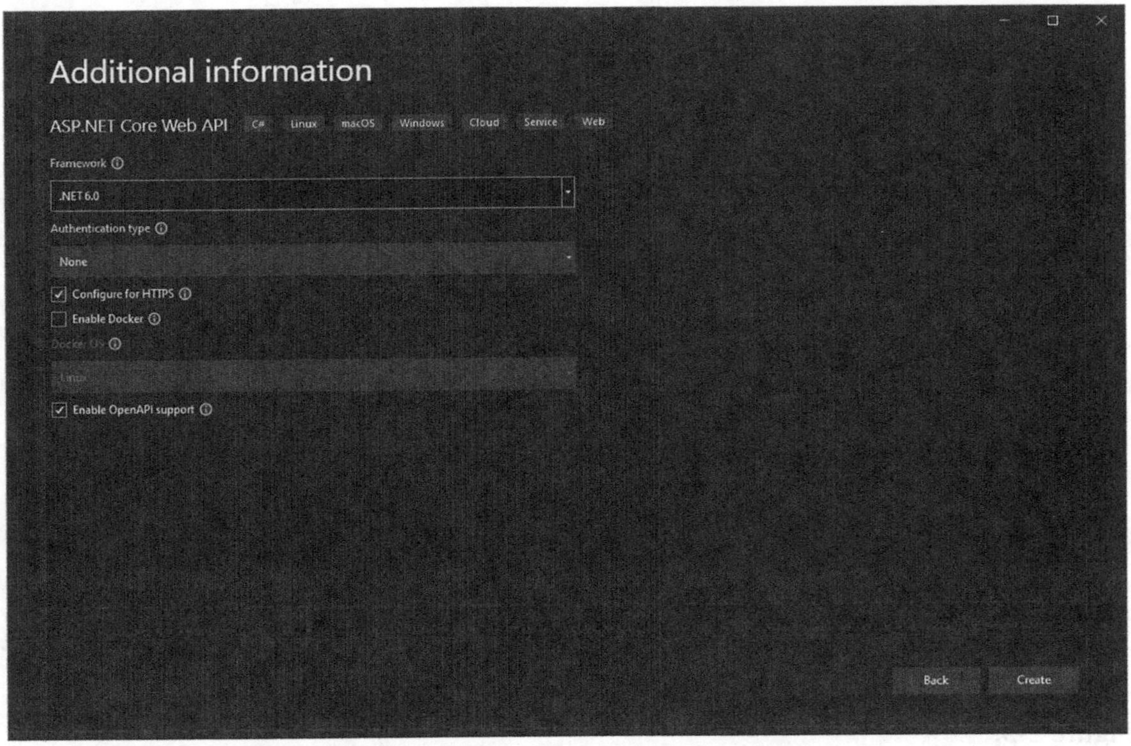

Figure 2-7. *How to configure the ASP.NET Core Web API*

If you aren't familiar with Docker, it is an open source containerization platform. *Docker* enables developers to containerize their applications that combine application source code with all the operating system (OS) libraries and dependencies required to run the code in any environment. To learn more, visit `https://www.docker.com/why-docker`. As for OpenAPI, it's a specification that defines a standard, language-agnostic interface to RESTful APIs, allowing humans (and the machine) to discover and understand features of a service without reading the source code. For details, refer to `https://swagger.io/specification/`. Swagger is the set of tools built on top of OpenAPI.

To follow along with the example, check the boxes to configure for HTTPS and enable OpenAPI support and then click the Create button. Visual Studio will generate your project with a default template, including a *WeatherForecast* model and controller. Figure 2-8 shows the default project created by Visual Studio.

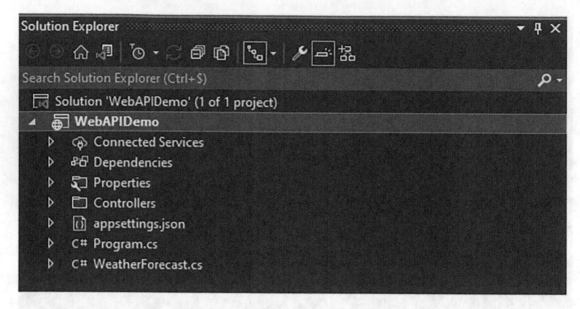

Figure 2-8. *Default ASP.NET Core WebAPI WeatherForecast template app*

Let's take a quick look at the controller, `WeatherForecastController.cs`, shown in Figure 2-9.

```
WeatherForecastController.cs ⊕ ×
WebAPIDemo                                    ⌄ ◆WebAPIDemo.Controllers.WeatherForecastController  ⌄ ◆Summaries        ⌄
    1   using Microsoft.AspNetCore.Mvc;
    2
    3   namespace WebAPIDemo.Controllers
    4   {
    5       [ApiController]
    6       [Route("[controller]")]
        3 references
    7       public class WeatherForecastController : ControllerBase
    8       {
    9           private static readonly string[] Summaries = new[]
   10           {
   11           "Freezing", "Bracing", "Chilly", "Cool", "Mild", "Warm", "Balmy", "Hot", "Sweltering", "Scorching"
   12       };
   13
   14           private readonly ILogger<WeatherForecastController> _logger;
   15
            0 references
   16           public WeatherForecastController(ILogger<WeatherForecastController> logger)
   17           {
   18               _logger = logger;
   19           }
   20
   21           [HttpGet]
            0 references
   22           public IEnumerable<WeatherForecast> Get()
   23           {
   24               return Enumerable.Range(1, 5).Select(index => new WeatherForecast
   25               {
   26                   Date = DateTime.Now.AddDays(index),
   27                   TemperatureC = Random.Shared.Next(-20, 55),
   28                   Summary = Summaries[Random.Shared.Next(Summaries.Length)]
   29               })
   30               .ToArray();
   31           }
   32       }
   33   }
```

Figure 2-9. *The WeatherForecastController class*

Let's take a look at the Program.cs file, the entry point of the application. As you can see in Figure 2-10, we previously opted to enable OpenAPI, and Swagger UI is using it.

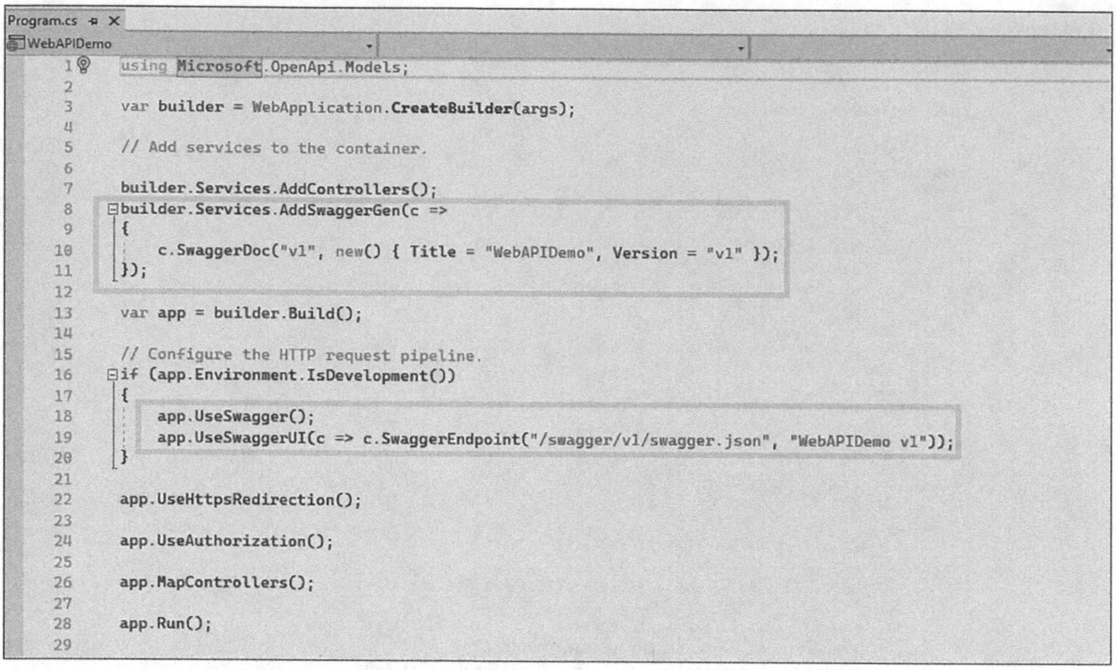

```
Program.cs  -¤ X
WebAPIDemo
    1    using Microsoft.OpenApi.Models;
    2
    3    var builder = WebApplication.CreateBuilder(args);
    4
    5    // Add services to the container.
    6
    7    builder.Services.AddControllers();
    8    builder.Services.AddSwaggerGen(c =>
    9    {
   10        c.SwaggerDoc("v1", new() { Title = "WebAPIDemo", Version = "v1" });
   11    });
   12
   13    var app = builder.Build();
   14
   15    // Configure the HTTP request pipeline.
   16    if (app.Environment.IsDevelopment())
   17    {
   18        app.UseSwagger();
   19        app.UseSwaggerUI(c => c.SwaggerEndpoint("/swagger/v1/swagger.json", "WebAPIDemo v1"));
   20    }
   21
   22    app.UseHttpsRedirection();
   23
   24    app.UseAuthorization();
   25
   26    app.MapControllers();
   27
   28    app.Run();
   29
```

Figure 2-10. *Startup.cs file configured with OpenAPI (Swagger)*

Visual Studio will open the browser with the OpenAPI web page and display all endpoints within the app if you run the app. At this point, it will show only the WeatherForecast GET endpoint. To try it, click the Execute button and view the data returned in the Response section, as shown in Figure 2-11.

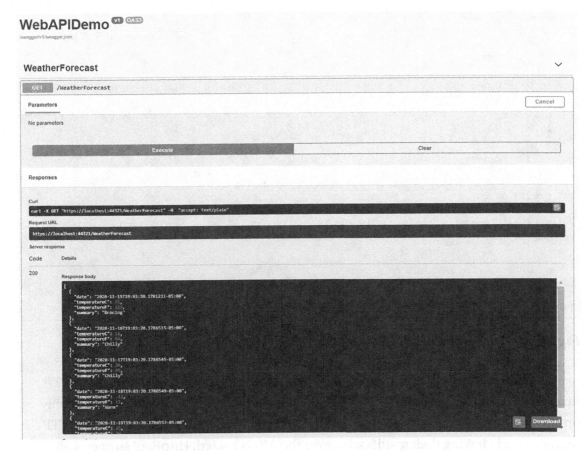

Figure 2-11. *Swagger UI web page*

The Swagger UI web page is open by default. When we enabled OpenAPI, Visual Studio configured it to open in launchSettings.json with the "launchUrl" value, as shown in Figure 2-12.

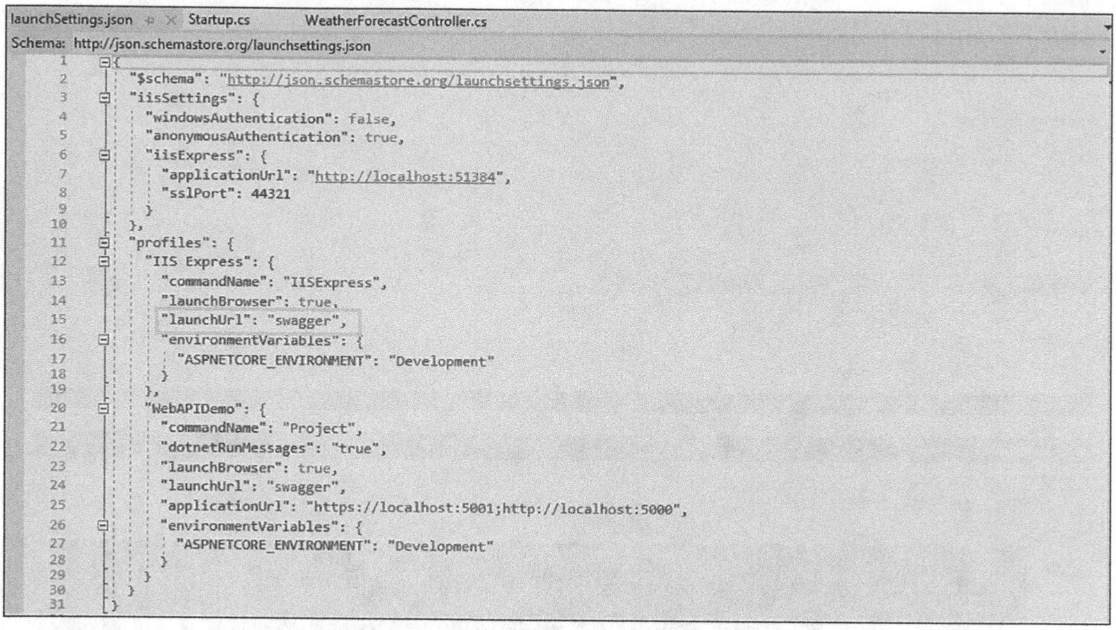

Figure 2-12. *"launchUrl" parameter set to "swagger" value*

In addition to Swagger, it is possible to use a command-line tool, *HttpRepl (HTTP Read-Eval-Print Loop)*, which is lightweight, cross-platform, and can be used not only on ASP.NET Core APIs but also other kinds of APIs. This tool is used for making HTTP requests and viewing their results wherever the API is hosted. HttpRepl supports all of the following verbs: DELETE, GET, HEAD, OPTIONS, PATCH, POST, and PUT.

To install HttpRepl, run the following command in a PowerShell window:

```
dotnet tool install -g Microsoft.dotnet-httprepl
```

If you want to discover all the commands supported by this tool, enter the following command:

```
httprepl --help
```

Figure 2-13 shows the commands available in the output window.

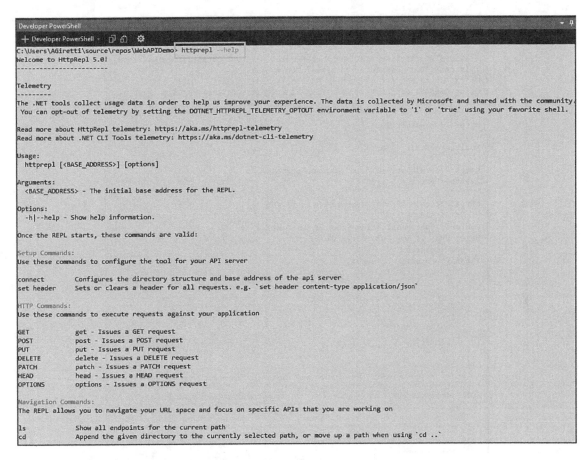

Figure 2-13. *Available commands for HttpRepl*

Figure 2-14 shows the exploration, navigation, and execution of the endpoints available in the API you want to discover. Endpoints are known because of the parsing of the swagger.json file, which is done automatically by typing the command (connection to the API) shown in Listing 2-10.

Listing 2-10. Connection to the Local API Base URL

```
httprepl https://localhost:5001
```

Note in Figure 2-14 that HttpRepl uses MS-DOS commands for endpoint exploration, navigation, and execution, such as ls to list endpoints (listing files in a directory in Windows) and cd to position itself on an endpoint (moving to a directory in Windows).

```
Developer PowerShell                                              ▼  ⋢
 + Developer PowerShell ▾    ⟙ ⟘    ⚙

C:\Users\AGiretti\source\repos\WebAPIDemo> httprepl https://localhost:5001
(Disconnected)> connect https://localhost:5001
Using a base address of https://localhost:5001/
Using OpenAPI description at https://localhost:5001/swagger/v1/swagger.json
For detailed tool info, see https://aka.ms/http-repl-doc

https://localhost:5001/> ls
.                 []
WeatherForecast   [GET]

https://localhost:5001/> cd weatherForecast
/weatherForecast    [GET]

https://localhost:5001/weatherForecast> get
HTTP/1.1 200 OK
Content-Type: application/json; charset=utf-8
Date: Sun, 29 Nov 2020 02:23:42 GMT
Server: Kestrel
Transfer-Encoding: chunked

[
  {
    "date": 11/29/2020 9:23:43 PM,
    "temperatureC": 3,
    "temperatureF": 37,
    "summary": "Sweltering"
  },
  {
    "date": 11/30/2020 9:23:43 PM,
    "temperatureC": -17,
    "temperatureF": 2,
    "summary": "Chilly"
  },
  {
    "date": 12/1/2020 9:23:43 PM,
    "temperatureC": 5,
    "temperatureF": 40,
    "summary": "Hot"
  },
  {
    "date": 12/2/2020 9:23:43 PM,
    "temperatureC": -14,
    "temperatureF": 7,
    "summary": "Cool"
  },
  {
    "date": 12/3/2020 9:23:43 PM,
    "temperatureC": -8,
    "temperatureF": 18,
    "summary": "Cool"
```

Figure 2-14. *Exploration, navigation, and execution of API endpoints*

Finally, if you do not want to use the generated Swagger web page or HttpRepl, you can use a tool named Postman, which is a GUI for generating HTTP requests to test the endpoints of a given API. This tool allows you to configure all the possible parameters of a request, such as the URL, headers, verbs, query string, and body. To download Postman, go to https://www.postman.com. Figure 2-15 shows what the Postman interface looks like.

Figure 2-15. *Postman GUI tool*

The most popular of these three tools is Postman, maybe you already know it, but I admit that using HttpRepl online is quite lovely, and if you are a fan of command-line tools, this one is for you. Especially if you are a Linux pro! If you are not, I hope this section has tempted you to try HttpRepl.

ASP.NET Core MVC

ASP.NET Core MVC enables you to create web applications.

ASP.NET MVC first became part of the .NET ecosystem in 2008. Originally, ASP. NET WebForms appeared in 2002. The framework was based on events (click, page load, etc.), so it tended to be complex, heavy, and inefficient. Microsoft's quest to create a lightweight and more efficient ASP.NET framework resulted in ASP.NET MVC. ASP. NET MVC follows the *Model-View-Controller (MVC)* pattern (previously discussed) and introduces many advantages to ASP.NET (and ASP.NET Core), such as the following:

- Clean architecture with the *separation of concerns (SoC)* principle

- Efficient and easy combination with JavaScript libraries like JQuery or Prototype.js

- *Search engine optimization (SEO)*, ASP.NET Core Routing feature provides more affinities with search engines

- No application state

- Complete control of HTML rendering, unlike ASP.NET WebForms

- *Test-driven development (TDD)* capabilities

In ASP.NET Core, MVC is architected like this:

1. *Model* is the component in the MVC design pattern that manages data to be displayed in the view component.

2. *View* is the component used to display the model data.

3. *Controller* is the component in an ASP.NET MVC application used to handle the incoming HTTP request generated by a user action. The controller deals with the model and view through an *Action*, which is a controller method and then sends the response to the user.

Figure 2-16 gives an overview of the MVC pattern.

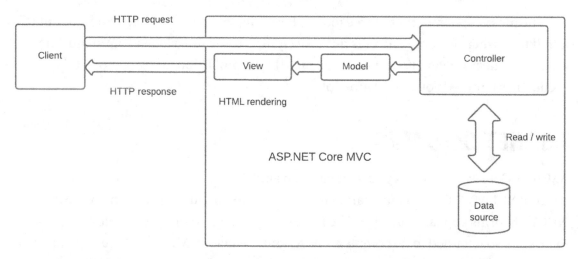

Figure 2-16. *ASP.NET Core MVC architecture*

How do you create an ASP.NET Core MVC application? Similar to the instructions for ASP.NET Core WebAPI earlier in the chapter, you need to create a new project in Visual Studio 2022 by selecting the dedicated template: ASP.NET Core Web App (Model-View-Controller), as shown in Figure 2-17.

Figure 2-17. *Create an ASP.NET Core MVC application*

From here, you'll repeat the same steps as the ASP.NET Core Web API creation, choosing .NET 6 as the runtime and choosing customization options such as setting the authentication type, configuring for HTTPS, enabling Docker, and enabling OpenAPI support.

After you click the Create button, Visual Studio creates the default application with CSS, JavaScript, and other static assets in the wwwroot folder. Controllers, models, and views are listed in their respective folders, as shown in Figure 2-18.

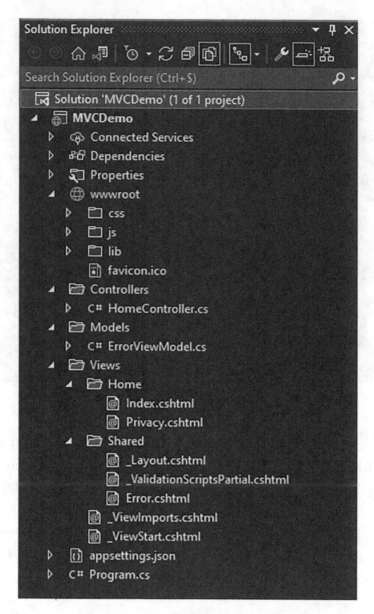

Figure 2-18. *The default template of ASP.NET Core MVC*

The HomeController class is created by default and implements the Index page as well as a Privacy page and an Error page, as shown in Figure 2-19.

```
HomeController.cs ↔ X
MVCDemo                                    ▾ ⚙ MVCDemo.Controllers.HomeController        ▾ ⚙_logger                ▾
    1    ⊟using Microsoft.AspNetCore.Mvc;
    2     using MVCDemo.Models;
    3     using System.Diagnostics;
    4
    5    ⊟namespace MVCDemo.Controllers
    6     {
            3 references
    7    ⊟    public class HomeController : Controller
    8         {
    9             private readonly ILogger<HomeController> _logger;
   10
              0 references
   11    ⊟        public HomeController(ILogger<HomeController> logger)
   12             {
   13                 _logger = logger;
   14             }
   15
              0 references
   16    ⊟        public IActionResult Index()
   17             {
   18                 return View();
   19             }
   20
              0 references
   21    ⊟        public IActionResult Privacy()
   22             {
   23                 return View();
   24             }
   25
   26             [ResponseCache(Duration = 0, Location = ResponseCacheLocation.None, NoStore = true)]
              0 references
   27    ⊟        public IActionResult Error()
   28             {
   29                 return View(new ErrorViewModel { RequestId = Activity.Current?.Id ?? HttpContext.TraceIdentifier });
   30             }
   31         }
   32     }
```

Figure 2-19. *The HomeController created by default, with the Index(), Privacy() and Error() Actions*

If you look at the Program.cs file, shown in Figure 2-20, you'll see that other features specific to ASP.NET Core MVC were added, such as default routing rules, error pages and views, and middleware to enable MVC controllers.

```
Program.cs ⊕ ×
MVCDemo
    1    var builder = WebApplication.CreateBuilder(args);
    2
    3    // Add services to the container.
    4    builder.Services.AddControllersWithViews();
    5
    6    var app = builder.Build();
    7
    8    // Configure the HTTP request pipeline.
    9    if (!app.Environment.IsDevelopment())
   10    {
   11        app.UseExceptionHandler("/Home/Error");
   12        // The default HSTS value is 30 days. You may want to change this for production scenarios, see https://aka.ms/aspnetcore-hsts.
   13        app.UseHsts();
   14    }
   15
   16    app.UseHttpsRedirection();
   17    app.UseStaticFiles();
   18
   19    app.UseRouting();
   20
   21    app.UseAuthorization();
   22
   23    app.MapControllerRoute(
   24        name: "default",
   25        pattern: "{controller=Home}/{action=Index}/{id?}");
   26
   27    app.Run();
   28
```

Figure 2-20. *Default Program.cs file in ASP.NET Core MVC*

ASP.NET views use the Razor syntax, which is straightforward: a mix between C#
and HTML. You can invoke C# code in Razor Pages using the @ symbol, as shown in
Figure 2-21 (the `Error.cshtml` file that displays the error page).

```
Error.cshtml ⊕ ×
    1    @model ErrorViewModel
    2    @{
    3        ViewData["Title"] = "Error";
    4    }
    5
    6    <h1 class="text-danger">Error.</h1>
    7    <h2 class="text-danger">An error occurred while processing your request.</h2>
    8
    9    @if (Model?.ShowRequestId ?? false)
   10    {
   11        <p>
   12            <strong>Request ID:</strong> <code>@Model?.RequestId</code>
   13        </p>
   14    }
   15
   16    <h3>Development Mode</h3>
   17    <p>
   18        Swapping to <strong>Development</strong> environment will display more detailed information about the error that occurred.
   19    </p>
   20    <p>
   21        <strong>The Development environment shouldn't be enabled for deployed applications.</strong>
   22        It can result in displaying sensitive information from exceptions to end users.
   23        For local debugging, enable the <strong>Development</strong> environment by setting the <strong>ASPNETCORE_ENVIRONMENT</strong>
   24        and restarting the app.
   25    </p>
```

Figure 2-21. `Error.cshtml` *view with C# instructions and data binding*

The `launchSettings.json` file is the same as for the ASP.NET Core Web API project.
If you run the project, you'll land on the Index page, the default launch page for when
the application starts, as shown in Figure 2-22.

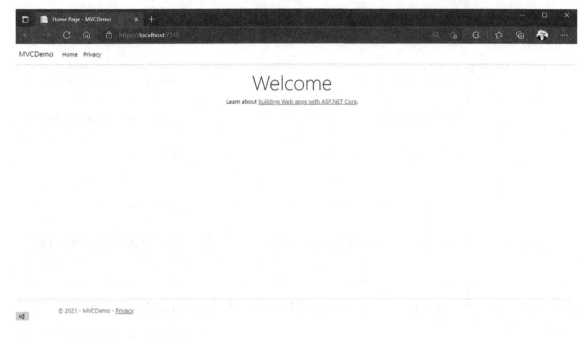

Figure 2-22. *Default Index page*

If you configure the `"launchUrl"` property with another page, the application starts on that page. If nothing is specified, the Index page is the default start page.

ASP.NET Core Razor Pages

ASP.NET Core Razor Pages enables you to create web applications with complete control of HTML, just as ASP.NET Core MVC does. ASP.NET Core Razor Pages and ASP.NET Core MVC are similar but also have their differences.

The main similarities lie with Razor's views. Both ASP.NET Core MVC and ASP.NET Core Razor Pages render HTML pages with the Razor syntax, but ASP.NET Core Razor Pages doesn't have a model or controller. Instead, a "code-behind" C# class sits behind a Razor view. Figure 2-23 shows the comparison between ASP.NET Core MVC and Razor Pages.

ASP.NET Core MVC   ASP.NET Core Razor Pages

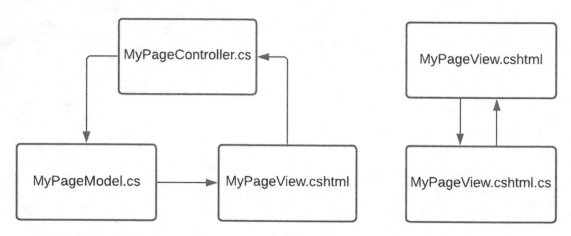

Figure 2-23. *Difference between ASP.NET Core MVC and ASP.NET Core Razor Pages*

The code-behind class acts like a controller. It implements HTTP handlers instead of *Actions* and communicates with the view using a *Model* inherited from a `PageModel` class that exposes objects like `ControllerBase` does for MVC. We'll talk more about this later in this section.

If you are wondering how to decide whether to choose ASP.NET Core Razor Pages or ASP.NET Core MVC in any particular scenario, the following discussion provides some guidance.

Choose ASP.NET Core MVC if you need to do the following:

- Build dynamic server views in the same application

- Work with a single-page application (SPA) model

- Use REST APIs with Asynchronous JavaScript and XML (AJAX) queries

ASP.NET Core Razor Pages works well for the following scenarios:

- No use of REST endpoints

- Simple and basic data manipulation

Choosing ASP.NET Core Razor Pages brings other advantages like:

- Better organization (view and its code-behind versus view, controller, model, and routing)

- Single responsibility (clean and clear endpoint responsibility with GET, POST, PUT, etc. endpoints versus Actions in MVC controllers)

- Less complexity than MVC (like no TempData, ViewData concepts, and more)

- Possibility to reuse UI components with Blazor

Creating an ASP.NET Core Razor Pages application is similar to creating applications in ASP.NET Core Web API and MVC, previously discussed in this chapter. You start the process by selecting ASP.NET Core Web App in Visual Studio 2022, as shown in Figure 2-24. Then click the Next button, and you'll have the same customization options as offered for ASP.NET Core MVC to configure your app.

Figure 2-24. *Select ASP.NET Core Web App*

After choosing your customization options and clicking the Create button, Visual Studio creates the default app shown in Figure 2-25. It looks like an MVC web application without models and views. Code-behind classes are now coupled to their respective Razor views.

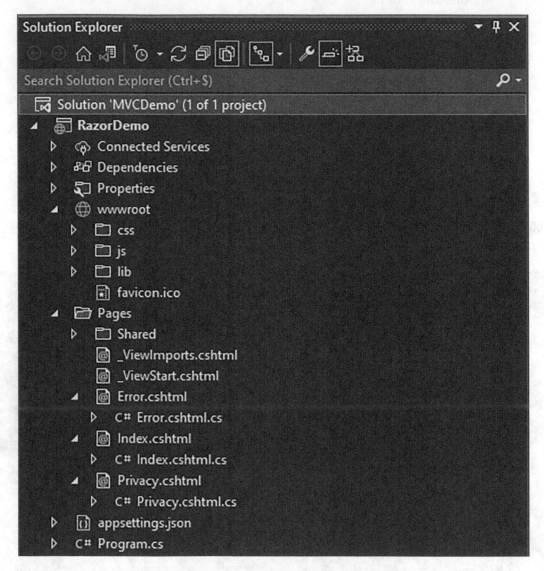

Figure 2-25. *The default ASP.NET Core Razor Pages template*

As discussed previously, controllers and models make way in Razor Pages for a PageModel class, where endpoints act as Actions in the ASP.NET Core MVC world. The default template generated by Visual Studio only implements the OnGet() method—it serves the requested page with the GET verb. You can implement all the HTTP verbs you desire, as shown in Figure 2-26.

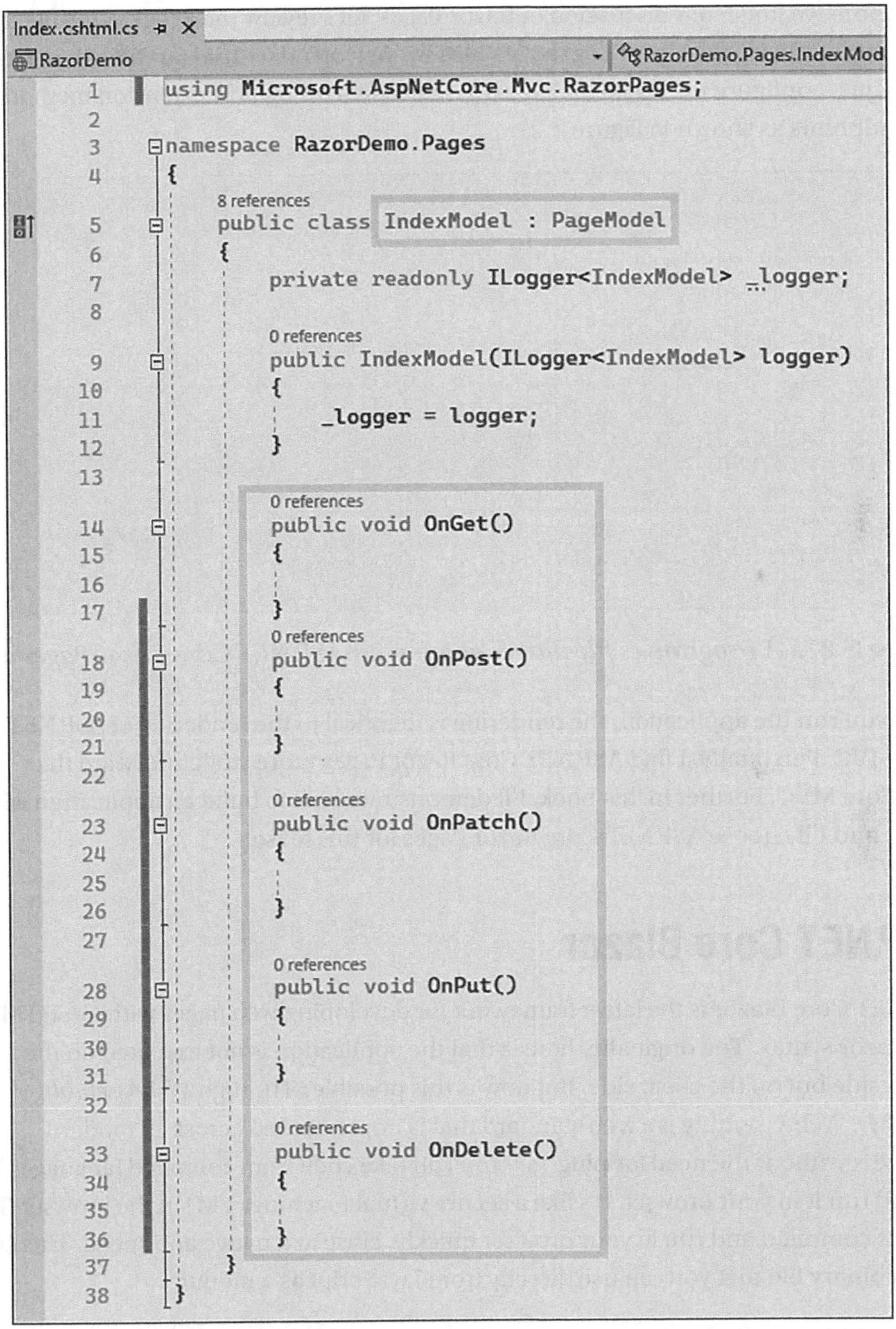

```
Index.cshtml.cs  ⊐  ×
RazorDemo                                          ▾  ⊀ RazorDemo.Pages.IndexMod
    1       using Microsoft.AspNetCore.Mvc.RazorPages;
    2
    3       ⊟namespace RazorDemo.Pages
    4        {
               8 references
    5        ⊟    public class IndexModel : PageModel
    6             {
    7                 private readonly ILogger<IndexModel> _logger;
    8
                     0 references
    9        ⊟        public IndexModel(ILogger<IndexModel> logger)
   10                 {
   11                     _logger = logger;
   12                 }
   13
                     0 references
   14        ⊟        public void OnGet()
   15                 {
   16
   17                 }
                     0 references
   18        ⊟        public void OnPost()
   19                 {
   20
   21                 }
   22
                     0 references
   23        ⊟        public void OnPatch()
   24                 {
   25
   26                 }
   27
                     0 references
   28        ⊟        public void OnPut()
   29                 {
   30
   31                 }
   32
                     0 references
   33        ⊟        public void OnDelete()
   34                 {
   35
   36                 }
   37             }
   38        }
```

Figure 2-26. *A PageModel class with its all HTTP verbs available for implementation*

63

Before we finish our discussion of Razor Pages, let's review the `Program.cs` file. It looks similar to all the other `Program.cs` files we've worked with so far. To activate Razor Pages, just configure the `AddRazorPages()` and `MapRazorPages()` extension methods for the endpoints as shown in Figure 2-27.

```
var builder = WebApplication.CreateBuilder(args);

// Add services to the container.
builder.Services.AddRazorPages();

var app = builder.Build();

// Configure the HTTP request pipeline.
if (!app.Environment.IsDevelopment())
{
    app.UseExceptionHandler("/Error");
    // The default HSTS value is 30 days. You may want to change this for production scenarios, see https://aka.ms/aspnetcore-hsts.
    app.UseHsts();
}

app.UseHttpsRedirection();
app.UseStaticFiles();

app.UseRouting();

app.UseAuthorization();

app.MapRazorPages();

app.Run();
```

Figure 2-27. *A Program.cs file that configures an ASP.NET Core Razor Pages app*

If you run the application, the rendering is identical to the rendering of ASP.NET Core MVC. Personally, I find ASP.NET Core Razor Pages more straightforward than ASP. NET Core MVC. Further in this book, I'll demonstrate how to build an application with gRPC, and I'll choose ASP.NET Core Razor Pages for this reason.

ASP.NET Core Blazor

ASP.NET Core Blazor is the latest framework for developing web pages with C#, HTML, and Razor syntax. The originality here is that the application is not executed on the server side but on the client side. But how is this possible? Through *WebAssembly (WASM)*! WebAssembly is a web standard that is implemented across all modern browsers without the need for plug-ins. You can take code from compiled languages like C# and run it in your browser. It's like a secure virtual machine (VM) in the browser. The code is compiled and run in your browser quickly, close to a native app speed. This code is in a binary file that you can use directly from JavaScript as a module.

Blazor is a framework that supports building components and web pages on top of WebAssembly. The name Blazor comes from the contraction of "browser" and "Razor," the HTML templating engine described in the previous section. Blazor is a single-page application framework that runs on .NET (with Mono) in the browser. Figure 2-28 shows the Blazor client-side stack.

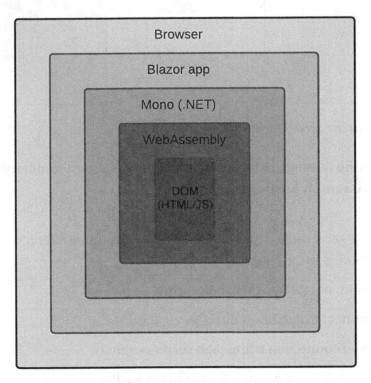

Figure 2-28. *The Blazor client-side stack*

ASP.NET Core Blazor is not limited to WebAssembly. Blazor also supports a server model. With the Blazor Server hosting model, the app is executed on the server from within an ASP.NET Core app. All interactions with the server are handled over a SignalR connection. Figure 2-29 shows the Blazor server-side stack.

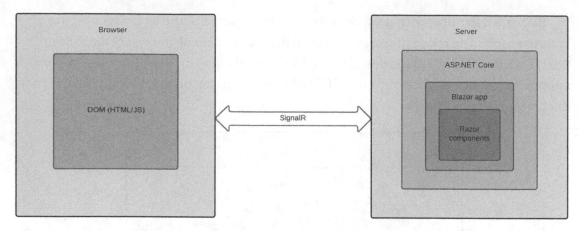

Figure 2-29.   *Blazor server-side stack*

Why choose one hosting model or the other? Here is a short summary.

Blazor WebAssembly hosting model

Pros:

- No .NET server-side dependency. The app is running after it's downloaded to the client.

- The client, not the server, handles work.

- Can connect to databases directly.

- Can store connection strings and secrets securely.

- Can access Windows and .NET Framework APIs.

- An ASP.NET Core web server isn't needed.

Cons:

- Depends on the browser's capability, and WebAssembly support is required.

- Needs to download the entire app before it runs, so it takes longer to start.

Blazor Server hosting model

Pros:

- Faster loading; no need to download the entire app before.

- Takes full advantage of server capabilities, like a regular ASP.NET Core app.

- Works with any browser.

Cons:

- Lots of interaction with the server might slow the experience sometimes.

- If the client connection breaks, like a standard ASP.NET Core app, it stops working.

- Needs to handle client state like a regular ASP.NET Core app.

- An ASP.NET Core server is necessary to serve the app.

Mobile developers are not forgotten, because Blazor also supports *Progressive Web Application (PWA)* development. If you are not familiar with PWA development, a PWA is a website that looks and behaves like a native mobile application. It can

- Load fast

- Send push notifications

- Work offline

- Access device features, such as compass, GPS, etc.

A PWA offers additional benefits:

- No installation required (and no need to push the app on stores like Google Play)

- Fully responsive, runs well on any devices (phones, tablets)

In this book, we will build an application with Blazor WebAssembly and gRPC-Web, so I'm not going to mention server-side Blazor further. It's not relevant because a Blazor Server App is simply an ASP.NET Core app.

Now, let's create a Blazor app with WebAssembly. To create a Blazor app (client side), select Blazor WebAssembly App in Visual Studio 2022, as shown in Figure 2-30.

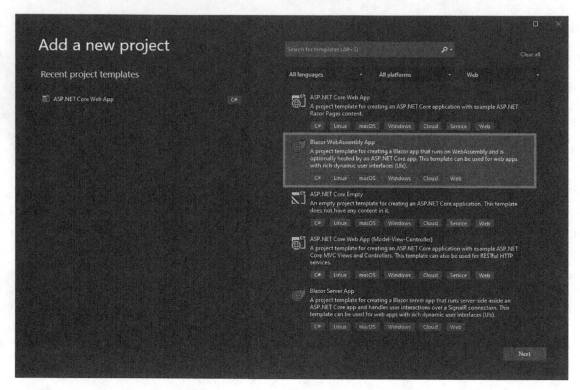

Figure 2-30.   *Create a Blazor app*

After selecting Blazor WebAssembly App and clicking Next, Visual Studio enables you to customize your app, like any ASP.NET Core app, but suggests two unique options for Blazor WebAssembly, as shown in Figure 2-31. If you enable ASP.NET Core hosted, the ASP.NET Core server serves up the client and provides a great place to host APIs. If you enable the Progressive Web Application option, you can deliver an app experience through the Web, built using standard web technologies including HTML, CSS, and JavaScript. PWA is intended to work on any platform that uses a standards-compliant browser, including desktop and mobile devices.

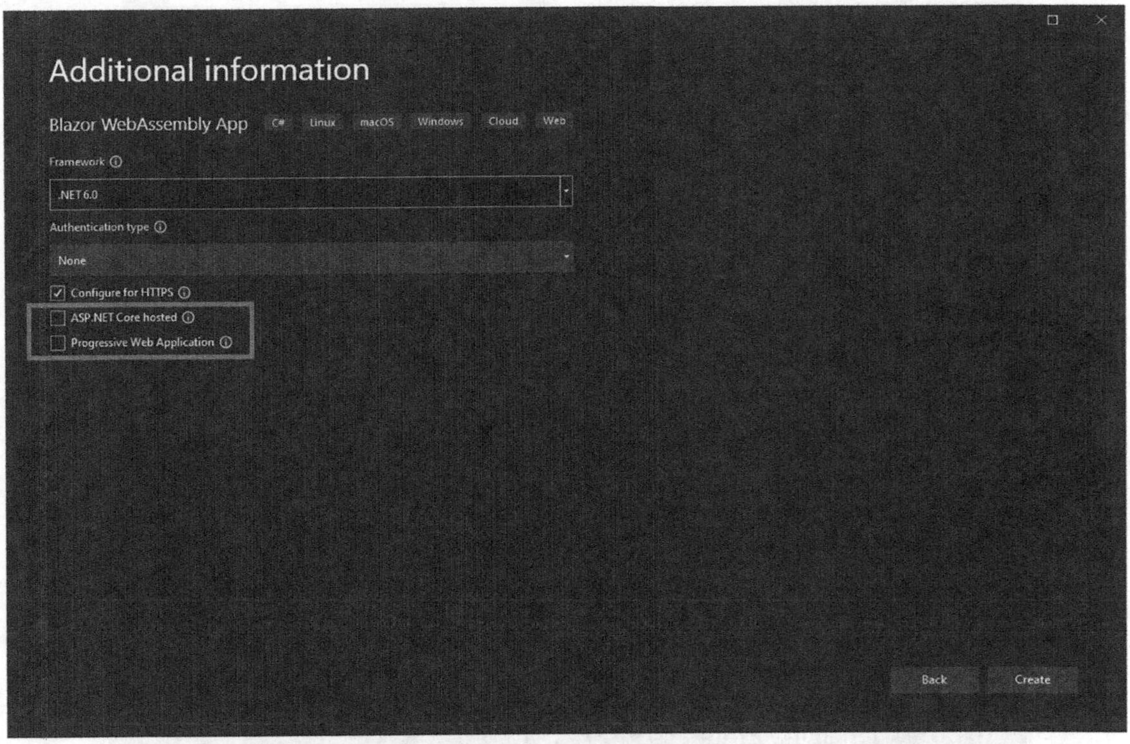

Figure 2-31. *Customize a Blazor app (WebAssembly)*

After you select your desired options and click Create, Visual Studio creates your app with HTML, CSS content, Razor Pages (notice this time the file extension is `.razor`, unlike ASP.NET MVC and Razor Pages, which are `.cshtml`), a `Program.cs` file, and an entry point component named `App.razor`. Figure 2-32 shows a default Blazor app configured for WebAssembly.

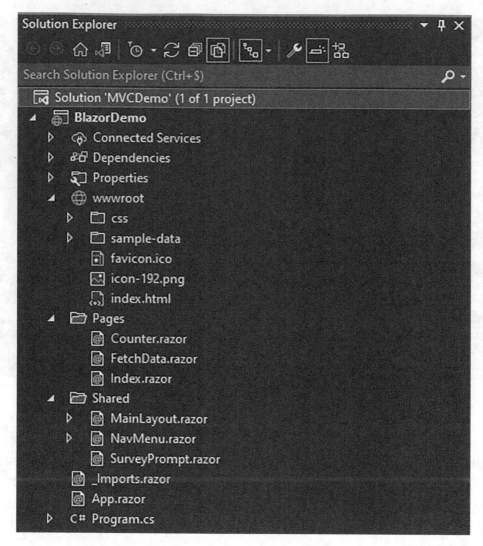

Figure 2-32. *A Blazor WebAssembly app*

Let's take a look at the entry point. As you can see, the Razor syntax remains the same compared to ASP.NET Core MVC and Razor Pages. However, the Razor Page file contains Blazor components that are missing in .cshtml files (MVC/Razor Pages), as shown in Figure 2-33.

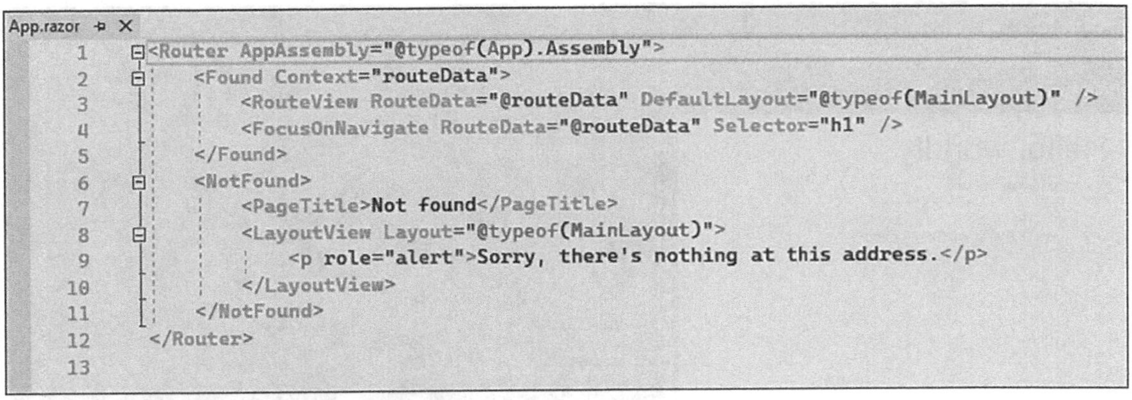

```
App.razor  ✛  ✕
    1    ⊟<Router AppAssembly="@typeof(App).Assembly">
    2    ⊟    <Found Context="routeData">
    3    │        <RouteView RouteData="@routeData" DefaultLayout="@typeof(MainLayout)" />
    4    │        <FocusOnNavigate RouteData="@routeData" Selector="h1" />
    5    │    </Found>
    6    ⊟    <NotFound>
    7    │        <PageTitle>Not found</PageTitle>
    8    ⊟        <LayoutView Layout="@typeof(MainLayout)">
    9    │            <p role="alert">Sorry, there's nothing at this address.</p>
   10    │        </LayoutView>
   11    │    </NotFound>
   12    </Router>
   13
```

Figure 2-33. *App.razor page*

Note that for Blazor WebAssembly apps, `Program.cs` is different from other `Program.cs` files for regular ASP.NET Core project types. In a WebAssembly scenario, ASP.NET Core configures and runs a *WebAssemblyHost* instead with a *WebAssemblyHostBuilder*, asynchronously to avoid browser blocking the UI thread, as shown in Figure 2-34.

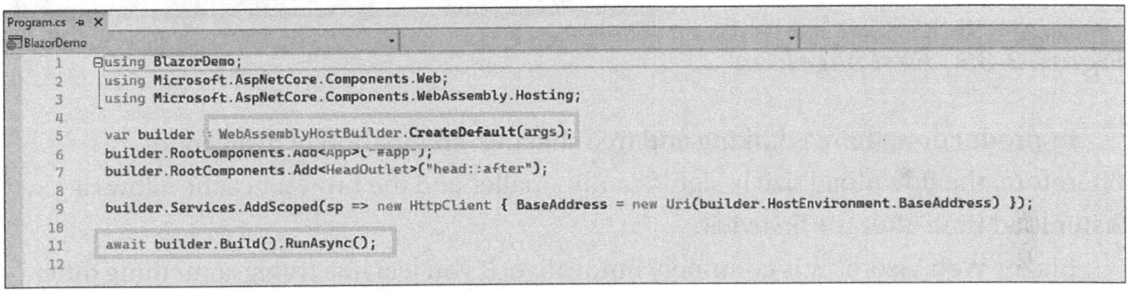

```
Program.cs  ✛  ✕
⊟BlazorDemo
    1    ⊟using BlazorDemo;
    2     using Microsoft.AspNetCore.Components.Web;
    3     using Microsoft.AspNetCore.Components.WebAssembly.Hosting;
    4
    5     var builder = WebAssemblyHostBuilder.CreateDefault(args);
    6     builder.RootComponents.Add<App>("#app");
    7     builder.RootComponents.Add<HeadOutlet>("head::after");
    8
    9     builder.Services.AddScoped(sp => new HttpClient { BaseAddress = new Uri(builder.HostEnvironment.BaseAddress) });
   10
   11     await builder.Build().RunAsync();
   12
```

Figure 2-34. *A Blazor WebAsssembly Program.cs file*

If you run the Blazor app, you'll notice all the DLLs are downloaded when loading the app (only in development mode), as shown in Figure 2-35.

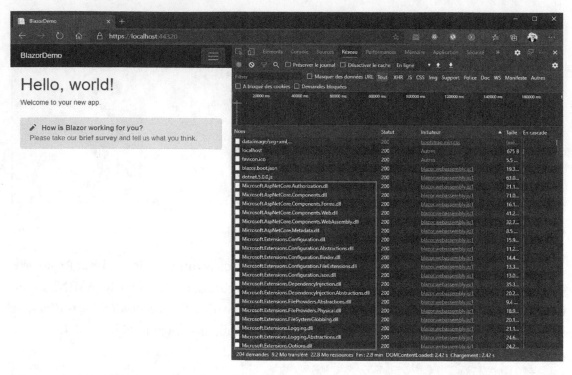

Figure 2-35. *First page load*

In production, there is linking and tree shaking (elimination of dead code). Therefore, the download size is significantly smaller and the browser cache allows a faster load time after the first visit.

Blazor WebAssembly is genuinely innovative. If you feel like trying something other than JavaScript/TypeScript, Blazor WebAssembly is the right choice!

ASP.NET Core SignalR

ASP.NET Core SignalR allows web apps to maintain a persistent connection and enable developers to add event notification functionality. So, when a new event is triggered, the app generates a notification to the user. This allows new web applications that require high-frequency updates from the server, such as real-time gaming. While this is a great way to make the web app much more engaging and intuitive, what exactly is SignalR? SignalR is a real-time, cross-browser, and open source two-way RPC protocol. So, each side in the connection can invoke procedures on the other side of the connection.

SignalR uses WebSockets when available and will gracefully fall back to other techniques like Ajax long polling; the application code remains the same whatever the fallback method used. As depicted in Figure 2-29 in the previous section, SignalR makes Blazor Server work.

SignalR provides an API for creating server-to-client *Remote Procedure Calls (RPCs)* that invoke JavaScript functions client side, like a browser or an Electron app which allows desktop application development with JavaScript. SignalR is also compatible with other client platforms, like C# in WPF. It also automatically handles connection management, such as connection/disconnection events, and lets the developer simultaneously broadcast messages to all connected clients. You can also send messages to specific clients. The connection between the client and server is persistent, unlike a classic HTTP connection, which is reestablished for each communication. From the server side, you define methods within a Hub that calls the client code. From the client side, you define methods within a Hub proxy that are called from the server, as shown in Figure 2-36.

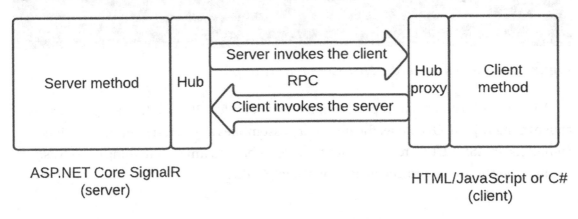

Figure 2-36. *ASP.NET Core SignalR client/server interaction*

Let's explore how to create an ASP.NET Core SignalR application. Unlike other projects in this chapter, there is no template for SignalR. You have to choose the ASP.NET Core Empty template, as Figure 2-37 shows.

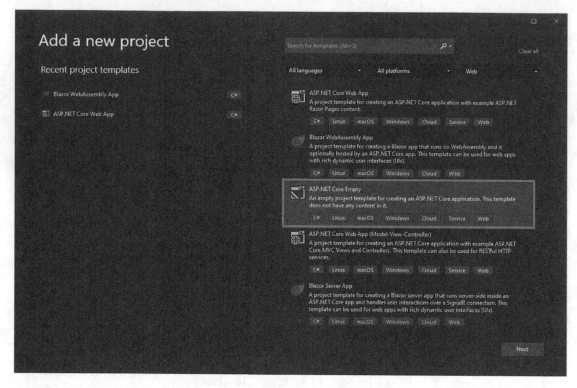

Figure 2-37. *Create an ASP.NET Core Empty app*

Visual Studio creates your project and only adds a few files, such as `Program.cs` and `appsettings.json`. Of course, the necessary assemblies are already imported—since SignalR is an ASP.NET Core component, we don't have to import anything ourselves. Figure 2-38 shows the project created by Visual Studio.

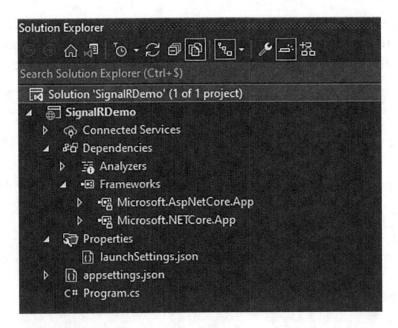

Figure 2-38. *ASP.NET Core app for SignalR*

Now, we must configure the application ourselves. To create our first Hub, we'll create a new class called MyHub.cs that we'll put in a dedicated Hubs directory. Before writing our method, we need to import the Microsoft.AspNetCore.SignalR namespace and inherit our MyHub class from the Hub class. We can then create our SendMessage method, which takes two parameters. The latter method will send all the connected clients a message using the ReceivedMessage client method. This example is shown in Figure 2-39.

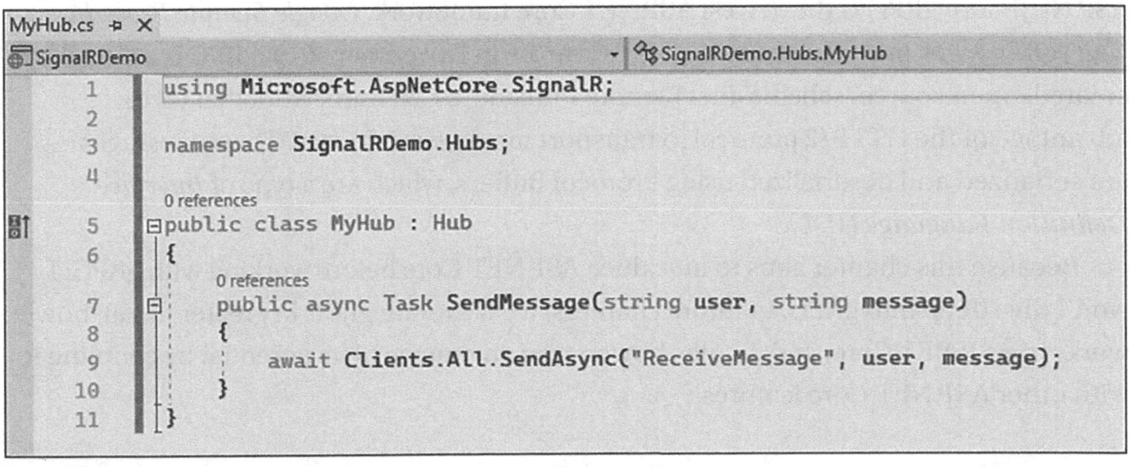

```
using Microsoft.AspNetCore.SignalR;

namespace SignalRDemo.Hubs;

public class MyHub : Hub
{
    public async Task SendMessage(string user, string message)
    {
        await Clients.All.SendAsync("ReceiveMessage", user, message);
    }
}
```

Figure 2-39. *Create a Hub class and a server method*

Finally, we need to configure our `Program.cs` file to enable SignalR with the `AddSignalR` extension method and related endpoints by declaring each Hub in the ASP. NET Core pipeline with the `MapHub` extension method, as shown in Figure 2-40.

```
Program.cs  ⊣ ×
SignalRDemo                                              ▾
     1    using SignalRDemo.Hubs;
     2
     3    var builder = WebApplication.CreateBuilder(args);
     4
     5    builder.Services.AddSignalR();
     6
     7    var app = builder.Build();
     8
     9    app.MapHub<MyHub>("/myhub");
    10
    11    app.MapGet("/", () => "Hello World!");
    12
    13    app.Run();
    14
```

Figure 2-40. *Configure the Program.cs for enabling SignalR endpoints*

ASP.NET Core gRPC

ASP.NET Core gRPC is the newest ASP.NET Core framework. *Google Remote Procedure Call (gRPC)* was introduced on ASP.NET Core 3.1 in November 2019. gRPC is a Google-created, open source, schema-first Remote Procedure Call framework that takes advantage of the HTTP/2 protocol to transport messages in binary. These messages are serialized and deserialized using Protocol Buffers, which are a type of *Interface Definition Language (IDL)*.

Because this chapter aims to introduce ASP.NET Core before working with gRPC, I won't dive deep into gRPC. In future chapters, we'll explore gRPC in greater detail, how it works in ASP.NET Core, and, finally, how to take advantage of its potential by coupling it with other ASP.NET Core features.

ASP.NET Core Minimal APIs

ASP.NET Core 6 introduces a new feature that is not a new framework like Blazor or gRPC, but I want to tell you about it because it's a feature that I like and I think you will too: minimal APIs.

Why do I like minimal APIs? For the simple reason that sometimes I have to write minimalistic APIs, one or two endpoints maximum with data to manipulate quite simply. How do minimal APIs work? There is no need to implement controllers, and only one file is necessary: the `Program.cs` file (which, as you already know, enables you to start an application with a minimal configuration). Note that all the ASP.NET Core pipeline remains the same: the dependency injection system, and the middleware that follows one another and manages HTTP requests and responses.

To get started, create an ASP.NET Core Empty project, as shown in Figure 2-41.

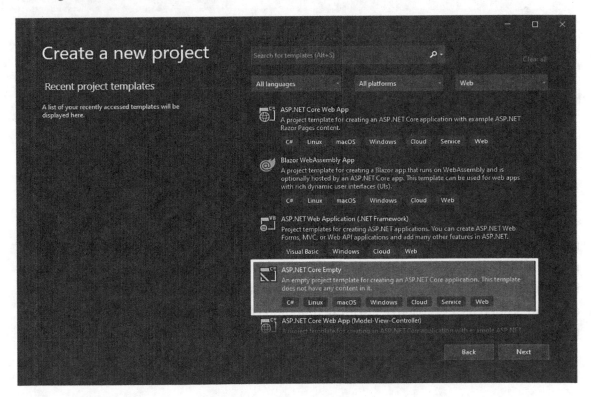

Figure 2-41. *Create an ASP.NET Core Empty project*

After you have named your project and clicked Create, Visual Studio 2022 will create the a minimalistic project with its default endpoint "Hello World", as shown in Figure 2-42.

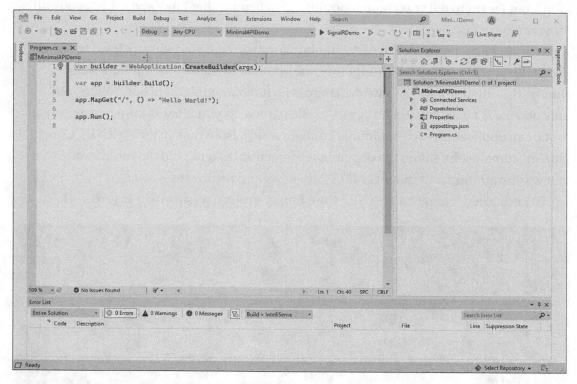

Figure 2-42. *Minimalistic ASP.NET Core project*

Figure 2-43 shows the minimal API configured to serve the Swagger documentation to reveal the "Hello" endpoint declared in the Program.cs file. Dependency injection is used for the *IHelloService* declared at the top of the file as a scoped service. C# 10 also introduces a new feature that allows developers to decorate lambdas expression with attributes, such as a FromRoute attribute that maps the route attribute *name* to the string parameter name.

```
IHelloService.cs        Program.cs

MinimalApiDemo

 1    using Microsoft.AspNetCore.Builder;
 2    using Microsoft.AspNetCore.Mvc;
 3    using Microsoft.Extensions.DependencyInjection;
 4    using Microsoft.Extensions.Hosting;
 5    using Microsoft.OpenApi.Models;
 6    using MinimalApiDemo.Services;
 7
 8    // Configure services
 9    var builder = WebApplication.CreateBuilder(args);
10
11    builder.Services.AddScoped<IHelloService, HelloService>();
12
13    builder.Services.AddEndpointsApiExplorer();
14
15    builder.Services.AddSwaggerGen(c =>
16    {
17        c.SwaggerDoc("v1", new OpenApiInfo { Title = "Api", Version = "v1" });
18    });
19
20    // Configure and enable middlewares
21    var app = builder.Build();
22
23    if (app.Environment.IsDevelopment())
24    {
25        app.UseDeveloperExceptionPage();
26    }
27
28    app.UseSwagger();
29    app.UseSwaggerUI(c => c.SwaggerEndpoint("/swagger/v1/swagger.json", "Api v1"));
30
31    app.MapGet("/{name}", ([FromRoute] string name, IHelloService service) => service.Hello(name));
32
33    // Run the app
34    app.Run();
```

Figure 2-43. *An example minimal API that uses dependency injection attributes on lambdas and serves as an endpoint with its Swagger documentation*

Figure 2-44 shows the Swagger UI generated from the code shown in Figure 2-43.

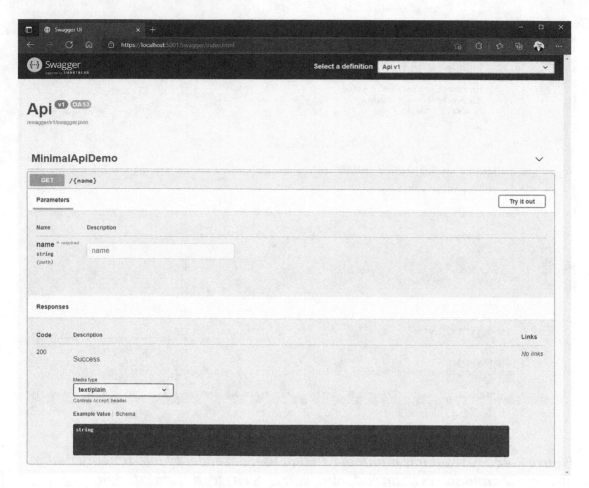

Figure 2-44. *An example of a minimal API Swagger UI*

I like this way of developing APIs. I use it almost automatically, as long as the project is not too big. I suggest you give it a try. Later in this book, we will return to it because inside our gRPC application, I will expose REST endpoints in our gRPC application. You will see that will be very practical in the use scenario that I will propose to you.

Summary

In this chapter, you've learned what ASP.NET Core is, its basics, and the frameworks it supports. ASP.NET Core is a vibrant framework. All kinds of web technologies are supported and well documented by Microsoft, which is why it's my favorite web application development framework, and I hope you enjoy it just as much as I do.

Throughout this book, you'll see how I'll mix gRPC and gRPC-web with technologies I introduced in this chapter to take advantage of the robust framework that is ASP. NET Core.

PART II

gRPC Fundamentals

CHAPTER 3

Understanding the gRPC Specification

Before we jump into the power of gRPC and ASP.NET Core, it is essential that you learn the gRPC specification and how it works. This is crucial because gRPC is much different from other technologies that you may be accustomed to working with, such as web APIs and *Simple Object Access Protocol (SOAP)* services. The gRPC specification is language-agnostic, which means that this specification not only is implemented with ASP.NET Core, but also can be integrated with other stacks like Java, PHP, and Node.js.

We'll cover the following content in this chapter:

- Introduction to Remote Procedure Calls

- gRPC concepts

- Introduction to the HTTP/2 protocol

- Benefits, drawbacks, and use cases

Introduction to Remote Procedure Calls

Remote Procedure Call (RPC) is a network protocol for establishing procedure calls on a remote computer using an application server—also known as a client/server model. The first description *of Remote Procedure Call* dates back to 1976 in the RFC 707 standard (`https://www.rfc-editor.org/info/rfc707`). Understanding the RPC principles and the RFC 707 standard was helpful for me to understand gRPC. It's always good to understand the basis of a system.

© Anthony Giretti 2022
A. Giretti, *Beginning gRPC with ASP.NET Core 6*, https://doi.org/10.1007/978-1-4842-8008-9_3

With RPC, a client invokes a *function*, a server procedure with parameters. When the server receives the request, it sends the required response back to the client. The client waits for the server to respond and cannot perform other operations until the server has finished the request. Figure 3-1 shows the RPC model principle.

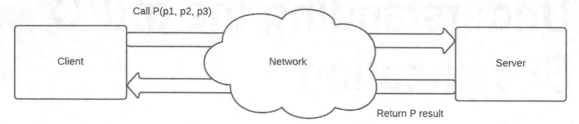

Figure 3-1. *The RPC model principle*

You need to understand that gRPC is influenced by this RPC model established long before gRPC. However, an important question to address is how an RPC call differs from a REST API call. After all, if you are accustomed to working with REST APIs, that could be a point of reference in your way of thinking.

- In an RPC API, an entity's feature is exposed (such as an entity creation or deletion) over a procedure, a function that has input parameters and returns a result. There is no significant dependency on HTTP verbs and URLs.

- In a REST API, an entity is considered a resource and uses HTTP verbs and specific URLs to expose operations on this resource. RESTful convention tends to encourage developers to use specific verbs in a particular situation: GET to retrieve data, POST to create data, PUT to replace data, PATCH to update data, and DELETE to delete data. Developers commonly use these verbs to perform *Create, Retrieve, Update, Delete (CRUD)* operations on data. REST is reliant on HTTP status codes. For example, if successful, a GET operation returns HTTP 200 OK status or HTTP 404 (NotFound) if the resource has not been found.

Despite the differences between these two protocols, they both use HTTP! With this basic knowledge of RPC, let's move on to gRPC concepts and learn how gRPC works.

gRPC Concepts

When I discover new technologies, I like to learn their history, and I will share the gRPC history with you. gRPC is an open source RPC framework initially developed by Google. The project started in the 2000s, and Google made it open source in 2014. gRPC uses Protocol Buffers (Protobuf) as the Interface Description Language, and message serialization and deserialization are done in *binary* over an HTTP/2 connection (I'll dive into specifics in a subsequent section). gRPC allows developers to build client/server applications with a wide choice of programming languages, such as:

- Java
- C
- C++
- Node.js (JavaScript/TypeScript)
- Python
- Ruby
- GO
- Dart
- PHP
- C#

Like any Remote Procedure Call, gRPC defines one or several procedures(s) that can be called remotely with their input parameter. On the server side, a gRPC server runs, which exposes functions to handle client calls. The client is implemented from a any language among languages shown above that supports the same gRPC methods (stubs) as the server.

Protocol Buffers

The gRPC client is aware of the available gRPC procedures (functions) and their input/output parameters (messages) due to sharing Protocol Buffers between the client and the server, which are language descriptors—much like *WSDL* for SOAP web services such as *Windows Communication Foundation (WCF)*, which is a Microsoft SOAP implementation. Chapter 8 will cover WCF and how it differs from gRPC.

The Protocol Buffers are stored in a .proto file. Listing 3-1 gives an example of the Protobuf syntax to build a service named *CountryService*, which exposes a procedure called GetById(), taking itself a message parameter named CountrySearchRequest and returning a message named CountryReply.

Listing 3-1. CountryService Described with the Protobuf Syntax

```
syntax = "proto3";

service CountryService {
  rpc GetById (CountrySearchRequest) returns (CountryReply) {}
}

message CountrySearchRequest {
    int32 CountryId = 1;
}

message CountryReply {
    int32 Id = 1;
    string Name = 2;
    string Description = 3;
}
```

You define the syntax using the syntax keyword, define services with the service and rpc keywords, and define entities with the message keyword. The next chapter will detail the Protobuf syntax and how a stub (client generated in a particular language) is made.

gRPC Channel

Any request to a gRPC server from any client is made through a *channel*. A gRPC channel is used to establish a connection to the server and allow Remote Procedure Calls. A *Channel* requires the following information to be initialized:

- The address of the remote host
- The port
- Connection credentials

A *channel* supports the configuration of the server's connection credentials and the credentials for each RPC request made to the server.

Three types of connection are supported:

- **SSL/TLS**: *Secure Sockets Layer (SSL)* and *Transport Layer Security (TLS)* are both cryptographic protocols that encrypt data and authenticate a connection when transferring data over the Internet. To use SSL/TLS, you need to install an SSL/TLS certificate on your web server. It includes a public key and a private key that authenticate your server and allow it to encrypt and decrypt data.

- **ALTS**: *Application Layer Transport Security (ALTS)* is an authentication and encryption protocol designed by Google that uses the Diffie-Hellman key exchange system. It looks like TLS, but both the client and the server need the certificate.

- **Token-based authentication**: This is used to authenticate a user from a token named *JWT (JSON Web Token)*, which contains the identity of a user issued by a third-party identity manager and not by the application itself. The initiator of the request will ask the server for a token, then pass it in the headers of the HTTP request. The client will validate its authenticity by reading the metadata provided for the third-party identity server, by checking the signature of the token received (check that the token actually comes from the supposed issuer). This is the type of authentication most commonly used for web applications.

Most of the time, the credentials for each RPC request made to the server are configured on the calls themselves, especially when using tokens. In the .NET implementation of gRPC, Microsoft encapsulates this in its custom gRPC client implementation. You just have to add your JWT within your request headers on the procedure call.

Finally, a channel supports options such as the maximum size of messages sent or messages received. If you want to learn all available options, go to the gRPC GitHub repository: `https://grpc.github.io/grpc/core/group__grpc__arg__keys.html`.

Listing 3-2 shows the creation of a channel in C# (whatever the .NET framework used) with a custom SSL certificate (`myCertificate.pem`, which includes the public certificate) and an option that limits the size of received messages to 5 MB. Then this channel is used to initialize a client (stub) that has been auto-generated from Protocol Buffers.

Listing 3-2. Creation of a Secured gRPC Channel in C# with Limitation of Messages Size

```
var channel = new Channel("https://localhost:5001", new
SslCredentials("myCertificate.pem"), new [] {
              new ChannelOption("grpc.max_receive_message_
              length","5242880") // 5 MB
          });
var countryClient = new CountryServiceClient(channel);
```

Listing 3-3 shows the same channel without any encryption or authentication (this is *not recommended*—always use HTTPS).

Listing 3-3. Creation of an Unsecured gRPC Channel in C#

```
var channel = new Channel("https://localhost:5001", ChannelCredentials.
Insecure, new [] {
              new ChannelOption("grpc.max_receive_message_
              length","5242880") // 5 MB
          });
var countryClient = new CountryServiceClient(channel);
```

In Chapter 7, we'll revisit that piece of code, and I'll show you all the required dependencies to write this *Channel* in C# for .NET Framework. In the case of .NET 6, it will be quite different.

While using the created *Channel*, you can check its status. It has a property named State that can have the following values:

- Idle

- Connecting (to the remote server)

- Ready (to handle RPCs)

- TransientFailure: An error occurred, but the error is not fatal, and the *Channel* can be reused, after returning to Ready state over the ConnectAsync method with a C# client

- Shutdown: A fatal error occurred, or the *Channel* has been shut down programmatically

Types of gRPC Services

gRPC supports four types of calls to the server:

- Unary

- Server-streaming

- Client-streaming

- Bidirectional

Unlike a REST API, which only supports unary type calls (the client sends a request, and the server receives it and returns the response with its status to the client), gRPC supports all four types, as described next.

Unary Calls

The client initiates the remote procedure call with the method name, metadata, and the request message. Then the server returns the response with the gRPC status, the response message, and metadata. Figure 3-2 shows the unary RPC sequence diagram.

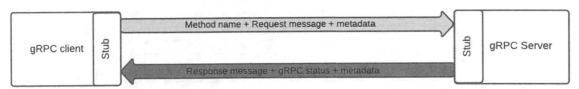

Figure 3-2. *Unary RPC sequence*

Server-Streaming Calls

The client initiates the remote procedure call with the method name, metadata, and the request message. Then it receives a streaming response from the server. The request's status is sent to the client at the end of the streaming response (all data has been transmitted to the client along with its metadata). Figure 3-3 shows the server-streaming RPC sequence diagram.

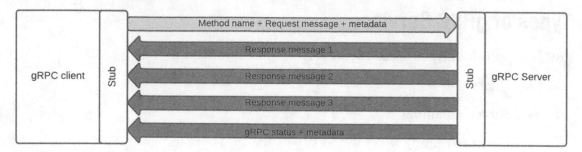

Figure 3-3. *Server-streaming RPC sequence*

Client-Streaming Calls

The client initiates the remote procedure call with the method name and metadata. Then the client sends streaming messages. However, the server can send the request status code and metadata before sending the client's messages. If a problem occurs on the server and it has already sent the status and metadata, detecting errors is difficult. Figure 3-4 shows the client-streaming RPC sequence diagram.

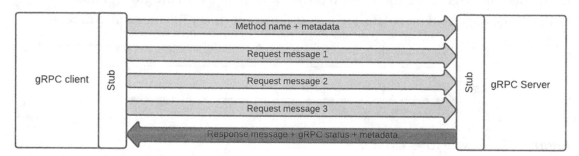

Figure 3-4. *Client-streaming RPC sequence*

Bidirectional Streaming Calls

Each party sends its messages by streaming, and this can be done in parallel, which means there is no order in which client/server messages are sent and received. The client initiates the remote procedure call with the method name and metadata. Then the server can respond to it immediately by returning the status and its metadata (or when the client has finished sending all of its messages). Figure 3-5 shows the bidirectional streaming RPC sequence diagram.

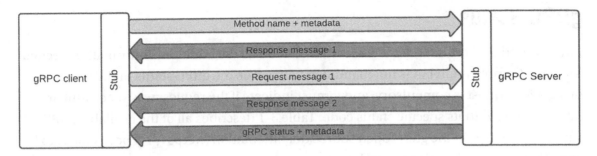

Figure 3-5. *Bidirectional streaming RPC sequence*

Later in this book, you'll discover how to implement these sequences in C#.

Trailers

gRPC allows metadata to be used in the form of trailers. Trailers are HTTP request headers but work differently. In a gRPC request, the Headers and Trailers are sent at the beginning of the request before the data (messages). In a gRPC response, the headers are received at the start of the response before the data (message), and trailers are received at the end with the gRPC status. This is not the HTTP status of the request but represents the status of the gRPC request, much like an HTTP status). To support streaming, the metadata must be sent after the streamed response is completed. Trailers allow transport between the client and any data type but always contain the gRPC status. Figure 3-6 summarizes how headers, data, and trailers are sent to and received from the server.

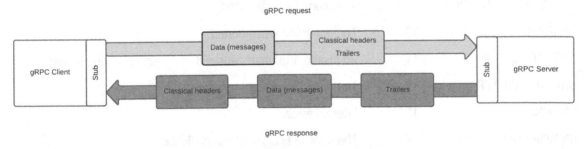

Figure 3-6. *Headers, Data, Trailers over gRPC requests and responses sequence diagram*

gRPC Status

I mentioned that trailers are metadata that contain all the additional information needed for a gRPC application but is not mandatory. However, the gRPC status in the response of a gRPC request is compulsory, and it must indicate if the request was successful or not and why, with its specific status code. Table 3-1 describes all of the available gRPC statuses, as listed in the gRPC open source documentation (`https://grpc.github.io/ grpc/core/md_doc_statuscodes.html`).

Table 3-1. *gRPC Statuses*

Code	Number	Description
OK	0	Success.
CANCELLED	1	The operation was cancelled.
UNKNOWN	2	Unknown error.
INVALID_ARGUMENT	3	The client specified an invalid argument.
DEADLINE_EXCEEDED	4	The deadline expired before the operation could complete.
NOT_FOUND	5	The requested entity was not found.
ALREADY_EXISTS	6	The entity already exists.
PERMISSION_DENIED	7	The caller doesn't have the required permission.
RESOURCE_EXHAUSTED	8	The requested resource has been exhausted.
FAILED_PRECONDITION	9	A precondition has failed.
ABORTED	10	The operation was aborted.
OUT_OF_RANGE	11	An invalid argument causes that exception during its cast.
UNIMPLEMENTED	12	The operation is not implemented.
INTERNAL	13	Internal error.
UNAVAILABLE	14	The service is currently unavailable.
DATA_LOSS	15	Unrecoverable data loss or corruption.
UNAUTHENTICATED	16	The request does not have valid authentication credentials for the operation.

Deadline and Cancellation

With gRPC, it is possible, just like a REST call with an HttpClient in .NET, to specify a timeout. In the gRPC specification, this is called a *Deadline* (a maximum execution time for a request). If the *Deadline* is exceeded, the client throws a DEADLINE_EXCEED gRPC error status. Then, the server will abort the request. In the .NET ecosystem, a *Cancellation Token* is generated server-side, allowing the cancellation to be propagated to the underlying services.

If no *Deadline* is specified in a .NET stub, the request will continue its execution until it is completed. No *Deadline* duration is specified by default. Figure 3-7 shows the workflow of a gRPC request with a 5-second deadline in a .NET context.

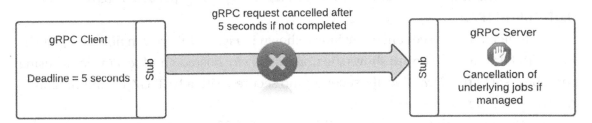

Figure 3-7. *Deadline exceeded workflow in a .NET implementation*

gRPC Requests and Responses over HTTP/2

With a basic knowledge of gRPC concepts, let's explore how gRPC works through HTTP/2 framing.

We already know that gRPC works like this:

- It uses the classic headers of an HTTP request.

- It uses specific headers called trailers.

- The response contains the gRPC status in the trailers, informing the client of the result of the request.

- The response is encoded in binary.

However, gRPC also sends an HTTP request to the server as follows:

- It works with TLS (in other words, HTTPS). It works also without TLS, which is not recommended. In this book I will always use HTTPS.

- It uses POST exclusively.

- The Content-Type is "application/grpc" or "application/grpc+proto" or "application/grpc+json".

- It uses an Authority header, which is the server domain name.

- It uses a Path header, which is the RPC URI.

- The HTTP status of the response is always 200 OK from the moment the server processes the request. However, if the server does not process the request because of unavailability, it could then return Service Unavailable 503.

If you are curious to learn more, you can read the complete operation of gRPC with the HTTP/2 framing on GitHub: https://github.com/grpc/grpc/blob/master/doc/PROTOCOL-HTTP2.md.

As depicted in the sequence previously shown in Figure 3-6, we can now complete it with HTTP frames. Figure 3-8 shows the *CountryService* hosted on a local machine, using port 5001, set with a *Deadline* of 5 seconds and secured with a JWT. GZIP compression is enabled, and the call succeeds.

On the request, the *end of stream (EOS)* flag (END_STREAM) set on the DATA frame signifies that no more data is expected. In the case of streaming, this flag is set on the last DATA frame sent to the server. The *end of headers (EOH)* flag (END_OF_HEADERS) signifies all headers have been sent to the server.

On the response, the EOH is the same as the request, but the last frame that sends *Trailers* to the client means that no more headers exist and no more data is expected to be sent.

In both request and response, <Length-Prefixed Message> represents the data (message), with some associated metadata (which is different from Trailers).

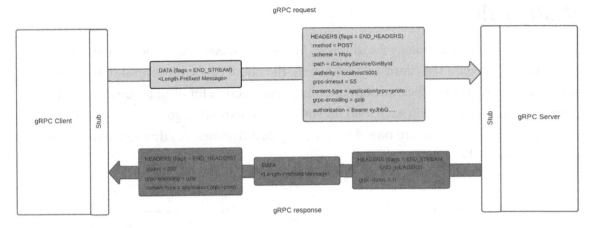

Figure 3-8. *gRPC request and response with the related HTTP frames*

Introduction to the HTTP/2 Protocol

The benefits of gRPC can be attributed to the robust capabilities of HTTP/2, which set it apart from HTTP/1.

HTTP was born in the 1990s. HTTP has evolved since then but any revolutionary changes. The latest version of HTTP/1 is HTTP/1.1, which has been around for 15 years but is no longer suited to the growing needs of today's Web. The main goal of HTTP/2 is to increase the performance and robustness of the HTTP network protocol by reducing the processing latency of HTTP requests with new strategies for delivering data between a client and a server, such as:

- Multiplexing
- Compression and binary data transport
- Flow control
- Server push

Multiplexing

Multiplexing is a new strategy for dialogue between a server and a client. With the same connection between the client and the server, the client can send several requests to the server. It's much more efficient than opening a connection for each request, as HTTP/1 does. You certainly want to save load on your server, so that's a great feature of HTTP/2. gRPC streaming requests are based on this. Figure 3-9 shows this difference between HTTP/2 and HTTP/1.9

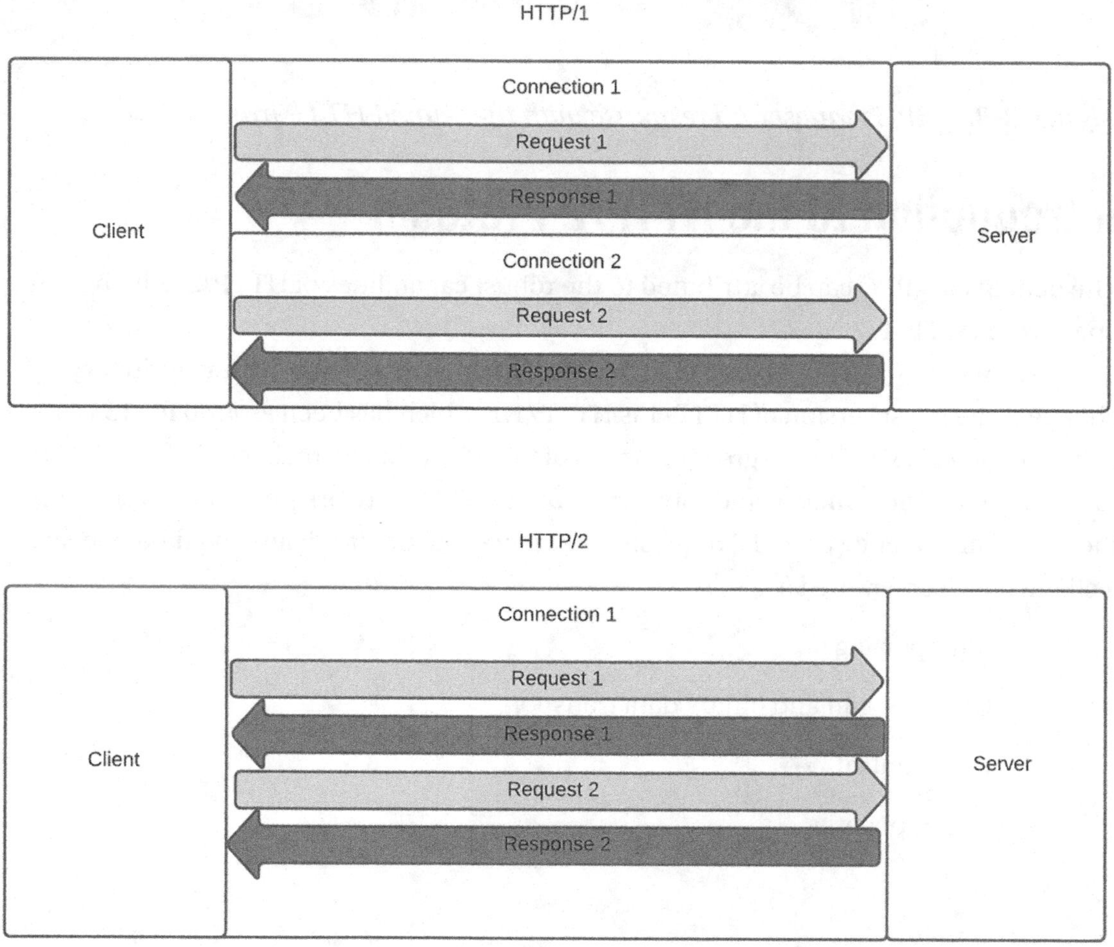

Figure 3-9. *Multiplexing in HTTP/2 versus HTTP/1*

Compression and Binary Data Transport

HTTP/2 allows data transport in binary and incidentally allows efficient compression (repeated strings of bytes offer remarkable compression efficiency). This is reflected in performance:

- Network latency is reduced because the data is less voluminous.

- Network traffic is reduced and allows better use of the network.

As we have already seen, gRPC is also based on this principle.

In HTTP/2, headers can be compressed with the *HPACK* specification. This specification is described in the RFC 7541 standard (`https://tools.ietf.org/html/rfc7541`).

Flow Control

HTTP/2 allows you to prioritize the data flow between the client and the server. The client decides on the priority to be given to a flow. This allows the server to optimize the network resources for the processing of the flow and the latency. The gRPC documentation does not specify whether this strategy is used.

Server Push

HTTP/2 supports server push, but it doesn't work the same as SignalR (introduced in Chapter 2) push (which is an RPC framework and uses WebSockets), because HTTP/2 server push relies on (obviously) HTTP. gRPC does not support this communication strategy.

Benefits, Drawbacks, and Use Cases

Throughout this chapter, you learned how gRPC works with its inherent behavior and performance benefit, taking advantage of HTTP/2. If we take a step back to observe better what gRPC is and can do, we can understand its main benefits and drawbacks compared to a SOAP web service or even REST.

Benefits

While SOAP is based on XML and REST is common with JSON, gRPC uses binary, which enables it to perform better than SOAP and JSON (binary serialization/deserialization uses less memory than JSON serialization/deserialization, and the same payload serialized in binary is 40% lighter than its JSON serialized version).

Regarding convenience, REST cannot provide two-way streaming, while gRPC and SOAP (WCF, for example) support it, but gRPC offers it over HTTP/2, which is an undeniable advantage. Note that SOAP supports different types of transport, unlike REST and gRPC, such as SMTP and FTP.

Drawbacks

Unlike REST, gRPC is not compatible with browsers because of HTTP/2. HTTP/2 is not fully supported in today's browsers because they can't interpret binary data. The binary data that gRPC renders also make debugging impossible for humans but more secure because binary is hard to decode without knowing the schema. However, later in this book, we will dive into gRPC-web, a particular implementation of gRPC to overcome browsers incompatibility. This lack of compatibility is the main drawback of gRPC.

Lastly, gRPC is not cacheable like SOAP, but REST is, which is a clear disadvantage of gRPC. However, there is another way to implement caching: using an in-memory cache instead of an HTTP cache. Microsoft describes this alternative here: `https://docs.microsoft.com/en-us/aspnet/core/performance/caching/memory?view=aspnetcore-6.0`.

Table 3-2 gives a summary of the comparison between gRPC, REST, and SOAP.

Table 3-2. *Comparison Between gRPC, REST, and SOAP*

	gRPC	REST	SOAP
Browser support	No	Yes	No
HTTP/2 support	Yes	Yes	Yes
Human readability	No	Yes	Yes
Exchange format	Binary	JSON /XML	XML
Performance	High	Medium	Low
Caching	No	Yes	No
Bidirectional streaming	Yes	No	Yes

Use Cases

From the comparison in Table 3-2, you better understand the advantages and disadvantages of gRPC. You can imagine common scenarios for gRPC compared to other types of services. gRPC services can replace the architectures in service mode and machine-to-machine microservices (back end to back end). gRPC can replace REST and SOAP in the following types of applications (illustrated in Figure 3-10):

- API to API, often used in complex architectures that require many services talking to others. No browser is needed, so gRPC could be a great fit there.

- A monolithic application in a service-oriented architecture (SOA), like the preceding scenario; if the browser does not call services, gRPC could also be a great fit.

- Background jobs (Windows service, CRON, etc.) connected to one or more web service(s), which is purely a back-end scenario; gRPC could replace REST or SOAP web services.

- A browser web app connected to a service or microservices over a REST API acting as a proxy. This scenario is more common than you might think. For example, a browser may talk directly to a single REST API, but the latter may talk to many back-end services. No browser is needed, so once again, gRPC may be a great fit.

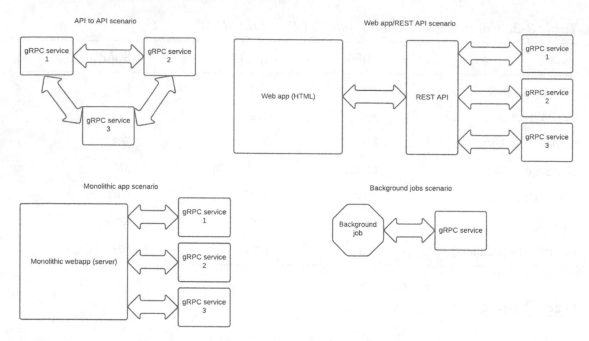

Figure 3-10. gRPC use cases

Summary

In this chapter, you discovered the operating principle of gRPC, its advantages, and its disadvantages, enabling you to understand which scenarios might be more advantageous to use gRPC in place of REST or SOAP services. Finally, you learned about the benefits of HTTP/2. If you want to learn more about the comparison of gRPC and REST APIs, Microsoft summarizes it well at `https://docs.microsoft.com/en-us/aspnet/core/grpc/comparison?view=aspnetcore-6.0`.

In the next chapter, we'll look in more depth at Protocol Buffers by exploring the syntax of this Interface Description Language and how to generate a stub.

CHAPTER 4

Protobufs

So far, you've discovered the fundamentals of .NET 6, ASP.NET Core 6, and gRPC. You're almost ready to develop gRPC applications with ASP.NET Core. First, though, you need to understand language Protocol Buffers, the topic of this chapter. That will enable you to build your first gRPC service in the next chapter.

In this chapter, you will learn about the following:

- About Protocol Buffers
- Individual declarations
- Services declarations
- Messages declarations

Note   All C# code in this chapter has been developed with Visual Studio 2022 and the Visual Studio gRPC service template. Chapters 5 and 7 will show how to generate server and client C# stubs.

About Protocol Buffers

Protocol Buffers language, as you will see, is a relatively simple language. One takeaway is that messages do not support inheritance. If you want to define messages that are similar to each other, you cannot make them inherit from a base message.

A Protobuf file contains three main sections:

- Individual declarations such as the choice of the language version, options, and import another proto file (.proto is the extension of a protobuf file)
- Services declaration
- Messages declaration

© Anthony Giretti 2022
A. Giretti, *Beginning gRPC with ASP.NET Core 6*, https://doi.org/10.1007/978-1-4842-8008-9_4

I will show you how to define a `CountryService` class in a Protobuf file and the generated code after compilation. A Protobuf file is complete when the three Protobuf sections are defined, as described in the rest of this chapter.

Individual Declarations

You must **always** define the version of the Protobuf syntax you want to use. There are three versions of this syntax:

- Proto3
- Proto2
- Proto1 (deprecated)

In this chapter (and for the rest of the book), I will only focus on version 3 (proto3). Although version 2 (proto2) is not deprecated, it is still recommended to use version 3. For example, version 3 brings new features such as JSON encoding, *Well-Known Types*, and strict UTF-8 enforcement.

A Protobuf file begins with the definition of the syntax, with the `syntax` keyword, as shown in Listing 4-1.

Listing 4-1. Definition of the Proto3 Syntax

```
syntax = "proto3";
```

Protocol Buffers language lets you define namespaces for your services and messages, using the `package` keyword. The generated code will be encapsulated within a namespace, its name matches the package name setup into the proto file. In Listing 4-2, the package name is specified as `gRPCDemo.v1`.

Listing 4-2. Protobuf file defined with gRPCDemo.v1 Package Name

```
syntax = "proto3";

package gRPCDemo.v1;
```

The generated code gives the result shown in Listing 4-3, which corresponds to messages generated in C#. Protocol Buffers compilation generates two files: one for messages and another one for services. We haven't defined a message yet, but the generated file contains code needed for reflection information (`FileDescriptor` and `CountryReflection`). I'll expand on this later in this section.

Listing 4-3. Generated Messages File from a Proto File Defined with gRPCDemo.v1 Package Name

```
// <auto-generated>
//     Generated by the protocol buffer compiler.  DO NOT EDIT!
//     source: Protos/country.proto
// </auto-generated>
#pragma warning disable 1591, 0612, 3021
#region Designer generated code

using pb = global::Google.Protobuf;
using pbc = global::Google.Protobuf.Collections;
using pbr = global::Google.Protobuf.Reflection;
using scg = global::System.Collections.Generic;
namespace GRPCDemo.V1 {

  /// <summary>Holder for reflection information generated from Protos/
  country.proto</summary>
  public static partial class CountryReflection {

    #region Descriptor
    /// <summary>File descriptor for Protos/country.proto</summary>
    public static pbr::FileDescriptor Descriptor {
      get { return descriptor; }
    }
    private static pbr::FileDescriptor descriptor;

    static CountryReflection() {
      byte[] descriptorData = global::System.Convert.FromBase64String(
          string.Concat(
            "ChRQcm90b3MvY291bnRyeS5wcm90bxILZ1JQQORlbW8udjFiBnByb3RvMw=="));
```

```
    descriptor = pbr::FileDescriptor.FromGeneratedCode(descriptorData,
        new pbr::FileDescriptor[] { },
        new pbr::GeneratedClrTypeInfo(null, null, null));
    }
    #endregion

  }
}
```

```
#endregion Designer generated code
```

The C# namespace is generated from the package name with the initial casing. If special characters exist, like an underscore, they will be removed. Unlike C#, where dashes or question marks are legal, they are strictly forbidden in Protobuf syntax. Dots are allowed and not removed after compilation.

The package keyword is optional, so it's possible not to use it at all. If you do this, C# generated code won't be encapsulated in a particular namespace. With C#, the generated code will belong to the *global* namespace, so your services and messages are invokable, as shown in Listing 4-4.

Listing 4-4. Instantiate a Class from Global Namespace

```
var instance = new global::SomeService();
```

I *don't recommend* using global namespaces, so I strongly suggest that you define a namespace with the package keyword or with an option named csharp_namespace (Protocol Buffers allows some options like defining a C# namespace with the option keyword), as shown in Listing 4-5.

Listing 4-5. Defining optional C# Apress.Sample.gRPC namespace

```
syntax = "proto3";

package gRPCDemo.v1;

option csharp_namespace = "Apress.Sample.gRPC";
```

Now, you might be wondering about the possible values of this option. It allows the generated namespace to be overriden in C# with the package's name. The file generated in C# for messages and services will have the namespace Apress.Sample.gRPC rather than gRPCDemo.v1. So, if we use the csharp_namespace option, what is the use of the *package* name? The *package* name will be used to give a name to the generated service, and this name will be used to **generate the URL**, which will be invoked during the call to the remote procedure. (Chapter 6 will cover this in more detail.) Listing 4-6 shows the services file generated in C#. I removed all code and left only the service name and namespace for clarity.

Listing 4-6. Generated C# Namespace and Service Name

```
// <auto-generated>
//      Generated by the protocol buffer compiler.  DO NOT EDIT!
//      source: Protos/country.proto
// </auto-generated>
#pragma warning disable 0414, 1591
#region Designer generated code

using grpc = global::Grpc.Core;
namespace Apress.Sample.gRPC {
  public static partial class CountryService
  {
    static readonly string __ServiceName = "gRPCDemo.v1.CountryService";
  }
}
#endregion
```

Note that the gRPCDemo.v1.CountryService value is populated from concatenating the package name and the service name defined in the Protobuf file, as shown in Listing 4-7.

Listing 4-7. Defining a Service Named CountryService

```
syntax = "proto3";

package gRPCDemo.v1;

option csharp_namespace = "Apress.Sample.gRPC";

service CountryService {
  rpc GetById (CountrySearchRequest) returns (CountryReply) {}
}
```

If a package name is not set, then the __ServiceName property will have the value of CountryService.

To view all options, visit the Google Protocol Buffers documentation at this URL: https://developers.google.com/protocol-buffers/docs/proto3#options.

We'll get back to individual declarations in the "Messages Declaration" section. I'll introduce you to the import keyword, designed to import other messages from other Protobuf files.

Services Declaration

The services declaration is the second part of a Protobuf file. Here, we declare the name of the service, as well as its procedures and their parameters. The service's name is preceded by the service keyword and encapsulates all the service functions with brackets. Each function is preceded by the RPC keyword and followed by the signature of the input message in parentheses, then followed by the return keyword indicating the output message, also in parentheses, as shown in Listing 4-8.

Listing 4-8. Services Declaration Pattern

```
service ServiceName {
  rpc FunctionName1 (InputMessage1) returns (OutputMessage1) {}
  rpc FunctionName2 (InputMessage2) returns (OutputMessage2) {}
}
```

In the previous chapter I introduced you to the four types of RPC services available with gRPC. I'll show you how to define these different services in a Protobuf file. When a service sends or receives a streamed message, it prefixes the messages declaration with the stream keyword, as shown in Listing 4-9.

Listing 4-9. Declare a Unary Function, Client-Streaming Function, Server-Streaming Function, and Bidirectional Streaming Function

```
service ServiceName {
  rpc UnaryFunction (InputMessage1) returns (OutputMessage1) {}
  rpc ClientStreamingFunction (stream InputMessage2) returns
  (OutputMessage2) {}
```

```
rpc ServerStreamingFunction (InputMessage3) returns (stream
OutputMessage3) {}
rpc BidirectionalStreamingFunction (stream InputMessage4) returns
(stream OutputMessage4) {}
}
```

Imagine building a service, still the same for the moment, CountryService, with a function for each type of service:

- Creation of several countries in bidirectional streaming, client streaming for each country to be created, and server streaming in response for each country created

- Deletion of several countries in client streaming and receipt of a message from the server once client streaming is done

- Country search that sends search parameters in a message and expects found countries in server streaming as a response

- Search for a country by its identifier in a unary call, and send and receive a message

Listing 4-10 shows the Protobuf file's syntax definition, package name, C# namespace, and services. In the meantime, use this naming convention:

- Function name is prefixed with an explicit action name

- Input messages are suffixed with Request, indicating the client origin of the message

- Output messages are suffixed with Reply, indicating the server origin of the message

This convention is not mandatory, but I recommend establishing a convention to keep some clarity in your code.

Listing 4-10. Definition of CountryService

```
service CountryService {
  rpc GetById(CountryByIdRequest) returns (CountryReply) {}
  rpc Delete(stream CountryRequest) returns (CountryDeletionReply) {}
```

```
rpc Search(CountrySearchRequest) returns (stream CountryReply) {}
rpc Create(stream CountryCreateRequest) returns (stream
CountryCreationReply) {}
}
```

Listing 4-11 shows generated RPC functions. I modified the code to show only the four generated methods (GetById(), Delete(), Search(), and Create()) defined in the generated CountryServiceBase class (stub). Note that CountryServiceBase is abstract, and when you write your gRPC services, you need to override RPC functions because their default implementation throws an exception with *UNIMPLEMENTED* status. An RpcException is the specific exception returned each time an exception is thrown while the gRPC application runs. In later chapters, we'll cover RpcException in detail.

Listing 4-11. CountryServiceBase Class and GetById(), Delete(), Search(), and Create() RPC Functions

```
/// <summary>Base class for server-side implementations of CountryService</
summary>
[grpc::BindServiceMethod(typeof(CountryService), "BindService")]
public abstract partial class CountryServiceBase
{
    public virtual global::System.Threading.Tasks.Task<global::Apress.
    Sample.gRPC.CountryReply> GetById(global::Apress.Sample.gRPC.
    CountryByIdRequest request, grpc::ServerCallContext context)
    {
        throw new grpc::RpcException(new grpc::Status(grpc::StatusCode.
        Unimplemented, ""));
    }

    public virtual global::System.Threading.Tasks.Task<global::Apress.
    Sample.gRPC.CountryDeletionReply> Delete(grpc::IAsyncStreamRea
    der<global::Apress.Sample.gRPC.CountryRequest> requestStream,
    grpc::ServerCallContext context)
    {
        throw new grpc::RpcException(new grpc::Status(grpc::StatusCode.
        Unimplemented, ""));
    }
```

```
public virtual global::System.Threading.Tasks.Task
Search(global::Apress.Sample.gRPC.CountrySearchRequest request, gr
pc::IServerStreamWriter<global::Apress.Sample.gRPC.CountryReply>
responseStream, grpc::ServerCallContext context)
{
    throw new grpc::RpcException(new grpc::Status(grpc::StatusCode.
    Unimplemented, ""));
}

public virtual global::System.Threading.Tasks.Task Create(grpc::
IAsyncStreamReader<global::Apress.Sample.gRPC.CountryCreateRequest>
requestStream, grpc::IServerStreamWriter<global::Apress.Sample.gRPC.
CountryCreationReply> responseStream, grpc::ServerCallContext context)
{
    throw new grpc::RpcException(new grpc::Status(grpc::StatusCode.
    Unimplemented, ""));
}
}
```

In the previous chapter, we compared gRPC services and REST services. Unlike REST, the gRPC service is not based on verbs, so we cannot associate an operation with a verb. It's now *your responsibility* to create your own conventions to clarify which operations perform which actions.

Messages Declaration

This section introduces you to the message declaration syntax. Then, you'll be ready to create gRPC services with ASP.NET Core!

The message declaration syntax supports the following:

- Scalar type values

- Collections

- Enumerations

- Nested types

- Import types

- Any, Value, Wrappers, dates, and times (Well-Known Types)

- Bytes

- One of

- Empty messages

- Comments

This same syntax does not support the following:

- Message inheritance, so sometimes you have to rewrite redundant code (similar messages).

- Message validation, the proto3 syntax (unlike proto2), does not allow you to define verifications. They must be implemented in your client application and/or gRPC server.

- The absence of a message as the parameter of a function; indeed, even if you have no parameter to send to the server or to return to the client, it is mandatory to create an empty message without properties.

And finally, all messages share the same rule: any message must be defined with the message keyword, and each property is *optional* by default. Each message must be assigned a position required for the serialization/deserialization process and must be *unique*. Any generated message inherits from the IMessage<T> interface, which gives the generated C# class the identity of a message resulting from a compilation from the Protobuf language. Listing 4-12 shows a CountryReply message with three properties.

Listing 4-12. CountryReply Message

```
syntax = "proto3";

package gRPCDemo.v1;

option csharp_namespace = "Apress.Sample.gRPC";

message CountryReply {
    int32 Id = 1;
    string Name = 2;
    string Description = 3;
}
```

Scalar Type Values

Once compiled, I'll list all the scalar variables supported by the Protocol Buffers syntax and their type in C#. Please note that these variables cannot be declared directly as a parameter in an RPC function but instead must be declared in a message in the current Protobuf file or imported from another. It's essential to know them. They are crucial in any project. I included in Table 4-1 their default value when the developer does not set them.

Table 4-1. *Protocol Buffer Supported Types and Their Default Values*

Protocol Buffer Type	C# Type	C# Default Value
double	double	0
float	float	0
int32	int	0
int64	long	0
uint32	uint	0
uint64	ulong	0
sint32	int	0
sint64	long	0
fixed32	unit	0
fixed64	ulong	0
sfixed32	int	0
sfixed64	long	0
bool	bool	false
string	string	string.Empty
bytes	ByteString	empty bytes

Collections

Collections, also essential in any project type, are supported in the Protobuf syntax with the following two types:

- Lists
- Dictionaries

113

Lists

To declare a list in a message, the keyword to use is repeated. Once the code is generated in C#, the type will be generated in Repeated<T>. Listing 4-13 gives an example of a CountrySearchRequest message containing a list of CountryId of type int32.

Listing 4-13. CountrySearchRequest Message with Repeated int32 CountryId

```
syntax = "proto3";

package gRPCDemo.v1;

option csharp_namespace = "Apress.Sample.gRPC";

message CountrySearchRequest {
    repeated int32 CountryIds = 1;
}
```

Listing 4-14 shows the generated code; as you can see, CountryIds is a typed RepeatedField<int>.

Listing 4-14. CountrySearchRequest Message Generated in C#

```
public const int CountryIdsFieldNumber = 1;
private static readonly pb::FieldCodec<int> _repeated_countryIds_codec =
pb::FieldCodec.ForInt32(10);
private readonly pbc::RepeatedField<int> countryIds_ = new
pbc::RepeatedField<int>();
[global::System.Diagnostics.DebuggerNonUserCodeAttribute]
public pbc::RepeatedField<int> CountryIds {
  get { return countryIds_; }
}
```

RepeatedField<T> is a sealed class (another class cannot inherit from it) from the Google.Protobuf assembly that implements many C# interfaces, such as IList<T>, ICollection<T>, IEnumerable<T>, IEnumerable, IList, ICollection, IEquatable<RepeatedField<T>>, IReadOnlyList<T>, and IReadOnlyCollection<T>, and another interface, IDeepCloneable<RepeatedField<T>>, from the same Google.Protobuf assembly, which allows cloning. Figure 4-1 shows the methods and properties that the RepeatedField<T> class exposes.

```
using System;
using System.Collections;
using System.Collections.Generic;
using System.Reflection;
using System.Runtime.CompilerServices;
using System.Security;

namespace Google.Protobuf.Collections
{
    ...public sealed class RepeatedField<T> : IList<T>, ICollection<T>, IEnumerable<T>,
    {
        public RepeatedField();

        ...public T this[int index] ...
        ...public int Count { get; }
        ...public int Capacity { get; set; }
        ...public bool IsReadOnly { get; }

        ...public void Add(T item);
        ...public void Add(IEnumerable<T> values);
        ...public void AddEntriesFrom(CodedInputStream input, FieldCodec<T> codec);
        ...public void AddEntriesFrom(ref ParseContext ctx, FieldCodec<T> codec);
        ...public void AddRange(IEnumerable<T> values);
        ...public int CalculateSize(FieldCodec<T> codec);
        ...public void Clear();
        ...public RepeatedField<T> Clone();
        ...public bool Contains(T item);
        ...public void CopyTo(T[] array, int arrayIndex);
        ...public override bool Equals(object obj);
        ...public bool Equals(RepeatedField<T> other);
        ...public IEnumerator<T> GetEnumerator();
        ...public override int GetHashCode();
        ...public int IndexOf(T item);
        ...public void Insert(int index, T item);
        ...public bool Remove(T item);
        ...public void RemoveAt(int index);
        ...public override string ToString();
        ...public void WriteTo(ref WriteContext ctx, FieldCodec<T> codec);
        ...public void WriteTo(CodedOutputStream output, FieldCodec<T> codec);
    }
}
```

Figure 4-1. *The Repeated<T> class*

In practice, it acts like a list, so working with RepeatedField<T> fields is shown in Listing 4-15.

Listing 4-15. Read/Write CountrySearchRequest Message

```
using Apress.Sample.gRPC;
namespace Server
{
    public class Program
    {
        public static void Main(string[] args)
        {
            // Write
            var countrySearchRequest = new CountrySearchRequest();
            countrySearchRequest.CountryIds.Add(1);
            countrySearchRequest.CountryIds.Add(2);
            countrySearchRequest.CountryIds.Add(3);

            // Read
            foreach (var countryId in countrySearchRequest.CountryIds)
            {
                // code
            }
        }
    }
}
```

Dictionaries

Who has never needed a dictionary? Nobody! To declare a dictionary, you need to use the map<TKey, TValue> keyword, which, once generated in C#, will give you a MapField.

Listing 4-16 shows the example of a CountryReply message having as a property a dictionary with a key of type int32 (TKey) and its associated value (TValue) of type string.

Listing 4-16. CountryReply Message with a Dictionary Property

```
syntax = "proto3";

package gRPCDemo.v1;

option csharp_namespace = "Apress.Sample.gRPC";

message CountryReply {
    map<int32, string> countries = 1;
}
```

Listing 4-17 shows the generated code.

Listing 4-17. countries field generated code

```
public const int CountriesFieldNumber = 1;
private static readonly pbc::MapField<int, string>.Codec _map_countries_
codec = new pbc::MapField<int, string>.Codec(pb::FieldCodec.ForInt32(8, 0),
pb::FieldCodec.ForString(18, ""), 10);
private readonly pbc::MapField<int, string> countries_ = new
pbc::MapField<int, string>();
[global::System.Diagnostics.DebuggerNonUserCodeAttribute]
public pbc::MapField<int, string> Countries {
    get { return countries_; }
}
```

If you view the same assembly, you'll see that MapField<TKey, TValue> implements IDictionary<TKey, TValue> but also implements IEquatable<T> like many C# collection interfaces (as well as the IDeepCloneable<MapField<TKey, TValue>> interface from the Google.Protobuf assembly). Figure 4-2 shows the methods and properties that the MapField<TKey, TValue> class exposes.

```
namespace Google.Protobuf.Collections
{
    public sealed class MapField<TKey, TValue> : IDeepCloneable<MapField<TKey, TValue>>, IDiction
    {
        public MapField();

        public TValue this[TKey key] ...
        public int Count { get; }
        public ICollection<TValue> Values { get; }
        public ICollection<TKey> Keys { get; }
        public bool IsReadOnly { get; }

        public void Add(TKey key, TValue value);
        public void Add(IDictionary<TKey, TValue> entries);
        public void AddEntriesFrom(CodedInputStream input, Codec codec);
        public void AddEntriesFrom(ref ParseContext ctx, Codec codec);
        public int CalculateSize(Codec codec);
        public void Clear();
        public MapField<TKey, TValue> Clone();
        public bool ContainsKey(TKey key);
        public override bool Equals(object other);
        public bool Equals(MapField<TKey, TValue> other);
        public IEnumerator<KeyValuePair<TKey, TValue>> GetEnumerator();
        public override int GetHashCode();
        public bool Remove(TKey key);
        public override string ToString();
        public bool TryGetValue(TKey key, out TValue value);
        public void WriteTo(CodedOutputStream output, Codec codec);
        public void WriteTo(ref WriteContext ctx, Codec codec);

        public sealed class Codec
        {
            public Codec(FieldCodec<TKey> keyCodec, FieldCodec<TValue> valueCodec, uint mapTag);
        }
    }
}
```

Figure 4-2. *The* `MapField<TKey, TValue>` *class*

Reading and writing on `MapField<TKey, TValue>` fields act like a C# dictionary. Each item added to the `MapField<TKey, TValue>` field is a `KeyValuePair<TKey, TValue>`. Listing 4-18 shows the `CountryReply` message.

Listing 4-18. Read/Write `CountryReply` Message

```
using Apress.Sample.gRPC;
namespace Server;

// Write
var countryReply = new CountryReply();
countryReply.Countries.Add(1, "Canada");
```

```
countryReply.Countries.Add(2, "USA");
countryReply.Countries.Add(3, "Mexico");

// Read
foreach (var country in countryReply.Countries) // country:
KeyValuePair<int, string>
{
    var countryId = country.Key;
    var CountryName = country.Value;
}
```

Enumerations

Enumerations syntax is identical (enum keyword and key/value association) to a C#
enumeration and can be used as a property in a message. You won't get lost here.
Enumerations are essential to keep code clean and help you avoid hard-coding values
in your code. Plus, it allows you to keep values defined in one place. Listing 4-19 shows a
Continent enumeration. Note here that the value 0 .. n (through 6 here) do not represent
the position for serialization/deserialization.

Listing 4-19. Continent Enumeration

```
syntax = "proto3";

package gRPCDemo.v1;

option csharp_namespace = "Apress.Sample.gRPC";

message CountryReply {
    int32 CountryId = 1;
    Continent Continent = 2;
}

enum Continent {
    Unknown = 0;
    NorthAmerica = 1;
    SouthAmerica = 2;
    Europe = 3;
```

```
    Africa = 4;
    Asia = 5;
    Australia = 6;
}
```

Note   Unlike C# (in terms of syntax analogy), the association of a key to a value (constant) is mandatory in Protobuf and must start at 0 to service the default value.

Enumerations with Protobuf support a practical feature that I greatly appreciate, *aliases*. Several keys can be associated with the same constant value. You need to set the option allow_alias = true within the enumerator, as shown in Listing 4-20.

Listing 4-20. Continent Enumeration Declared with Aliases Australia/Oceania

```
syntax = "proto3";

package gRPCDemo.v1;

option csharp_namespace = "Apress.Sample.gRPC";

message CountryReply {
    int32 CountryId = 1;
    Continent Continent = 2;
}

enum Continent {
    option allow_alias = true;
    Unknown = 0;
    NorthAmerica = 1;
    SouthAmerica = 2;
    Europe = 3;
    Africa = 4;
    Asia = 5;
    Australia = 6;
    Oceania = 6;
}
```

The generated code will look as shown in Listing 4-21.

Listing 4-21. Generated Continent Enumeration

```
public enum Continent {
  [pbr::OriginalName("Unknown")] Unknown = 0,
  [pbr::OriginalName("NorthAmerica")] NorthAmerica = 1,
  [pbr::OriginalName("SouthAmerica")] SouthAmerica = 2,
  [pbr::OriginalName("Europe")] Europe = 3,
  [pbr::OriginalName("Africa")] Africa = 4,
  [pbr::OriginalName("Asia")] Asia = 5,
  [pbr::OriginalName("Australia")] Australia = 6,
  [pbr::OriginalName("Oceania", PreferredAlias = false)] Oceania = 6,
}
```

You'll notice that the C# enum is created, but each item has an attribute set named OriginalName defined within the Google.Protobuf assembly, as shown in Figure 4-3.

```
assembly Google.Protobuf, Version=3.13.0.0, Culture=neutral, PublicKeyToken=a7d26565bac4d604

  using System;

namespace Google.Protobuf.Reflection
  {
      ...public class OriginalNameAttribute : Attribute
      {
          ...public OriginalNameAttribute(string name);

          ...public string Name { get; set; }
          ...public bool PreferredAlias { get; set; }
      }
  }
```

Figure 4-3. The OriginalName attribute

The last thing to mention is the ability to reserve Protobuf enumeration values to prevent breaking code in future updates. I do not recommend adding breaking changes in your proto files but instead recommend using API versioning. However, if you are interested in reserved values, review the Google documentation: https://developers. google.com/protocol-buffers/docs/proto3#reserved_values.

Nested Types

The protocol buffer support syntax supports nested types. Depending on your programming habits, you can nest your messages in a single message. For example, you can nest enumerations in a message, but you have to use a different case on the property name (not the same as the type declared). Listing 4-22 shows nested `CountryReply` and `Continent` messages.

Listing 4-22. Nested `CountryReply` and `Continent` Messages

```
syntax = "proto3";

package gRPCDemo.v1;

option csharp_namespace = "Apress.Sample.gRPC";

message CountryReply {
    message Continent {
        string Name = 1;
    }

    int32 CountryId = 1;
    Continent continent = 2; // Not working if Continent property name
                                declared with the same case of its type
}
```

Import Types

Fortunately, you can store your type definitions in separate files, which supports the notion of reusability. I think you will agree that you may often have to use the same message for several services. As with any programming language, arranging classes is essential to maintain code clarity.

With the language Protocol Buffers, you can import a type with the keyword `import` and then declare the Protobuf file's path to import. This path is relative to the compilation's execution directory by the *Protocol Buffer Compiler (Protoc)*. Still, Protoc needs to know where are stored all Protobufs, an option to locate them can be set up, and Chapter 12 will cover that by showing an example with manual execution of *Protoc*, unlike Visual Studio, which manages all by itself, and Chapters 5 and 7 will cover that. Listing 4-23 shows the same `CountryReply` Protobuf file importing the `Continent` Protobuf file.

Listing 4-23. CountryReply Proto File Importing Continent Proto File

```
syntax = "proto3";

package gRPCDemo.v1;

option csharp_namespace = "Apress.Sample.gRPC";

import "continent.proto";

message CountryReply {
    int32 CountryId = 1;
    Continent continent = 2;
}
```

Any, Value, Struct, Wrappers, Dates, and Times (Well-Known Types)

Any, Value, Struct, Wrappers, dates, and *times* are types that have a particular behavior and require special treatment. They cannot be compiled as-is in C# and therefore need to be encapsulated in specific features so that the .NET runtime knows what to do with them. To do this, Google has provided proto files to import; then, during compilation, .NET can interpret them with C# extensions, which are called *Protobuf's Well-Known Types* extensions.

Any

Any fields (or properties) are typed but not "strongly typed" fields. The type is not known in advance, which means that we can pass any type in an Any field, but we will have to infer its type to know its type. Any is intended for any arbitrary message types but *not primitive types*. C# will not allow you to pack an object into it if it doesn't implement the IMessage interface.

Let's revisit our example with the CountryReply message containing a field that could be typed Continent or anything else but declared as Any.

Note   You must have the proto definition to infer the type. The message descriptor is required to infer the type that is implemented in generated code.

To declare a field of type Any (google.protobuf.Any), you must import the proto file "google/protobuf/any.proto" as shown in Listing 4-24. You don't need to have the file physically somewhere on your computer. The file is known from the Protobuf compiler as a "global variable."

Listing 4-24. CountryReply with Any field supposedly to be a Continent Type

```
syntax = "proto3";

package gRPCDemo.v1;

option csharp_namespace = "Apress.Sample.gRPC";

import "google/protobuf/any.proto";

message CountryReply {
    int32 CountryId = 1;
    google.protobuf.Any Whatever = 2; // Could be Continent type or could
                                      be something
}
```

Recall the FileDescriptor introduced at the beginning of this chapter in the context of Listing 4-3. As I mentioned, FileDescriptor is used for reflection, a Protobuf file contains messages, and the FileDescriptor contains *Base64 encoded* the signature of all types included inside it. They are generated from each message's name and properties, making them a unique signature (for a given namespace). This FileDescriptor is an array of GeneratedClrTypeInfo type objects containing the signature of each message. To access a given message's signature (description), you can invoke a static property generated when compiling the Protobuf file. An example of the Continent message, Continent.Descriptor, is shown in Figure 4-4.

```
namespace Apress.Sample.gRPC {

/// <summary>Holder for reflection information generated from Protos/continent.proto</summary>
public static partial class ContinentReflection {

  #region Descriptor
  /// <summary>File descriptor for Protos/continent.proto</summary>
  public static pbr::FileDescriptor Descriptor {
    get { return descriptor; }
  }
  private static pbr::FileDescriptor descriptor;

  static ContinentReflection() {
    byte[] descriptorData = global::System.Convert.FromBase64String(
      string.Concat(
        "ChZQcm90b3MvY29udGluZW50LnByb3RvEgtBDRGVtby52MSI3Cg1Db250",
        "aW51bnQSEwoLQ29udGluZW50SWQYASABKAUSFQoNQ29udGluZW50TmFtZRgC",
        "IAEoCUIVagISQXByZXNzLlNhbXBsZS5nUlBDYg2wcm90bzM="));
    descriptor = pbr::FileDescriptor.FromGeneratedCode(descriptorData,
      new pbr::FileDescriptor[] { },
      new pbr::GeneratedClrTypeInfo(null, null, new pbr::GeneratedClrTypeInfo[] {
        new pbr::GeneratedClrTypeInfo(typeof(global::Apress.Sample.gRPC.Continent), global::Apress.Sample.gRPC.Continent.Parser, new[]{ "ContinentId", "ContinentName" }, null, null, null, null)
      }));
  }
  #endregion

}
#region Messages
public sealed partial class Continent : pb::IMessage<Continent>
#if !GOOGLE_PROTOBUF_REFSTRUCT_COMPATIBILITY_MODE
  , pb::IBufferMessage
#endif
{
  private static readonly pb::MessageParser<Continent> _parser = new pb::MessageParser<Continent>(() => new Continent());
  private pb::UnknownFieldSet _unknownFields;
  [global::System.Diagnostics.DebuggerNonUserCodeAttribute]
  public static pb::MessageParser<Continent> Parser { get { return _parser; } }

  [global::System.Diagnostics.DebuggerNonUserCodeAttribute]
  public static pbr::MessageDescriptor Descriptor {
    get { return global::Apress.Sample.gRPC.ContinentReflection.Descriptor.MessageTypes[0]; }
  }

  [global::System.Diagnostics.DebuggerNonUserCodeAttribute]
  pbr::MessageDescriptor pb::IMessage.Descriptor {
    get { return Descriptor; }
  }
```

Figure 4-4. *The Continent message descriptor*

This descriptor allows us to infer the Any type from the Whatever field of the
CountryReply message. Listing 4-25 shows the different ways to infer the desired type.

Listing 4-25. Infer Continent Message

```
using Apress.Sample.gRPC;
using Google.Protobuf.WellKnownTypes;

namespace Server;

// Write
var country = new CountryReply();
country.Whatever = Any.Pack(new Continent
{
    ContinentId = 1,
    ContinentName = "North America"
});
```

```
// Read
Continent continent;
if (country.Whatever.Is(Continent.Descriptor))
{
    continent = country.Whatever.Unpack<Continent>();
}
// OR
country.Whatever.TryUnpack(out continent);
```

To start, you need to import the namespace `Google.Protobuf.WellKnownTypes`, which is part of the `Google.Protobuf` assembly.

As Listing 4-25 shows, to pass from client to server or from server to client a message containing an `Any` type, you need to use the `Any` class exposing a `Pack` method that serializes any object to type `ByteString` (array of bytes). On the other side, you must use the `Unpack` method, which takes care of the byte array's serialization in the desired type. To make the deserialization reliable, you can test whether a message corresponds to a specific type using the method `Is()`, which takes the descriptor as a parameter, `Continent.Descriptor`. You can directly use the `tryUnpack` method, which will return null if the deserialization fails. An exciting feature, isn't it? You may love it. Sometimes, I need to infer type because I'm not sure what I will receive, which makes this feature very welcome!

Wrappers

By default, the Protobuf syntax does not allow nullable fields, and if you fail to pass a value to your scalar types, they will have a default value. A nullable boolean in .NET (`bool?`) has no equivalent in the Protobuf language. To overcome this, there are *Well-Known Type wrappers* that allow compatibility with nullable fields in .NET. Table 4-2, which is based on Microsoft's documentation (`https://docs.microsoft.com/en-us/ aspnet/core/grpc/protobuf?view=aspnetcore-6.0`), shows all wrapper types.

Table 4-2. *Wrapper Types for .NET (source: Microsoft)*

C# Type	Well-Known Type Wrapper
bool?	google.protobuf.BoolValue
double?	google.protobuf.DoubleValue
float?	google.protobuf.FloatValue
int?	google.protobuf.Int32Value
long?	google.protobuf.Int64Value
uint?	google.protobuf.UInt32Value
ulong?	google.protobuf.UInt64Value
string	google.protobuf.StringValue
ByteString	google.protobuf.BytesValue

To use wrappers, you have to import the "google/protobuf/wrappers.proto" proto file, as shown in Listing 4-26.

Listing 4-26. Import wrappers.proto

```
syntax = "proto3";

package gRPCDemo.v1;

option csharp_namespace = "Apress.Sample.gRPC";

import "google/protobuf/wrappers.proto";

message Continent {
    int32 ContinentId = 1;
    string ContinentName = 2;
    google.protobuf.BoolValue IsSeparatedByASea = 3
}
```

The generated code gives the expected type (bool?) for the IsSeparatedByASea field, as shown in Listing 4-27.

Listing 4-27. IsSeparatedByASea Field Generated Code

```
/// <summary>Field number for the "IsSeparatedByASea" field.</summary>
public const int IsSeparatedByASeaFieldNumber = 3;
private static readonly pb::FieldCodec<bool?> _single_isSeparatedByASea_
codec = pb::FieldCodec.ForStructWrapper<bool>(26);
private bool? isSeparatedByASea_;
[global::System.Diagnostics.DebuggerNonUserCodeAttribute]
public bool? IsSeparatedByASea {
    get { return isSeparatedByASea_; }
    set {
        isSeparatedByASea_ = value;
    }
}
```

Value

You can pass messages with fields whose type was not known in advance. You can also pass messages with fields that are not typed, such as dynamic objects that can take any scalar values we saw previously, and collections null values are allowed.

To do so, import the proto file "google/protobuf/struct.proto" and declare the dynamic type as google.protobuf.Value. Listing 4-28 shows the CountryReply message with dynamic fields.

Listing 4-28. CountryReply Message with Dynamic Fields

```
syntax = "proto3";

package gRPCDemo.v1;

option csharp_namespace = "Apress.Sample.gRPC";

import "google/protobuf/struct.proto";

message CountryReply {
    google.protobuf.Value CountryId = 1;
    google.protobuf.Value Continent = 2;
}
```

Listing 4-29 shows the generated code.

Listing 4-29. CountryReply Message Generated Code

```
/// <summary>Field number for the "CountryId" field.</summary>
public const int CountryIdFieldNumber = 1;
private global::Google.Protobuf.WellKnownTypes.Value countryId_;
[global::System.Diagnostics.DebuggerNonUserCodeAttribute]
public global::Google.Protobuf.WellKnownTypes.Value CountryId {
  get { return countryId_; }
  set {
    countryId_ = value;
  }
}

/// <summary>Field number for the "Continent" field.</summary>
public const int ContinentFieldNumber = 2;
private global::Google.Protobuf.WellKnownTypes.Value continent_;
[global::System.Diagnostics.DebuggerNonUserCodeAttribute]
public global::Google.Protobuf.WellKnownTypes.Value Continent {
  get { return continent_; }
  set {
    continent_ = value;
  }
}
```

The generated type in C# is Value and belongs to the Google.Protobuf.
WellKnownTypes namespace, which belongs itself to the Google.Protobuf assembly.
This type inherits from the IMessage<T>, IMessage, IEquatable<T>, IDeepCloneable<T>,
and IBufferMessage interfaces that all belong to the Google.Protobuf assembly, except
for IEquatable<T>, which comes from the .NET System.Runtime assembly.

To write and read dynamic values, we have a set of methods available. Table 4-3
shows the available write static functions.

Table 4-3. *Available Write Static Functions*

Type	Method	Comment
Number	Value.ForNumber	Support all .NET number types
String	Value.ForString	
Objects	Value.ForStruct	Not the same type as C# structs
Boolean	Value.ForBool	
Null	Value.ForNull	
Collections	Value.ForList	

Struct is a bit special: it's *not at all the native C# type*. Struct in Protobuf is a Well-Known Type that inherits from the same interfaces as Value, as shown in Figure 4-5.

```
assembly Google.Protobuf, Version=3.13.0.0, Culture=neutral, PublicKeyToken=a7d26565bac4d604
using [...]
namespace Google.Protobuf.WellKnownTypes
{
    ...public sealed class Struct : IMessage<Struct>, IMessage, IEquatable<Struct>, IDeepCloneable<Struct>, IBufferMessage
    {
        ...public const int FieldsFieldNumber = 1;

        ...public Struct();
        ...public Struct(Struct other);

        ...public static MessageParser<Struct> Parser { get; }
        ...public static MessageDescriptor Descriptor { get; }
        ...public MapField<string, Value> Fields { get; }

        ...public int CalculateSize();
        ...public Struct Clone();
        ...public override bool Equals(object other);
        ...public bool Equals(Struct other);
        ...public override int GetHashCode();
        ...public void MergeFrom(Struct other);
        ...public void MergeFrom(CodedInputStream input);
        ...public override string ToString();
        ...public void WriteTo(CodedOutputStream output);
    }
}
```

Figure 4-5. *The Struct type*

Each Struct property is set in a dictionary named Fields, typed MapField<TKey, TValue>. Listing 4-30 shows how to populate the CountryReply message defined above.

Listing 4-30. Fill the Dynamic CountryReply Message

```
using Apress.Sample.gRPC;
using Google.Protobuf.WellKnownTypes;
using System;

namespace Server;

var country = new CountryReply();
country.CountryId = Value.ForNumber(1);
country.Continent = Value.ForStruct(new Struct
{
    Fields = {
        ["ContinentId"] = Value.ForNumber(1),
        ["ContinentName"] = Value.ForString("North America"),
        ["IsSeparatedByASea"] = Value.ForBool(false)
    }
});
```

The read Value type is straightforward. The Value type has a set of properties that exposes its value in the wanted type. Table 4-4 shows the available properties.

Table 4-4. *Available Read Properties*

Type	Method	Comment
Number	NumberValue	Exposes number value as Double .NET type
String	StringValue	
Objects	StructValue	Needs to access a property from the Fields dictionary property
Boolean	BoolValue	
Null	NullValue	
Collections	ListValue	

Continuing with the same dynamic CountryReply message, I offer an example of implementation on the program's side that will read this message. Assume that we want to populate domain objects from a dynamic message. Listing 4-31 shows what that would look like.

Listing 4-31. Map Dynamic CountryReply to Domain Objects

```
using Apress.Sample.gRPC;
using System;

namespace Server;

var country = new CountryReply(); // Received filled from a gRPC call

// Read
var countryModel = new CountryModel
{
    CountryId = Convert.ToInt32(country.CountryId.NumberValue),
    Continent = new ContinentModel
    {
        CountryId = Convert.ToInt32(country.Continent.StructValue.
        Fields["ContinentId"].NumberValue),
        ContinentName = country.Continent.StructValue.
        Fields["ContinentId"].StringValue,
        IsSeparatedByASea = country.Continent.StructValue.
        Fields["ContinentId"].BoolValue,
    }
};

public class CountryModel
{
    public int CountryId { get; set; }
    public ContinentModel Continent { get; set; }
}

public class ContinentModel
{
    public int CountryId { get; set; }
    public string ContinentName { get; set; }
    public bool IsSeparatedByASea { get; set; }
}
```

Dates and Times

The .NET types DateTimeOffset, DateTime, and TimeSpan have no equivalent in Protobuf languages, so Protobuf provides some Well-Known Types to manage these unsupported types in .NET.

TimeSpan requires you to import the "google/protobuf/duration.proto" file and DateTime/DateTimeOffset require you to import the "google/protobuf/timestamp. proto" file. Table 4-5 is based on Microsoft documentation (https://docs.microsoft. com/en-us/aspnet/core/grpc/protobuf?view=aspnetcore-5.0#dates-and-times) and shows each .NET type has a related Protobuf Well-Known Type.

Table 4-5. *Date and Times Types in .NET and Their Equivalent Protobuf Well-Known Type Extensions (source: Microsoft)*

.NET Type	Protobuf Well-Known Type
DateTimeOffset	google.protobuf.Timestamp
DateTime	google.protobuf.Timestamp
TimeSpan	google.protobuf.Duration

Listing 4-32 shows a FlightBooking message that defines a booking ID, flight duration, and the departure time.

Listing 4-32. FlightBooking Message

```
syntax = "proto3";

package gRPCDemo.v1;

option csharp_namespace = "Apress.Sample.gRPC";

import "google/protobuf/duration.proto";
import "google/protobuf/timestamp.proto";

message FlightBooking {
    int32 BookingId = 1;
    google.protobuf.Duration FlightDuration = 2;
    google.protobuf.Timestamp DepartureTime = 3;
}
```

Listing 4-33 shows generated FlightDuration and DepartureTime fields.

Listing 4-33. Generated FlightDuration and DepartureTime Fields

```
/// <summary>Field number for the "FlightDuration" field.</summary>
public const int FlightDurationFieldNumber = 2;
private global::Google.Protobuf.WellKnownTypes.Duration flightDuration_;
[global::System.Diagnostics.DebuggerNonUserCodeAttribute]
public global::Google.Protobuf.WellKnownTypes.Duration FlightDuration {
  get { return flightDuration_; }
  set {
    flightDuration_ = value;
  }
}

/// <summary>Field number for the "departureTime" field.</summary>
public const int DepartureTimeFieldNumber = 3;
private global::Google.Protobuf.WellKnownTypes.Timestamp departureTime_;
[global::System.Diagnostics.DebuggerNonUserCodeAttribute]
public global::Google.Protobuf.WellKnownTypes.Timestamp DepartureTime {
  get { return departureTime_; }
  set {
    departureTime_ = value;
  }
}
```

The Timestamp type inherits from the IMessage<Timestamp>, IMessage, IEquatable<Timestamp>, IDeepCloneable<Timestamp>, IBufferMessage, ICustomDiagnosticMessage, and IComparable<Timestamp> interfaces. Figure 4-6 shows the methods and properties that the Timestamp class exposes.

```csharp
namespace Google.Protobuf.WellKnownTypes
{
    public sealed class Timestamp : IMessage<Timestamp>, IMessage, IEquatable<Timestamp>
    {
        public const int SecondsFieldNumber = 1;
        public const int NanosFieldNumber = 2;

        public Timestamp();
        public Timestamp(Timestamp other);

        public static MessageDescriptor Descriptor { get; }
        public static MessageParser<Timestamp> Parser { get; }
        public long Seconds { get; set; }
        public int Nanos { get; set; }

        public static Timestamp FromDateTime(DateTime dateTime);
        public static Timestamp FromDateTimeOffset(DateTimeOffset dateTimeOffset);
        public int CalculateSize();
        public Timestamp Clone();
        public int CompareTo(Timestamp other);
        public override bool Equals(object other);
        public bool Equals(Timestamp other);
        public override int GetHashCode();
        public void MergeFrom(Timestamp other);
        public void MergeFrom(CodedInputStream input);
        public DateTime ToDateTime();
        public DateTimeOffset ToDateTimeOffset();
        public string ToDiagnosticString();
        public override string ToString();
        public void WriteTo(CodedOutputStream output);

        public static Timestamp operator +(Timestamp lhs, Duration rhs);
        public static Duration operator -(Timestamp lhs, Timestamp rhs);
        public static Timestamp operator -(Timestamp lhs, Duration rhs);
        public static bool operator ==(Timestamp a, Timestamp b);
        public static bool operator !=(Timestamp a, Timestamp b);
        public static bool operator <(Timestamp a, Timestamp b);
        public static bool operator >(Timestamp a, Timestamp b);
        public static bool operator <=(Timestamp a, Timestamp b);
        public static bool operator >=(Timestamp a, Timestamp b);
    }
}
```

Figure 4-6. *The Timestamp class*

The Duration type inherits from the IMessage<Duration>, IMessage, IEquatable<Duration>, IDeepCloneable<Duration>, IBufferMessage, ICustomDiagnosticMessage, and IComparable<Duration> interfaces. Figure 4-7 shows the methods and properties that the Duration class exposes.

```
namespace Google.Protobuf.WellKnownTypes
{
    ...public sealed class Duration : IMessage<Duration>, IMessage, IEquatable<Duration>
    {
        ...public const int SecondsFieldNumber = 1;
        ...public const int NanosFieldNumber = 2;
        ...public const int NanosecondsPerSecond = 1000000000;
        ...public const int NanosecondsPerTick = 100;
        ...public const long MaxSeconds = 315576000000;
        ...public const long MinSeconds = -315576000000;

        ...public Duration();
        ...public Duration(Duration other);

        ...public static MessageDescriptor Descriptor { get; }
        ...public static MessageParser<Duration> Parser { get; }
        ...public long Seconds { get; set; }
        ...public int Nanos { get; set; }

        ...public static Duration FromTimeSpan(TimeSpan timeSpan);
        ...public int CalculateSize();
        ...public Duration Clone();
        ...public bool Equals(Duration other);
        ...public override bool Equals(object other);
        ...public override int GetHashCode();
        ...public void MergeFrom(Duration other);
        ...public void MergeFrom(CodedInputStream input);
        ...public string ToDiagnosticString();
        ...public override string ToString();
        ...public TimeSpan ToTimeSpan();
        ...public void WriteTo(CodedOutputStream output);

        ...public static Duration operator +(Duration lhs, Duration rhs);
        ...public static Duration operator -(Duration value);
        ...public static Duration operator -(Duration lhs, Duration rhs);
    }
}
```

Figure 4-7. *Duration class*

Listing 4-34 shows how to write and read the FlightBooking message set with TimeStamp and Duration Well-Known Types.

Listing 4-34. Read/Write FlightBooking Message

```
using Apress.Sample.gRPC;
using Google.Protobuf.WellKnownTypes;
using System;
```

```
namespace Server;

// Write
var flightBooking = new FlightBooking();
flightBooking.BookingId = 1;
flightBooking.FlightDuration = Duration.FromTimeSpan(new TimeSpan(2, 0, 0));
// 2h
flightBooking.DepartureTime = Timestamp.FromDateTime(DateTime.
SpecifyKind(new DateTime(2021, 7, 1), DateTimeKind.Utc)); // July 1st
2021 or FromDateTimeOffset(DateTime.SpecifyKind(new DateTime(2021, 7, 1),
DateTimeKind.Utc));

// Read
var bookingId = flightBooking.BookingId;
var bookingDuration = flightBooking.FlightDuration.ToTimeSpan();
var bookingDepartureTime = flightBooking.DepartureTime.ToDateTime();
// or TodateTimeOffset()
```

To set the `FlightDuration` field, which is typed `Duration` and corresponds to a `TimeSpan` in .NET, the `Duration` class exposes the static method `FromTimeSpan()`. It takes in parameter the .NET TimeSpan object.

Set `DepartureTime` field which is typed `Timestamp` and corresponds to `DateTime/DateTimeOffset` types in .NET use from `Timestamp` class `FromDateTime()` static method, and pass in parameter the a .NET `DateTime` or `DateTimeOffset` object.

On the other side, when you read `Duration` and `Timestamp` Protobuf Well-Known Types, invoke the `ToTimeSpan()` method on a field typed `Duration` to give a .NET `TimeSpan`, and invoke the `ToDateTime()` or `ToDateTimeOffset()` method on a field typed `Timestamp` to give a .NET `DateTime` or `DateTimeOffset`.

Bytes

Protobuf language (and gRPC) support binary payloads transport (yes, gRPC can transport binary data within binary payloads). The most obvious example I can give you is the file upload/download process. Let's consider the `CountryImageUpload` message, which contains the FileName, the MimeType, and the file content in binary. Keeping MIME type information is always helpful, especially if your gRPC app serves a file to an ASP.NET Core app, which itself will serve a file to the browser. You'll need to tell the latter app what kind of file is being downloaded.

Listing 4-35 shows the CountryImageUpload proto file.

Listing 4-35. CountryImageUpload Message

```
syntax = "proto3";

package gRPCDemo.v1;

option csharp_namespace = "Apress.Sample.gRPC";

message CountryImageUpload {
    string FileName = 1;
    string MimeType = 2;
    bytes Content = 3;
}
```

Listing 4-36 shows the generated code, in which FileName and MimeType are generated as C# strings and the Content field is generated as a Protobuf ByteString. Notice that the ByteString default value is ByteString.Empty, as I mentioned earlier in this chapter. I lightened the generated code for more clarity.

Listing 4-36. CountryImageUpload Message

```
/// <summary>Field number for the "FileName" field.</summary>
public const int FileNameFieldNumber = 1;
private string fileName_ = "";
[global::System.Diagnostics.DebuggerNonUserCodeAttribute]
public string FileName {
   get { return fileName_; }
   set {
       fileName_ = pb::ProtoPreconditions.CheckNotNull(value, "value");
   }
}

/// <summary>Field number for the "MimeType" field.</summary>
public const int MimeTypeFieldNumber = 2;
private string mimeType_ = "";
[global::System.Diagnostics.DebuggerNonUserCodeAttribute]
```

```csharp
public string MimeType {
    get { return mimeType_; }
    set {
        mimeType_ = pb::ProtoPreconditions.CheckNotNull(value, "value");
    }
}

/// <summary>Field number for the "Content" field.</summary>
public const int ContentFieldNumber = 3;
private pb::ByteString content_ = pb::ByteString.Empty;
[global::System.Diagnostics.DebuggerNonUserCodeAttribute]
public pb::ByteString Content {
    get { return content_; }
    set {
        content_ = pb::ProtoPreconditions.CheckNotNull(value, "value");
    }
}
```

The ByteString C# type (which is not a Well-Known Type) inherits from the IEnumerable<byte>, IEnumerable, and IEquatable<ByteString> .NET interfaces. Figure 4-8 shows the methods and properties that the ByteString class exposes.

```
namespace Google.Protobuf
{
    public sealed class ByteString : IEnumerable<byte>, IEnumerable, IEquatable<ByteString>
    {
        public byte this[int index] ...
        public static ByteString Empty { get; }
        public ReadOnlySpan<byte> Span { get; }
        public bool IsEmpty { get; }
        public int Length { get; }
        public ReadOnlyMemory<byte> Memory { get; }

        public static ByteString CopyFrom(params byte[] bytes);
        public static ByteString CopyFrom(byte[] bytes, int offset, int count);
        public static ByteString CopyFrom(ReadOnlySpan<byte> bytes);
        public static ByteString CopyFrom(string text, Encoding encoding);
        public static ByteString CopyFromUtf8(string text);
        public static ByteString FromBase64(string bytes);
        public static ByteString FromStream(Stream stream);
        public static Task<ByteString> FromStreamAsync(Stream stream, CancellationToken cancellationToken = default);
        public void CopyTo(byte[] array, int position);
        public CodedInputStream CreateCodedInput();
        public override bool Equals(object obj);
        public bool Equals(ByteString other);
        public IEnumerator<byte> GetEnumerator();
        public override int GetHashCode();
        public string ToBase64();
        public byte[] ToByteArray();
        public string ToString(Encoding encoding);
        public string ToStringUtf8();
        public void WriteTo(Stream outputStream);

        public static bool operator ==(ByteString lhs, ByteString rhs);
        public static bool operator !=(ByteString lhs, ByteString rhs);
    }
}
```

Figure 4-8. *The ByteString class*

Read/write operations on the ByteString type are straightforward. The Protobuf
language exposes the static method CopyFrom on the ByteString class and the
ToByteArray on a ByteString instance object. The ByteString class offers other
alternatives to bytes, such as Base64 (FromBase64/ToBase64 methods) or Stream
usage (FromStream/FromStreamAsync/WriteTo methods). Listing 4-37 shows a read/
write sample with the CountryImageUpload message. This sample simulates a .png file
upload/download.

Listing 4-37. Read/Write on CountryImageUpload Message

```
using Apress.Sample.gRPC;
using Google.Protobuf;
using System.IO;
using System.Threading.Tasks;

namespace Server;
```

```
// Write
var uploadFile = new CountryImageUpload();
uploadFile.FileName = "Canada_flag.png";
uploadFile.MimeType = "image/png";
uploadFile.Content = ByteString.CopyFrom(File.ReadAllBytes("C:\\countries\\
flags\\Canada_flag.png"));
uploadFile.Content = await ByteString.FromStreamAsync(new FileStream("C:\\
countries\\flags\\Canada_flag.png", FileMode.Open)); // from Stream async
// uploadFile.Content = ByteString.FromStream(new FileStream("C:\\
countries\\flags\\Canada_flag.png", FileMode.Open)); // from Stream
// uploadFile.Content = ByteString.FromBase64("MDExMTExMDAwMDAwMTEwMTAw
MTAxMDEwMTAxMDEwMTAxMTAxMTAxMDA...."); // from base64 encoded file

// Read
var fileName = uploadFile.FileName;
var mimeType = uploadFile.MimeType;
var contentInBytes = uploadFile.Content.ToByteArray();
var contentInBase64 = uploadFile.Content.ToBase64();
var contentInStream = new MemoryStream();
uploadFile.Content.WriteTo(contentInStream);
```

One of

One of is an exciting feature. When a service fails, the Protobuf language makes it possible to intelligently manage the information sent back to the customer.

Let's take a concrete example. A user searches for a country by name, but no country is found (input error or the user entered a continent name). The service will return a typed error response without returning an exception to the client, and in this particular case, the error message is the alternative information. Alternative answers are not limited in number. The initial search can be a country, but alternatively can be a continent or an error. The role of the feature *One of* here is to allow the setup of a single message as a response; that is, if a continent is found from the input search name, neither the country will be set nor the error, and if an error is encountered, neither the country nor the continent will be set. This mechanism saves memory by not serving unset objects. Note that the fields subject to a grouping uniqueness with *One of* must be wrapped in a named *One of* statement.

Listing 4-38 shows the use of the *Oneof* feature on the CountryOrContinentReply message allowing the search for a country or a continent or an error if nothing is found; each message is stored in its proto file.

Listing 4-38. CountryOrContinentReply Message

```
syntax = "proto3";

package gRPCDemo.v1;

option csharp_namespace = "Apress.Sample.gRPC";

import "Protos/country.proto";
import "Protos/continent.proto";
import "Protos/error.proto";

message CountryOrContinentReply {
    oneof countryOrContinent {
        Country Country = 1;
        Continent Continent = 2;
        Error Error = 3;
    }
}
```

Listings 4-39, 4-40, and 4-41 show, respectively, the Country, Continent, and Error messages in their dedicated proto file.

Listing 4-39. The Country Message

```
syntax = "proto3";

package gRPCDemo.v1;

option csharp_namespace = "Apress.Sample.gRPC";

message Country {
    int32 CountryId = 1;
    string CountryName = 2;
}
```

Listing 4-40. The Continent Message

```
syntax = "proto3";

package gRPCDemo.v1;

option csharp_namespace = "Apress.Sample.gRPC";

message Continent {
    int32 ContinentId = 1;
    string ContinentName = 2;
}
```

Listing 4-41. The Error Message

```
syntax = "proto3";

package gRPCDemo.v1;

option csharp_namespace = "Apress.Sample.gRPC";

message Error {
    string SearchContent = 1;
    string Message = 2;
}
```

If we observe the generated code, we see that it's simply a *switch* / *case* statement of three possible types (defined by *enum*) to be returned, as shown in Listing 4-42. I voluntarily lightened the generated code.

Listing 4-42. Generated CountryOrContinent Message

```
[global::System.Diagnostics.DebuggerNonUserCodeAttribute]
public CountryOrContinentReply(CountryOrContinentReply other) : this() {
    switch (other.CountryOrContinentCase) {
        case CountryOrContinentOneofCase.Country:
            Country = other.Country.Clone();
            break;
        case CountryOrContinentOneofCase.Continent:
            Continent = other.Continent.Clone();
            break;
```

```
      case CountryOrContinentOneofCase.Error:
        Error = other.Error.Clone();
        break;
   }
   _unknownFields = pb::UnknownFieldSet.Clone(other._unknownFields);
}

[global::System.Diagnostics.DebuggerNonUserCodeAttribute]
public CountryOrContinentReply Clone() {
   return new CountryOrContinentReply(this);
}

/// <summary>Field number for the "Country" field.</summary>
public const int CountryFieldNumber = 1;
[global::System.Diagnostics.DebuggerNonUserCodeAttribute]
public global::Apress.Sample.gRPC.Country Country {
   get { return countryOrContinentCase_ == CountryOrContinentOneofCase.
   Country ? (global::Apress.Sample.gRPC.Country) countryOrContinent_
   : null; }
   set {
       countryOrContinent_ = value;
       countryOrContinentCase_ = value == null ?
       CountryOrContinentOneofCase.None : CountryOrContinentOneofCase.
       Country;
   }
}

/// <summary>Field number for the "Continent" field.</summary>
public const int ContinentFieldNumber = 2;
[global::System.Diagnostics.DebuggerNonUserCodeAttribute]
public global::Apress.Sample.gRPC.Continent Continent {
   get { return countryOrContinentCase_ == CountryOrContinentOneofCase.
   Continent ? (global::Apress.Sample.gRPC.Continent) countryOrContinent_
   : null; }
```

```
    set {
        countryOrContinent_ = value;
        countryOrContinentCase_ = value == null ?
        CountryOrContinentOneofCase.None : CountryOrContinentOneofCase.
        Continent;
    }
}

/// <summary>Field number for the "Error" field.</summary>
public const int ErrorFieldNumber = 3;
[global::System.Diagnostics.DebuggerNonUserCodeAttribute]
public global::Apress.Sample.gRPC.Error Error {
    get { return countryOrContinentCase_ == CountryOrContinentOneofCase.
    Error ? (global::Apress.Sample.gRPC.Error) countryOrContinent_ : null; }
    set {
        countryOrContinent_ = value;
        countryOrContinentCase_ = value == null ?
        CountryOrContinentOneofCase.None :
        CountryOrContinentOneofCase.Error;
    }
}

private object countryOrContinent_;
/// <summary>Enum of possible cases for the "countryOrContinent"
oneof.</summary>
public enum CountryOrContinentOneofCase {
    None = 0,
    Country = 1,
    Continent = 2,
    Error = 3,
}
```

Let's simulate a search that matches a Continent message result. Listing 4-43 shows how to set the Continent response and read the Continent response message. It results in a *switch / case statement* to determine what kind of type is returned by the server.

Listing 4-43. Read/Write the Continent Message from
CountryOrContinentReply Message

```
using Apress.Sample.gRPC;
using System;

namespace Server;

// Write
var countryOrContinentReply = new CountryOrContinentReply();
countryOrContinentReply.Continent = new Continent
{
    ContinentId = 1,
    ContinentName = "Americas"
};

// Read
switch (countryOrContinentReply.CountryOrContinentCase)
{
    case CountryOrContinentReply.CountryOrContinentOneofCase.Country:
        Console.Write("Country found.");
        break;
    case CountryOrContinentReply.CountryOrContinentOneofCase.Continent:
        Console.Write("Continent found.");
        break;
    case CountryOrContinentReply.CountryOrContinentOneofCase.Error:
        Console.Write("None of country or continent found");
        break;
    default:
        throw new ArgumentException("Unhandled response");
}
```

This is especially useful when you know in advance what you can return to the
customer based on certain conditions. For example, this can be used when you want
to return typed data, something did not happen as expected, for example, an error, and
you send an alternate data back to the client. It's completely different from Value, which
allows you to manipulate untyped objects, or Any when you have no idea what you are
manipulating even though it is typed data.

Empty Messages

As I previously mentioned, sometimes we call remote procedures without any parameters. However, the Protobuf language makes it mandatory to pass parameters in these functions. You have two possibilities:

- Create yourself a message without any properties

- Use a Protobuf Well-Known Type named Empty

Listing 4-44 shows the CountryService that define a GetAll RPC function that takes, as input parameter, a custom message, the EmptyRequest message.

Listing 4-44. CountryService Using EmptyRequest Custom Empty Message

```
syntax = "proto3";
package gRPCDemo.v1;

option csharp_namespace = "Apress.Sample.gRPC";

service CountryService {
    rpc GetAll(EmptyRequest) returns (CountriesReply) {}
}

message EmptyRequest {

}

message CountriesReply {
    repeated CountryReply = 1;
}

message CountryReply {
    int32 CountryId = 1;
    string CountryName = 2;
}
```

Once compiled, you need to instantiate the generated class and pass it as is to the RPC call, as shown in Listing 4-45.

Listing 4-45. Instantiate and Pass EmptyRequest Message to RPC Function

```
// ....

var emptyRequest = new EmptyRequest();

var countries = await countryClient.GetAllAsync(emptyRequest);
```

Instead of using your empty message, you can use the Empty Protobuf Well-Known Type message. You have to import it with the path google/protobuf/Empty.proto and use it like this: google.protobuf.Empty.

Protoc knows it, and you don't need to have it stored somewhere on your computer. Listing 4-46 shows how to proceed.

Listing 4-46. CountryService Using google.protobuf.Empty Message

```
syntax = "proto3";

package gRPCDemo.v1;

option csharp_namespace = "Apress.Sample.gRPC";

import "google/protobuf/Empty.proto";

service CountryService {
    rpc GetAll(google.protobuf.Empty) returns (CountryReplies) {}
}

message CountryReplies {
    repeated CountryReply = 1;
}

message CountryReply {
    int32 CountryId = 1;
    string CountryName = 2;
}
```

Like the EmptyRequest custom message, all you need to do is to instantiate it and pass it as is to the RPC call, as shown in Listing 4-47.

Listing 4-47. Instantiate and Pass google.protobuf.Empty Message to RPC Function

```
// .....

var emptyRequest = new Empty();

var countries = await countryClient.GetAllAsync(emptyRequest);
```

Comments

You can easily add comments to your Protobuf files, and it's often useful. I have tons of comments in my code. Like in C#, you can use the syntax shown in Listing 4-48.

Listing 4-48. Comments Syntax

```
/* Comment here */
and
// Comment here
```

Listing 4-49 shows the Error message commented out with both types of allowed syntax.

Listing 4-49. Comments Error Message

```
/*
Author: Anthony Giretti
Example for Apress book
*/
syntax = "proto3";

package gRPCDemo.v1;

option csharp_namespace = "Apress.Sample.gRPC";

// The Error message entity
message Error {
    string SearchContent = 1; // The initial search keyword
    string Description = 2; // The error description
}
```

The commented code is reported to the C# generated class, as shown in Listing 4-50. Note that only commented code will be reported to the generated class. Comments that don't surround any code, such as the header comment shown in the previous listing, won't be part of the generated code. I voluntarily lightened the generated code.

Listing 4-50. Generated Error Message Class with Comments Set in the Proto File

```
/// <summary>
/// The Error message entity
/// </summary>
public sealed partial class Error : pb::IMessage<Error>
{
    /// <summary>Field number for the "SearchContent" field.</summary>
    public const int SearchContentFieldNumber = 1;
    private string searchContent_ = "";
    /// <summary>
        /// The initial search keyword
        /// </summary>
    [global::System.Diagnostics.DebuggerNonUserCodeAttribute]
    public string SearchContent {
      get { return searchContent_; }
      set {
        searchContent_ = pb::ProtoPreconditions.CheckNotNull(value,
        "value");
      }
    }

    /// <summary>Field number for the "Description" field.</summary>
    public const int DescriptionFieldNumber = 2;
    private string description_ = "";
        /// <summary>
        /// The error description
        /// </summary>
```

```
[global::System.Diagnostics.DebuggerNonUserCodeAttribute]
public string Description {
  get { return description_; }
  set {
      description_ = pb::ProtoPreconditions.CheckNotNull(value, "value");
  }
}
}
```

Summary

In this chapter, you have seen all the power of the Protocol Buffers language. As you discovered, there is no limit to what you can transport in two systems that communicate with each other. In the following chapters, you will find out how to create a server (and client) application from the sample features you learned in this chapter. Exploration of the most exciting aspects of gRPC and ASP.NET Core is finally about to begin!

Summary

In this chapter...

PART III

gRPC and ASP.NET Core

Creating an ASP.NET Core gRPC Application

Here we are at the heart of the matter. Up to this point, you have discovered the prerequisites for building a gRPC service with ASP.NET Core by exploring .NET 6, ASP. NET Core 6, the fundamentals of gRPC, and the Protocol Buffers language, which is essential for any gRPC service creation (whatever the final language or framework used). It's time to put into practice everything you have learned in the previous chapters.

In this chapter, you will learn how to do the following:

- Create an ASP.NET Core gRPC application

- Create and compile Protobuf files

- Write, configure, and expose gRPC services, and register dependencies

- Test using gRPCurl and gRPCui tools

- Manage errors, handle responses, and perform logging

- Perform messages validation

- Explore support of ASP.NET Core gRPC on Microsoft Azure

Create an ASP.NET Core gRPC Application

In this section, I will show you how to create a server gRPC application with Visual Studio 2022. Note that discussion of an ASP.NET Core gRPC application refers to the server part that exposes the service, not the client that consumes it. Chapter 7 will demonstrate how to create a client with a console application in .NET 6.

© Anthony Giretti 2022
A. Giretti, *Beginning gRPC with ASP.NET Core 6*, https://doi.org/10.1007/978-1-4842-8008-9_5

To start, It is necessary to use Visual Studio 2022 to create a gRPC application with ASP.NET Core 6. Open Visual Studio 2022 and select the ASP.NET Core gRPC Service template. You can type **grpc** in the search bar to find it more quickly, as shown in Figure 5-1.

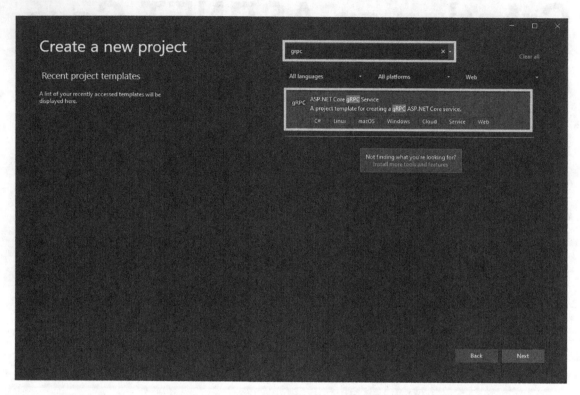

Figure 5-1. *Find and select the ASP.NET Core gRPC Services template*

Once you have selected it, click Next to move to the configuration options, shown in Figure 5-2. Name your project, select the location where to create your application, name your solution, and then click Next.

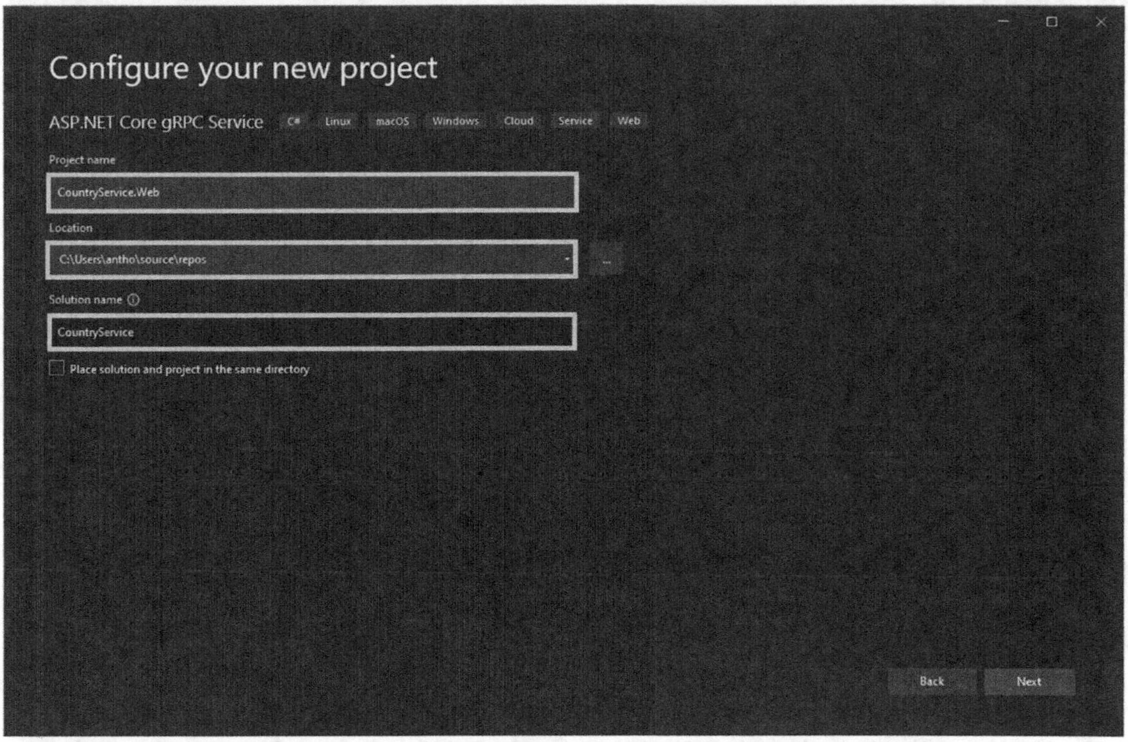

Figure 5-2. *Set the project name, solution name, and application location on the disk*

The last step is to choose the .NET 6 runtime, as shown in Figure 5-3. We won't use Docker here, so click Create.

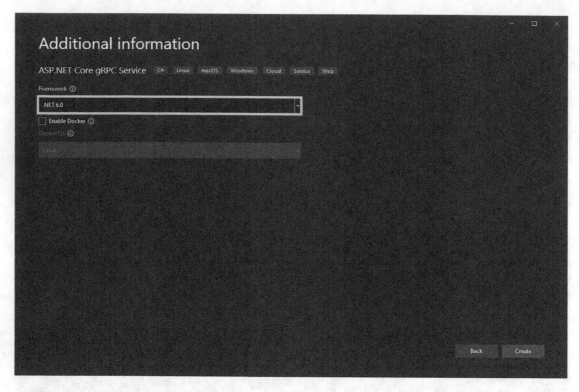

Figure 5-3. *Select .NET 6 runtime*

Visual Studio generates the solution with the default files, such as the standard ASP.NET Core files introduced in Chapter 2 (`lauchSettings.json`, `Program.cs`, and `appsettings.json`). There are extra files that you won't need. You can delete the following files, which are default files created by Visual Studio:

- `greet.proto`

- `GreeterService.cs`

I will show you how to create a Protobuf file, compile it, and write the related gRPC service from the generated code.

Regarding NuGet packages, you do not need to install anything. Everything is ready to write, compile, and write gRPC services from generated code. The three main packages included with the template are

- `Google.Protobuf`: Used for generated code (Google Protobuf types and Well-Known Types).

- `Grpc.Asp.NetCore.Server.ClientFactory`: Includes all you need to write a gRPC service in ASP.NET Core, including the necessity to write gRPC clients within the ASP.NET Core gRPC application (you might need to connect to another gRPC service, for example) with the `Grpc.Net.ClientFactory` package. `Grpc.Net.ClientFactory` is the package we will use to write a gRPC client in any .NET application.

- `Grpc.Tools`: Contains all proto files (references) you might want to import in your proto file (Well-Known Types, for example, as you have seen in the previous chapter).

Figure 5-4 shows the default ASP.NET Core gRPC template generated by Visual Studio.

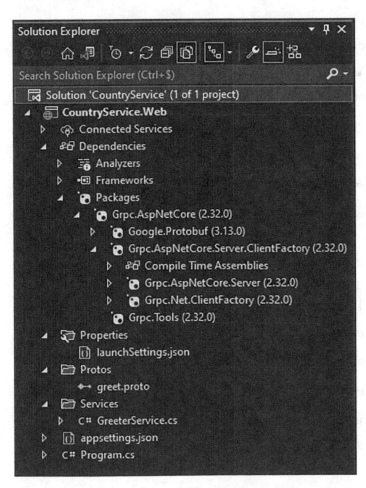

Figure 5-4. *The default ASP.NET Core gRPC application template*

Create and Compile Protobuf Files

This section will teach you how to create and compile a Protobuf file to describe a set of services in Visual Studio. I will continue the same example from the previous chapters. Together, we will build a service (class) called `CountryService` that enables users to create, update, delete and find countries, and import a file containing a list of countries to be saved in a database.

I will create CRUD operations with all possible gRPC services (introduced in Chapter 3): *unary*, *client-streaming*, *server-streaming*, and *bidirectional streaming*. Streaming services provide significant performance gains when transporting large amounts of data, whether from the client to the server or from the server to the client (or bidirectionally). To do so, here are the services that we will implement:

- Create a list of multiple countries that will be imported with a bidirectional service (creation/creation confirmation sent to the client)

- Delete one or more countries with a client-streaming service

- Retrieve all countries with a server-streaming service

- Get a country with a unary service

- Update a country with a unary service

A country has properties such as the following:

- ID

- Name

- Description

- Flag (image)

- Creation date

- Update date

Listing 5-1 shows the `country.proto` file to be created.

Listing 5-1. country.proto File

```
syntax = "proto3";

package gRPCDemo.v1;

option csharp_namespace = "Apress.Sample.gRPC";

import "google/protobuf/empty.proto";
import "google/protobuf/timestamp.proto";

service CountryService {
    rpc GetAll(google.protobuf.Empty) returns (stream CountryReply) {}
    rpc Get(CountryIdRequest) returns (CountryReply) {}
    rpc Delete(stream CountryIdRequest) returns (google.protobuf.Empty) {}
    rpc Update(CountryUpdateRequest) returns (google.protobuf.Empty) {}
    rpc Create(stream CountryCreationRequest) returns (stream
    CountryCreationReply) {}
}

message CountryReply {
    int32 Id = 1;
    string Name = 2;
    string Description = 3;
    bytes Flag = 4;
    google.protobuf.Timestamp CreateDate = 5;
    google.protobuf.Timestamp UpdateDate = 6;
}

message CountryIdRequest {
    int32 Id = 1;
}

message CountryUpdateRequest {
    int32 Id = 1;
    string Description = 3;
    google.protobuf.Timestamp UpdateDate = 6;
}
```

```
message CountryCreationRequest {
        string Name = 2;
        string Description = 3;
        bytes Flag = 4;
        google.protobuf.Timestamp CreateDate = 5;
}

message CountryCreationReply {
        int32 Id = 1;
        string Name = 2;
}
```

Let's go now to Visual Studio and create country.proto. Right-click the Protos folder in the Solution Explorer, choose Add, and click New Item, as shown in Figure 5-5.

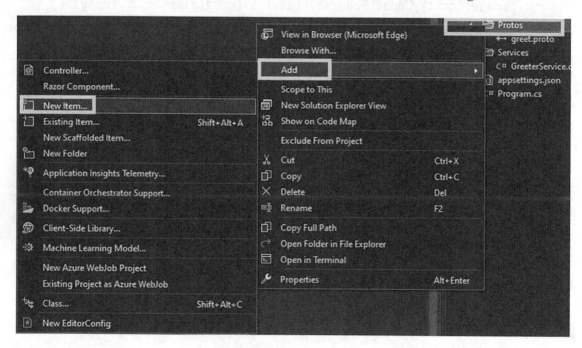

Figure 5-5. *Add a new item to the solution*

The Add New Item window opens, as shown in Figure 5-6. Scroll down and select the Protocol Buffer File type and name the file **country.proto**. Then click the Add button.

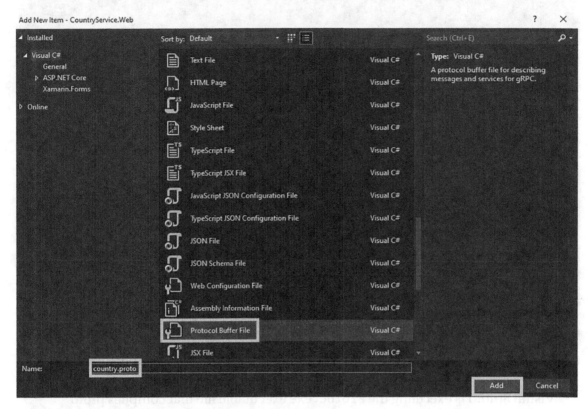

Figure 5-6. *Add a Protocol Buffer file (country.proto)*

Add the Protocol Buffers code (Listing 5-1) within the country.proto file (ensure that it's registered in the CountryService.Web.csproj file) like this:

```
<ItemGroup>
  <Protobuf Include="Protos\country.proto" Link="country.proto"
  GrpcServices="Server" />
</ItemGroup>
```

Then compile the solution by running the command **dotnet build** in the Terminal window. The build should succeed, as shown in Figure 5-7.

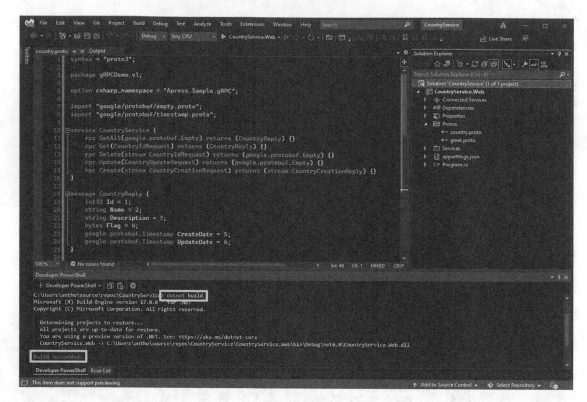

Figure 5-7. *Running* dotnet build *command in Terminal window*

Visual Studio is executing the Protoc.exe executable file that compiles proto files to C# stubs behind the scenes. The reason why I did not give many details in the previous chapter is that Visual Studio handles its execution. You don't need to learn *Protoc* commands. You can check detailed compilation logs in the Output window to see what Visual Studio does, as shown in Figure 5-8. The Protoc command requires absolute paths to be executed on Windows, so I cut the command for easier readability.

Figure 5-8. *The Protoc command execution handled by Visual Studio*

Even If Visual Studio manages everything for you, you can override many compilation options. If you are interested, you can read the following tutorial on GitHub: https://github.com/grpc/grpc/blob/master/src/csharp/BUILD-INTEGRATION.md.

Once the compilation is done, go to the `obj/Debug/.NET6.0/Protos` folder (in your solution folder) and you should see two generated files, as mentioned in Chapter 4:

- `Country.cs`: Contains messages compiled to C#

- `CountryGrpc.cs`: Contains the services definition compiled to C#

Figure 5-9 shows the generated files in the `{SolutionPath}/obj/Debug/.net6.0/Protos` folder.

Figure 5-9. *Generated files*

The combination of these two files is named *gRPC stubs*, aka Protocol Buffers compiled into a specific language, C# here.

Now you are ready to write the concrete implementation of `CountryService`!

Write, Configure, and Expose gRPC Services

As you have just read, the services are now compiled into gRPC stubs (in C#). Now you must write the services from the `abstract` class (a base class that cannot be instantiated directly) generated by Protoc. Listing 5-2 shows the abstract `CountryServiceBase` class generated in the `CountryGrpc.cs` file.

Listing 5-2. CountryServiceBase Class

```
[grpc::BindServiceMethod(typeof(CountryService), "BindService")]
public abstract partial class CountryServiceBase
{
    public virtual global::System.Threading.Tasks.Task GetAll(global::
    Google.Protobuf.WellKnownTypes.Empty request, grpc::IServerStream
    Writer<global::Apress.Sample.gRPC.CountryReply> responseStream,
    grpc::ServerCallContext context)
```

```
{
    throw new grpc::RpcException(new grpc::Status(grpc::StatusCode.
    Unimplemented, ""));
}

public virtual global::System.Threading.Tasks.Task<global::Apress.
Sample.gRPC.CountryReply> Get(global::Apress.Sample.gRPC.
CountryIdRequest request, grpc::ServerCallContext context)
{
    throw new grpc::RpcException(new grpc::Status(grpc::StatusCode.
    Unimplemented, ""));
}

public virtual global::System.Threading.Tasks.Task<global::Google.
Protobuf.WellKnownTypes.Empty> Delete(grpc::IAsyncStreamReader
<global::Apress.Sample.gRPC.CountryIdRequest> requestStream,
grpc::ServerCallContext context)
{
    throw new grpc::RpcException(new grpc::Status(grpc::StatusCode.
    Unimplemented, ""));
}

public virtual global::System.Threading.Tasks.Task<global::Google.
Protobuf.WellKnownTypes.Empty> Update(global::Apress.Sample.gRPC.
CountryUpdateRequest request, grpc::ServerCallContext context)
{
    throw new grpc::RpcException(new grpc::Status(grpc::StatusCode.
    Unimplemented, ""));
}

public virtual global::System.Threading.Tasks.Task Create(grpc::IAs
yncStreamReader<global::Apress.Sample.gRPC.CountryCreationRequest>
requestStream, grpc::IServerStreamWriter<global::Apress.Sample.gRPC.
CountryCreationReply> responseStream, grpc::ServerCallContext context)
```

```
    {
        throw new grpc::RpcException(new grpc::Status(grpc::StatusCode.
        Unimplemented, ""));
    }
}
```

To write the gRPC services, create a new class in your Services folder as shown in Figure 5-10.

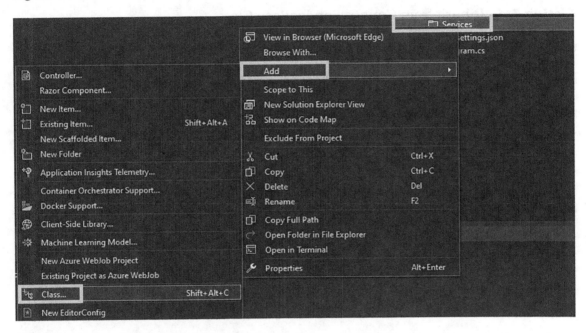

Figure 5-10. *Create a new class*

Name the new class **CountryGrpcService** and click Create. Once created, it should look like Listing 5-3.

Listing 5-3. CountryGrpcService Class Newly Created

```
namespace CountryService.Web.Services
{
    public class CountryGrpcService
    {
    }
}
```

Note that by default the file-scoped namespace is not applied, so you can remove the brackets below the namespace declaration. The next step is to implement the CountryGrpcService gRPC service to inherit from the CountryServiceBase class. This class is nested to the generated CountryService that belongs to the Apress.Sample.gRPC namespace. To make the code clearer, I'm using the static statement to shorten the declaration Apress.Sample.gRPC.CountryService.CountryServiceBase, as shown in Listing 5-4.

Listing 5-4. Inherit from CountryServiceBase Class

```
using static Apress.Sample.gRPC.CountryService;

namespace CountryService.Web.Services;

public class CountryGrpcService : CountryServiceBase
{
}
```

Next, copy and paste the CountryServiceBase virtual methods in Listing 5-2 and make the following modifications:

- Replace the virtual keyword with override because you are rewriting methods

- Remove the global::System.Threading.Tasks namespace because it's already imported as a using statement at the top of the file

- Remove the global::Google.Protobuf.WellKnownTypes namespace from every declared Empty type and add it once in the using statement at the top of the file

- Remove global::Apress.Sample.gRPC everywhere and add it as a using statement as well

- Remove all remaining grpc:: namespaces and import the Grpc.Core namespace as a using statement instead

- Add the async keyword before the Task keyword

After that quick cleanup, the CountryGrpcService class should look like Listing 5-5.

Listing 5-5. CountryService Exposing Wanted gRPC Services

```
using Apress.Sample.gRPC;
using Google.Protobuf.WellKnownTypes;
using Grpc.Core;
using static Apress.Sample.gRPC.CountryService;

namespace CountryService.Web.Services;

public class CountryGrpcService : CountryServiceBase
{
    public override async Task GetAll(Empty request, IServerStreamWriter
    <CountryReply> responseStream, ServerCallContext context)
    {
        throw new RpcException(new Status(StatusCode.Unimplemented, ""));
    }

    public override async Task<CountryReply> Get(CountryIdRequest request,
    ServerCallContext context)
    {
        throw new RpcException(new Status(StatusCode.Unimplemented, ""));
    }

    public override async Task<Empty> Delete(IAsyncStreamReader<CountryId
    Request> requestStream, ServerCallContext context)
    {
        throw new RpcException(new Status(StatusCode.Unimplemented, ""));
    }

    public override async Task<Empty> Update(CountryUpdateRequest request,
    ServerCallContext context)
    {
        throw new RpcException(new Status(StatusCode.Unimplemented, ""));
    }
```

```
public override async Task Create(IAsyncStreamReader<CountryCreation
Request> requestStream, IServerStreamWriter<CountryCreationReply>
responseStream, ServerCallContext context)
{
    throw new RpcException(new Status(StatusCode.Unimplemented, ""));
}

}
```

This code is ready to run, but it will only return a gRPC status of
UNIMPLEMENTED to the client. To return an error status (all statuses except *OK* were
introduced in Chapter 3), you have to throw an RpcException that takes in parameter
a StatusCode and a string that you can add details within. We'll delve a bit further into
error management later in this chapter.

You may notice that each gRPC function takes a message (Empty or designed by
you) in input and returns a message (Empty or created by you) when it's not streamed
in output. Input- and output streamed messages are not returned by the gRPC
function but are parameters of the function. Any input streamed message is typed
IAsyncStreamReader<TMessage>, and any output streamed message is typed IServer
StreamWriter<TMessage>.

The ServerContext parameter is the gRPC HttpContext containing all contextual
information of the current request, even user data if a user is authenticated. We'll return
to this parameter in Chapter 14, where I'll explain authentication in ASP.NET Core gRPC.

This code is ready to run, but it's not ready to be exposed to the Web yet. To expose
it, you'll have to go to the Program.cs file and declare the service in the UseEndpoints
middleware, as shown in Listing 5-6.

Listing 5-6. Configuring Program.cs file to Expose CountryGrpcService

```
using CountryService.Web.Services;

var builder = WebApplication.CreateBuilder(args);

// Add services to the container.
builder.Services.AddGrpc();

var app = builder.Build();

app.MapGrpcService<CountryGrpcService>();
```

```
// Configure the HTTP request pipeline.
app.MapGet("/", () => "Communication with gRPC endpoints must be made
through a gRPC client. To learn how to create a client, visit: https://
go.microsoft.com/fwlink/?linkid=2086909");

app.Run();
```

To complete your gRPC service, add a service layer that manages CRUD operations on a Country entity and write your gRPC services class with that service. Let's name it CountryManagementService. You'll need to register it into the ASP.NET Core dependency injection system, inject it within the CountryGrpcService constructor that needs to be added. ASP.NET Core gRPC supports dependency injection like any ASP.NET Core apps, as you've seen in Chapter 2. To guide you as smoothly as possible writing these gRPC services, we'll write a simple CountryManagementService class that exposes a hard-coded collection of countries. We'll revisit that service in Chapter 9, where you'll learn to build a fully layered app with a database, a data access layer, a service layer, and *Data Transfer Objects (DTO)* as domain entities, and discover dependency injection best practices.

Listing 5-7 shows the CountryManagementService class with basic CRUD operations. I'm implementing asynchronous operations with async and await keywords.

Listing 5-7. Simple CountryManagementService Class

```
using Google.Protobuf.WellKnownTypes;
using Apress.Sample.gRPC;

namespace CountryService.Web;

public class CountryManagementService
{
    private readonly List<CountryReply> _countries = new(); // C# 9 syntax
    "Improved target typing"

    public CountryManagementService()
    {
        _countries.Add(new CountryReply { Id = 1, Name = "Canada",
        Description = "Canada has at least 32 000 lakes", CreateDate =
        Timestamp.FromDateTime(DateTime.SpecifyKind(new DateTime(2021,
        1, 2), DateTimeKind.Utc)) });
```

```csharp
        _countries.Add(new CountryReply { Id = 2, Name = "USA", Description
        = "Yellowstone has 300 to 500 geysers", CreateDate = Timestamp.
        FromDateTime(DateTime.SpecifyKind(new DateTime(2021, 1, 2),
        DateTimeKind.Utc)) });
        _countries.Add(new CountryReply { Id = 3, Name = "Mexico",
        Description = "Mexico is crossed by Sierra Madre Oriental and
        Sierra Madre Occidental mountains", CreateDate = Timestamp.
        FromDateTime(DateTime.SpecifyKind(new DateTime(2021, 1, 2),
        DateTimeKind.Utc)) });
    }

    public async Task<IEnumerable<CountryReply>> GetAllAsync()
    {
        return await Task.FromResult(_countries.ToArray());
    }

    public async Task<CountryReply> GetAsync(CountryIdRequest country)
    {
        return await Task.FromResult(_countries.FirstOrDefault(x => x.Id ==
        country.Id));
    }

    public async Task DeleteAsync(IEnumerable<CountryIdRequest> countries)
    {
        var ids = countries.Select(x => x.Id).ToList();
        _countries.RemoveAll(x => ids.Contains(x.Id));

        await Task.CompletedTask;
    }

    public async Task UpdateAsync(CountryUpdateRequest country)
    {
        var countryToUpdate = _countries.FirstOrDefault(x => x.Id ==
        country.Id);
        if (countryToUpdate != null)
        {
            countryToUpdate.Description = country.Description;
            countryToUpdate.UpdateDate = country.UpdateDate;
        }
```

```
        await Task.CompletedTask;
    }

    public async Task<IEnumerable<CountryCreationReply>> CreateAsync(List
    <CountryCreationRequest> countries)
    {
        var countryCreationReply = new CountryCreationReply();
        var newCountries = new List<CountryReply>();
        var count = _countries.Count;
        countries.ForEach(country => {
            var existingCountry = _countries.FirstOrDefault(x => x.Name ==
            country.Name);
            if (existingCountry == null)
            {
                newCountries.Add(new CountryReply
                {
                    Id = ++count,
                    Name = country.Name,
                    Description = country.Description,
                    Flag = country.Flag,
                    CreateDate = Timestamp.FromDateTime(DateTime.
                    SpecifyKind(new DateTime(2021, 1, 2),
                    DateTimeKind.Utc))

                });
            }
        });
        _countries.AddRange(newCountries);

        return await Task.FromResult(newCountries.Select(x => new
        CountryCreationReply { Id = x.Id, Name = x.Name }).ToList());
    }
}
```

To use the *CountryManagementService* class consume it in the gRPC services you have created before, you must register it in the dependency injection system, as shown in Listing 5-8. Note that the service is registered in Singleton lifetime, which means only one instance of the service will be created, so any operation on the country hard-coded list will be kept in memory unless you stop and restart the app.

Listing 5-8. Registering the CountryManagementService Class as Singleton

```
using CountryService.Web;
using CountryService.Web.Services;

var builder = WebApplication.CreateBuilder(args);

// Add services to the container.
builder.Services.AddGrpc();
builder.Services.AddSingleton<CountryManagementService>();

var app = builder.Build();

app.MapGrpcService<CountryGrpcService>();
// Configure the HTTP request pipeline.
app.MapGet("/", () => "Communication with gRPC endpoints must be made
through a gRPC client. To learn how to create a client, visit: https://
go.microsoft.com/fwlink/?linkid=2086909");

app.Run();
```

Next, you need to add a constructor in the CountryGrpcService class if you have not done so yet and inject the CountryManagementService class in the constructor. Then you can write your gRPC service final implementation. As you can see, it's straightforward to read or write streamed messages. Use the ReadAllAsync() method on the IAsyncStreamReader<T> parameter and the WriteAsync method on the IAsyncStreamWriter<T> parameter, then iterate on items. *Unary* services are the simplest to implement, as shown in Listing 5-9.

Listing 5-9. The CountryGrpcService Class Implemented with Several gRPC Services

```
using Apress.Sample.gRPC;
using Google.Protobuf.WellKnownTypes;
using Grpc.Core;
using static Apress.Sample.gRPC.CountryService;

namespace CountryService.Web.Services;

public class CountryGrpcService : CountryServiceBase
{
    private readonly CountryManagementService _countryManagementService;

    public CountryGrpcService(CountryManagementService countryManagement
    Service)
    {
        _countryManagementService = countryManagementService;
    }

    public override async Task GetAll(Empty request, IServerStreamWriter
    <CountryReply> responseStream, ServerCallContext context)
    {
        // Streams all found countries to the client
        var countries = await _countryManagementService.GetAllAsync();
        foreach (var country in countries)
        {
            await responseStream.WriteAsync(country);
        }
        await Task.CompletedTask;
    }

    public override async Task<CountryReply> Get(CountryIdRequest request,
    ServerCallContext context)
    {
        // Send a single country to the client in the gRPC response
        return await _countryManagementService.GetAsync(request);
    }
```

```csharp
public override async Task<Empty> Delete(IAsyncStreamReader<CountryId
Request> requestStream, ServerCallContext context)
{
    // Read and store all streamed input messages
    var countryIdRequestList = new List<CountryIdRequest>();
    await foreach (var countryIdRequest in requestStream.
    ReadAllAsync())
    {
        countryIdRequestList.Add(countryIdRequest);
    }
    // Delete in one shot all streamed countries
    await _countryManagementService.DeleteAsync(countryIdRequestList);
    return new Empty();
}

public override async Task<Empty> Update(CountryUpdateRequest request,
ServerCallContext context)
{
    // read input message from the gRPC request
    await _countryManagementService.UpdateAsync(request);
    return new Empty();
}

public override async Task Create(IAsyncStreamReader<CountryCreation
Request> requestStream, IServerStreamWriter<CountryCreationReply>
responseStream, ServerCallContext context)
{
    // Read and store all streamed input messages before performing
      any action
    var countryCreationRequestList = new List<CountryCreation
    Request>();
    await foreach (var countryCreationRequest in requestStream.
    ReadAllAsync())
    {
        countryCreationRequestList.Add(countryCreationRequest);
    }
```

```
// Call in one shot the countryManagementService that will perform
    creation operations
var createdCountries = await _countryManagementService.CreateAsync(
countryCreationRequestList);

// Stream all created countries to the client
foreach (var country in createdCountries)
{
    await responseStream.WriteAsync(country);
}
    }
}
```

The following task is optional, but it's possible to add some options to change/ improve your gRPC service's behavior. Chapter 3 introduced you the procedure for adding some options within a gRPC *Channel* class used to build a gRPC client, and you can do the same server-side. You can apply the following options globally (on each service once) or on a specific service:

- MaxSendMessageSize: Corresponds to the maximum size in bytes of the message sent by the server. If no value is set, the size is not limited, and if a value is set and the message exceeds that limit, an RpcException will be raised.

- MaxReceivedMessageSize: The same as the previous option except for the message sent to the server. If no value is set, the default value set is 4 MB. To set the value to unlimited, you must set it to null. An RpcException will be raised if the size exceeds the limit.

- CompressionProviders: A collection of compression providers. When no provider is set, the default compression used is Gzip. You can customize the Gzip compression and/or add your compression provider.

- ResponseCompressionAlgorithm: The string value of the algorithm to be applied for message compression. If not set, the selected algorithm will be the first in the CompressionProviders collection that matches the client's algorithm over the grpc-accept-encoding header. Gzip is the default compression algorithm. It doesn't need to be added to the CompressionProviders collection.

- ResponseCompressionLevel: The compression level passed to the compression provider. If not set, the compression provider should implement a default compression level.

Listing 5-10 illustrate the custom compression provider based on the Brotli compression algorithm.

Listing 5-10. A Custom gRPC Compression Provider Using Brotli

```
using Grpc.Net.Compression;
using System.IO;
using System.IO.Compression;

namespace CountryService.gRPC.Compression;

public class BrotliCompressionProvider : ICompressionProvider
{
    private readonly CompressionLevel? _compressionLevel;

    public BrotliCompressionProvider(CompressionLevel compressionLevel)
    {
        _compressionLevel = compressionLevel;
    }

    public BrotliCompressionProvider()
    {
    }

    public string EncodingName => "br"; // Must match grpc-accept-encoding

    public Stream CreateCompressionStream(Stream outputStream,
    CompressionLevel? compressionLevel)
    {
        if (_compressionLevel.HasValue)
            return new BrotliStream(outputStream, compressionLevel ??
            _compressionLevel.Value, true);

        else if (!_compressionLevel.HasValue && compressionLevel.HasValue)
            return new BrotliStream(outputStream, compressionLevel.
            Value, true);
```

```
        return new BrotliStream(outputStream, CompressionLevel.
        Fastest, true);
    }

    public Stream CreateDecompressionStream(Stream stream)
    {
        return new BrotliStream(stream, CompressionMode.Decompress);
    }
}
```

Note   The Brotli compression algorithm provides highly efficient compression, higher than Gzip. I strongly recommend using it.

Listing 5-11 shows message size and compression options in the Program.cs file.

Listing 5-11. Message Size and Compression Options

```
builder.Services.AddGrpc(options => {
            options.MaxReceiveMessageSize = 6291456; // 6 MB
            options.MaxSendMessageSize = 6291456; // 6 MB
            options.CompressionProviders = new List<ICompression
            Provider>
            {
BrotliCompressionProvider(CompressionLevel.Optimal) // br
            };
            options.ResponseCompressionAlgorithm = "br"; // grpc-
            accept-encoding, and must match the compression provider
            declared in CompressionProviders collection
            options.ResponseCompressionLevel = CompressionLevel.
            Optimal; // compression level used if not set on the
            provider
});
```

Tip   Although the `MaxSendMessageSize` and `MaxReceiveMessageSize` options are optional, it's highly recommended to consider using them to limit resources and keep performance and stability to an acceptable level.

There are three more options that I haven't talked about yet: `EnableDetailedErrors`, `Interceptors`, and `IgnoreUnknownServices`. I'll introduce them in the next section because they are more closely related to logging and tracing and/or error management.

Test Using gRPCurl and gRPCui Tools

gRPCurl and *gRPCui* are similar tools that allow developers to test their gRPC services. gRPCurl is the *curl* tool for gRPC services that is a command-line tool for invoking remote URI. You can learn more about the curl tool here: `https://curl.se/`). gRPCui is based on gRPCurl. It's merely a graphical user interface (GUI) built on gRPCurl, which runs behind the scenes.

Throughout this section, we'll continue to use the `gRPC.v1.CountryService` that we have been using since the beginning of this book.

gRPCurl

gRPCurl is a great tool that allows you to call your gRPC endpoints like Postman, for example, but offers more than that: it enables you to list available services and describe them (showing services definition). To be able to do that, it needs to know the services definition (protos). There are two ways to provide this to gRPCurl:

- Passing to gRPCurl command-line proto files as arguments

- Using reflection with *gRPC reflection*

In this book, I'll only introduce the usage of gRPCurl with gRPC reflection because it's the easiest way to proceed. ASP.NET Core natively supports it.

First, you need to install the `Grpc.AspNetCore.Server.Reflection` Nuget package from the Package Manager window with the command shown in Listing 5-12.

Listing 5-12. Install `Grpc.AspNetCore.Server.Reflection`

```
Install-Package Grpc.AspNetCore.Server.Reflection
```

Figure 5-11 shows the command executed in the Package Manager window.

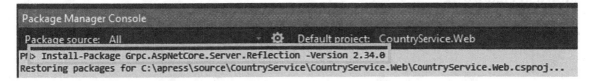

Figure 5-11. *Install* `Grpc.AspNetCore.Server.Reflection` *from Package Manager window*

Once you have installed `Grpc.AspNetCore.Server.Reflection`, go to the `Program.cs` file to register the gRPC reflection with the `AddGrpcReflection` method and apply it with the `MapGrpcReflectionService` method on endpoints, as shown in Listing 5-13 (I removed options added in the previous section for more clarity).

Listing 5-13. Register and Apply gRPC Reflection

```
using CountryService.Web;
using CountryService.Web.Services;

var builder = WebApplication.CreateBuilder(args);

// Add services to the container.
builder.Services.AddGrpc();
builder.Services.AddGrpcReflection();
builder.Services.AddSingleton<CountryManagementService>();

var app = builder.Build();

app.MapGrpcReflectionService();
app.MapGrpcService<CountryGrpcService>();
// Configure the HTTP request pipeline.
app.MapGet("/", () => "Communication with gRPC endpoints must be made
through a gRPC client. To learn how to create a client, visit: https://
go.microsoft.com/fwlink/?linkid=2086909");

app.Run();
```

The gRPC server is ready to request gRPCurl, but the latter is not set yet. Because it's a tool implemented with the *Go* programming language, you have to install Go to run it. You can download Go `https://golang.org/doc/install`.

If you are using Windows, you have to run the installer that you just downloaded, as shown in Figure 5-12.

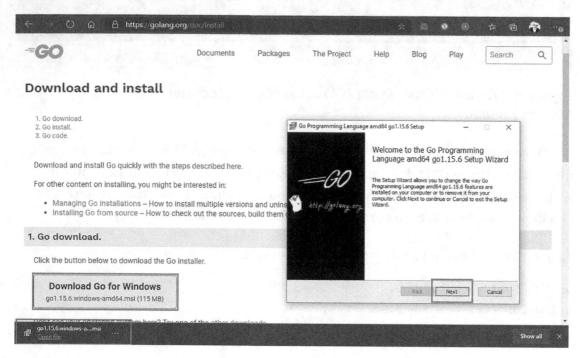

Figure 5-12. *Install Go on Windows*

Ensure that Go is installed in your Windows Environments Variables. If you don't know how to proceed, you can follow a complete tutorial at `https://www.geeksforgeeks.org/how-to-install-go-on-windows/`.

You can now download and install gRPCurl with two commands in a PowerShell command window, as shown in Listing 5-14.

Listing 5-14. Download and Install gRPCurl via Command Line

```
go get github.com/fullstorydev/grpcurl/...
go install github.com/fullstorydev/grpcurl/cmd/grpcurl@latest
```

Tip   I suggest running PowerShell as Administrator. PowerShell did not work for me on my computer without doing so.

If everything goes well, no error message appears, and you should be able to run the grpcurl -help command as shown in Figure 5-13.

```
 Administrator: Windows PowerShell
Windows PowerShell
Copyright (C) Microsoft Corporation. All rights reserved.

Try the new cross-platform PowerShell https://aka.ms/pscore6

PS C:\WINDOWS\system32> go get github.com/fullstorydev/grpcurl/...
PS C:\WINDOWS\system32> go install github.com/fullstorydev/grpcurl/cmd/grpcurl
PS C:\WINDOWS\system32> grpcurl -help
Usage:
        C:\Users\anthony.giretti\go\bin\grpcurl.exe [flags] [address] [list|describe] [symbol]

The 'address' is only optional when used with 'list' or 'describe' and a
protoset or proto flag is provided.

If 'list' is indicated, the symbol (if present) should be a fully-qualified
service name. If present, all methods of that service are listed. If not
present, all exposed services are listed, or all services defined in protosets.

If 'describe' is indicated, the descriptor for the given symbol is shown. The
symbol should be a fully-qualified service, enum, or message name. If no symbol
is given then the descriptors for all exposed or known services are shown.

If neither verb is present, the symbol must be a fully-qualified method name in
'service/method' or 'service.method' format. In this case, the request body will
be used to invoke the named method. If no body is given but one is required
(i.e. the method is unary or server-streaming), an empty instance of the
method's request type will be sent.

The address will typically be in the form "host:port" where host can be an IP
address or a hostname and port is a numeric port or service name. If an IPv6
address is given, it must be surrounded by brackets, like "[2001:db8::1]". For
Unix variants, if a -unix=true flag is present, then the address must be the
path to the domain socket.

Available flags:
  -H value
        Additional headers in 'name: value' format. May specify more than one
        via multiple flags. These headers will also be included in reflection
        requests requests to a server.
  -allow-unknown-fields
        When true, the request contents, if 'json' format is used, allows
        unkown fields to be present. They will be ignored when parsing
        the request.
  -authority string
        The authoritative name of the remote server. This value is passed as the
        value of the ":authority" pseudo-header in the HTTP/2 protocol. When TLS
        is used, this will also be used as the server name when verifying the
        server's certificate. It defaults to the address that is provided in the
        positional arguments.
  -cacert string
        File containing trusted root certificates for verifying the server.
        Ignored if -insecure is specified.
  -cert string
        File containing client certificate (public key), to present to the
        server. Not valid with -plaintext option. Must also provide -key option.
  -connect-timeout float
        The maximum time, in seconds, to wait for connection to be established.
        Defaults to 10 seconds.
  -d string
```

Figure 5-13. *Verify gRPCurl installation with the* grpcurl -help *command*

You can now test your gRPC ASP.NET Core app. Don't forget to run your app first, as shown in Figure 5-14, with the dotnet run command.

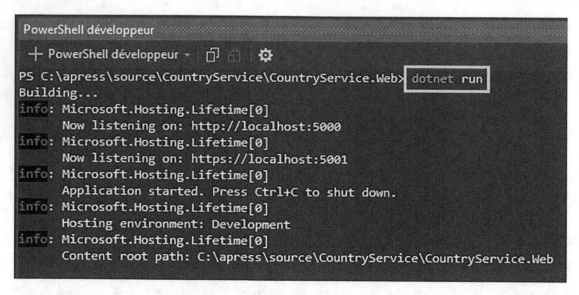

Figure 5-14. *Run ASP.NET Core gRPC application*

In another PowerShell window, type the command shown in Listing 5-15 to list all gRPC services your app is exposing.

Listing 5-15. List of gRPC Services Exposed by the App

```
grpccurl localhost:{yourport} list
```

Figure 5-15 shows the output result.

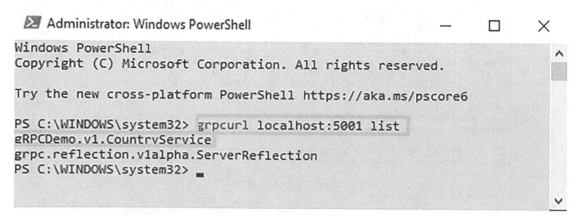

Figure 5-15. *Listing exposed gRPC services*

As expected, the output result is gRPC.v1.CountryService. Recall that we set the package directive value to gRPCDemo.v1 in the country.proto file, and as you can see, it prefixes the gRPC service CountryService.

From this, you can now reuse the same command by adding the service name as the argument to list each RPC function of that service, as shown in Listing 5-16.

Listing 5-16. List RPC Functions with gRPCurl list Command

```
grpccurl localhost:{yourport} list gRPCDemo.v1.CountryService
```

Figure 5-16 shows the output result.

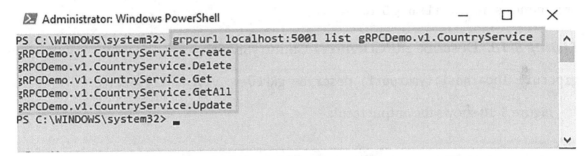

Figure 5-16. Listing RPC function output result with gRPCurl list command

As expected again, all RPC functions we have defined previously are listed here. If you now want to get the description of an RPC function, you can do so with the describe command argument, which takes the RPC function full name as an argument, as shown in Listing 5-17 using as an example the gRPCDemo.v1.CountryService.Create RPC function.

Listing 5-17. Get the gRPCDemo.v1.CountryService.Create RPC Function Description with the describe Command Argument

```
grpccurl localhost:{yourport} describe gRPCDemo.v1.CountryService.Create
```

Figure 5-17 shows the output result that is the Create function proto definition.

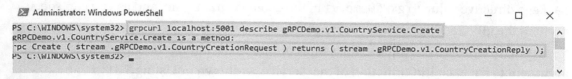

Figure 5-17. *The gRPCDemo.v1.CountryService.Create function definition output*

You can even use the describe command argument on gRPCDemo.v1.CountryService, which gives you more detailed information on that service than the list command argument, as shown in Listing 5-18.

Listing 5-18. Describe gRPCDemo.v1.CountryService

```
grpccurl localhost:{yourport} describe gRPCDemo.v1.CountryService
```

Figure 5-18 shows the output result.

```
Administrator: Windows PowerShell                                    —    □    ×
PS C:\WINDOWS\system32> grpcurl localhost:5001 describe gRPCDemo.v1.CountryService
gRPCDemo.v1.CountryService is a service:
service CountryService {
  rpc Create ( stream .gRPCDemo.v1.CountryCreationRequest ) returns ( stream .gRPCDemo.v1.CountryCreationReply );
  rpc Delete ( stream .gRPCDemo.v1.CountryIdRequest ) returns ( .google.protobuf.Empty );
  rpc Get ( .gRPCDemo.v1.CountryIdRequest ) returns ( .gRPCDemo.v1.CountryReply );
  rpc GetAll ( .google.protobuf.Empty ) returns ( stream .gRPCDemo.v1.CountryReply );
  rpc Update ( .gRPCDemo.v1.CountryUpdateRequest ) returns ( .google.protobuf.Empty );
}
PS C:\WINDOWS\system32>
```

Figure 5-18. *Describe the gRPCDemo.v1.CountryService output result*

And now, what about messages description? It's also possible to fetch them with the same command. Like RPC functions, you have to pass the full name of the message as an argument; for example, Listing 5-19 shows getting the description of the gRPCDemo.v1.CountryCreationRequest message.

Listing 5-19. Get the gRPCDemo.v1.CountryCreationRequest Message Description

```
grpccurl localhost:{yourport} describe gRPCDemo.v1.CountryCreationRequest
```

Figure 5-19 shows the output result for the gRPCDemo.v1.CountryCreationRequest message.

```
Administrator: Windows PowerShell                                    —    □    ×

PS C:\WINDOWS\system32> grpcurl localhost:5001 describe gRPCDemo.v1.CountryCreationRequest
gRPCDemo.v1.CountryCreationRequest is a message:
message CountryCreationRequest {
  string Name = 2;
  string Description = 3;
  bytes Flag = 4;
  .google.protobuf.Timestamp CreateDate = 5;
}
PS C:\WINDOWS\system32>
```

Figure 5-19. *The gRPCDemo.v1.CountryCreationRequest message description output*

It's time to test your endpoints! gRPCurl supports empty message requests (no parameters), empty message responses, streaming requests, and streaming responses. All data passed in parameters can be in JSON format or text. I'll show you examples in JSON format for purposes of readability. Google well documents the JSON representation of your message at https://developers.google.com/protocol-buffers/docs/proto3#json.

For example, let's test the GetAll() RPC function that doesn't take parameters and stream a collection of the CountryReply message. An argument that matches the desired RPC function should match the following pattern: *{ServiceFullName}/{FunctionName}*.

Listing 5-20 shows the command to invoke the GetAll gRPC endpoint.

Listing 5-20. Invoke GetAll gRPC Endpoint

```
grpcurl localhost:{yourport} gRPCDemo.v1.CountryService/GetAll
```

Figure 5-20 shows the output result of the command. Note that results have been streaming one by one to the output.

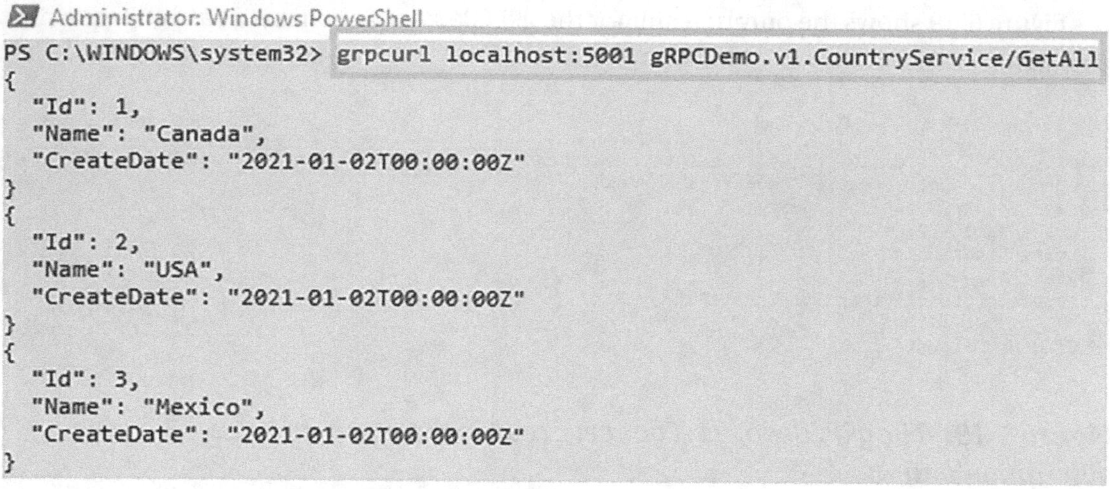

```
Administrator: Windows PowerShell

PS C:\WINDOWS\system32> grpcurl localhost:5001 gRPCDemo.v1.CountryService/GetAll
{
  "Id": 1,
  "Name": "Canada",
  "CreateDate": "2021-01-02T00:00:00Z"
}
{
  "Id": 2,
  "Name": "USA",
  "CreateDate": "2021-01-02T00:00:00Z"
}
{
  "Id": 3,
  "Name": "Mexico",
  "CreateDate": "2021-01-02T00:00:00Z"
}
```

Figure 5-20. *The* GetAll *invocation output result*

Let's now try a unary function, like the Get gRPC endpoint. This gRPC endpoint takes as a parameter the CountryIdRequest message. When you try to call a gRPC function with parameters, you have to add the argument -d followed by the JSON representation of the message *before* the gRPC endpoint's full name. Listing 5-21 shows the parameterized command to invoke the Get gRPC endpoint (note that a backslash must escape double quotes).

Listing 5-21. Invoke Get gRPC Endpoint with CountryIdRequest Message

```
grpcurl localhost:{yourport} -d '{\"\Id" : 1}' gRPCDemo.
v1.CountryService/Get
```

Figure 5-21 shows the output result after the Get gRPC endpoint invocation.

```
Administrator: Windows PowerShell                                    —    □    ×

PS C:\WINDOWS\system32> grpcurl -d '{\"Id\": 1}' localhost:5001 gRPCDemo.v1.CountryService/Get
{
  "Id": 1,
  "Name": "Canada",
  "CreateDate": "2021-01-02T00:00:00Z"
}
PS C:\WINDOWS\system32>
```

Figure 5-21. Get *invocation output result*

As a last test here, let's try a client-streaming function, the `Delete` gRPC endpoint. This function takes as a parameter a streamed `CountryIdRequest` message. To pass a collection of messages streamed into a gRPC request, you have to concatenate the message's JSON representation. Don't be confused with an array of parameters that is the way to pass a collection of the same message on a non-streamed request. Listing 5-22 shows the command to invoke the `Delete` gRPC endpoint with two streamed `CountryIdRequest` messages:

Listing 5-22. Invoke the `Delete` gRPC Endpoint with Two Streamed `CountryIdRequest` Messages

```
grpcurl localhost:{yourport} -d '{\"\Id" : 1}{\"\Id" : 2}' gRPCDemo.
v1.CountryService/Delete
```

Figure 5-22 shows the `Delete` gRPC endpoint invocation output result.

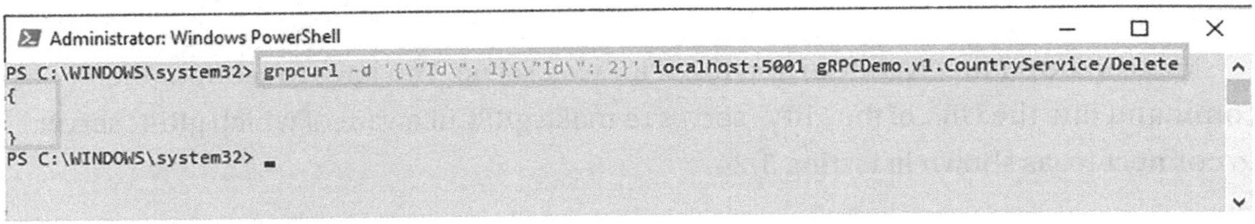

Figure 5-22. *Delete invocation output result*

As expected, the returned message is an empty JSON object.

This tutorial introduced you to gRPCurl. I did not cover all its capabilities. However, if you want to learn more about gRPCurl capabilities, you can read the GitHub documentation here: `https://github.com/fullstorydev/grpcurl#installation`.

I find this tool very useful, but some people won't like it because it's a command-line tool. Many developers (except Linux developers, maybe) might prefer gRPCui, the focus of the next section.

gRPCui

gRPCui is another excellent tool to test your ASP.NET Core gRPC app. In terms of functionalities, it's the same as gRPCurl. It's merely a UI built on top of it, similar to Swagger for REST services. If you are more comfortable with a GUI than a command-line tool, gRPCui is made for you!

To download and install gRPCui, run the two commands (as Administrator, as with gRPCurl) shown in Listing 5-23.

Listing 5-23. Download and Install gRPCui from a Command Line

```
go get github.com/fullstorydev/grpcui/...
go install github.com/fullstorydev/grpcui/cmd/grpcui@latest
```

If the download and installation succeed, no error should be displayed, as shown in Figure 5-23.

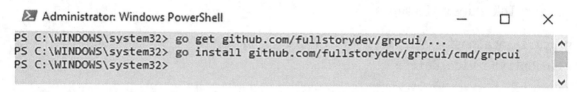

Figure 5-23. *Download and install gRPCui*

You can now launch gRPCui and test if it's well set up. You have to set from the command line the URL of the gRPC server to make gRPCui aware of which gRPC server to connect to, as shown in Listing 5-24.

Listing 5-24. Launch gRPCui and Specify gRPC Server URL

```
grpcui localhost:{yourport}
```

The command should receive a response with a successful message and give you the local URL of the GUI. Then your default browser should open that URL automatically, as shown in Figure 5-24.

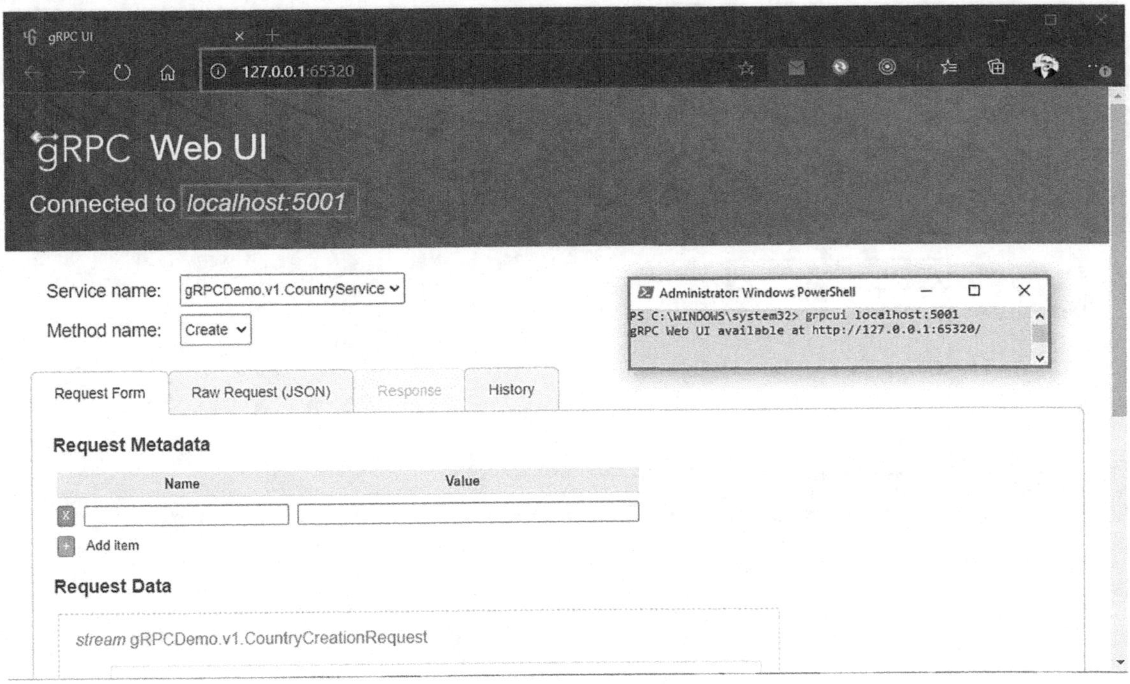

Figure 5-24. Launch gRPCui from a command line

It's super simple to invoke a gRPC function: select the method name in the drop-
down list first, fill in the Request Metadata fields, and then set the Request Timeout field.
Figure 5-25 shows the GetAll() function invocation form, which does not have any
input message.

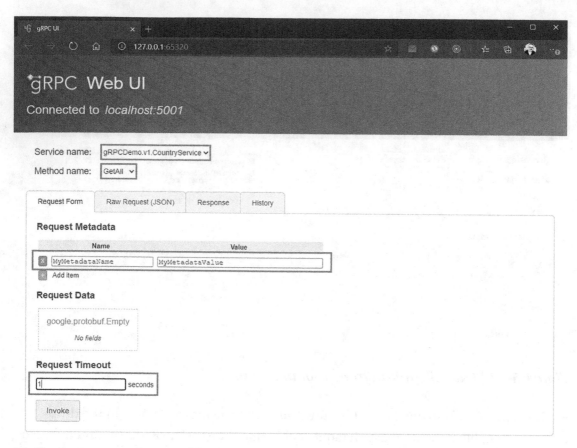

Figure 5-25.   *Invoke* GetAll *gRPC function via gRPCui form*

Click the Invoke button, and the results will appear in the Response panel. Displayed results are

- Response Headers

- Response Data

- Response Trailers

Figure 5-26 shows output results after GetAll gRPC function invocation in gRPCui.

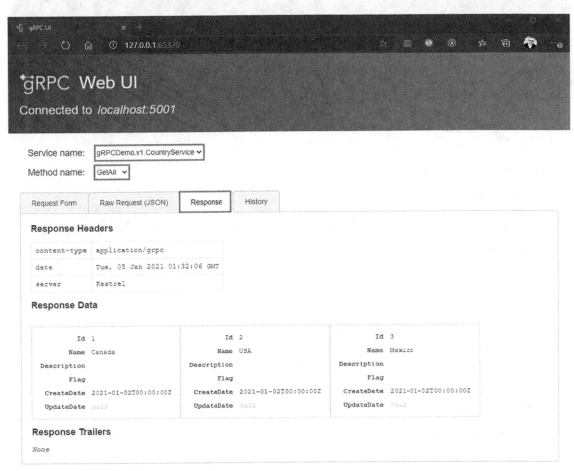

Figure 5-26. *The GetAll() gRPC function invocation results in gRPCui*

Setting up streamed request messages is straightforward as well. If you test the
Delete() gRPC function with gRPCui again, you'll see that it's intuitive. You need to fill a
collection of CountryIdRequest and gRPCui streams them for you. Figure 5-27 shows the
request form to invoke the Delete() gRPC function.

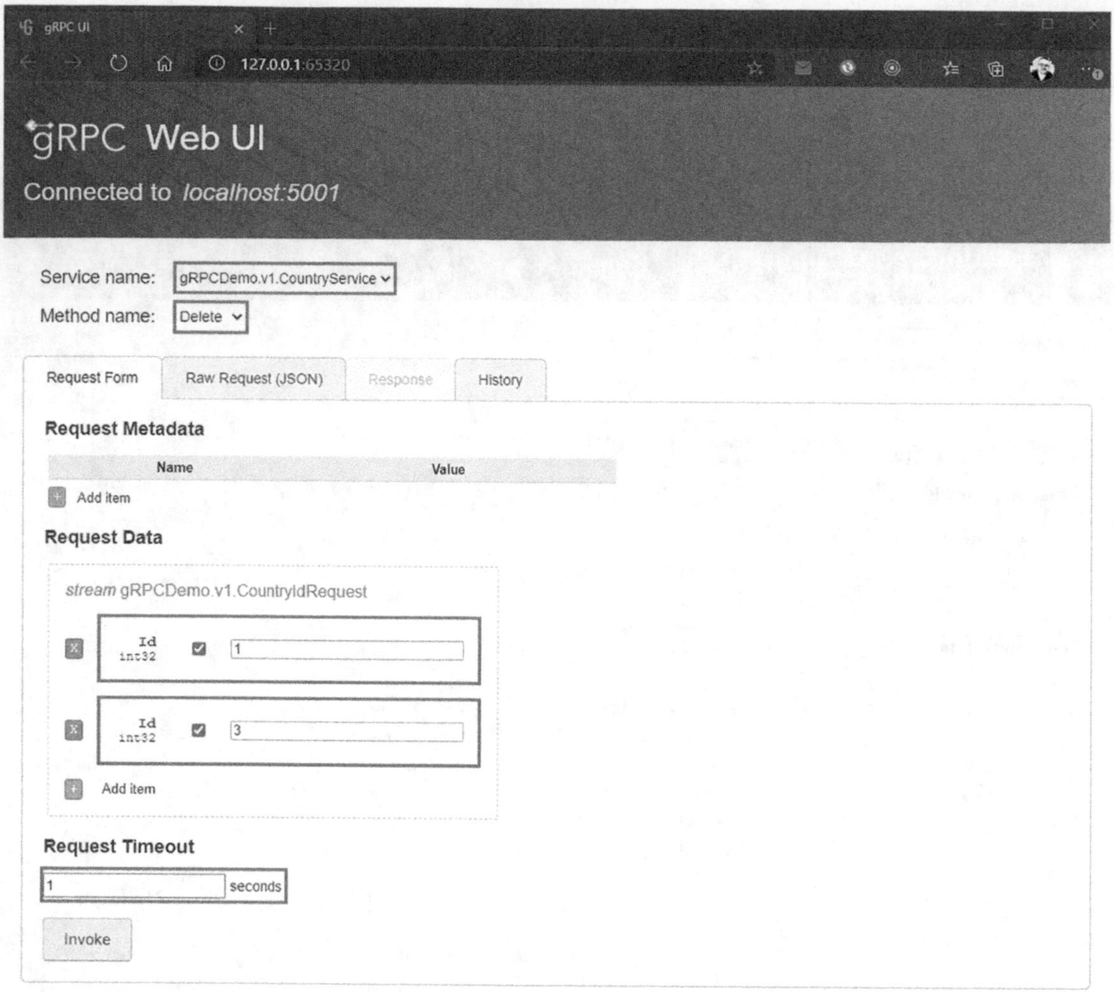

Figure 5-27. *Invoke* `Delete` *gRPC function over gRPCui form*

After clicking the Invoke button, you can verify the response panel's response status. As expected for this function, there is no data in the response (`Empty` message), as shown in Figure 5-28.

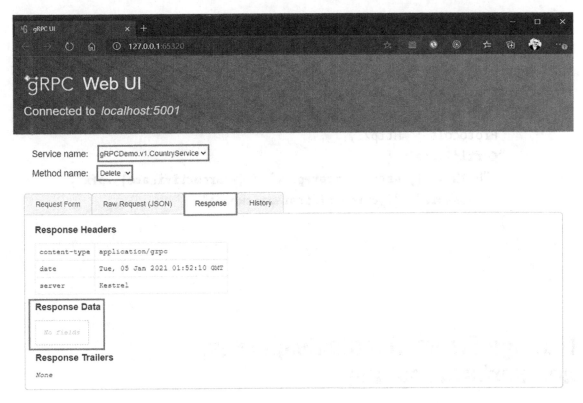

Figure 5-28. *The* `Delete()` *gRPC function invocation results in gRPCui*

This tutorial introduced you to gRPCui. I did not cover all its capabilities. However, if you want to learn more about gRPCui capabilities, you can read the GitHub documentation: `https://github.com/fullstorydev/grpcui#installation`.

TLS Certificates

So far, in the examples with gRPCurl and gRPCui, no HTTPS certificates were configured because ASP.NET Core in development mode has an HTTPS certificate by default. Therefore, you do not need to configure any one on Kestrel. However, once in production, you will need to configure a certificate for Kestrel in the `appsettings.json` file, as shown in Listing 5-25.

Listing 5-25. Configure an HTTPS Certificate on Kestrel

```
"Kestrel": {
    "Endpoints": {
      "HttpsInlineCertFile": {
        "Url": "https: // localhost: 5001",
        "Protocols": "Http2",
        "Certificate": {
          "Path": "{yourcertificatepath} / {yourcertificate} .pfx",
          "Password": "{yourcertificatepassword}"
        }
      }
    }
  }
```

Manage Errors, Handle Responses, and Perform Logging

Suppose that you are developing an application and things are not going as expected. Your application encounters an unexpected behavior that causes a crash. You are faced with an *exception*. On ASP.NET Core gRPC, it's possible to handle exceptions easily, and I'll show how in this section.

Let's consider that a gRPC endpoint like GetAll raises an exception with the simple example shown in Listing 5-26.

Listing 5-26. GetAll Raises an Unexpected Exception

```
public override async Task GetAll(Empty request, IServerStreamWriter
<CountryReply> responseStream, ServerCallContext context)
{
    /////////// simulating an exception here ///////////
    throw new Exception("Something got really wrong here");

    // Streams all found countries to the client
    var countries = await _countryManagementService.GetAllAsync();
    foreach (var country in countries)
```

```
{
    await responseStream.WriteAsync(country);
}
await Task.CompletedTask;
}
```

As you can see, the error is not handled, which means nothing is done to continue the app's regular operation. Figure 5-29 shows the gRPCui client receiving the error from the server.

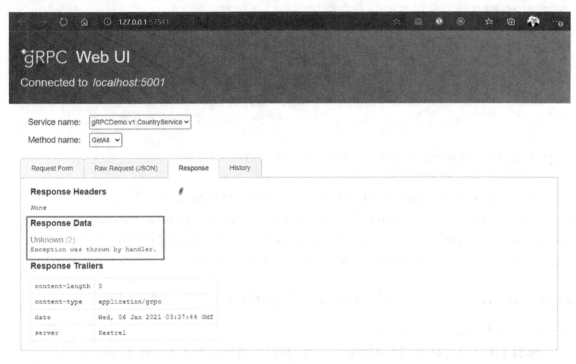

Figure 5-29. *Client receiving error from the server*

As you can see, the server sent an UNKNOWN (2) gRPC status, and the client is not aware of what happened server side. However, on the server side, the error has been logged correctly by default (we'll get back to logging a bit later), as shown in Figure 5-30.

```
C:\apress\source\CountryService\CountryService.Web\bin\Debug\net5.0\CountryService.Web.exe                      —     □    ×
        Request starting HTTP/2 POST https://localhost:5001/gRPCDemo.v1.CountryService/GetAll application/grpc -
info: Microsoft.AspNetCore.Routing.EndpointMiddleware[0]
        Executing endpoint 'gRPC - /gRPCDemo.v1.CountryService/GetAll'
     : Grpc.AspNetCore.Server.ServerCallHandler[6]
      Error when executing service method 'GetAll'.
     System.Exception: Something got really wrong here
        at CountryService.Web.Services.CountryGrpcService.GetAll(Empty request, IServerStreamWriter`1 responseSt
ream, ServerCallContext context) in C:\apress\source\CountryService\CountryService.Web\Services\CountryGrpcServic
e.cs:line 23
        at Grpc.Shared.Server.ServerStreamingServerMethodInvoker`3.Invoke(HttpContext httpContext, ServerCallCon
text serverCallContext, TRequest request, IServerStreamWriter`1 streamWriter)
        at Grpc.Shared.Server.ServerStreamingServerMethodInvoker`3.Invoke(HttpContext httpContext, ServerCallCon
text serverCallContext, TRequest request, IServerStreamWriter`1 streamWriter)
        at Grpc.AspNetCore.Server.Internal.CallHandlers.ServerStreamingServerCallHandler`3.HandleCallAsyncCore(H
ttpContext httpContext, HttpContextServerCallContext serverCallContext)
        at Grpc.AspNetCore.Server.Internal.CallHandlers.ServerCallHandlerBase`3.<HandleCallAsync>g__AwaitHandleC
all|8_0(HttpContextServerCallContext serverCallContext, Method`2 method, Task handleCall)
info: Microsoft.AspNetCore.Routing.EndpointMiddleware[1]
        Executed endpoint 'gRPC - /gRPCDemo.v1.CountryService/GetAll'
info: Microsoft.AspNetCore.Hosting.Diagnostics[2]
        Request finished HTTP/2 POST https://localhost:5001/gRPCDemo.v1.CountryService/GetAll application/grpc - -
200 0 application/grpc 25.8858ms
```

Figure 5-30. *The logged error on the server side*

There is nothing on the client side that helps to make the link with the error on the server side, but we can definitely do something to remedy this. First, we can enable an option that allows error details to be sent to the client. Listing 5-27 shows the EnableDetailedError option enabled in the Program.cs file.

Listing 5-27. Enabling EnableDetailedError in the Program.cs File

```
services.AddGrpc(options => {
    options.EnableDetailedErrors = true; // Enabling error details
    options.MaxReceiveMessageSize = 6291456;
    options.MaxSendMessageSize = 6291456;
    options.CompressionProviders = new List<ICompressionProvider>
    {
        new GzipCompressionProvider(CompressionLevel.Optimal), // gzip
        new BrotliCompressionProvider(CompressionLevel.Optimal) // br
    };
    options.ResponseCompressionAlgorithm = "br";
    options.ResponseCompressionLevel = CompressionLevel.Optimal;
});
```

If you retry now, you should see more information about the error sent from the server, as shown in Figure 5-31.

Figure 5-31. *Detailed errors enabled and displayed client side*

Caution   It's always helpful to get more information from the server when an error occurs, but keep in mind that you have to be careful with this so as not to expose clients' sensitive data!

OK, it was helpful to get some more details. Still, it's not enough. We need to handle the error correctly on the server side because the client has received an UNKNOWN gRPC status, which is not relevant—it's too generic, and the server should be more precise on the status to be sent. Let's go back to the gRPC endpoint and improve this by handling any error with a try/catch statement and the RpcException designed for gRPC error handling. RpcException should return the correct gRPC status. The response should contain in the Trailers a correlationId: Imagine, you can send that id (for debugging purpose) to the developers working on the server app. You really could do a great team job by identifying and fixing issues encountered more easily by linking the client error log and the server error log. While catching the real error and handling it with a proper RpcException, you are losing the original error. In that case, logging must be performed to log the error and its correlationId.

Listing 5-28 shows the GetAll endpoint rearranged with logging (ILogger is injected by constructor allows performing logging within the service), error handling with a try/catch statement, managed response with RpcException setup with INTERNAL gRPC status, an error message sent to the client, a correlationId sent over trailers, and another error message dedicated for server logging (not sent to the client).

Listing 5-28. Handling, Logging gRPC Error and Managing Response with an RpcException and INTERNAL gRPC Status

```
using Apress.Sample.gRPC;
using Google.Protobuf.WellKnownTypes;
using Grpc.Core;
using static Apress.Sample.gRPC.CountryService;

namespace CountryService.Web.Services;

public class CountryGrpcService : CountryServiceBase
{
    private readonly CountryManagementService _countryManagementService;
    private readonly ILogger<CountryGrpcService> _logger;

    public CountryGrpcService(CountryManagementService,
    ILogger<CountryGrpcService> logger)
    {
        _countryManagementService = countryManagementService;
        _logger = logger;
    }

    public override async Task GetAll(Empty request, IServerStreamWriter
    <CountryReply> responseStream, ServerCallContext context)
    {
        try
        {
            /////////////// Something is going wrong here ////////////
            throw new Exception("Something got really wrong here");
```

```
        // Streams all found countries to the client
        var countries = await _countryManagementService.GetAllAsync();
        foreach (var country in countries)
        {
            await responseStream.WriteAsync(country);
        }
        await Task.CompletedTask;
    }
    catch (Exception e)
    {
        var correlationId = Guid.NewGuid();
        _logger.LogError(e, "CorrelationId: {0}", correlationId);

        var trailers = new Metadata();
        trailers.Add("CorrelationId", correlationId.ToString());
        // Adding the correlation to Response Trailers

        throw new RpcException(new Status(StatusCode.Internal,
        $"Error message sent to the client with a CorrelationId:
        {correlationId}"), trailers,
                            "Error message that will appear in log
                            server");

    }
............
    }
}
```

Server logs should now include a correlationId that will help to correlate server and client errors. Server logs also contain the original error (exception + error message) and the RpcException (logged as info and not as fail) with the error message we set up. Figure 5-32 shows the server logs arranged with these improvements.

Figure 5-32. *Server-side error handled with a custom message and a* `correlationId`

In the meantime, Figure 5-33 shows what the client received.

Figure 5-33. *Client-side error handled with a custom message, a* `correlationId`, *and a proper gRPC status*

It's better, isn't it? But we can do even better. It's possible with interceptors!

Interceptors are another option that can be set in the gRPC configuration in the `Program.cs` file. What's an interceptor? It's a kind of middleware that defines, in *one place*, pieces of code to be executed at each gRPC request. It operates only during a gRPC request execution, unlike ASP.NET Core middlewares that are operating all over the ASP.NET Core request lifecycle. What does it mean concretely? ASP.NET Core middlewares run before any gRPC interceptor. Still, the main difference is that the message is not serialized to bytes yet in Interceptors, unlike middleware that can access the bytes message content.

An interceptor is a class that must inherit the Interceptor abstract class, and can be applied globally or specifically on a particular service. Several Interceptors can be defined and are executed in the order in which they are declared. A custom Interceptor allows you to define specific behavior for each kind of gRPC service. The `Interceptor` abstract class provides four virtual methods that can be overridden:

- `UnaryServerHandler`

- `ClientStreamingServerHandler`

- `ServerStreamingServerHandler`

- `DuplexStreamingServerHandler`

Note that interceptors support *dependency injection*, and we can use the `ILogger` interface there. Listing 5-29 shows a custom interceptor that handles errors and manages them with the proper gRPC status.

Listing 5-29. Custom Interceptor that Handles Errors and Manages gRPC Status Properly

```
using Grpc.Core;
using Grpc.Core.Interceptors;
using CountryService.Web.Interceptors.Helpers;

namespace CountryService.Web.Interceptors;

public class ExceptionInterceptor : Interceptor
{
    private readonly ILogger<ExceptionInterceptor> _logger;
    private readonly Guid _correlationId;
```

```csharp
public ExceptionInterceptor(ILogger<ExceptionInterceptor> logger)
{
    _logger = logger;
    _correlationId = Guid.NewGuid();
}

public override async Task<TResponse> UnaryServerHandler<TRequest,
TResponse>(
    TRequest request,
    ServerCallContext context,
    UnaryServerMethod<TRequest, TResponse> continuation)
{
    try
    {
        return await continuation(request, context);
    }
    catch (Exception e)
    {
        throw e.Handle(context, _logger, _correlationId);
    }
}

public override async Task<TResponse> ClientStreamingServerHandler
<TRequest, TResponse>(
    IAsyncStreamReader<TRequest> requestStream,
    ServerCallContext context,
    ClientStreamingServerMethod<TRequest, TResponse> continuation)
{
    try
    {
        return await continuation(requestStream, context);
    }
    catch (Exception e)
    {
        throw e.Handle(context, _logger, _correlationId);
    }
}
```

```
public override async Task ServerStreamingServerHandler<TRequest,
TResponse>(
    TRequest request,
    IServerStreamWriter<TResponse> responseStream,
    ServerCallContext context,
    ServerStreamingServerMethod<TRequest, TResponse> continuation)
{
    try
    {
        await continuation(request, responseStream, context);
    }
    catch (Exception e)
    {
        throw e.Handle(context, _logger, _correlationId);
    }
}

public override async Task DuplexStreamingServerHandler<TRequest,
TResponse>(
    IAsyncStreamReader<TRequest> requestStream,
    IServerStreamWriter<TResponse> responseStream,
    ServerCallContext context,
    DuplexStreamingServerMethod<TRequest, TResponse> continuation)
{
    try
    {
        await continuation(requestStream, responseStream, context);
    }
    catch (Exception e)
    {
        throw e.Handle(context, _logger, _correlationId);
    }
}
}
```

Error management is handled entirely within the Handle extension method that returns an RpcException with the proper gRPC status and error message sent to the client. This logic is defined into a custom class named ExceptionHelpers and manages specifically exceptions depending on their types, like SQL timeouts, generic SQL errors, generic timeout exceptions, and even RPC exceptions thrown by another piece of code or default exceptions, as shown in Listing 5-30.

Listing 5-30. Exception Management Provided by a Custom ExceptionHelpers Class

```
using Grpc.Core;
using Microsoft.Data.SqlClient;

namespace CountryService.Web.Interceptors.Helpers;

public static class ExceptionHelpers
{
    public static RpcException Handle<T>(this Exception exception,
    ServerCallContext context, ILogger<T> logger, Guid correlationId) =>
        exception switch
        {
            TimeoutException => HandleTimeoutException((TimeoutException)
            exception, context, logger, correlationId),
            SqlException => HandleSqlException((SqlException)exception,
            context, logger, correlationId),
RpcException => HandleRpcException((RpcException)exception, context,
logger, correlationId),
            _ => HandleDefault(exception, context, logger, correlationId)
        };

    private static RpcException HandleTimeoutException<T>(TimeoutException
    exception, ServerCallContext context, ILogger<T> logger, Guid
    correlationId)
    {
        logger.LogError(exception, $"CorrelationId: {correlationId} - A
        timeout occurred");
        Status status;
```

```
    status = new Status(StatusCode.Internal, "An external resource did
    not answer within the time limit");

    return new RpcException(status, CreateTrailers(correlationId));
}

private static RpcException HandleSqlException<T>(SqlException
exception, ServerCallContext context, ILogger<T> logger, Guid
correlationId)
{
    logger.LogError(exception, $"CorrelationId: {correlationId} - An
    SQL error occurred");
    Status status;

    if (exception.Number == -2)
    {
        status = new Status(StatusCode.DeadlineExceeded, "SQL
        timeout");
    }
    else
    {
        status = new Status(StatusCode.Internal, "SQL error");
    }
    return new RpcException(status, CreateTrailers(correlationId));
}

private static RpcException HandleDefault<T>(Exception exception,
ServerCallContext context, ILogger<T> logger, Guid correlationId)
{
    logger.LogError(exception, $"CorrelationId: {correlationId} - An
    error occurred");
    return new RpcException(new Status(StatusCode.Internal, exception.
    Message), CreateTrailers(correlationId));
}
```

```
private static RpcException HandleRpcException<T>(RpcExcepti
on exception, ServerCallContext context, ILogger<T> logger, Guid
correlationId)
{
            logger.LogError(exception, $"CorrelationId:
            {correlationId} - An error occurred");
    var trailers = exception.Trailers;
    trailers.Add(CreateTrailers(correlationId)[0]);
    return new RpcException(new Status(exception.StatusCode, exception.
    Message), trailers);
}

/// <summary>
///  Adding the correlation to Response Trailers
/// </summary>
/// <param name="correlationId"></param>
/// <returns></returns>
private static Metadata CreateTrailers(Guid correlationId)
{
    var trailers = new Metadata();
    trailers.Add("CorrelationId", correlationId.ToString());
    return trailers;
}
}
```

I love that way of handling errors. Suppose you have another kind of error to manage. In that case, it will be easy to add it in the extension class designed for this and keep the ExceptionInterceptor class readable and maintainable.

Note that this code sample uses a C# 9 improved pattern matching named "Simple pattern matching" that allows that allows you to omit the discard parameter within the switch statement when a type matches. To learn more about it, check out my blog post at https://anthonygiretti.com/2020/06/23/introducing-c-9-improved-pattern-matching/.

Listing 5-31 shows the ExceptionInterceptor registration within the Interceptors collection option in the Program.cs file.

Listing 5-31. Set Up the ExceptionInterceptor Registration

```
builder.Services.AddGrpc(options => {
    options.EnableDetailedErrors = true;
    options.MaxReceiveMessageSize = 6291456; // 6 MB
    options.MaxSendMessageSize = 6291456; // 6 MB
    options.CompressionProviders = new List<ICompressionProvider>
    {
        new GzipCompressionProvider(CompressionLevel.Optimal), // gzip
        new BrotliCompressionProvider(CompressionLevel.Optimal) // br
    };
    options.ResponseCompressionAlgorithm = "br"; // grpc-accept-encoding
    options.ResponseCompressionLevel = CompressionLevel.Optimal; //
    compression level used if not set on the provider
    options.Interceptors.Add<ExceptionInterceptor>(); // Register custom
    ExceptionInterceptor interceptor
});
```

You can now perform a cleanup within your gRPC services. No need to use try/catch statements anymore. But the choice is up to you. Both ways to handle errors in a gRPC service are valid. Listing 5-32 shows the GetAll gRPC endpoint cleared.

Listing 5-32. The GetAll gRPC endpoint cleared from any error handling and response management

```
public override async Task GetAll(Empty request, IServerStreamWriter
<CountryReply> responseStream, ServerCallContext context)
{
    /////////////// Something is going wrong here ///////////////
    throw new TimeoutException("Something got really wrong here");

    // Streams all found countries to the client
    var countries = await _countryManagementService.GetAllAsync();
    foreach (var country in countries)
    {
        await responseStream.WriteAsync(country);
    }
    await Task.CompletedTask;
}
```

Server logs are still efficient, as shown in Figure 5-34.

Figure 5-34. *Server logs after performing error handling in the ExceptionInterceptor Interceptor*

And client side as well, as shown in Figure 5-35.

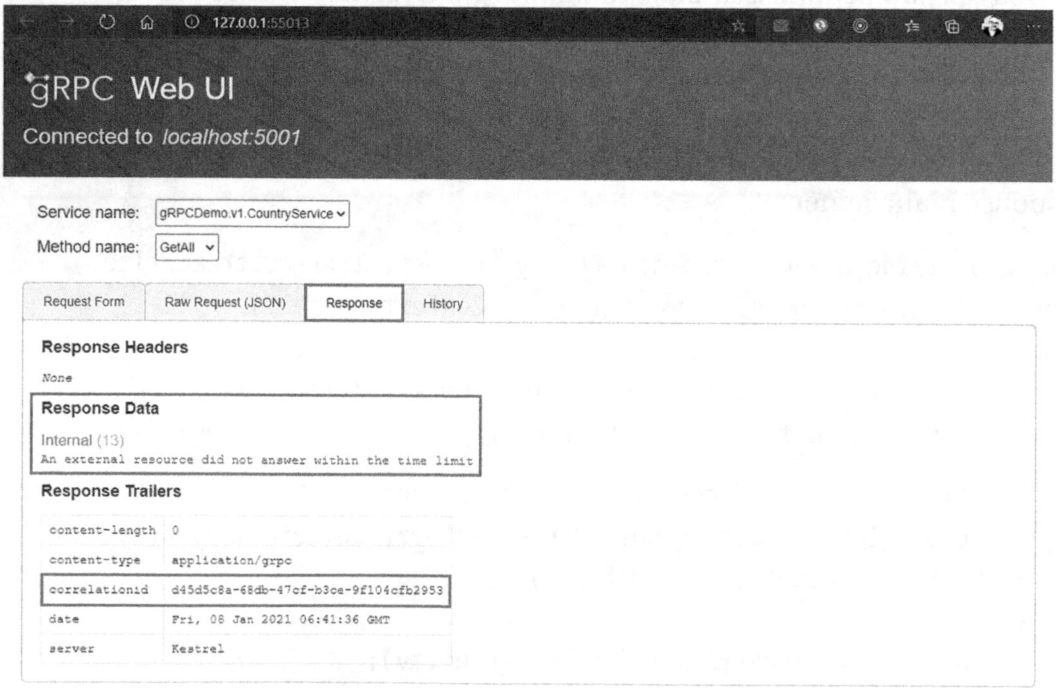

Figure 5-35. *Client response after performing error handling in the ExceptionInterceptor Interceptor*

Sometimes the client Protobufs definition doesn't match the server Protobufs description because there is a version mismatch between them. Calls on unknown services result from an UNKNOWN gRPC status in the response. It's possible to ignore that kind of error and provide your custom answer using ASP.NET Core middlewares.

Enabling the IgnoreUnknownServices option will allow the request to go through the next middleware declared after the gRPC endpoint middleware declaration. Without that option set to true, when an unknown service or method is invoked, the server returns the gRPC response immediately with the UNIMPLEMENTED gRPC status. It doesn't go through the next middleware. Listing 5-33 shows IgnoreUnknownServices enabled and a custom middleware that handles the gRPC response with a NOTFOUND gRPC status.

Listing 5-33. Enable IgnoreUnknownServices Option and Set Up a Custom ASP.NET Core Middleware to Handle the Response

```
using System.IO.Compression;
using ICompressionProvider = Grpc.Net.Compression.ICompressionProvider;
using GzipCompressionProvider = Grpc.Net.Compression.
GzipCompressionProvider;
using BrotliCompressionProvider = CountryService.Web.Compression.
BrotliCompressionProvider;
using CountryService.Web.Services;

using CountryService.Web.Interceptors;
using Grpc.Core;
using CountryService.Web;

var builder = WebApplication.CreateBuilder(args);

// Add services to the container.
builder.Services.AddGrpc(options => {
    options.EnableDetailedErrors = true;
    options.IgnoreUnknownServices = true;
    options.MaxReceiveMessageSize = 6291456; // 6 MB
    options.MaxSendMessageSize = 6291456; // 6 MB
    options.CompressionProviders = new List<ICompressionProvider>
            {
                new GzipCompressionProvider(CompressionLevel.
                Optimal), // gzip
```

```
                    new BrotliCompressionProvider(CompressionLevel.
                    Optimal) // br
            };
    options.ResponseCompressionAlgorithm = "br"; // grpc-accept-encoding
    options.ResponseCompressionLevel = CompressionLevel.Optimal; //
    compression level used if not set on the provider
    options.Interceptors.Add<ExceptionInterceptor>(); // Register custom
    ExceptionInterceptor interceptor
});

builder.Services.AddGrpcReflection();
builder.Services.AddSingleton<CountryManagementService>();

var app = builder.Build();

app.MapGrpcReflectionService();
app.MapGrpcService<CountryGrpcService>();
// Configure the HTTP request pipeline.
app.MapGet("/", () => "Communication with gRPC endpoints must be made
through a gRPC client. To learn how to create a client, visit: https://
go.microsoft.com/fwlink/?linkid=2086909");

app.Use(async (context, next) =>
{
    context.Response.ContentType = "application/grpc";
    context.Response.Headers.Add("grpc-status", ((int)StatusCode.NotFound).
    ToString());
    await next();
});

app.Run();
```

Be very careful here, because this middleware will run, and you'll have to perform your own rules to not interfere with the gRPC response. For example, while streaming data, you'll receive streaming data server side while receiving a NOTFOUND gRPC status.

Figure 5-36 shows the response client side when IgnoreUnknownServices is not enabled.

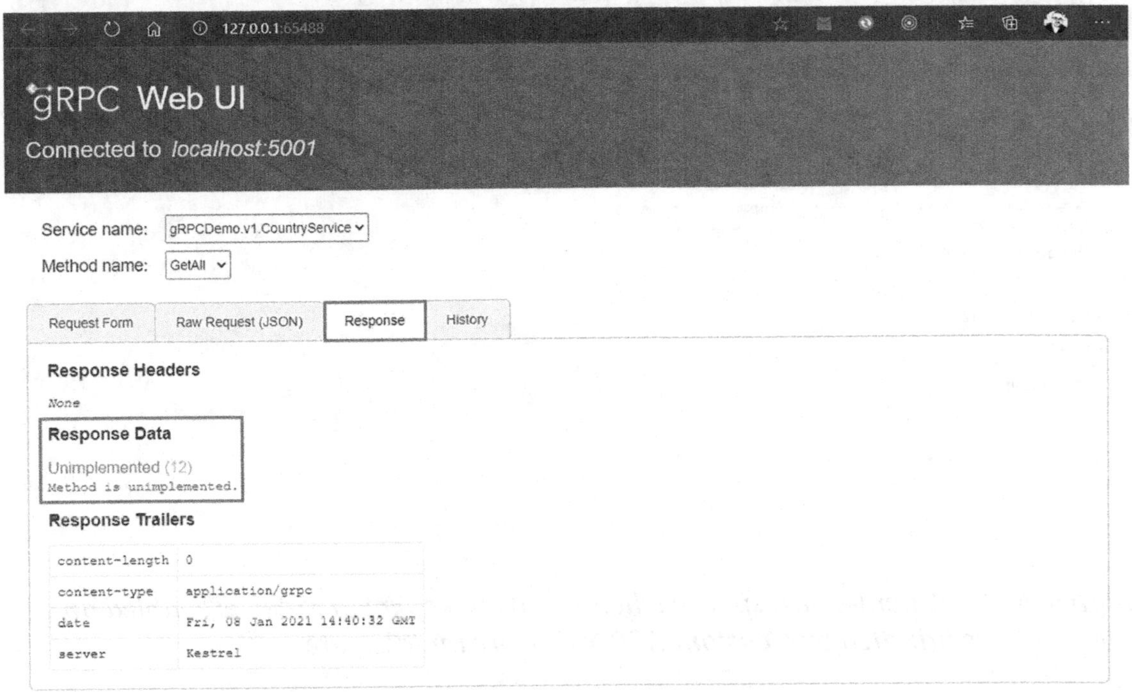

Figure 5-36. *Client-side response when IgnoreUnknownServices is not enabled*

Figure 5-37 shows the response client side when IgnoreUnknownServices is enabled and the response is handled into an ASP.NET Core middleware.

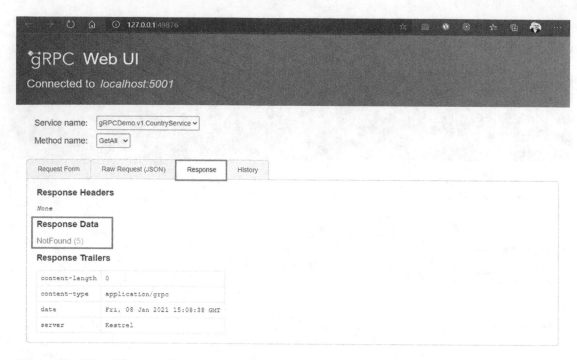

Figure 5-37. *Client-side response when* IgnoreUnknownServices *is enabled and the response handled by a custom ASP.NET Core middleware*

As you can see, you have options to handle unknown services. I have no preference between handling them or not, except that I have less code to type if I don't configure unknown services!

Perform Message Validation

Validating user input is very important because users can be clumsy or even malicious and bypass specific application business rules. This section shows you how to verify the data entered by a user in ASP.NET Core gRPC. First, be aware that there is no native validation in the ASP.NET Core gRPC framework. For example, if you are familiar with data annotations such as required attributes applied to C# object properties, be aware that this is inoperative here. But then how do you accomplish it? Well, I have the solution! I designed a Nuget package that you can download with the following command:

```
Install-Package Calzolari.Grpc.AspNetCore.Validation
```

At the time of this writing, the package has been downloaded 44,000 times, and I have received very few bug reports, so let's say it's pretty reliable, and I invite you to use it. It works in a relatively simple way. This package is based on the FluentValidation library, which makes it possible to identify an object even before it has been passed into the function called by the client by recognizing its signature. You can find the documentation on its syntax here: https://fluentvalidation.net/; you will need it to create your validation rules in ASP.NET Core gRPC. This package was initially developed for ASP.NET Core MVC, WebAPI type applications, and I reuse the same mechanics to apply it to gRPC by taking advantage of interceptors, allowing an object sent by the client to be intercepted and validated before any RPC function is executed. If the validation succeeds, the code is executed as expected. Otherwise, an RpcException is thrown with an InvalidArgument gRPC status.

Let's create a validator that validates the CountryCreationRequest message, where the Name property is mandatory, as is the Description property, which must be longer than five characters. Listing 5-34 shows the CountryCreateRequestValidator that performs the validation.

Listing 5-34. The CountryCreateRequestValidator Class

```
using Apress.Sample.gRPC;
using FluentValidation;

namespace CountryService.Web.Validator;

public class CountryCreateRequestValidator : AbstractValidator<Country
CreationRequest>
{
    public CountryCreateRequestValidator()
    {
        RuleFor(request => request.Name).NotEmpty().WithMessage("Name is
        mandatory.");
        RuleFor(request => request.Description).MinimumLength(5).
        WithMessage("Description is mandatory and be longer than 5
        characters");
    }
}
```

As you can see, it's pretty simple. We next need to register the validator in the dependency injection system in the `Program.cs` file. We also need to enable the validation feature with the `EnableMessageValidation()` extension method within the gRPC options and configure the validation feature within the dependency injection system with the `EnableMessageValidation()` extension method. Listing 5-35 shows the validation enabled in the ASP.NET Core gRPC app and the `CountryCreateRequestValidator` class registered in the `Program.cs` file.

Listing 5-35. Enabling Input Validation on ASP.NET Core gRPC and the CountryCreateRequestValidator Class

```
using System.IO.Compression;
using ICompressionProvider = Grpc.Net.Compression.ICompressionProvider;
using BrotliCompressionProvider = CountryService.Web.Compression.
BrotliCompressionProvider;
using CountryService.Web.Services;
using CountryService.Web.Interceptors;
using CountryService.Web;
using Calzolari.Grpc.AspNetCore.Validation;
using CountryService.Web.Validator;

var builder = WebApplication.CreateBuilder(args);

// Add services to the container.
builder.Services.AddGrpc(options => {
    options.EnableDetailedErrors = true;
    options.MaxReceiveMessageSize = 6291456; // 6 MB
    options.MaxSendMessageSize = 6291456; // 6 MB
    options.CompressionProviders = new List<ICompressionProvider>
                {
                    new BrotliCompressionProvider(CompressionLevel.
                    Optimal) // br
                };
```

```
    options.ResponseCompressionAlgorithm = "gzip"; // grpc-accept-encoding
    options.ResponseCompressionLevel = CompressionLevel.Optimal;
    // compression level used if not set on the provider
    options.Interceptors.Add<ExceptionInterceptor>();
    // Register custom ExceptionInterceptor interceptor
    options.EnableMessageValidation();
});
builder.Services.AddGrpcValidation();
builder.Services.AddValidator<CountryCreateRequestValidator>();
builder.Services.AddGrpcReflection();
builder.Services.AddSingleton<CountryManagementService>();

var app = builder.Build();

app.MapGrpcReflectionService();
app.MapGrpcService<CountryGrpcService>();
// Configure the HTTP request pipeline.
app.MapGet("/", () => "Communication with gRPC endpoints must be made
through a gRPC client. To learn how to create a client, visit: https://
go.microsoft.com/fwlink/?linkid=2086909");

app.Run();
```

Let's test what this looks like. Using gRPCui, try to create a country without complying with the rule that says the country description must be more than five characters; for this example, type **leaf**, as shown in Figure 5-38.

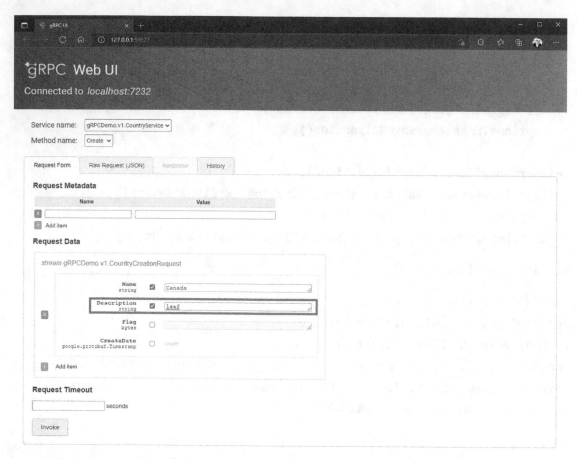

Figure 5-38. *Attempting to create a country without adhering to the five-character-minimum rule in the Description field*

You should expect to receive an error from the server stating that the description length is too short, and this is indeed what happens, as shown in Figure 5-39.

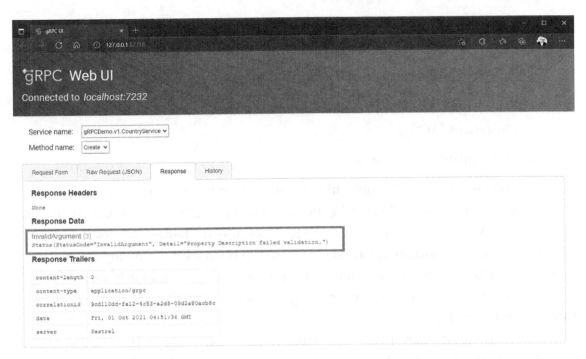

Figure 5-39. *Validation error returned by the server because the Description field entry is too short*

As you can see, an INVALIDARGUMENT is returned by the server with a validation message previously defined in the CountryCreateRequestValidator class.

This is pretty cool and perfectly fulfills the job of a validator that gRPC does not implement natively. This validation can be applied to all types of gRPC services. If you want to understand how this library works, the source code is freely available and can be consulted here: https://github.com/AnthonyGiretti/grpc-aspnetcore-validator. You can even contribute to the project if you wish! We will revisit this library in Chapter 7; a client-side library is also available.

Support of ASP.NET Core gRPC on Microsoft Azure

While this book doesn't cover cloud hosting on Microsoft Azure (nor AWS or GCP), I still want to touch on it here so that you are aware of some Azure services that you can use with ASP.NET Core gRPC.

There are four main ways to host ASP.NET Core applications on Microsoft Azure:

- Hosting on a Windows Virtual machine or Linux Virtual machine

- Hosting on a Windows App Service or Linux App Service

- Hosting on a Windows Docker container with Azure Container Instances (ACI)

- Hosting on a Kubernetes cluster

Regarding hosting a gRPC application on an *AppService*, be aware that Azure AppServices are not compatible with gRPC because of HTTP/2 and the response trailers at the time of writing. Internet Information Services (IIS), the famous Microsoft web server, is also not compatible for the same reasons. If you are interested in following the progress on this subject, Microsoft regularly updates its documentation here: `https://docs.microsoft.com/en-us/aspnet/core/grpc/aspnetcore?view=aspnetcore-5.0&tabs=visual-studio`.

Regarding ACI, it's a bit special: ACI supports gRPC and HTTP/2, but ACI doesn't provide static IP addresses, which change at each container deployment or restart. To figure that capability, ACI needs a component named Azure Application Gateway, which is a web traffic load balancer. At the time of writing, the latter doesn't support HTTP/2 traffic to the back end; only traffic coming from clients to the AppGateway is supported. If you want to learn more about ACI and AppGateway, Microsoft provides excellent documentation here: `https://docs.microsoft.com/en-us/azure/container-instances/` and `https://docs.microsoft.com/en-us/azure/application-gateway/`.

Regarding *Azure Virtual Machines*, there is no limitation on gRPC application hosting. As long as you are self-hosting your ASP.NET Core gRPC application in Kestrel, the cross-platform web server for ASP.NET Core, unlike IIS, is not cross-platform. If you want to learn more about Azure Virtual Machines, you can read the complete documentation here: `https://docs.microsoft.com/en-us/azure/virtual-machines/`.

And finally, *Azure Kubernetes Service (AKS)*, a service that allows managing Kubernetes clusters, supports gRPC and HTTP/2. If you want to learn more about AKS, Microsoft also provides excellent documentation at `https://docs.microsoft.com/en-us/azure/aks/`. If you are not familiar with Kubernetes, which is an open source system designed for deployment automation, scaling, and managing a containerized application, you can discover its features here: `https://kubernetes.io/`.

Summary

Since Chapter 4, you have learned a lot, but almost everything you need to know about protobufs to build any gRPC service effectively.

Chapter 5, meanwhile, allowed you to show how to build your services. You also learned how to configure them according to your needs, I think, in particular, about performance optimizations of the serialization and the volume of data to transfer.

You saw how it's essential to handle errors properly, including validating inputs, because, as you know, gRPC always returns an HTTP 200 OK status even in the event of an error. Hence, you have to be vigilant about error handling by allowing the client to manage errors as much as possible on the client side. Finally, you saw that testing the services with a tool such as gRPCui or gRPCurl (without coding any client in C#) is also very useful and efficient for your development.

In the next chapter, I will talk about versioning gRPC services, and then you will be ready to build web applications while implementing gRPC clients to access data.

CHAPTER 6

API Versioning

Developing APIs often leads you to have different versions of APIs, especially when delivering to several consumers. For example, some may need a specific version, some use a particular version, and some might want to stay on the bleeding edge. As a result, API developers need to maintain different versions of the same API. In this chapter, I will explain to you how to:

- Version gRPC services
- Expose the versions of your Protobuf files with minimal APIs

Version gRPC Services

Recall from Chapter 4 the package directive in the Protobuf files. This directive enables us to manage our version of APIs. Imagine that we have two versions of our CountryService Protobuf example. One controls the country flag and the deletion capability, and the second does not because we will handle them in another dedicated service. Listings 6-1 and 6-2 show how you should declare CountryService version 1 and CountryService version 2, respectively.

Listing 6-1. CountryService v1 Protobuf

```
syntax = "proto3";

package gRPCDemo.v1;

option csharp_namespace = "Apress.Sample.gRPC.v1";

import "google/protobuf/empty.proto";
import "google/protobuf/timestamp.proto";
```

223

© Anthony Giretti 2022
A. Giretti, *Beginning gRPC with ASP.NET Core 6*, https://doi.org/10.1007/978-1-4842-8008-9_6

```
service CountryService {
    rpc GetAll(google.protobuf.Empty) returns (stream CountryReply) {}
    rpc Get(CountryIdRequest) returns (CountryReply) {}
    rpc Delete(stream CountryIdRequest) returns (google.protobuf.Empty) {}
    rpc Update(CountryUpdateRequest) returns (google.protobuf.Empty) {}
    rpc Create(stream CountryCreationRequest) returns (stream
    CountryCreationReply) {}
}

message CountryReply {
    int32 Id = 1;
    string Name = 2;
    string Description = 3;
    bytes Flag = 4;
    google.protobuf.Timestamp CreateDate = 5;
    google.protobuf.Timestamp UpdateDate = 6;
}

message CountryIdRequest {
    int32 Id = 1;
}

message CountryUpdateRequest {
    int32 Id = 1;
    string Description = 3;
    google.protobuf.Timestamp UpdateDate = 6;
}

message CountryCreationRequest {
    string Name = 2;
    string Description = 3;
    bytes Flag = 4;
    google.protobuf.Timestamp CreateDate = 5;
}
```

```
message CountryCreationReply {
      int32 Id = 1;
      string Name = 2;
}
```

Listing 6-2. CountryService v2 Protobuf

```
syntax = "proto3";

package gRPCDemo.v2;

option csharp_namespace = "Apress.Sample.gRPC.v2";

import "google/protobuf/empty.proto";
import "google/protobuf/timestamp.proto";

service CountryService {
    rpc GetAll(google.protobuf.Empty) returns (stream CountryReply) {}
    rpc Get(CountryIdRequest) returns (CountryReply) {}
    rpc Update(CountryUpdateRequest) returns (google.protobuf.Empty) {}
    rpc Create(stream CountryCreationRequest) returns (stream
    CountryCreationReply) {}
}

message CountryReply {
      int32 Id = 1;
      string Name = 2;
      string Description = 3;
      google.protobuf.Timestamp CreateDate = 5;
      google.protobuf.Timestamp UpdateDate = 6;
}

message CountryIdRequest {
      int32 Id = 1;
}
```

```
message CountryUpdateRequest {
    int32 Id = 1;
    string Description = 3;
    google.protobuf.Timestamp UpdateDate = 6;
}

message CountryCreationRequest {
    string Name = 2;
    string Description = 3;
    google.protobuf.Timestamp CreateDate = 5;
}

message CountryCreationReply {
    int32 Id = 1;
    string Name = 2;
}
```

As you can see, since you are defining your CountryService version 1 and version 2, there is no conflict between the same names such as CountryService or CountryCreationService because each of the namespaces contains the entities Apress. Sample.gRPC.v1 and Apress.Sample.gRPC.v2. Combining the package and csharp_ namespace keywords will allow you to write different versions of a service, with different URLs for gRPC endpoints. The package directive is meant to define different gRPC URLs without any conflict to your C# code since the use of csharp_namespace directive will allow you to isolate your different versions into different C# namespaces.

I suggest storing each version in its folder named with the corresponding version, as shown in Figure 6-1, for better organization.

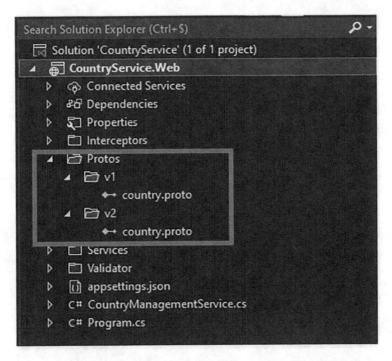

Figure 6-1. *Organize* `country.proto` *files in separate folders that match their version*

After compiling, Protoc will generate a C# stub in its folder, as shown in Figure 6-2.

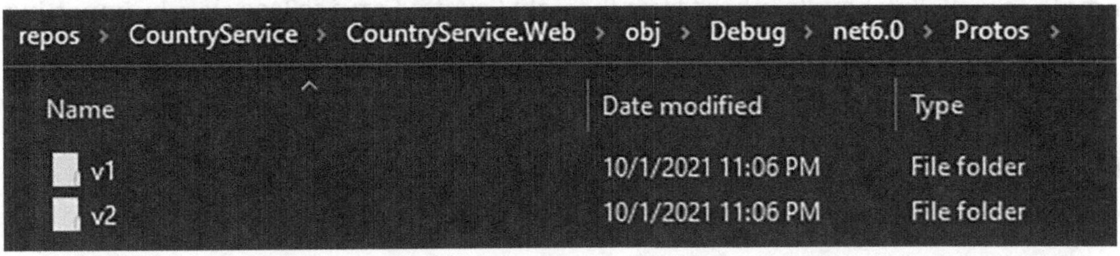

repos > CountryService > CountryService.Web > obj > Debug > net6.0 > Protos >		
Name ^	Date modified	Type
v1	10/1/2021 11:06 PM	File folder
v2	10/1/2021 11:06 PM	File folder

Figure 6-2. *C# stubs generated in their respective folder that matches their version*

Now, for writing the CountryGrpcService class, you can follow the same pattern as above by creating CountryGrpcService.cs files in separate folders that match their version, as shown in Figure 6-3.

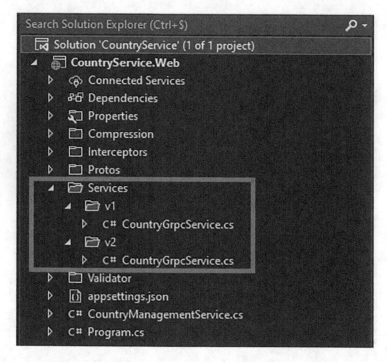

Figure 6-3. *Organize* `CountryGrpcService.cs` *files in separate folders that match their version*

Writing the implementation of each version of the `CountryGrpcService` class is quite simple as well. You have to inherit from the right `CountryServiceBase` class by importing the right namespace for the version you want to write, as shown in Listing 6-3 for v1 and Listing 6-4 for v2 (I voluntarily lightened the code to focus on the namespaces).

Listing 6-3. Import Version 1 of the `CountryServiceBase` Class and Write Version 1 of the `CountryGrpcService` Class

```
using Apress.Sample.gRPC.v1;

namespace CountryService.Web.Services.v1;

public class CountryGrpcService : Apress.Sample.gRPC.v1.CountryService.
CountryServiceBase
{
    // Implementation
}
```

Listing 6-4. Import Version 2 of the CountryServiceBase Class and Write Version 2 of the CountryGrpcService Class

```
using Apress.Sample.gRPC.v2;

namespace CountryService.Web.Services.v2;

public class CountryGrpcService : Apress.Sample.gRPC.v2.CountryService.
CountryServiceBase
{
    // Implementation
}
```

The last thing you have to do is register each version of the `CountryGrpcService` class as a gRPC service in the `Program.cs` file, as shown in Listing 6-5 (I voluntarily lightened the code to focus on namespaces (and the usage of C# *aliases*).

Listing 6-5. Register Versions 1 and 2 of CountryGrpcService gRPC Service

```
using System.IO.Compression;
using ICompressionProvider = Grpc.Net.Compression.ICompressionProvider;
using BrotliCompressionProvider = CountryService.Web.Compression.
BrotliCompressionProvider;
using CountryService.Web.Interceptors;
using CountryService.Web;
using Calzolari.Grpc.AspNetCore.Validation;
using CountryService.Web.Validator;
using v1 = CountryService.Web.Services.v1;
using v2 = CountryService.Web.Services.v2;

var builder = WebApplication.CreateBuilder(args);

// Add services to the container.
builder.Services.AddGrpc(options => {
    options.EnableDetailedErrors = true;
    options.MaxReceiveMessageSize = 6291456; // 6 MB
    options.MaxSendMessageSize = 6291456; // 6 MB
```

```
        options.CompressionProviders = new List<ICompressionProvider>
                {
                        new BrotliCompressionProvider(CompressionLevel.
                        Optimal) // br
                };
        options.ResponseCompressionAlgorithm = "br"; // grpc-accept-encoding
        options.ResponseCompressionLevel = CompressionLevel.Optimal;
        // compression level used if not set on the provider
        options.Interceptors.Add<ExceptionInterceptor>();
        // Register custom ExceptionInterceptor interceptor
        options.EnableMessageValidation();
});
builder.Services.AddGrpcValidation();
builder.Services.AddValidator<CountryCreateRequestValidator>();
builder.Services.AddGrpcReflection();
builder.Services.AddSingleton<CountryManagementService>();

var app = builder.Build();

app.MapGrpcReflectionService();
app.MapGrpcService<v1.CountryGrpcService>();
app.MapGrpcService<v2.CountryGrpcService>();

app.MapGet("/", () => "Communication with gRPC endpoints must be made
through a gRPC client. To learn how to create a client, visit: https://
go.microsoft.com/fwlink/?linkid=2086909");

app.Run();
```

If you now test your application with gRPCui, you'll see that you can access both services, as shown in Figure 6-4.

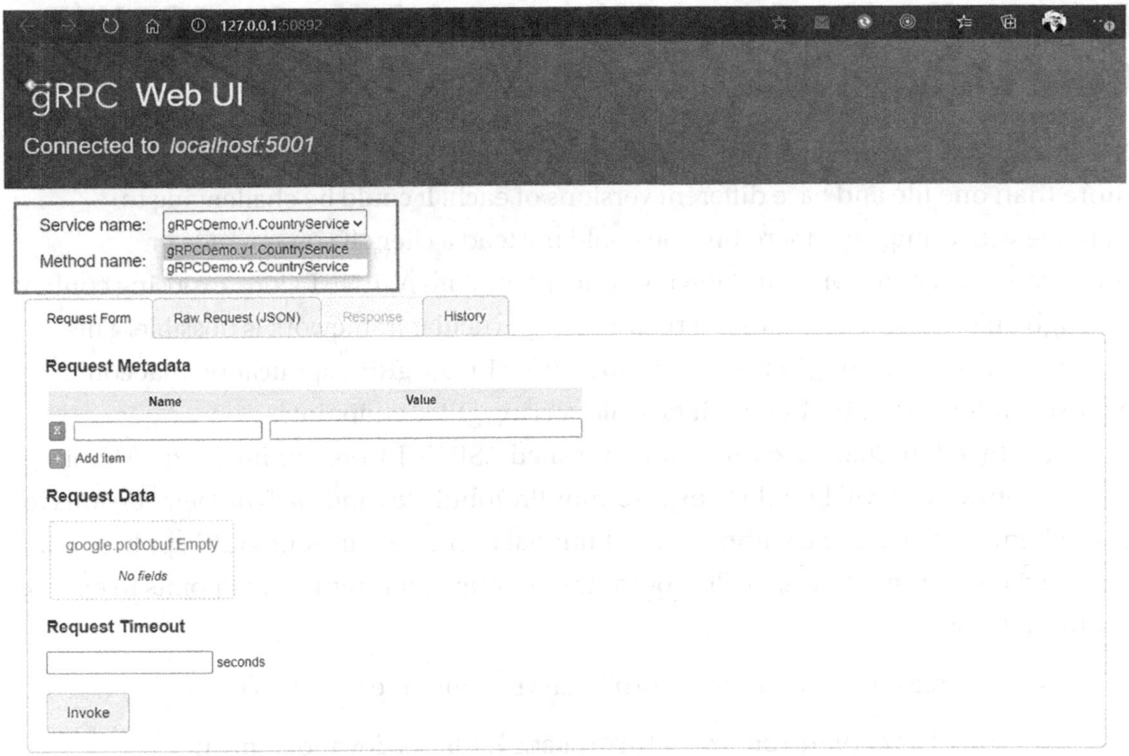

Figure 6-4.

Invoke both versions of the GetAll gRPC endpoint, and you should see that they are targeting their respective version by checking the URL called by gRPCui, as shown in Figure 6-5.

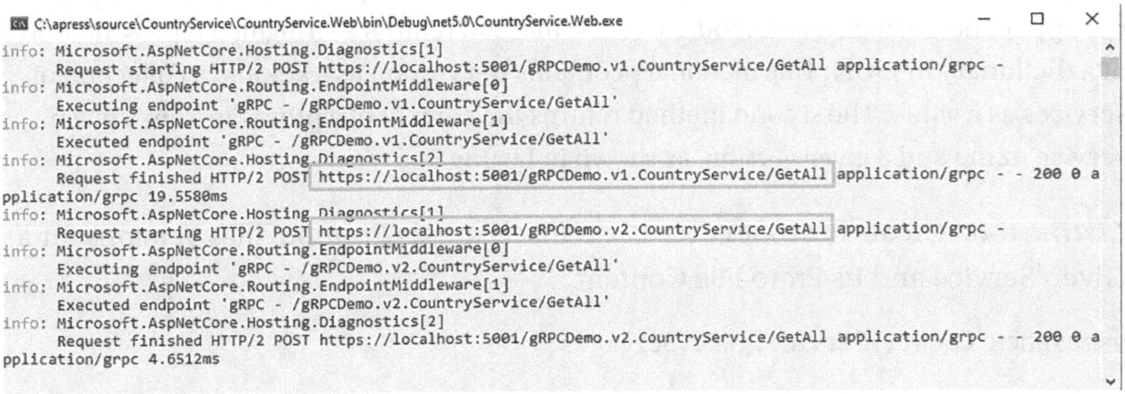

Figure 6-5. *Invoke Versions 1 and 2 of the* GetAll *gRPC endpoint*

Expose the Versions of Your Protobuf with ASP.NET Core Minimal APIs

It is not always easy to share Protobuf files with clients, especially if you have more than one file and have different versions of each. It could be challenging to manage versioning, and therefore you could mislead a client if you upgrade or downgrade a version without notifying your client. With ASP.NET Core, exposing content through an endpoint that does not require any particular framework is possible. This is particularly interesting in the case of an ASP.NET Core gRPC application that could expose content with REST endpoints while serving gRPC endpoints.

Introduced in Chapter 2, this feature is called ASP.NET Core minimal APIs. Thanks to this feature, you will be able to expose your Protobuf files and each of their versions to your clients with ease and without any additional framework in your gRPC application.

Based on minimal APIs, I will show how to implement three GET endpoints to expose Protobuf files:

- /protos: Exposes in JSON format all versions for each service.

- /protos/v{version:int}/{protoName}: Allows downloading the Protobuf file for a given version of a given service. Minimal APIs URL pattern supports templated routes (accept route parameters).

- /protos/v{version:int}/{protoName}/view: Allows services to serve the Protobuf file in text format for a given version of a given service.

Let's implement a new ProtoService class. This service parses a "Protos" folder in the application using two methods. The first method returns a stringified representation of a dictionary in JSON. This dictionary contains the version as a key and a collection of services as a value. The second method returns the content of a proto file from a given service name and a given version, as shown in Listing 6-6.

Listing 6-6. Create ProtoService Class that Exposes Protobuf files Versions for a Given Service and Its Proto File Content

```
namespace CountryService.gRPC.Services;

public class ProtoService
{
    private readonly string _baseDirectory;
```

```csharp
public ProtoService(IWebHostEnvironment webHost)
{
    _baseDirectory = webHost.ContentRootPath;
}

public Dictionary<string, IEnumerable<string>> GetAll() =>
    Directory.GetDirectories($"{_baseDirectory}/protos")
            .Select(x => new { version = x, protos = Directory.
            GetFiles(x).Select(Path.GetFileName) })
            .ToDictionary(o => Path.GetRelativePath("protos",
            o.version), o => o.protos);

public string Get(int version, string protoName)
{
    var filePath = $"{_baseDirectory}/protos/v{version}/{protoName}";
    var exist = File.Exists(filePath);

    return exist ? filePath : null;
}

public async Task<string> ViewAsync(int version, string protoName)
{
    var filePath = $"{_baseDirectory}/protos/v{version}/{protoName}";
    var exist = File.Exists(filePath);

    return exist ? await File.ReadAllTextAsync(filePath) :
    string.Empty;
}
}
```

Register your ProtoService class and write the endpoints as shown in Listing 6-7.

Listing 6-7. Register ProtoService and Write Minimal Endpoints to Expose Protobuf files Version and Files Content

```csharp
using System.IO.Compression;
using ICompressionProvider = Grpc.Net.Compression.ICompressionProvider;
using BrotliCompressionProvider = CountryService.Web.Compression.
BrotliCompressionProvider;
```

```
using CountryService.Web.Interceptors;
using CountryService.Web;
using Calzolari.Grpc.AspNetCore.Validation;
using CountryService.Web.Validator;
using v1 = CountryService.Web.Services.v1;
using v2 = CountryService.Web.Services.v2;
using CountryService.gRPC.Services;

var builder = WebApplication.CreateBuilder(args);

// Add services to the container.
builder.Services.AddGrpc(options => {
    options.EnableDetailedErrors = true;
    options.MaxReceiveMessageSize = 6291456; // 6 MB
    options.MaxSendMessageSize = 6291456; // 6 MB
    options.CompressionProviders = new List<ICompressionProvider>
                {
                    new BrotliCompressionProvider(CompressionLevel.
                    Optimal) // br
                };
    options.ResponseCompressionAlgorithm = "br"; // grpc-accept-encoding
    options.ResponseCompressionLevel = CompressionLevel.Optimal; //
    compression level used if not set on the provider
    options.Interceptors.Add<ExceptionInterceptor>(); // Register custom
    ExceptionInterceptor interceptor
    options.EnableMessageValidation();
});
builder.Services.AddGrpcValidation();
builder.Services.AddSingleton<ProtoService>();
builder.Services.AddValidator<CountryCreateRequestValidator>();
builder.Services.AddGrpcReflection();
builder.Services.AddSingleton<CountryManagementService>();

var app = builder.Build();

app.MapGrpcReflectionService();
app.MapGrpcService<v1.CountryGrpcService>();
```

```
app.MapGrpcService<v2.CountryGrpcService>();

app.MapGet("/protos", (ProtoService protoService) =>
{
    return Results.Ok(protoService.GetAll());
});
app.MapGet("/protos/v{version:int}/{protoName}", (ProtoService
protoService, int version, string protoName) =>
{
    var filePath = protoService.Get(version, protoName);

    if (filePath != null)
        return Results.File(filePath);

    return Results.NotFound();
});
app.MapGet("/protos/v{version:int}/{protoName}/view", async (ProtoService
protoService, int version, string protoName) =>
{
    var text = await protoService.ViewAsync(version, protoName);

    if (!string.IsNullOrEmpty(text))
        return Results.Text(text);

    return Results.NotFound();
});

app.Run();
```

If you open a browser and call these endpoints, you should get all versions for the country.proto file as shown in Figure 6-6 and the content of country.proto as shown in Figure 6-7.

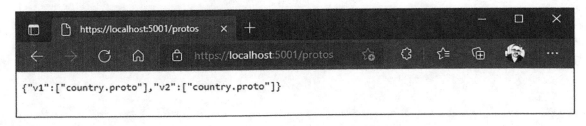

Figure 6-6. *Get all versions of country.proto via /protos endpoint*

```
□    □ https://localhost:5001/protos/v1  ×    +                        —    □    ×

←    →    C    ⌂    🔒 https://localhost:5001/protos/...    ⭐    ⚙    ⟆    ⊞    🐶    ...

syntax = "proto3";

package gRPCDemo.v1;

option csharp_namespace = "Apress.Sample.gRPC.v1";

import "google/protobuf/empty.proto";
import "google/protobuf/timestamp.proto";

service CountryService {
        rpc GetAll(google.protobuf.Empty) returns (stream CountryReply) {}
        rpc Get(CountryIdRequest) returns (CountryReply) {}
        rpc Delete(stream CountryIdRequest) returns (google.protobuf.Empty) {}
        rpc Update(CountryUpdateRequest) returns (google.protobuf.Empty) {}
        rpc Create(stream CountryCreationRequest) returns (stream CountryCreationReply) {}
}

message CountryReply {
        int32 Id = 1;
        string Name = 2;
        string Description = 3;
        bytes Flag = 4;
        google.protobuf.Timestamp CreateDate = 5;
        google.protobuf.Timestamp UpdateDate = 6;
}

message CountryIdRequest {
        int32 Id = 1;
}

message CountryUpdateRequest {
        int32 Id = 1;
        string Description = 3;
        google.protobuf.Timestamp UpdateDate = 6;
}

message CountryCreationRequest {
        string Name = 2;
        string Description = 3;
        bytes Flag = 4;
        google.protobuf.Timestamp CreateDate = 5;
}

message CountryCreationReply {
        int32 Id = 1;
        string Name = 2;
}
```

Figure 6-7. Get country.proto file content via /protos/v{version:int}/
{protoName}/view endpoint

Summary

This chapter has taught you how to expose your customers to your Protobuf files easily. It is a simple, fast, and efficient solution, but it is not the only option. For example, you can proceed differently to automate sending a Protobuf file to your clients in FTP or create file storage and send the link to your clients. I found that the possibility of creating REST endpoints without a particular framework and exposing Protobuf files was the best example.

You have learned how to create a server-side gRPC application and distribute your proto files. Next you will learn how to create .NET 6 applications that use gRPC services. See you in Chapter 7!

CHAPTER 7

Create a gRPC Client

You learned everything you need to know in the previous chapters to build an ASP.NET Core gRPC server application. Now we will tackle the client part: how to create a client, consume data coming from a gRPC server, handle errors, and much more (in fact, the whole base of gRPC on the client side) with a console application in .NET 6 before going more into the concrete task of building a complete web application in the following chapters. In this chapter, you'll learn how to

- Create a console application

- Compile Protobuf files and generate gRPC clients

- Consume gRPC services with .NET 6

- Optimize performance

- Get message validation errors from the server

© Anthony Giretti 2022
A. Giretti, *Beginning gRPC with ASP.NET Core 6*, https://doi.org/10.1007/978-1-4842-8008-9_7

Create a Console Application

We'll start by creating a gRPC client with a console application. I always start by testing my functionality quickly with a console application. It's quick and easy, so let's go! Figure 7-1 shows the Visual Studio template to create a console application.

Figure 7-1. *Select the Console Application template*

Click Next, and then configure the project name as **CountryService.Client** and choose the project location, as shown in Figure 7-2.

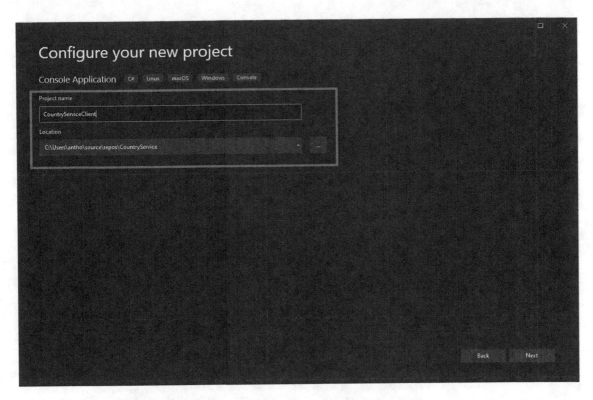

Figure 7-2. *Configure project name and project location*

Click Next, and Visual Studio 2022 will display a window named "Additional information" that allows you to choose the runtime you want to use, .NET 6.0 here, as shown in Figure 7-3.

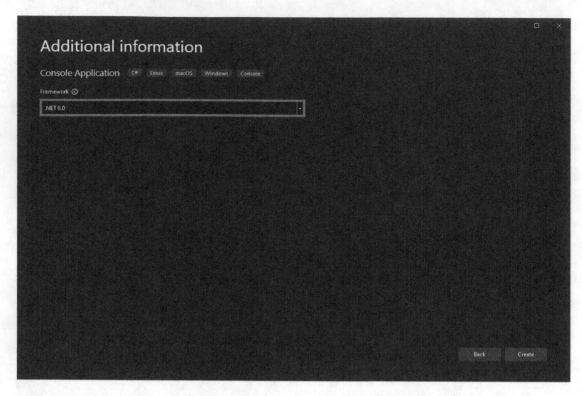

Figure 7-3. *Select the .NET 6.0 runtime*

Click Create, and Visual Studio will create your .NET 6 console application.

To get ready to create a .NET 6 gRPC client, you need to download these NuGet packages:

- `Google.Protobuf`: Provides all Google Protobuf classes like Well-Known Types

- `Grpc.Net.ClientFactory`: Provides the .NET 6 HTTP client factory to create gRPC clients (encapsulates the gRPC `Channel` class, for example)

- `Grpc.Tools`: Allows Protobufs compilation

To download these packages, use the commands shown in Listing 7-1.

Listing 7-1. Download `Google.Protobuf`, `Grpc.Net.ClientFactory`, and `Grpc.Tools` NuGet packages

```
Install-Package Google.Protobuf
Install-Package Grpc.Net.ClientFactory
Install-Package Grpc.Tools
```

If you have followed all previous steps correctly, your `CountryServiceClient.csproj` file should look like the content shown in Figure 7-4, and that means you are ready to create a gRPC client in .NET 6.

```
CountryServiceClient.csproj ⊕ X
 1  <Project Sdk="Microsoft.NET.Sdk">
 2
 3    <PropertyGroup>
 4      <OutputType>Exe</OutputType>
 5      <TargetFramework>net6.0</TargetFramework>
 6      <ImplicitUsings>enable</ImplicitUsings>
 7      <Nullable>enable</Nullable>
 8    </PropertyGroup>
 9
10    <ItemGroup>
11      <PackageReference Include="Google.Protobuf" Version="3.18.0" />
12      <PackageReference Include="Grpc.Net.ClientFactory" Version="2.39.0" />
13      <PackageReference Include="Grpc.Tools" Version="2.41.0">
14        <PrivateAssets>all</PrivateAssets>
15        <IncludeAssets>runtime; build; native; contentfiles; analyzers; buildtransitive</IncludeAssets>
16      </PackageReference>
17    </ItemGroup>
18
19  </Project>
20
```

Figure 7-4. *CountryServiceClient.csproj file configured to run with .NET 6 gRPC clients*

Compile Protobuf Files and Generate gRPC Clients

Like a server-side project, you have to add, manually or not, your Protobuf files to your .NET 6 client application. I suggest, for reasons of clarity, creating a Protos directory and possible subdirectories for versioning, as shown in Figure 7-5, with version 1 and version 2 of the country.proto file.

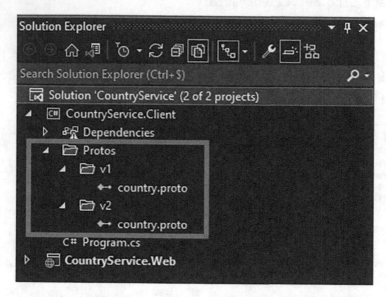

Figure 7-5. *Adding versions 1 and 2 of the* country.proto *file in Protos folder*

Client side, you have the option to add your Protobuf files other than manually. Recall that Chapter 6 showed you how to expose Protobuf files over REST endpoints. Now we are going to import them through the Visual Studio Service Reference wizard, and I'm sure you'll like this easy way to import your Protobuf files. Right-click the CountryService.Client project, select Add, and then click Service Reference, as shown in Figure 7-6.

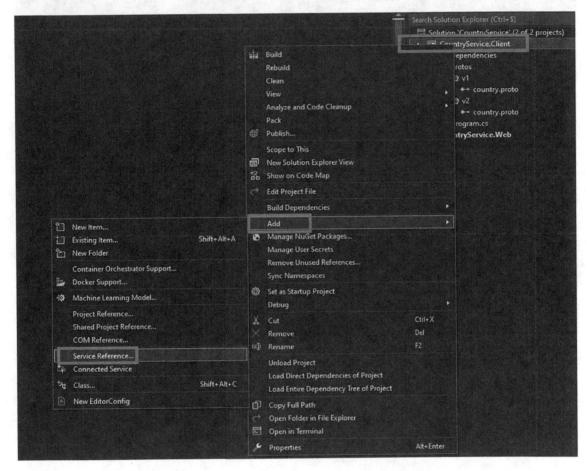

Figure 7-6. *Add service reference on .NET 6 console application*

Then the "Add service reference" window appears, as shown in Figure 7-7. For the gRPC client context, select gRPC. Note that you can add a WCF service and a REST service via the OpenAPI item.

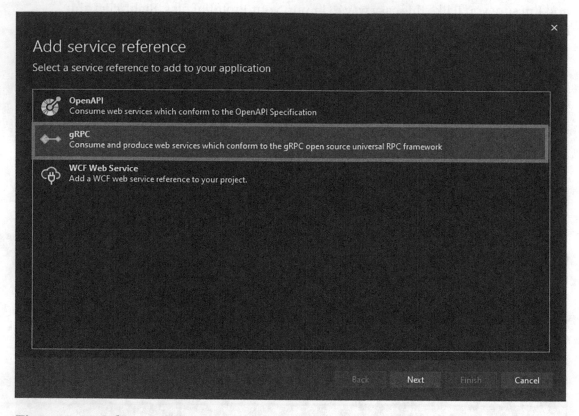

Figure 7-7. *Select gRPC in the "Add service reference" window*

Click the Next button and then provide the path to where the Protobuf file is stored on your computer, as shown in Figure 7-8. Ensure that the type of class to be generated is set to Client.

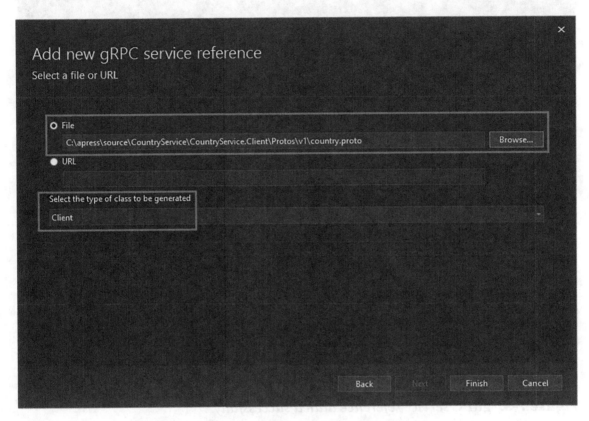

Figure 7-8. *Add new gRPC service reference from a file*

Click the Next button and then the gRPC service reference should be successfully added, as shown in Figure 7-9.

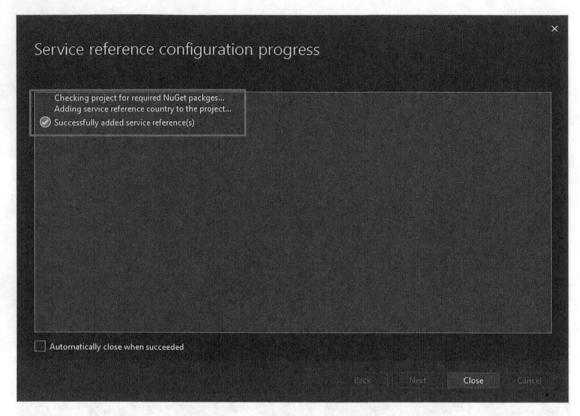

Figure 7-9. *gRPC service reference added successfully*

Finally, repeat this operation for each Protobuf file you want to add. As I previously mentioned, you can add new gRPC service references from a URL like the REST endpoint exposed with the minimal API feature of ASP.NET Core, as shown in Figure 7-10.

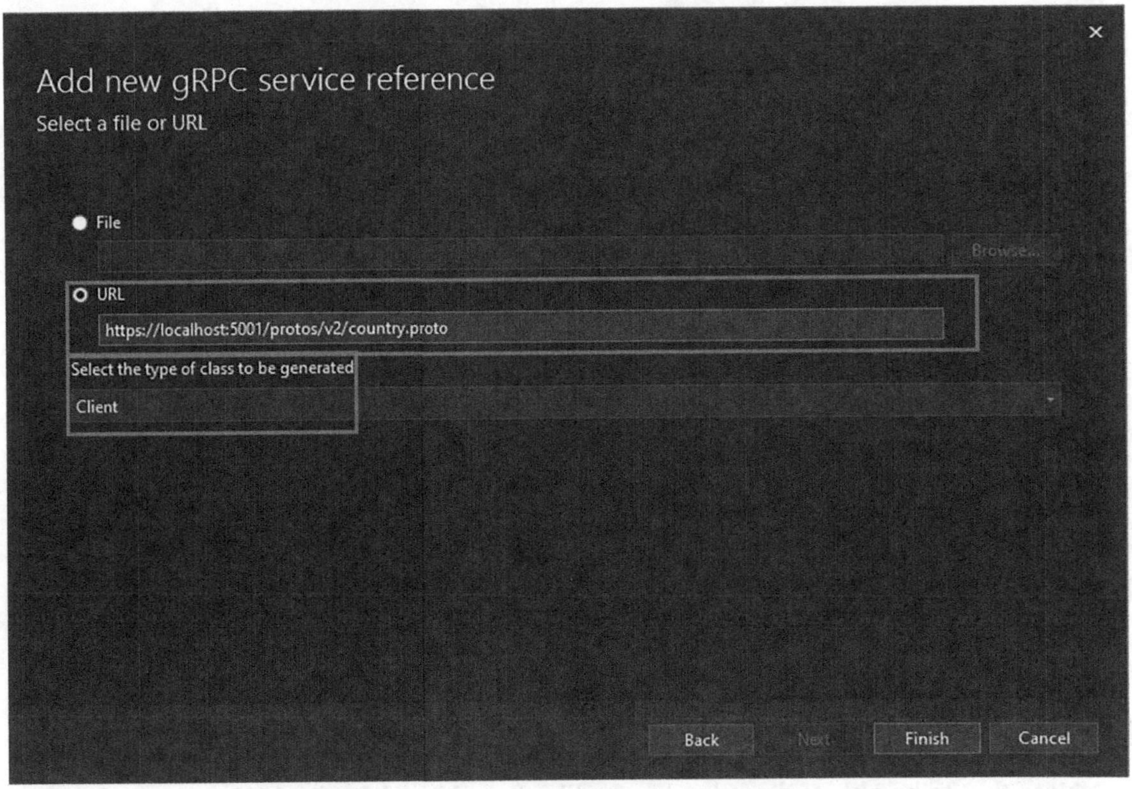

Figure 7-10. *Add new gRPC service reference from a URL*

Don't forget to modify the names of the C# namespaces to fit your needs. You may need it. For example, it's easy to keep the server C# namespace, which could be inappropriate for your client project. I'm sure you don't want to modify the names of the C# namespaces to fit your needs that you have not designed yourself. In my example, I'll keep the following namespaces in the Protobuf file, depending on the version:

```
option csharp_namespace = "Apress.Sample.gRPC.v1";
```

or

```
option csharp_namespace = "Apress.Sample.gRPC.v2";
```

Once you are done with your gRPC services referencing, you'll see all your referenced services in the Connected Services window, as shown in Figure 7-11. As you can see, `country.proto` version 1 has been referenced from a file, and `country.proto` version 2 has been referenced from a URL. For Protobuf files imported via a URL, you'll have to move the file to the correct version folder, as shown at the beginning of the section. Importation by URL drops it off at the `Protos` root folder.

Figure 7-11. *All referenced gRPC services are visible in the Connected Services window*

Note that to be able to download proto files from Visual Studio 2022, you need to ensure that server-side HTTP/1 is enabled (as well as HTTP/2) by adding within the `appsettings.json` file the configuration shown on Listing 7-2.

Listing 7-2. Enabling HTTP/1 and HTTP/2 in Kestrel Configuration in `appsettings.json`

```
{
  "AllowedHosts": "*",
  "Kestrel": {
    "EndpointDefaults": {
      "Protocols": "Http1AndHttp2"
    }
  }
}
```

Assuming you are done with Protobufs referencing, you can build your project, such as the server application it should generate (if you are using versioning) and a folder for each version that contains two files, one for the messages and another for the gRPC client. Figure 7-12 shows the Country.cs file containing the messages definition and the CountryGrpc.cs file containing the gRPC client definition. They are both in the v1 (version 1) folder.

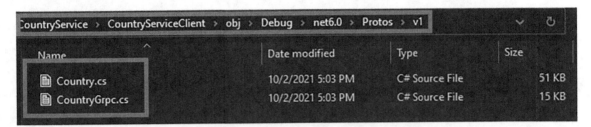

Figure 7-12. *Generated Country.cs and CountryGrpc.cs files in the v1 folder*

These files are similar to their server version, except CountryGrpc.cs contains the gRPC client. Listing 7-3 shows the generated CountryServiceClient class.

Listing 7-3. The Generated CountryServiceClient Class

```
/// <summary>Client for CountryService</summary>
public partial class CountryServiceClient : grpc::ClientBase<Country
ServiceClient>
{
    /// <summary>Creates a new client for CountryService</summary>
    /// <param name="channel">The channel to use to make remote
        calls.</param>
    public CountryServiceClient(grpc::ChannelBase channel) : base(channel)
    {
    }

    /// <summary>Creates a new client for CountryService that uses a custom
        <c>CallInvoker</c>.</summary>
    /// <param name="callInvoker">The callInvoker to use to make remote
        calls.</param>
```

```
public CountryServiceClient(grpc::CallInvoker callInvoker) :
base(callInvoker)
{
}

/// <summary>Protected parameterless constructor to allow creation of
    test doubles.</summary>
protected CountryServiceClient() : base()
{
}

// Other pieces of generated code
}
```

There are three different constructors. You can use each of them depending on how you are building your gRPC client:

- The parameterless constructor is protected, so you'll use it directly.

- The second constructor takes as a parameter a CallInvoker class that allows invoking a single gRPC function.

- The third constructor takes as a parameter a Channel class, which is the most often used, as we have seen in Chapter 4.

I'll show you how to create a gRPC client using the Channel class in the next section. Using the CallInvoker class is more recommended for more advanced gRPC developers, so I won't cover this part in this book.

Consume gRPC Services with .NET 6

We'll build together a simple gRPC client, and in this section I'll show you the basics before we create a complete web application in Chapter 9. We will therefore go step by step.

Listing 7-4 shows the creation of the CountryServiceClient class that takes as a parameters the Channel class. Note that this code sample uses the C# 9 *top-level statements* feature to build a lighter Program.cs file.

Listing 7-4. Instantiate the `CountryServiceClient` Class Using the `Channel` Class

```
using Grpc.Net.Client;
using static Apress.Sample.gRPC.v1.CountryService;

var channel = GrpcChannel.ForAddress("https://localhost:5001");
var countryClient = new CountryServiceClient(channel);
```

Creating a gRPC client in this way is the simplest method. You can add some options to the `Channel` class through an override of the `ForAddress()` method. For example, you can add a logger (and I'll show you how in the following code sample) that allows you to log certain information during a gRPC call. I won't describe right here all possible options, but I will show some of them in this chapter (like options for managing message size or compression) and introduce others, such as for security, in Chapter 14. Listing 7-5 shows the command to download the NuGet package that enables logging within a console application.

Listing 7-5. Install `Microsoft.Extensions.Logging.Console` Package That Enables Logging in Console Applications

```
Install-Package Microsoft.Extensions.Logging.Console
```

Listing 7-6 shows a `Channel` created using the `GrpcChannelOptions` class, allowing passing options to this `Channel`, here, a `LoggerFactory` which allows to implement and configure a logger. The `AddConsole()` method enables logging in the console, and the minimum level of logging is set to `Trace`, which enables any log for display.

Listing 7-6. Add a `LoggerFactory` to a `Channel` Class

```
using Grpc.Net.Client;
using Microsoft.Extensions.Logging;
using static Apress.Sample.gRPC.v1.CountryService;

var loggerFactory = LoggerFactory.Create(logging =>
{
    logging.AddConsole();
    logging.SetMinimumLevel(LogLevel.Trace);
});
```

```
var channel = GrpcChannel.ForAddress("https://localhost:5001", new
GrpcChannelOptions
{
    LoggerFactory = loggerFactory

});
var countryClient = new CountryServiceClient(channel);
```

If you now call a gRPC endpoint—for example, GetAll function, which is a server-streamed RPC function—you should see all logs (trace, debug, etc.), as shown in Figure 7-13.

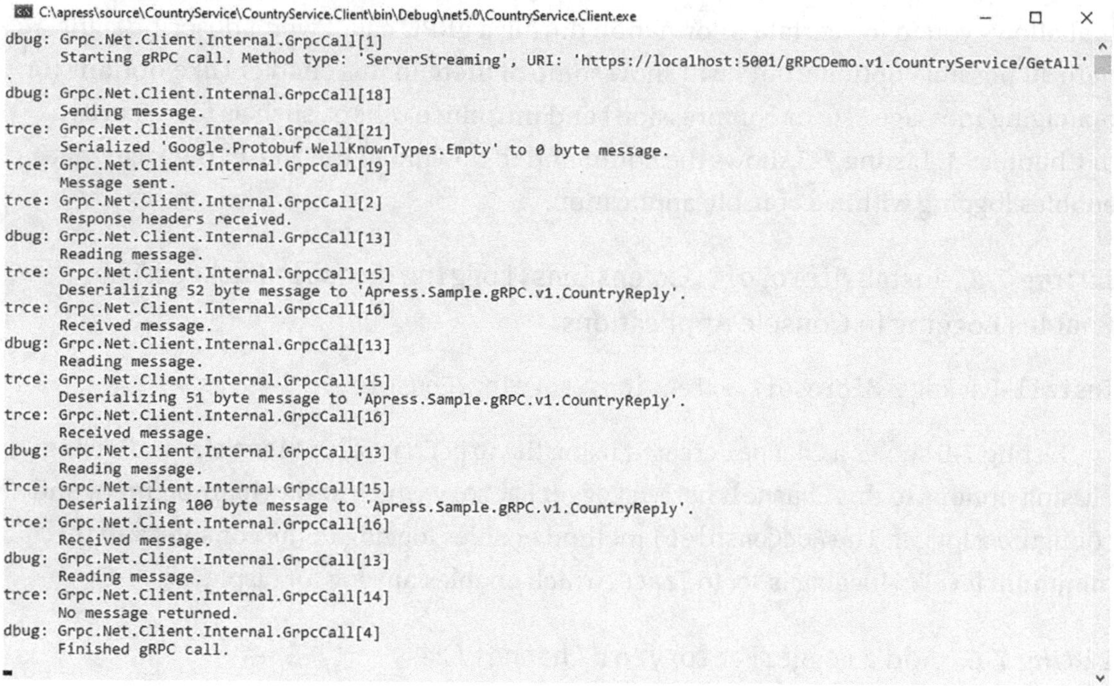

Figure 7-13. *Logging enabled in the console application*

You are now ready to consume the CountryServiceClient class. I'll show you how to invoke and consume returned data by using the following gRPC endpoints:

- GetAll: A server-streaming function

- Get: A unary function

- `Create`: A bidirectional streaming function

- `Delete`: A client-streaming function

The principle is the same as the server regarding streaming methods (client, server, and bidirectional). Streamed data to be read or written must be iterated:

- Streamed responses must be iterated with the `ReadAllAsync()` method.

- Streamed requests must be iterated with the `WriteAsync()` method.

Streaming methods also have some particularities:

- A gRPC function invocation is an object that implements the `IDisposable` interface. Then you have to dispose the invocation object after you read the response.

- A streamed gRPC function invocation is awaitable (async / await), but it doesn't have the *async* suffix on its method name. The streamed response reading/writing is asynchronous, and the call completion is asynchronous as well.

- When you finish streaming messages into a request to the gRPC server, you have to tell the server you are done with the streamed data transmission with the `CompleteAsync()` method.

- If you expect a non-streamed response at the end of client-streamed call execution, you have to use the `await` keyword on the invocation object to get the final response message. If it doesn't return any non-streamed response message, you have to use the `await` keyword anyway without getting any data. Finally, using `await` on a call object completes the call (tells the server the request is made).

Listing 7-7 shows the `GetAll` RPC method invocation, the asynchronous streamed response to be read, and headers and trailers accessed, respectively, from the `ResponseHeadersAsync` property (which is asynchronous) and `GetTrailers()` method (which is synchronous). Trailers must be read after completing the reading of streamed response messages. Headers can be read before.

Listing 7-7. The GetAll Function Invocation, the Streamed Response Read Asynchronously, and Headers and Trailers Read

```
using Google.Protobuf.WellKnownTypes;
using Grpc.Core;
using Grpc.Net.Client;
using Microsoft.Extensions.Logging;
using System;
using static Apress.Sample.gRPC.v1.CountryService;

var loggerFactory = LoggerFactory.Create(logging =>
{
    logging.AddConsole();
    logging.SetMinimumLevel(LogLevel.Trace);
});

var channel = GrpcChannel.ForAddress("https://localhost:5001", new
GrpcChannelOptions
{
    LoggerFactory = loggerFactory

});
var countryClient = new CountryServiceClient(channel);

using var serverStreamingCall = countryClient.GetAll(new Empty());
await foreach (var response in serverStreamingCall.ResponseStream.
ReadAllAsync())
{
    Console.WriteLine($"{response.Name}: {response.Description}");
}

// Read headers and trailers
var serverStreamingCallHeaders = await serverStreamingCall.Response
HeadersAsync;
var serverStreamingCallTrailers = serverStreamingCall.GetTrailers();
var myHeaderValue = serverStreamingCallHeaders.GetValue("myHeaderName");
var myTrailerValue = serverStreamingCallTrailers.GetValue("myTrailerName");
```

Note that I didn't used the explicit `Dispose()` method. Instead, I used the `using` keyword, which disposes automatically the `serverStreamingCall` object at the end of the statement.

Listing 7-8 shows the `Delete()` gRPC function invocation. Request messages are streamed. Once done, the `CompleteAsync()` method needs to be invoked, and the call is ended by awaiting the call object named here `clientStreamingCall`. Note that trailers can be read before the `ResponseAsync` property, unlike trailers, which can be read only *after* the `ResponseAsync` property.

Listing 7-8. The `Delete` gRPC Function Invocation, Read the Streamed Response, Complete Message Reading, Finish the Call, and Read Headers and Trailers

```
using Apress.Sample.gRPC.v1;
using Grpc.Net.Client;
using Microsoft.Extensions.Logging;
using System;
using System.Collections.Generic;
using static Apress.Sample.gRPC.v1.CountryService;

var loggerFactory = LoggerFactory.Create(logging =>
{
    logging.AddConsole();
    logging.SetMinimumLevel(LogLevel.Trace);
});

var channel = GrpcChannel.ForAddress("https://localhost:5001", new
GrpcChannelOptions
{
    LoggerFactory = loggerFactory

});
var countryClient = new CountryServiceClient(channel);
```

```
using var clientStreamingCall = countryClient.Delete();
var countriesToDelete = new List<CountryIdRequest>
{
    new CountryIdRequest {
        Id = 1
    },
    new CountryIdRequest {
        Id = 2
    }
};

// Write
foreach (var countryToDelete in countriesToDelete)
{
    await clientStreamingCall.RequestStream.WriteAsync(countryToDelete);
    Console.WriteLine($"Country with Id {countryToDelete.Id} set for
    deletion");
}

// Tells server that request streaming is done
await clientStreamingCall.RequestStream.CompleteAsync();

// Finish the call by getting the response
var emptyResponse = await clientStreamingCall.ResponseAsync;
// Read headers and Trailers
var clientStreamingCallHeaders = await clientStreamingCall.ResponseHeadersAsync;
var clientStreamingCallTrailers = clientStreamingCall.GetTrailers();
var myHeaderValue = clientStreamingCallHeaders.GetValue("myHeaderName");
var myTrailerValue = clientStreamingCallTrailers.GetValue("myTrailerName");

// var emptyResponse = await clientStreamingCall; // Works as well but
cannot read headers and Trailers
```

Listing 7-9 shows the Create RPC method, which is a bidirectional streaming function. A bidirectional RPC method combines the server-streaming reading feature and client-streaming writing feature. A bidirectional RPC method also needs to invoke the CompleteAsync() method to tell the server the client is done with streamed request messages and then read the server's streamed response. Headers can be read before completion of reading streamed response messages and trailers can be read *only* after. Note that I chose (for simplicity purposes) to stream all messages to the server before reading any response, but keep in mind it's possible to start reading server responses before all request messages have been sent.

Listing 7-9. The Create gRPC Function Invocation, Write Streamed Messages to the Request, Complete the Streaming Request, Read the Streamed Response, and Read Headers and Trailers

```
using Apress.Sample.gRPC.v1;
using Google.Protobuf.WellKnownTypes;
using Grpc.Core;
using Grpc.Net.Client;
using Microsoft.Extensions.Logging;
using System;
using System.Collections.Generic;
using static Apress.Sample.gRPC.v1.CountryService;

var loggerFactory = LoggerFactory.Create(logging =>
{
    logging.AddConsole();
    logging.SetMinimumLevel(LogLevel.Trace);
});

var channel = GrpcChannel.ForAddress("https://localhost:5001", new
GrpcChannelOptions
{
    LoggerFactory = loggerFactory

});
var countryClient = new CountryServiceClient(channel);

using var bidirectionnalStreamingCall = countryClient.Create();
var countriesToCreate = new List<CountryCreationRequest>
{
    new CountryCreationRequest {
        Name = "France",
```

```
        Description = "Western european country",
        CreateDate = Timestamp.FromDateTime(DateTime.SpecifyKind
        (DateTime.UtcNow, DateTimeKind.Utc))
    },
    new CountryCreationRequest {
        Name = "Poland",
        Description = "Eastern european country",
        CreateDate = Timestamp.FromDateTime(DateTime.SpecifyKind
        (DateTime.UtcNow, DateTimeKind.Utc))
    }
};

// Write
foreach (var countryToCreate in countriesToCreate)
{
    await bidirectionnalStreamingCall.RequestStream.WriteAsync
    (countryToCreate);
    Console.WriteLine($"Country {countryToCreate.Name} set for creation");
}

// Tells server that request streaming is done
await bidirectionnalStreamingCall.RequestStream.CompleteAsync();

// Read
await foreach (var createdCountry in bidirectionnalStreamingCall.Response
Stream.ReadAllAsync())
{
    Console.WriteLine($"{createdCountry.Name} has been created with Id:
    {createdCountry.Id}");
}

// Read headers and Trailers
var bidirectionnalStreamingCallHeaders = await bidirectionnalStreamingCall
.ResponseHeadersAsync;
var bidirectionnalStreamingCallTrailers = bidirectionnalStreamingCall
.GetTrailers();
```

```
var myHeaderValue = bidirectionnalStreamingCallHeaders.GetValue
("myHeaderName");
var myTrailerValue = bidirectionnalStreamingCallTrailers.GetValue
("myTrailerName");
```

Listing 7-10 shows the Get RPC method. This function can be called synchronously with the Get method or asynchronously with the GetAsync method. Only *Unary* methods have this specificity. The response is directly received after the gRPC function invocation. *Headers* can be read before the ResponseAsync property and *Trailers* can be read *only* after.

Listing 7-10. The Get gRPC Function Invocation (Synchronously and Asynchronously), the Read Directly from the Server's Response Message, and Read Headers and Trailers

```
using Apress.Sample.gRPC.v1;
using Grpc.Net.Client;
using Microsoft.Extensions.Logging;
using System;
using static Apress.Sample.gRPC.v1.CountryService;

var loggerFactory = LoggerFactory.Create(logging =>
{
    logging.AddConsole();
    logging.SetMinimumLevel(LogLevel.Trace);
});

var channel = GrpcChannel.ForAddress("https://localhost:5001", new
GrpcChannelOptions
{
    LoggerFactory = loggerFactory

});
var countryClient = new CountryServiceClient(channel);

var countryCall = countryClient.GetAsync(new CountryIdRequest { Id = 1 });
var country = await countryCall.ResponseAsync;
Console.WriteLine($"{country.Id}: {country.Name}");
```

```
// Read headers and Trailers
var countryCallHeaders = await countryCall.ResponseHeadersAsync;
var countryCallTrailers = countryCall.GetTrailers();
var myHeaderValue = countryCallHeaders.GetValue("myHeaderName");
var myTrailerValue = countryCallTrailers.GetValue("myTrailerName");

// var country = await countryClient.GetAsync(new CountryIdRequest { Id = 1
}); // Works as well but Headers and Trailers cannot be accessed
```

You may remember from Chapter 3 the introduction of *Deadlines*, which are timeouts and are configured on the client side. Listing 7-11 shows how, in any RPC method (unary, client streaming, server streaming, bidirectional streaming), to configure a deadline. If a deadline is exceeded, an exception of type RpcException will be thrown. Note that it is also possible to access trailers in an RpcException, as shown again in Listing 7-11.

Listing 7-11. Set a Deadline of 30 Seconds, Catch the Deadline Exception and Other Exceptions, and Get the Custom correlationId from Trailers Within an RpcException

```
using Apress.Sample.gRPC.v1;
using Grpc.Core;
using Grpc.Net.Client;
using Microsoft.Extensions.Logging;
using System;
using static Apress.Sample.gRPC.v1.CountryService;

var loggerFactory = LoggerFactory.Create(logging =>
{
    logging.AddConsole();
    logging.SetMinimumLevel(LogLevel.Trace);
});

var channel = GrpcChannel.ForAddress("https://localhost:5001", new
GrpcChannelOptions
{
    LoggerFactory = loggerFactory

});
```

```
var countryClient = new CountryServiceClient(channel);

var countryIdRequest = new CountryIdRequest { Id = 1 };
try
{
    var countryCall = countryClient.GetAsync(countryIdRequest, deadline:
    DateTime.UtcNow.AddSeconds(30));
    var country = await countryCall.ResponseAsync;
    Console.WriteLine($"{country.Id}: {country.Name}");

    // Read headers and Trailers
    var countryCallHeaders = await countryCall.ResponseHeadersAsync;
    var countryCallTrailers = countryCall.GetTrailers();
    var myHeaderValue = countryCallHeaders.GetValue("myHeaderName");
    var myTrailerValue = countryCallTrailers.GetValue("myTrailerName");
}
catch (RpcException ex) when (ex.StatusCode == StatusCode.DeadlineExceeded)
{
    Console.WriteLine($"Get country with Id: {countryIdRequest.Id} has
    timed out");
    var trailers = ex.Trailers;
    var correlationId = trailers.GetValue("correlationId");
}
catch (RpcException ex)
{
    Console.WriteLine($"An error occured while getting the country with Id:
    {countryIdRequest.Id}");
    var trailers = ex.Trailers;
    var correlationId = trailers.GetValue("correlationId");
}
```

A gRPC client allows developers to use *Interceptors* like the gRPC services server-side. That's a great thing because, for example, you can customize your logging message instead of using the LoggerFactory that is passed as a parameter in the gRPC Channel. gRPC client *Interceptors* work quite the same as gRPC server *Interceptors*, except the methods you have to implement are different:

- AsyncClientStreamingCall: The call *Interceptor* for client-streaming functions

- AsyncDuplexStreamingCall: The call *Interceptor* for bidirectional streaming functions

- AsyncServerStreamingCall: The call *Interceptor* for server-streaming functions

- AsyncUnaryCall: The call *Interceptor* for unary functions

As with the server Interceptors, you have to inherit from the Interceptor class. Listing 7-12 shows the TracerInterceptor that perform custom logging, for example.

Listing 7-12. TracerInterceptor That Perform Simple Tracing

```
using Grpc.Core;
using Grpc.Core.Interceptors;
using Microsoft.Extensions.Logging;

namespace CountryService.Client
{
    public class TracerInterceptor : Interceptor
    {
        private readonly ILogger<TracerInterceptor> _logger;

        public TracerInterceptor(ILogger<TracerInterceptor> logger)
        {
            _logger = logger;
        }

        public override AsyncClientStreamingCall<TRequest, TResponse> Async
        ClientStreamingCall<TRequest, TResponse>(ClientInterceptorContext
        <TRequest, TResponse> context, AsyncClientStreamingCallContinuation
        <TRequest, TResponse> continuation)
```

```csharp
    where TRequest : class
    where TResponse : class
{

    _logger.LogDebug($"Executing {context.Method.Name} {context.
    Method.Type} method on server {context.Host}");
    return continuation(context);
}

public override AsyncDuplexStreamingCall<TRequest, TResponse> Async
DuplexStreamingCall<TRequest, TResponse>(ClientInterceptorContext
<TRequest, TResponse> context, AsyncDuplexStreamingCallContinuation
<TRequest, TResponse> continuation)
    where TRequest : class
    where TResponse : class
{

    _logger.LogDebug($"Executing {context.Method.Name} {context.
    Method.Type} method on service {context.Method.ServiceName}");
    return continuation(context);
}

public override AsyncServerStreamingCall<TResponse> AsyncServerStre
amingCall<TRequest, TResponse>(TRequest request, ClientInterceptor
Context<TRequest, TResponse> context, AsyncServerStreamingCall
Continuation<TRequest, TResponse> continuation)
    where TRequest : class
    where TResponse : class
{

    _logger.LogDebug($"Executing {context.Method.Name} {context.
    Method.Type} method on service {context.Method.ServiceName}");
    return continuation(request, context);
}

public override AsyncUnaryCall<TResponse> AsyncUnaryCall<TRequest,
TResponse>(TRequest request, ClientInterceptorContext<TRequest,
TResponse> context, AsyncUnaryCallContinuation<TRequest, TResponse>
continuation)
    where TRequest : class
```

```
            where TResponse : class
      {

          _logger.LogDebug($"Executing {context.Method.Name} {context.
          Method.Type} method on service {context.Method.ServiceName}");
          return continuation(request, context);
      }
   }
}
```

To use the TracerInterceptor from Listing 7-12, create a logger from the LoggerFactory class, remove the latter from the gRPC *Channel,* and use the method Intercept() (on the same *Channel* instance) that takes as a parameter an instance of TracerInterceptor, which take itself an instance of the logger and passes it to the CountryServiceClient class constructor. Listing 7-13 shows how to use TracerInterceptor on the GetAll() RPC method.

Listing 7-13. Add TracerInterceptor to the CountryServiceClient Class Constructor

```
using CountryService.Client;
using Google.Protobuf.WellKnownTypes;
using Grpc.Core;
using Grpc.Core.Interceptors;
using Grpc.Net.Client;
using Microsoft.Extensions.Logging;
using System;
using static Apress.Sample.gRPC.v1.CountryService;

var loggerFactory = LoggerFactory.Create(logging =>
{
    logging.AddConsole();
    logging.SetMinimumLevel(LogLevel.Trace);
});
```

```
var logger = loggerFactory.CreateLogger<TracerInterceptor>();

var channel = GrpcChannel.ForAddress("https://localhost:5001");

var countryClient = new CountryServiceClient(channel.Intercept(new
TracerInterceptor(logger)));

using var serverStreamingCall = countryClient.GetAll(new Empty());
await foreach (var response in serverStreamingCall.ResponseStream.
ReadAllAsync())
{
    Console.WriteLine($"{response.Name}: {response.Description}");
}

logger.LogDebug("Call to GetAll function ended");
```

If you execute now the call on the GetAll function, you should see the logs in the console as shown in Figure 7-14.

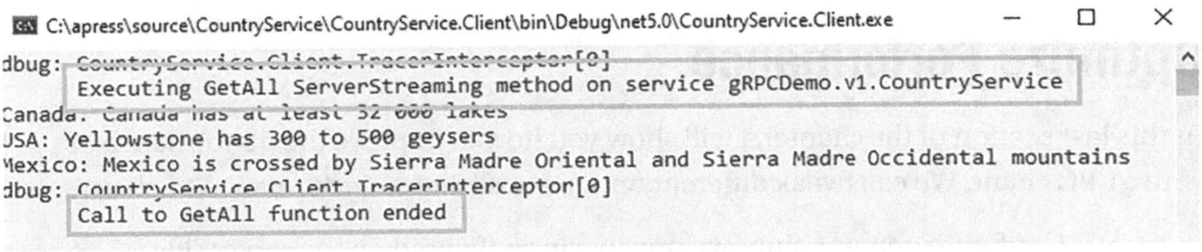

Figure 7-14. TracerInterceptor in action on GetAll function call

The last thing you should know is that, unlike the HttpClient class for REST calls, the gRPC client is not disposable, which means it doesn't inherit from the IDisposable interface. The gRPC *Channel* is **disposable**. Once you don't need your gRPC *Channel*, you should call Dispose() to close all active calls (then ensure you don't have active calls by waiting for all of them to complete) and dispose of the HttpMessageInvoker, which performs HTTP calls. You should also use the ShutDownAsync() method, which unregisters the gRPC *Channel*. Listing 7-14 shows how to dispose of and unregister the gRPC *Channel*.

Listing 7-14. Dispose and Unregister a gRPC Channel

```
var channel = GrpcChannel.ForAddress("https://localhost:5001");
var countryClient = new CountryServiceClient(channel);

// Perform calls

channel.Dispose();
await channel.ShutdownAsync();
```

Reusing the same gRPC *Channel* for all your clients helps keep good performance. The client doesn't reopen a new TCP connection after opening a new socket, negotiating TLS (a secure connection), and opening a new HTTP/2 connection. You have to ensure that your *Channel* is not disposed by avoiding calling ShutDownAsync() or Dispose() methods.

This isn't the only way to help performance. Keep reading to see more ways to optimize performance.

Optimize Performance

In this last section of the chapter, I will show you how to improve the performance of your gRPC client. We can tweak different options to optimize performance, such as:

- Configure compression (we previously configured on the server side, so now I will show you how to benefit activate it on the client side)

- Define the maximum message size

- Keep an HTTP/2 connection open to avoid the opening/closing cycle of a connection, which can prevent a certain delay

- Increase the number of HTTP/2 connections when the limit is reached to avoid calls being queued

Take Advantage of Compression

Chapter 5 showed you how to configure the compression on the server side, specifically with a custom compressor provider: Brotli. The compression was configured but not enabled until a client sends the accept-encoding request header,

HeaderGrpcAcceptEncoding. Listing 7-15 shows how to check the headers server side with the help of the GetHttpContext() method (which returns the HttpContext of the current gRPC request) on the ServerCallContext class.

Listing 7-15. Get Headers from the Current gRPC Request

```
var headers = context.GetHttpContext().Request.Headers;
```

When a client passes in the headers the accept-encoding header with the **"br"**value you should be able to see it server side, as shown in Figure 7-15.

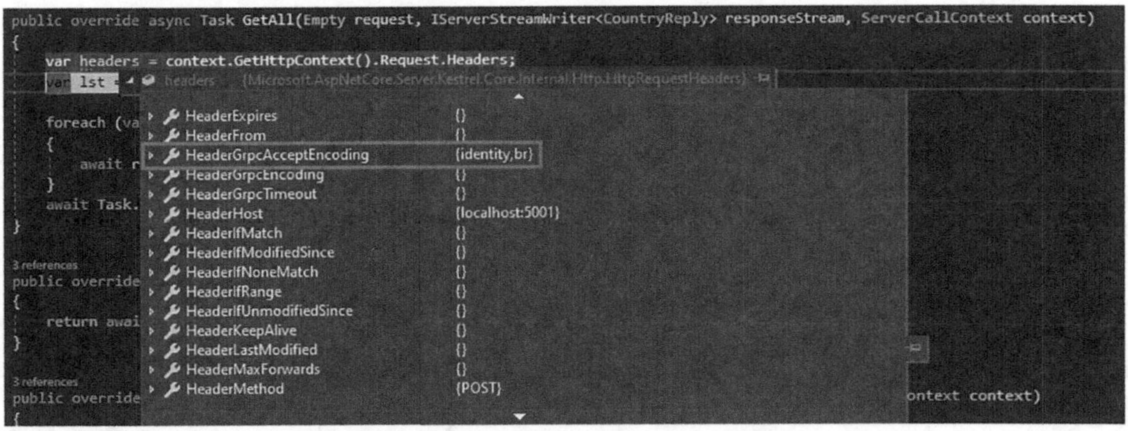

Figure 7-15. *Get HeaderGrpcAcceptEncoding server side*

To make the compression possible, you have to set up the compression client side by adding the Brotli compression into the *Channel* configuration, as shown in Listing 7-16. (FYI, Brotli is 20% more efficient than Gzip in terms of compression).

Listing 7-16. Enabling Brotli Compression on the gRPC Channel

```
using CountryService.Client.Compression;
using Google.Protobuf.WellKnownTypes;
using Grpc.Core;
using Grpc.Net.Client;
using Grpc.Net.Compression;
using Microsoft.Extensions.Logging;
using System;
using System.Collections.Generic;
using static Apress.Sample.gRPC.v1.CountryService;
```

269

```
var loggerFactory = LoggerFactory.Create(logging =>
{
    logging.AddConsole();
    logging.SetMinimumLevel(LogLevel.Trace);
});

var channel = GrpcChannel.ForAddress("https://localhost:5001", new
GrpcChannelOptions {
    LoggerFactory = loggerFactory,
    CompressionProviders = new List<ICompressionProvider>
    {
        new BrotliCompressionProvider()
    }
});

// var countryClient = new CountryServiceClient(channel.Intercept(new
TracerInterceptor(logger)));
var countryClient = new CountryServiceClient(channel);

using var serverStreamingCall = countryClient.GetAll(new Empty());
await foreach (var response in serverStreamingCall.ResponseStream.
ReadAllAsync())
{
    Console.WriteLine($"{response.Name}: {response.Description}");
}

channel.Dispose();
await channel.ShutdownAsync();
```

If you run your client (GetAll RPC method), the server should receive the HeaderGrpcAcceptEncoding header, which you can see in in the server logs, as shown in Figure 7-16.

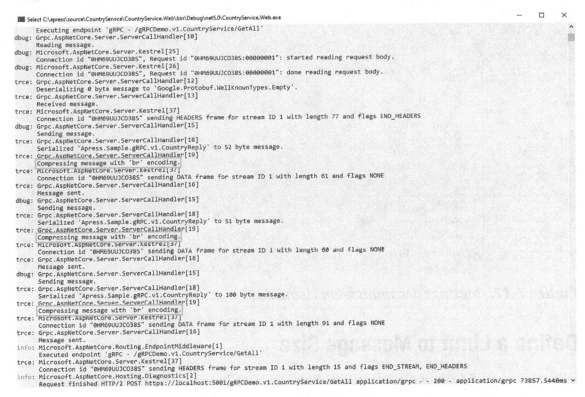

Figure 7-16. *Message compression in action when calling* GetAll *endpoint with Brotli compression provider enabled client side and configured server side*

Note that *only responses are compressed,* not request messages.

Naturally, the client decompresses messages, which you also can see in the logs, as shown in Figure 7-17.

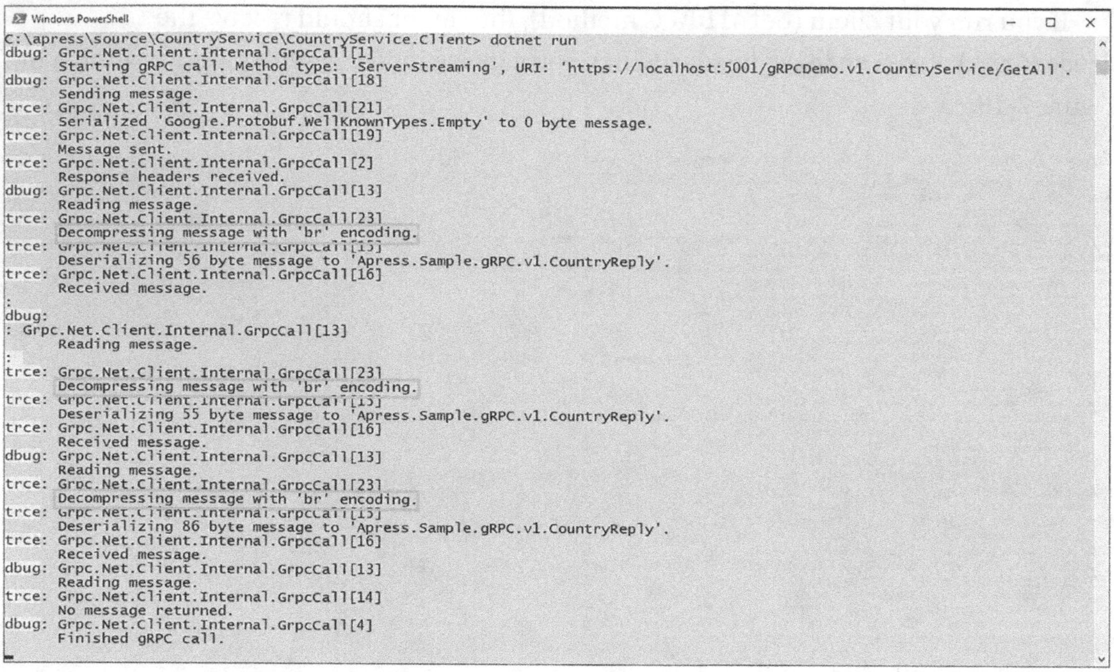

Figure 7-17. *Message decompression client side*

Define a Limit to Message Size

Like the server-side application, a gRPC client also can limit the size of the incoming and outgoing messages. It's configurable with the GrpcChannelOptions class, as shown in Listing 7-17.

Listing 7-17. Set the Maximum Size to 6 MB for Incoming and Outgoing Messages

```
using CountryService.Client.Compression;
using Grpc.Net.Client;
using Grpc.Net.Compression;
using Microsoft.Extensions.Logging;
using System;
using System.Collections.Generic;
using static Apress.Sample.gRPC.v1.CountryService;
```

```
var loggerFactory = LoggerFactory.Create(logging =>
{
    logging.AddConsole();
    logging.SetMinimumLevel(LogLevel.Trace);
});

var channel = GrpcChannel.ForAddress("https://localhost:5001", new
GrpcChannelOptions {
    LoggerFactory = loggerFactory,
    CompressionProviders = new List<ICompressionProvider>
    {
        new BrotliCompressionProvider()
    },
    MaxReceiveMessageSize = 6291456, // 6 MB,
        MaxSendMessageSize = 6291456 // 6 MB
});

var countryClient = new CountryServiceClient(channel);
```

An RpcException will be raised if the maximum size is exceeded.

Keep HTTP/2 Connections Open

Regular pings keep an HTTP/2 connection open. It may be a good idea to
prevent it from closing prematurely by keeping it open for a future call since
opening another connection may take some time. Listing 7-18 shows how to
configure a SocketHttpHandler to be bound to the HttpHandler property of the
GrpcChannelOptions class, that enable, on a *Channel*, regular pings to be made to the
server, every 15 seconds, for example:

Listing 7-18. Enabling Pings to the Server Every 15 Seconds to Keep Alive
HTTP/2 Connection

```
using Grpc.Net.Client;
using Microsoft.Extensions.Logging;
using System;
using System.Net.Http;
using static Apress.Sample.gRPC.v1.CountryService;
```

```
var loggerFactory = LoggerFactory.Create(logging =>
{
    logging.AddConsole();
    logging.SetMinimumLevel(LogLevel.Trace);
});

var handler = new SocketsHttpHandler
{
    KeepAlivePingDelay = TimeSpan.FromSeconds(15)
};

var channel = GrpcChannel.ForAddress("https://localhost:5001", new
GrpcChannelOptions {
    LoggerFactory = loggerFactory,
    HttpHandler = handler
});

// var countryClient = new CountryServiceClient(channel.Intercept(new
TracerInterceptor(logger)));
var countryClient = new CountryServiceClient(channel);
```

Note   You *must* perform at least one call to an RPC method to enable the ping; if you only create a *Channel* and/or only create a client without making any call, no ping will be sent to the server.

It's possible to set a limit to the reusability of an HTTP/2 connection. Listing 7-19 shows how to set a maximum idle time of 5 minutes for a connection to be reused; after 5 minutes, the idle connection will be closed and no more pings will be sent to the server. It's possible to set an infinite idle time.

Listing 7-19. Set Up a Maximum Idle Time of 5 Minutes for HTTP/2 Connections

```
using Grpc.Net.Client;
using Microsoft.Extensions.Logging;
using System;
using System.Net.Http;
using static Apress.Sample.gRPC.v1.CountryService;
```

```
var loggerFactory = LoggerFactory.Create(logging =>
{
    logging.AddConsole();
    logging.SetMinimumLevel(LogLevel.Trace);
});

var handler = new SocketsHttpHandler
{
        KeepAlivePingDelay = TimeSpan.FromSeconds(15),
        PooledConnectionIdleTimeout = TimeSpan.FromMinutes(5),
        // Timeout.InfiniteTimeSpan for infinite idle connection
};

var channel = GrpcChannel.ForAddress("https://localhost:5001", new
GrpcChannelOptions {
    LoggerFactory = loggerFactory,
    HttpHandler = handler
});

// var countryClient = new CountryServiceClient(channel.Intercept(new
TracerInterceptor(logger)));
var countryClient = new CountryServiceClient(channel);
```

Finally, I recommend ensuring that pings time out after a specified time period, because sometimes the server may be slow to answer, in which case the pings could flood the server if they don't have a timeout set. Listing 7-20 shows how to configure a timeout for pings to 5 seconds.

Listing 7-20. Configure a Timeout of 5 Seconds on Pings

```
using Grpc.Net.Client;
using Microsoft.Extensions.Logging;
using System;
using System.Net.Http;
using static Apress.Sample.gRPC.v1.CountryService;
```

```
var loggerFactory = LoggerFactory.Create(logging =>
{
    logging.AddConsole();
    logging.SetMinimumLevel(LogLevel.Trace);
});

var handler = new SocketsHttpHandler
{
            KeepAlivePingDelay = TimeSpan.FromSeconds(15),
        PooledConnectionIdleTimeout = TimeSpan.FromMinutes(5),
        // Timeout.InfiniteTimeSpan for infinite idle connection
    KeepAlivePingTimeout = TimeSpan.FromSeconds(5)
};

var channel = GrpcChannel.ForAddress("https://localhost:5001", new
GrpcChannelOptions {
    LoggerFactory = loggerFactory,
    HttpHandler = handler
});

// var countryClient = new CountryServiceClient(channel.Intercept(new
TracerInterceptor(logger)));
var countryClient = new CountryServiceClient(channel);
```

You can appreciate the regular ping with the logs, as shown in Figure 7-18.

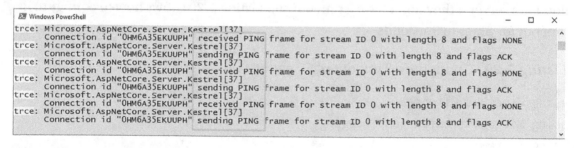

Figure 7-18. *Logging pings that are set up to fire every 15 seconds*

Increase HTTP/2 Maximum Connections

Like Kestrel, default servers enable 100 active requests simultaneously for a single HTTP/2 connection by default. A gRPC channel uses a single HTTP/2 connection, and sometimes the workload may require more than 100 concurrent requests. What happens if a single HTTP/2 connection receives more than 100 calls? They are queued and wait for active request processing to end. It's possible to bypass that limitation and tell a gRPC channel to open additional HTTP/2 connections if needed. Listing 7-21 shows how to enable multiple HTTP/2 connections for the same Channel over the SocketsHttpHandler class. Note that it can be combined with other SocketsHttpHandler options.

Listing 7-21. Enable Multiple HTTP/2 Connections on a gRPC Channel

```
using Grpc.Net.Client;
using Microsoft.Extensions.Logging;
using System;
using System.Net.Http;
using static Apress.Sample.gRPC.v1.CountryService;

var loggerFactory = LoggerFactory.Create(logging =>
{
    logging.AddConsole();
    logging.SetMinimumLevel(LogLevel.Trace);
});

var handler = new SocketsHttpHandler
{
        KeepAlivePingDelay = TimeSpan.FromSeconds(15),
        PooledConnectionIdleTimeout = TimeSpan.FromMinutes(5),
    KeepAlivePingTimeout = TimeSpan.FromSeconds(5),
        EnableMultipleHttp2Connections = true
};

var channel = GrpcChannel.ForAddress("https://localhost:5001", new
GrpcChannelOptions {
    LoggerFactory = loggerFactory,
    HttpHandler = handler
});
```

```
// var countryClient = new CountryServiceClient(channel.Intercept(new
TracerInterceptor(logger)));
var countryClient = new CountryServiceClient(channel);
```

Get Message Validation Errors from the Server

Chapter 5 introduced you to a solution to overcome the lack of native message validation in ASP.NET Core gRPC. As you can saw, the server throws an RpcException with the status INVALIDARGUMENT and a message with the errors concatenated together. In this section, I propose a solution that allows you to get the errors in a more-detailed way on the client side—that is, to receive the following in a structured way:

- The name of the property for which the validation error is raised

- The value of the property that caused the validation error

- The error message

I think you will agree it is beneficial to retrieve this information. You will interpret errors more easily than with the gRPC error message coming from the RpcException. To do so, download the required package with the following command:

```
Install-Package Calzolari.Grpc.Net.Client.Validation
```

This package exposes an extension method named GetValidationErrors(). If you use it, it will return a null result if there is no validation error. But I suggest you use it over a when statement that catches an INVALIDARGUMENT precisely. Then you'll have a catch block dedicated to validation errors, which makes the code cleaner, as shown in Listing 7-22.

Listing 7-22. Using GetValidationErrors on a catch Block

```
using Apress.Sample.gRPC.v1;
using Calzolari.Grpc.Net.Client.Validation;
using Google.Protobuf.WellKnownTypes;
using Grpc.Core;
using Grpc.Net.Client;
using Microsoft.Extensions.Logging;
using static Apress.Sample.gRPC.v1.CountryService;
```

```csharp
var loggerFactory = LoggerFactory.Create(logging =>
{
    logging.SetMinimumLevel(LogLevel.Trace);
});
var channel = GrpcChannel.ForAddress("https://localhost:5001", new
GrpcChannelOptions
{
    LoggerFactory = loggerFactory

});
var countryClient = new CountryServiceClient(channel);

using var bidirectionnalStreamingCall = countryClient.Create();

try
{
    var countriesToCreate = new List<CountryCreationRequest>
    {
        new CountryCreationRequest
        {
            Name = "Japan",
            Description = "",
            CreateDate =   Timestamp.FromDateTime(DateTime.SpecifyKind
            (DateTime.UtcNow, DateTimeKind.Utc))
        }
    };

    // Write
    foreach (var countryToCreate in countriesToCreate)
    {
        await bidirectionnalStreamingCall.RequestStream.WriteAsync
        (countryToCreate);
        Console.WriteLine($"Country {countryToCreate.Name} set for
        creation");
    }
```

```
    // Tells server that request streaming is done
    await bidirectionnalStreamingCall.RequestStream.CompleteAsync();

    // Read
    await foreach (var createdCountry in bidirectionnalStreamingCall.
    ResponseStream.ReadAllAsync())
    {
        Console.WriteLine($"{createdCountry.Name} has been created with Id:
        {createdCountry.Id}");
    }
}
catch (RpcException ex) when (ex.StatusCode == StatusCode.InvalidArgument)
{
    var errors = ex.GetValidationErrors();
    Console.WriteLine(ex.Message);
}
catch (RpcException ex)
{
    Console.WriteLine(ex.Message);
}
```

It's cleaner, isn't it?.

After executing this code, you'll get the result shown in Figure 7-19.

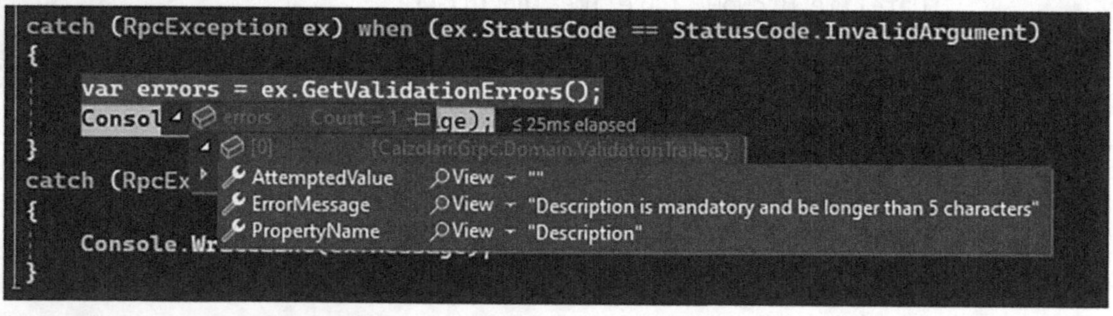

Figure 7-19. *Get detailed validation errors with the* GetValidationErrors *extension method*

If you are using my server-side package, I strongly encourage you to use the client-side package. It really helped me to debug validation errors returned by the server. Enjoy!

Summary

In this chapter, you learned the basics of generating C# stubs from local and remote proto files, configuring a *Channel*, creating a gRPC client, and performing a call with any gRPC function type. You learned as well how to take advantage of Interceptors client side and improve performance for high-load scenarios. I did not cover all gRPC client features in .NET 6. For example, I presented a simple console application. In Chapter 9, which is a complete ASP.NET Core 6 project, you'll learn more about gRPC clients in ASP.NET Core 6, especially how to use them with dependency injection and the gRPC client factory. You also learned how to set up a deadline, which is a significant feature, and cancel a request. Finally, I shared my validation package, which I hope will help you too. Before you start creating a gRPC application, in the next chapter, we will see together, for those are interested in, learn how to migrate with some basics tips a legacy WCF app to gRPC.

CHAPTER 8

From WCF to gRPC

Congratulations! At this point, you have learned the gRPC basics. If you aren't interested in migrating a Windows Communication Foundation (WCF) application to gRPC, you can go straight to Chapter 9. Otherwise, this chapter is intended for you, because you'll need to identify what and how to migrate from WCF to gRPC. Although I won't teach you WCF in this chapter, I'll guide you with some basics and resources to help you migrate from WCF to gRPC, which, as you'll see, is easy! In this chapter, you'll learn

- Differences and similarities between WCF and gRPC

- What and what not to migrate from WCF to gRPC

Differences and Similarities Between WCF and gRPC

WCF and gRPC work with a code generation approach, unlike REST. WCF is rather code-first oriented (gRPC is schema-first oriented because of the Protobuf file) because your first code your data contracts and your services. When you start your WCF application, it opens a *Web Services Description Language (WSDL)* file on the Internet to create a client proxy. But that's not all. Unlike gRPC, the configuration of a WCF endpoint is cumbersome. The endpoint XML configuration resides in a configuration file (like the endpoint URL, the type of binding, and the service behavior). There is no equivalent in gRPC, except for Kestrel configuration in the `appsetting.json` file or code within the *Channel* options configuration. (The next section provides an example of code migration from WCF to gRPC so that the process is not so vague.)

© Anthony Giretti 2022
A. Giretti, *Beginning gRPC with ASP.NET Core 6*, https://doi.org/10.1007/978-1-4842-8008-9_8

Unlike gRPC, WCF implements the *Simple Object Access Protocol (SOAP)*, which uses XML to exchange data, and implements *Representational State Transfer (REST)* architecture in what is commonly known as WCF REST (which generally is generally poorly understood by developers). Thus, whereas gRPC can transport data only with HTTP/2, WCF offers several transport protocols, such as:

- HTTP/1.1

- HTTP/1.1 with TLS

- Transmission Control Protocol (TCP)

- Named Pipe

- Message Queuing (MSMQ)

Table 8-1 shows each of the transport protocols offered by WCF, as well as the associated WCF bindings.

Table 8-1. *All Transport Protocols and Bindings Supported by WCF*

Transport Protocol	Encoding	WCF Bindings

HTTP 1.1/HTTPS 1.1	XML, Text (REST)	`BasicHttpBinding`
		`WSHttpBinding`
		`WSDualHttpBinding`
		`WSFederationHttpBinding`

TCP	Binary	`NetTcpBinding`
Named Pipe	Binary	`NetNamedPipeBinding`
MSMQ	Binary	`NetMsmqBinding` `MsmqIntegrationBinding`

A WCF binding is a way to transport data over the network. If you want to learn more about WCF bindings and each transport protocol, you can read this great article: `https://www.dotnettricks.com/learn/wcf/understanding-various-types-of-wcf-bindings`.

Table 8-1 doesn't include `CustomBinding`, which enables you to create your own binding rules if none of the listed bindings meet your needs. You can, for example, implement binary data transport in HTTP/1.1. I won't go further into this topic because there is no need to know this for gRPC, but understand that you can't customize the data transport in gRPC, whereas as you can with WCF.

WCF's variety of transport options is the opposite of gRPC with its unique transport with HTTP/2, which is not a disadvantage. It's even advantageous since gRPC *standardizes* data transport with a single protocol and, therefore, offers more simplicity while enjoying the *best possible performance* with HTTP/2 combined with binary data transport.

In terms of interoperability, both WCF and gRPC support many languages. Still, if we compare gRPC versus SOAP web services, we can see that many languages support SOAP:

- PHP

- Java

- Ruby

- Python

- JavaScript/TypeScript (Node.js)

- .NET

- C/C++

- Go (client only)

Go, introduced in Chapter 5, supports gRPC but doesn't support SOAP server side .NET 6 doesn't support WCF but supports SOAP clients.

Both gRPC and WCF are used to build back-end to back-end web services (and microservices). Both are not compatible with browsers as well.

Regarding security, WCF is compatible with Windows authentication, whereas gRPC is not compatible with Windows authentication due to HTTP/2. Both support JWT (JSON Web Token) authentication.

What and What Not to Migrate from WCF to gRPC

To help you understand how to migrate from WCF to gRPC, I will use the
CountryService example we have used so far. I'll use an original way to migrate from
WCF by showing you how CountryService would look in its WCF version.

If you are a WCF developer, you are already familiar with the DataContract,
DataMember, ServiceContract, OperationContract, and FaultContract attributes.
If you're a gRPC developer, you need to know that they are class attributes that are
equivalent (in their meaning) to the messages, services, rpc, and oneof Protobuf
keywords. You can define error messages in a Oneof property, and the FaultContract (a
particular DataContract) can take any type like Oneof. Table 8-2 shows that comparison.

Table 8-2. *WCF C# Attributes and Classes vs. Protobuf Keywords*

WCF	Protobuf
DataContract/DataMember	message
ServiceContract	service
OperationContract	rpc
FaultContract	oneof

Within the C# code, you can convert some functionality to gRPC. You can consider
the WCF headers IncomingMessageHeader class and OutgoingMessageHeader class to
be *Trailers* (Metadata class), and the FaultContract can be treated in C# code as an
RpcException, as shown in Table 8-3.

Table 8-3. *WCF C# Classes vs. Their gRPC Equivalent*

WCF	gRPC
MessageHeader/OutgoingMessageHeader	Metadata
MessageHeader/IncomingMessageHeader	Metadata
FaultContract	RpcException
IServiceBehavior, IErrorHandler, IParameterInspector, IOperationBehavior	Interceptor

The purpose of each of the four WCF interfaces in the final row of Table 8-3 is described here:

- IServiceBehavior: Allows calls to be intercepted on the operations of a given service

- IErrorHandler: Allows catching an error when calling an operation

- IParameterInspector: Allows parameters to be intercepted during a call to an operation

- IOperationBehavior: Allows intercepting a particular call on a service operation

To perform these same actions in gRPC, these four interfaces in WCF can be replaced with a gRPC interceptor, previously described in detail in Chapter 5. You already know that gRPC interceptors are very easy to implement and use. You can easily figure out how to migrate implementations of these four interfaces into one or more interceptors.

WCF supports four types of services like gRPC does. You can convert each type of WCF service to its gRPC equivalent, as shown in Table 8-4.

Table 8-4. *WCF Type of Service vs. Equivalent on gRPC*

WCF	gRPC
Request/reply	Unary
Duplex (with session and client callback interface)	Server streaming
Full duplex (with session)	Bidirectional
One-way	Unary without expected response

There is no equivalent for gRPC client streaming in WCF, so as a WCF developer, it's a good reason to jump to gRPC.

Let's see now what CountryService would look like as a WCF web service. Listing 8-1 shows the CountryService messages implemented in C# directly for WCF as DataContract, which includes the ErrorContract to be used as FaultContract.

Listing 8-1. CountryService Messages Implemented As DataContract, Including the ErrorContract to Handle Errors As a FaultContract

```csharp
using System;
using System.Runtime.Serialization;

namespace Contracts
{
    [DataContract]
    public class CountryReply
    {
        [DataMember]
        public int Id { get; set; }

        [DataMember]
        public string Name { get; set; }

        [DataMember]
        public string Description { get; set; }

        [DataMember]
        public byte[] Flag { get; set; }

        [DataMember]
        public DateTime CreateDate { get; set; }

        [DataMember]
        public DateTime UpdateDate { get; set; }
    }

    [DataContract]
    public class CountryIdRequest
    {
        [DataMember]
        public int Id { get; set; }
    }

    [DataContract]
    public class CountryUpdateRequest
    {
```

```
    [DataMember]
    public int Id { get; set; }

    [DataMember]
    public string Description { get; set; }

    [DataMember]
    public DateTime UpdateDate { get; set; }
}

[DataContract]
public class CountryCreationRequest
{
    [DataMember]
    public string Name { get; set; }

    [DataMember]
    public string Description { get; set; }

    [DataMember]
    public byte[] Flag { get; set; }

    [DataMember]
    public DateTime CreateDate { get; set; }
}
[DataContract]
public class CountryCreationReply
{
    [DataMember]
    public int Id { get; set; }

    [DataMember]
    public string Name { get; set; }
}

[DataContract]
public class ErrorContract
{
    [DataMember]
    public string CorrelationId { get; set; }
```

```
    [DataMember]
    public string Message { get; set; }
  }
}
```

The DataContract attribute must precede each message class, and DataMember must decorate each field of the message class. The DataMember indicates that the field is part of the DataContract and is serializable. Note that the Protobuf language doesn't have a similar keyword for this. Only the message property is needed to declare a field to be part of the message. However, with WCF, there is no need to order fields for serialization like in the Protobuf language.

Listing 8-2 shows the definition of the CountryService class using ServicesContract and OperationContract attributes. This example includes a FaultContract typed ErrorContract, which is the type of the FaultContract returned to the client in case of error. This example is the simplest way to implement in WCF. No streaming is required.

Listing 8-2. CountryService Definition with WCF Including a FaultContract of Type ErrorContract

```
[ServiceContract]
public interface ICountryService
{
    [OperationContract]
    [FaultContract(typeof(ErrorContract))]
    Task<CountryReply> Get(CountryIdRequest request);

    [OperationContract(IsOneWay = true)]
    [FaultContract(typeof(ErrorContract))]
    Task Update(CountryUpdateRequest request);

    [OperationContract]
    [FaultContract(typeof(ErrorContract))]
    Task<CountryReply> GetAll();

    [OperationContract(IsOneWay = true)]
    [FaultContract(typeof(ErrorContract))]
    Task Delete(List<CountryIdRequest> requestList);
```

```
[OperationContract]
[FaultContract(typeof(ErrorContract))]
Task<List<CountryCreationReply>> Create(List<CountryCreationRequest>
requestList);
}
```

Unlike gRPC, WCF doesn't require you to send an empty message when expecting a response. With WCF, adding `IsOneWay = true` suffices to tell the client that the server won't respond. This example doesn't use any streaming feature with WCF and doesn't require complicated operations. But with gRPC, it's possible to implement streaming to pass a collection of data between the client and the server for better performance, and the goal of this section is promoting gRPC streaming features.

Looking at the service's configuration, we saw in Chapter 7 that it is easy to configure gRPC with options. With WCF, the configuration is complicated. You must configure the services in an XML configuration file. In this file, you declare services in a section called `services`. You define behaviors, such as a timeout or error details, in a `behaviors` section. Finally, you transport data, like with compression and bindings, in a `bindings` section.

Listing 8-3 shows a `CountryService` WCF configuration. It limits the size of messages to 6 MB and enables Brotli compression. It also limits the request execution time to 30 seconds. To limit the execution time, the configuration authorizes the metadata and error transport with a custom binding. This method allows transporting compressed data with the HTTP protocol.

Listing 8-3. Server-Side XML Configuration of the WCF Version of CountryService

```
<system.serviceModel>
  <services>
    <service behaviorConfiguration="WebServiceBehavior" name="Country
    Service.Web.Services.V1.CountryService">
      <endpoint binding="customBinding" bindingConfiguration="custom
      Binding_ICountryService" contract="CountryService.Web.Services.
      V1.ICountryService"/>
      <endpoint address="mex" binding="mexHttpBinding"
      contract="IMetadataExchange"/>
    </service>
  </services>
```

```xml
  <behaviors>
    <serviceBehaviors>
      <behavior name="WebServiceBehavior">
        <serviceMetadata httpGetEnabled="true"/>
        <serviceDebug includeExceptionDetailInFaults="true"/>
        <serviceTimeouts transactionTimeout="00:30:00"/>
      </behavior>
    </serviceBehaviors>
    <endpointBehaviors>
      <behavior name="RestBehavior">
        <webHttp helpEnabled="true"/>
      </behavior>
    </endpointBehaviors>
  </behaviors>
  <extensions>
    <bindingElementExtensions>
      <add name="brotliMessageEncoding" type="CountryService.Web.
      Compression.BrotliCompressionProvider, CountryService.Web.
      Compression, Version=4.0.0.0, Culture=neutral, PublicKeyToken=null"/>
    </bindingElementExtensions>
  </extensions>
  <bindings>
    <customBinding>
      <binding name="customBinding_ICountryService"
      maxBufferPoolSize="6291456" maxBufferSize="6291456"
      maxReceivedMessageSize="6291456" receiveTimeout="00:30:00"
      sendTimeout="00:30:00">
        <brotliMessageEncoding innerMessageEncoding="textMessageEncoding"/>
        <readerQuotas maxDepth="32" maxStringContentLength="6291456"
        maxArrayLength="6291456" maxBytesPerRead="6291456"
        maxNameTableCharCount="6291456"/>
      </binding>
    </customBinding>
  </bindings>
  <serviceHostingEnvironment aspNetCompatibilityEnabled="true" multipleSite
  BindingsEnabled="true"/>
</system.serviceModel>
```

On the client side, WCF requires a configuration as well by code or in XML like the server part, the configuration need to define the service URL, and the binding required to define the compression provider, as shown in Listing 8-4.

Listing 8-4. Client-Side XML Configuration of the WCF Version of CountryService

```
<system.serviceModel>
  <extensions>
    <bindingElementExtensions>
      <add name="brotliMessageEncoding" type="CountryService.Web.
      Compression.BrotliCompressionProvider, CountryService.Web.
      Compression, Version=4.0.0.0, Culture=neutral, PublicKeyToken=null"/>
    </bindingElementExtensions>
  </extensions>
  <bindings>
    <customBinding>
      <binding name="customBinding_ICountryService"
      receiveTimeout="00:30:00" sendTimeout="00:30:00">
        <brotliMessageEncoding innerMessageEncoding="textMessageEncoding"/>
        <httpTransport hostNameComparisonMode="StrongWildca
        rd" manualAddressing="False" maxBufferPoolSize="6291456"
        maxBufferSize="6291456" maxReceivedMessageSize="6291456" authentica
        tionScheme="Anonymous" bypassProxyOnLocal="False" realm=""/>
      </binding>
    </customBinding>
  </bindings>
  <client>
    <endpoint address="https://localhost:5001/CountryService.
    svc" binding="customBinding" bindingConfiguration="customBin
    ding_ICountryService" contract="CountryService.Web.Services.
    V1.ICountryService" name="customBinding_ICountryService"/>
    <metadata>
      <policyImporters>
```

```
    <extension type="CountryService.Web.Compression.
    BrotliCompressionProvider, CountryService.Web.Compression,
    Version=4.0.0.0, Culture=neutral, PublicKeyToken=null"/>
      </policyImporters>
    </metadata>
  </client>
</system.serviceModel>
```

As you can see, the configuration is heavy, and I don't really like it. gRPC simplifies configuration. Except for the compression and message size limit, you don't need to migrate that part.

For headers, I previously showed you how to read and write into *Trailers*, the equivalent of which in WCF is the MessageHeader. I also previously showed you that you can read incoming headers with the IncomingMessageHeader class and write outgoing headers with the OutgoingMessageHeader class. Listing 8-5 shows how to read and write a correlationId into headers on the server side through the WCF OperationContext class, similar to the ServerCallContext with gRPC. I also take this opportunity to show you how to expose your endpoints as we would have done with the CountryGrpcService class.

Listing 8-5. Read and Write a correlationId into Headers Server side and Expose Endpoints with WCF

```
using System.Collections.Generic;
using System.ServiceModel;
using System.ServiceModel.Activation;
using System.ServiceModel.Channels;
using System.Threading.Tasks;
using Apress.Sample.WCF.v1;

namespace CountryService.Web.Services.V1
{
    [ServiceBehavior(InstanceContextMode = InstanceContextMode.PerCall)]
    [AspNetCompatibilityRequirements(RequirementsMode = AspNet
    CompatibilityRequirementsMode.Allowed)]
    public class CountryService : ICountryService
```

```
{
    private CountryManagementService _countryManagementService;

    public InvoiceServices(CountryManagementService
    countryManagementService)
    {
        _countryManagementService = countryManagementService;
    }

    public async Task<IEnumerable<CountryReply>> GetAllAsync()
    {
        // Read incoming header
        HttpRequestMessageProperty requestProperty = (HttpRequest
        MessageProperty)OperationContext.Current.IncomingMessage
        Properties[HttpRequestMessageProperty.Name];
        string correlationId = requestProperty.Headers
        ["correlationId"];

        // Write outgoing header
        MessageHeader outGoingHeader = MessageHeader.CreateHeader
        ("correlationId", "http://Microsoft.WCF.Documentation",
        correlationId);              OperationContext.Current.
        OutgoingMessageHeaders.Add(outGoingHeader);

        return _countryManagementService.GetAllAsync();
    }
}
}
```

You will notice that WCF has quite a few attributes that do not exist in gRPC. You will not need to migrate them to gRPC, such as the ServiceBehavior and the AspNetCompatibilityRequirements attributes. The rest remains the same, such as the GetAllAsync() method's body and the dependency injection of the CountryManagementService service.

Client side, it's pretty much the same piece of code. Within an OperationContextScope, you can read headers through the same OperationContext object as server side, as shown in Listing 8-6.

Listing 8-6. Read and Write into Headers Client Side Through an
OperationContextScope

```
using System.Collections.Generic;
using System.ServiceModel;
using System.ServiceModel.Channels;
using System.Threading.Tasks;
using Apress.Sample.WCF.v1;

namespace TIO.Automation
{
    class Program
    {
        static async Task Main(string[] args)
        {
            using (CountryServiceClient service = new CountryServiceClient
            ("customBinding_ICountryService"))
            {
                using (OperationContextScope scope = new OperationContext
                Scope(service.InnerChannel))
                {
                    // Read incoming header
                    HttpRequestMessageProperty requestProperty = (Http
                    RequestMessageProperty)OperationContext.Current.
                    IncomingMessageProperties[HttpRequestMessage
                    Property.Name];
                    string correlationId = requestProperty.
                    Headers["correlationId"];

                    // Write outgoing header
                    MessageHeader outGoingHeader = MessageHeader.
                    CreateHeader("correlationId", "http://Microsoft.WCF.
                    Documentation", correlationId);
                    OperationContext.Current.OutgoingMessageHeaders.
                    Add(outGoingHeader);
```

```
        IEnumerable<CountryReply> listClient = await service.
        GetAllAsync();
                }
            }
        }
    }
}
```

As you can see, for this part (headers), there are no considerable changes to make (only read/write classes differ).

Migrating a duplex or full-duplex WCF service is not complicated but cannot be done with gRPC in the same way. Unlike WCF, if you remember the previous chapter, gRPC doesn't have the notion of callback. A callback is a function that is executed by another function when a certain event happens. Streaming works without any callback, but let's see how would look like the Create() (which is a bidirectional streaming service) RPC method that accepts as a request parameter a streamed collection of CountryCreationRequest objects and sends back a streamed collection of CountryCreationReply objects.

Listing 8-7 shows the CreateAsync() method invoked by the client, and the server replies with a callback that notifies the client of the state of the creation. The concrete implementation of CreateAsync() is defined server side, and the concrete implementation of the ReplyAsync() callback method is defined client side. This process is the same for duplex services (server streaming). A callback is needed to notify the client.

Listing 8-7. WCF version of the Create Function Defined over a Full-Duplex Service

```
using System.ServiceModel;
using System.Threading.Tasks;
using Apress.Sample.WCF.v1;

namespace TIO.WebServices.Services.Interfaces
{
    [ServiceContract(SessionMode = SessionMode.Required,
    CallbackContract = typeof(ICountryServiceCallback))]
    public interface ICountryService
    {
        [OperationContract(IsOneWay = true)]
```

```
    Task CreateAsync(CountryCreationRequest request);
}

[ServiceContract]
public interface ICountryServiceCallback
{
    [OperationContract(IsOneWay = true)]
    Task ReplyAsync(CountryCreationReply reply);
}
}
```

gRPC streaming makes the code simpler compared to WCF, and I love it. You need to understand here that there is no callback to be implemented. You can easily migrate the server-side and client-side parts of your WCF application to gRPC using the `IServerStreamWriter` and `IAsyncStreamReader` interfaces, as I showed you in the Chapter 5.

For more guidance on migration from WCF to gRPC, the following excellent GitHub repository provides complete code samples of WCF services migrated to gRPC: `https:// github.com/dotnet-architecture/grpc-for-wcf-developers`.

One more thing: if you are a WCF developer and want to learn gRPC without learning Protobuf syntax, there is a great tool named `protobuf-net.Grpc` that allows you to create a gRPC service from WCF `DataContract` and `ServiceContract`. I personally don't use it, because I like Protobuf. If you are interested, you can read the tutorial on the `protobuf-net.Grpc` website: `https://protobuf-net.github.io/protobuf-net.Grpc/`.

Summary

In this short chapter, I have shown you the similarities and differences between WCF and gRPC. You have learned how to switch from WCF code-first orientation to Protobuf's schema-first orientation, how to switch from WCF headers to trailers, how to get rid of heavy XML configuration, and how to do away with duplex service callbacks to use gRPC streaming service. From there, you will be able to migrate to gRPC easily! You are now ready to build a complete gRPC application, and that's the goal of the next chapter!

CHAPTER 9

Import and Display Data with ASP.NET Core Razor Pages, Hosted Services, and gRPC

You have finally arrived at the chapter in which you will create a complete but simple application. I will teach you how to develop a web interface for managing a list of countries. Imagine a wiki, for example a wiki countries, that will be designed with ASP. NET Core Razor Pages for the web interface, a hosted service running in the background, gRPC as an API allowing you to manipulate the data between the database and the web interface, SQL Server for storing data, and Entity Framework Core for data access. Along with these steps, I'll also teach you some concepts such as how to layer (architecture) an application properly. This chapter covers the following:

- Scenario explanation
- Create and layer the ASP.NET Core gRPC application
- Set up an SQL Server database and use Entity Framework Core to access data
- Write the business logic and expose the Country gRPC service
- Create and layer the ASP.NET Core Razor application
- Upload a data file with a form and display and manage data on Razor Pages

© Anthony Giretti 2022
A. Giretti, *Beginning gRPC with ASP.NET Core 6*, https://doi.org/10.1007/978-1-4842-8008-9_9

Scenario Explanation

To help you fully understand what I will show you in this chapter, I will describe the overall solution to achieve our ends. We will have the following components:

1. A web page with Razor Pages to upload from a JSON file the list of countries from our wiki.

2. A second web page with Razor Pages to display the list of countries and delete them with a check box.

3. A third web page to update the description of a country

4. A background task (hosted service) that will allow you to manage the uploaded JSON file to feed the database with the countries data. This step is essential because it provides no blocking on the website while countries information are stored in the database.

5. A gRPC service to manage country data.

6. A SQL Server database on Azure, and Entity Framework Core, which is an *object-relational mapping (ORM)* tool that allows developers to abstract SQL queries into LINQ queries and create the database from code.

Figure 9-1 shows the solution architecture.

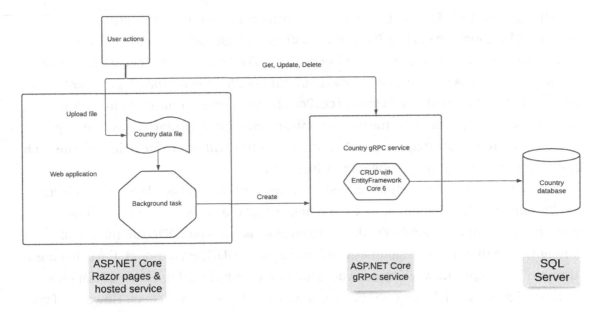

Figure 9-1. *The Countries wiki architecture diagram*

Don't be intimidated by the complexity of the diagram! We will gradually go through each step of the development of the application in detail, and I will explain to you why I offer you this solution in this way, it is promised you will like!

Create and Layer the ASP.NET Core gRPC Application

In this section we'll create our Country gRPC service with the following layers:

- CountryService.gRPC

- CountryService.DAL

- CountryService.BLL

- CountryService.Domain

Chapter 2 showed you how to create a gRPC service from the ASP.NET Core gRPC template, but now I want to show you good programming practices for adding C# projects to the solution in a manner that separates code responsibilities that will apply to the whole solution we'll design here.

The CountryService.gRPC layer is the C# project that contains the gRPC services. The CountryService.DAL project will contain all code related to data access. It's commonly named the *data access layer (DAL)*. The CountryService.BLL layer will include all business services, and is also commonly called the *business logic layer (BLL)*. The fourth layer, named CountryService.Domain, will contain only domain objects, meaning all classes shared by the whole application, regardless of the layer. This layer will also include all abstractions, such as interfaces that will be useful to decorrelate each layer from another by using dependency injection.

These four layers form what is called an *N-tier* application. Each layer (C# project) can be reused independently from each other, except the domain layer that contains abstractions. If you are familiar with the *domain-driven design (DDD)* architectural concept, note that my code samples won't implement DDD, even though I'm using the "domain" concept; my way to teach you good practices by layering your application is more straightforward. It's a good start, for now, to make your code clean. However, if you want to dive more into DDD architecture, the tutorial at the following link clearly teaches DDD: https://dzone.com/articles/ddd-part-i-introduction.

To create and add a DAL, a BLL, and a domain layer, right-click the solution name in Visual Studio (CountryService here), then select Add and click New Project, as shown in Figure 9-2.

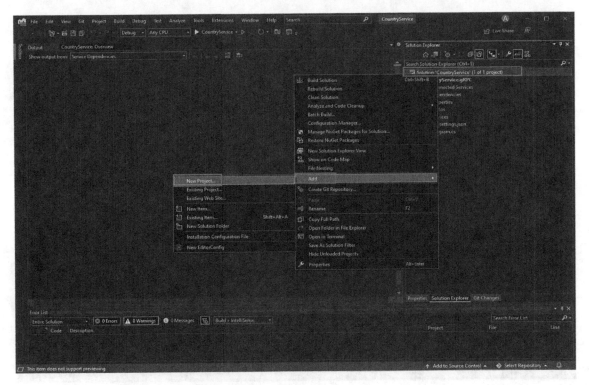

Figure 9-2. *Add a new project to the solution*

As shown in Figure 9-3, use the drop-down menus to filter the list and locate
the Class Library template. Create the first project (layer) using the template, as
demonstrated in previous chapters (e.g., Chapter 2), and then repeat the operation for
each of the other application layers.

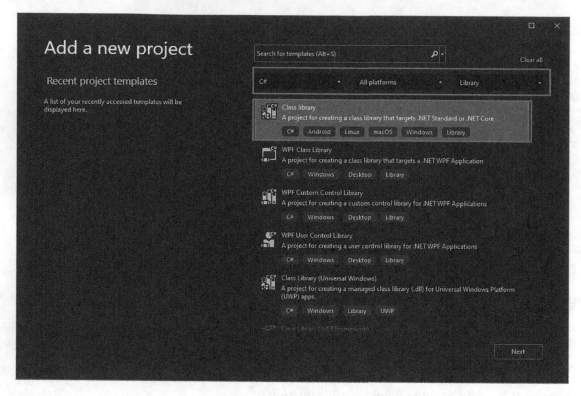

Figure 9-3. *Filtering to reveal the Class Library template*

Once you are done, the solution should look like as Figure 9-4 shows.

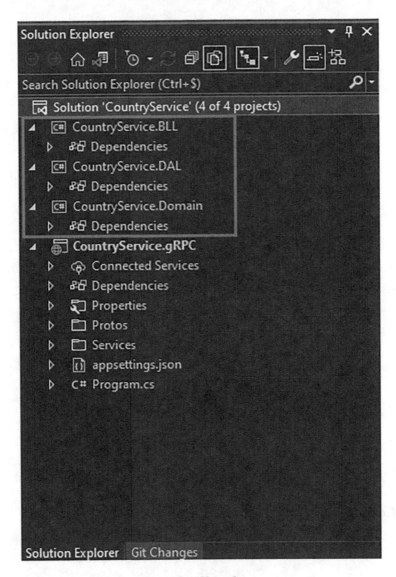

Figure 9-4. *Country gRPC service with all its layers*

Finally, we will define the relationships (dependencies) between each layer. The domain layer is at the top of the hierarchy (meaning that all the other layers depend on it), then comes the DAL BLL layers; they do not depend on each other since the Domain layer references the abstractions of each. The BLL layer only needs to know the abstractions of the DAL layer. Finally, the ASP.NET Core gRPC application layer depends on the DAL and BLL layers to configure the dependency injection of the latter. Figure 9-5 shows the dependency diagram.

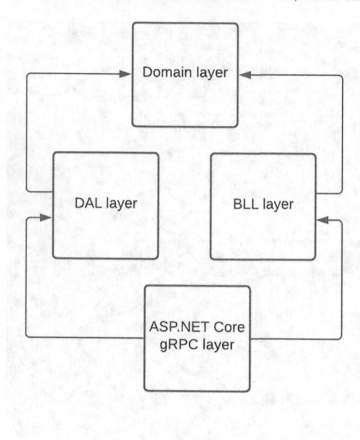

A depends on B

Layer A ⟶ Layer B

Figure 9-5. *Country gRPC service dependency diagram*

Adding a dependency can be done with just a few clicks. Open the Dependencies submenu of the project to which you want to add a dependency, then choose Add Project Reference and select the project you want to add as a dependency, as shown respectively in Figure 9-6 and Figure 9-7.

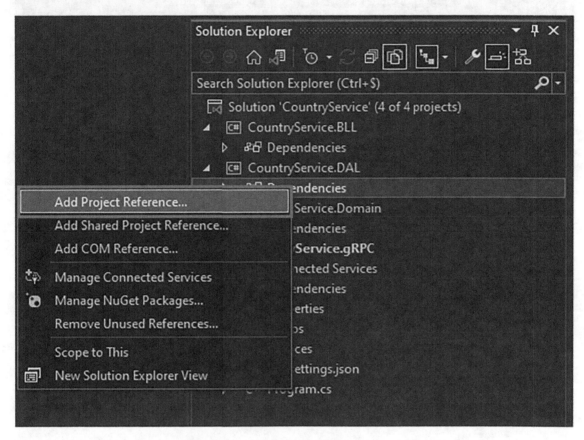

Figure 9-6. *Add Project Preference option from the context menu*

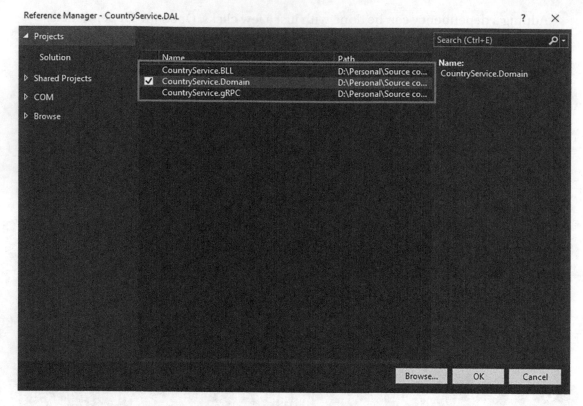

Figure 9-7. *Select and add a dependency to a layer*

If you have referenced dependencies correctly according to the dependency diagram shown in Figure 9-5, the CountryService.gRPC dependency tree should look like as Figure 9-8 shows.

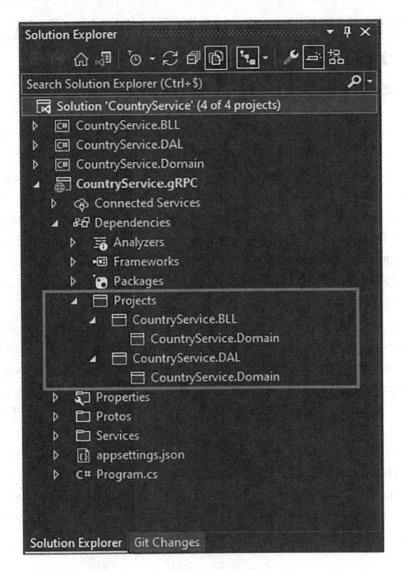

Figure 9-8. *The* `CountryService.gRPC` *dependency tree*

Now the solution is set up correctly. The next step is to set up the SQL Server database and implement the data access layer (DAL) with Entity Framework Core.

Set Up a SQL Server Database and Use Entity Framework Core to Access Data

Set Up a SQL Server Database

Let's start by building the foundation for our app, using the famous Microsoft SQL Server database. SQL Server is a *Relational Database Management System (RDBMS)* based on the *Structured Query Language (SQL)*. SQL Server supports management of queries made by users, most often through an application, as we will do here. However, to facilitate the development of our application, we will use the object-relational mapper (O/RM) Entity Framework Core, which will allow us to abstract SQL queries with *Language-Integrated Query (LINQ)*, so you will not have to write any SQL queries. The choice here of Microsoft SQL Server is natural, because .NET has a natural and long-standing affinity with it, and what is nice is that with the installation of Visual Studio, you get the Express version of SQL Server at the same time—it is a free version of SQL Server that is used for development purposes. However, although Visual Studio already has the necessary tools to view SQL Server databases, I recommend that you install and use *Microsoft SQL Server Management Studio (SSMS)*. This tool will allow you to do more afterward view and design a database, as it is complete in terms of features. The following link will enable you to consult its complete documentation but also to download it: `https://docs.microsoft.com/en-us/sql/ssms/download-sql-server-management-studio-ssms?view=sql-server-ver15`.

After you have installed SSMS, use the following server name to connect to the SQL Server Express database: (LocalDB)\MSSQLLocalDB. Figure 9-9 shows how to connect to the SQL Server Express database.

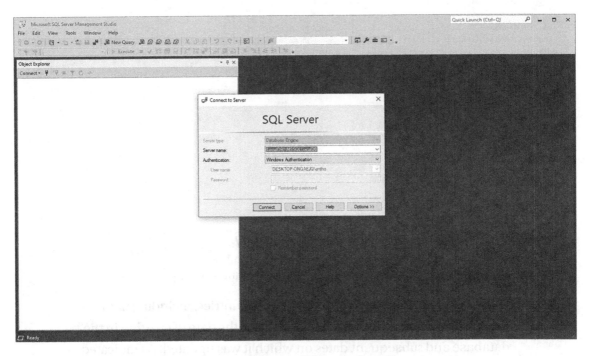

***Figure 9-9.** Connecting to the SQL Server Express database*

We'll return to SQL Server Management Studio later, once the database is created.

Using Entity Framework Core to Access Data

Entity Framework Core allows you to

- Design the database by code

- Seed the database by code

- Query the database with LINQ queries

I'll walk you through these steps. What's excellent about Entity Framework Core is that its documentation is easy to understand and use to develop your application, which I'm sure you'll appreciate as much as I do.

Design the Database by Code

To build our database, we need first to design its model. Figure 9-10 shows the model that represents three linked SQL tables and their respective properties.

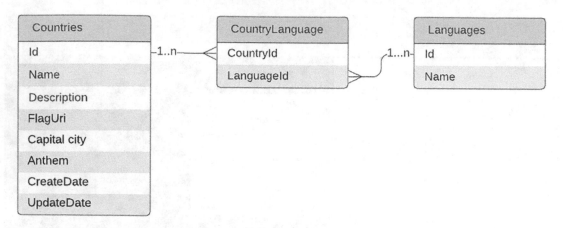

Figure 9-10. *The country service database model*

The following list describes the tables shown in Figure 9-10:

- `Countries`: Contains the properties of all countries, including name, description, capital city, anthem name, and the date of creation in the database and subsequent dates on which it was updated. As indicated by the FlagUri property, I chose to store the Uniform Resource Identifer (URI) [not URL] for locating the image of the country's flag instead of storing the actual flag image, to save space in the database. Flag photos are stored in a *content delivery network (CDN)*, a server that only serves static items, such as images, for performance purposes.

- `Languages`: Stores a language list that is used for reference purposes.

- `CountryLanguage`: Stores for a given country the languages spoken in that country. Some countries have several official languages or commonly used languages. In SQL, this table is a *many-to-many relationship* table.

Let's design these tables in C# entities that are used to generate the SQL database and mapped to the generated SQL tables while querying the database. Listing 9-1 shows the C# entity modeling.

Listing 9-1. C# Entities Model

```
namespace CountryService.DAL.Database.Entities;

public class Country
{
```

```
    public int Id { get; set; }
    public string Name { get; set; }
    public string Description { get; set; }
    public string FlagUri { get; set; }
    public string CapitalCity { get; set; }
    public string Anthem { get; set; }
    public DateTime CreateDate { get; set; }
    public DateTime? UpdateDate { get; set; }
    public ICollection<Language> Languages { get; set; }
}

public class Language
{
    public int Id { get; set; }
    public string Name { get; set; }
    public Icollection<Country> Countries { get; }
}

public class CountryLanguage
{
    public int CountryId { get; set; }
    public Country Country { get; set; }

    public int LanguageId { get; set; }
    public Language Language { get; set; }
}
```

To use Entity Framework Core will all its features, we have to download the following Nuget packages with the Visual Studio Package manager window in the CountryService. DAL project:

```
Install-Package Microsoft.EntityFrameworkCore.SqlServer
Install-Package Microsoft.EntityFrameworkCore.Tools
Install-Package Microsoft.EntityFrameworkCore.Design
```

Note   Installation of the `Microsoft.EntityFramework.Tools` package into the `CountryService.gRPC` project is required for the initial database creation and update.

313

Once you have installed these packages, we must define a class (database context class) that describes C# entities as entities queryable by to the SQL Server database and describes the SQL model to generate from these entities. These entities are commonly named "proxy" classes, DbSet in the Entity Framework Core nomenclature, a kind of interface between the app and the database.

We'll name that database context class CountryContext and inherit it from the DbContext class, the Entity Framework base class. The many-to-many relationship needs some configuration in a method named OnModelCreating(). Many-to-many relationships are pretty tricky because we will need to perform insertions into several tables while creating a country. I will show that a bit further. To learn more about many-to-many relationships with Entity Framework Core, you can read the tutorial here: https://docs.microsoft.com/en-us/ef/core/modeling/relationships?tabs=fluent-api%2Cfluent-api-simple-key%2Csimple-key#indirect-many-to-many-relationships.

Listing 9-2 shows the CountryContext class. Note that I placed the Microsoft.EntityFrameworkCore using statement in a GlobalUsings.cs file. You can find its content in Listing 9-8 at the end of this section.

Note   In each section in this chapter, I'll place using statements in a GlobalUsings.cs file that you can peruse at the end of the section. There is one GlobalUsings.cs file per C# project.

Listing 9-2. The CountryContext Class

```
namespace CountryService.DAL.Database;

public class CountryContext : DbContext
{
    public CountryContext(DbContextOptions<CountryContext> options) :
    base(options)
    {
    }
```

```
protected override void OnConfiguring(DbContextOptionsBuilder
opBuilder)
{
    opBuilder.UseSqlServer(@"Data Source=(LocalDB)\MSSQLLocalDB;Initial
    Catalog=CountryService;");
}

public DbSet<Country> Countries { get; set; }
public DbSet<Language> Languages { get; set; }
public DbSet<CountryLanguage> CountryLanguages { get; set; }

protected override void OnModelCreating(ModelBuilder modelBuilder)
{
    modelBuilder.Entity<CountryLanguage>()
                .HasKey(t => new { t.CountryId, t.LanguageId });

    modelBuilder.Entity<CountryLanguage>()
                .HasOne(cl => cl.Country)
                .WithMany(c => c.CountryLanguages)
                .HasForeignKey(cl => cl.CountryId);

    modelBuilder.Entity<CountryLanguage>()
                .HasOne(cl => cl.Language)
                .WithMany(c => c.CountryLanguages)
                .HasForeignKey(cl => cl.LanguageId);
}
}
```

Note that I used the LocalDB's connection string there, as shown in the previous section. If you are using a remote SQL Server database, please replace this connection string with the remote server's connection string.

The OnConfiguring() method allows you to set the SQL Server connection string to create the database from the entities model on your local development machine. To perform this operation, open the Package Manager Console window (from the View panel at the top screen of Visual Studio), select the CountryService.DAL project, and type the command **Add-Migration Initial**, as shown in Figure 9-11.

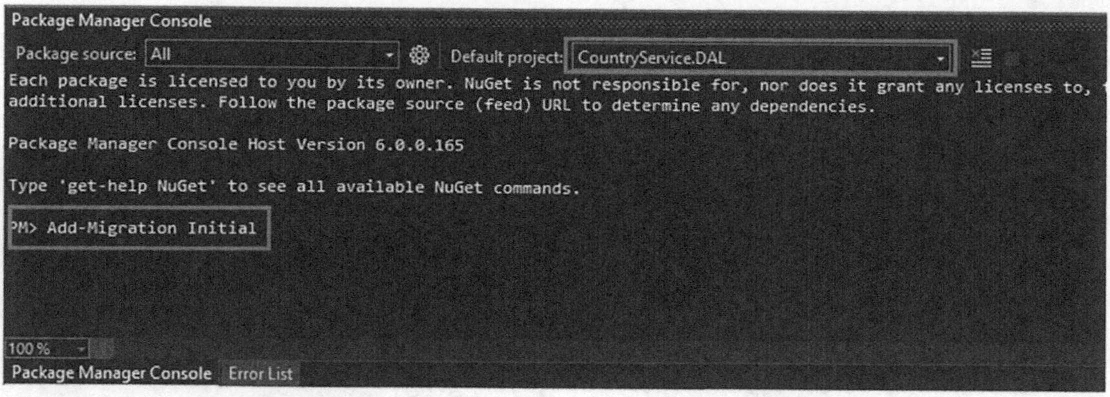

Figure 9-11. *Database initial creation*

If the operation succeeds, the console will output `Build succeed`, and Visual Studio will open the C# script to create the database in the folder named Migrations suffixed by _Initial.cs, as shown in Figure 9-12.

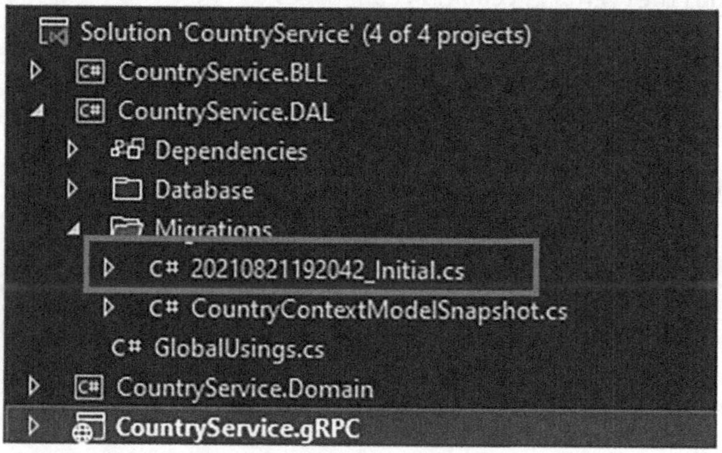

Figure 9-12. *The database initial creation file*

The CountryContextModelSnapshot.cs file is a snapshot of the current CountryServiceContext class for backup purposes.

The last step is to create the database on SQL Server from that file. The following command allows that: `Update-Database`. Figure 9-13 shows that the operation succeeded, and the output mentions the initial creation file applied.

```
Package Manager Console
Package source:  All          ▾  ⚙   Default project:  CountryService.DAL              ▾   ⟩≡
PM> Update-Database
Build started...
Build succeeded.
Applying migration '20210821192042_Initial'.
Done.
PM>
```

Figure 9-13.   *The initial migration file applied*

Looking at the database with SQL Server Management Studio, as shown in Figure 9-14, we can now appreciate our great work. We have created a SQL database with some C# code and some commands. This demonstrates the simplicity of Entity Framework Core, and that's why I love it! Note in Figure 9-14 that Entity Framework Core has created a table named `_EFMigrationsHistory`, which is a table that keeps a history of the evolving changes. This is needed for further database model updates.

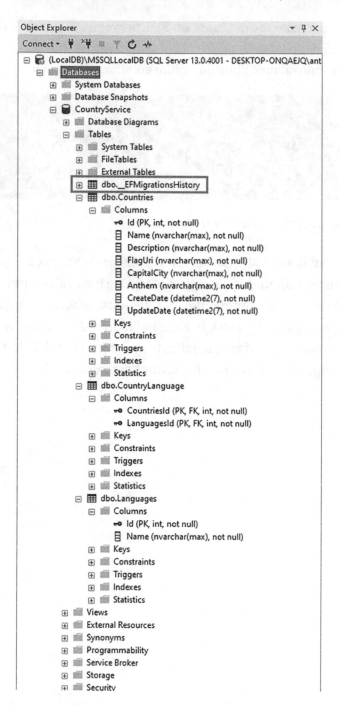

Figure 9-14. *The* CountryService *database created*

If it seems to you that Entity Framework Core is doing magic, this is a normal reaction. It implements many conventions that allow a minimum of code to see none to infer, for example, primary and foreign keys without defining them explicitly (identical field names are linked automatically between two tables for example). I won't describe all the conventions here. However, if you want to know more, you can check out the following blog: https://www.learnentityframeworkcore.com/conventions.

Seed the Database by Code

The CountryService database will be fed from a file that contains all countries' data. But the country data file won't contain languages' names, only their ID. Consequently, we need to feed the database with languages references (languages name) into the Languages table specifically. In this way, we will be able to identify what ID refers to. It looks awkward, but it happens very often: getting an ID of a particular thing from a data source that doesn't contain essential data and then identifying what the ID refers to. In our example, we will feed the Languages table from code with Entity Framework Core again, and you'll see that it will be convenient and simple.

Let's go back to the CountryContext class and add initial data for the Languages table within the OnModelCreating() method, as shown in Listing 9-3.

Listing 9-3. Seed the Languages SQL Table by Code

```
namespace CountryService.DAL.Database;

public class CountryContext : DbContext
{
    public CountryContext(DbContextOptions<CountryContext> options) :
    base(options)
    {
    }

    protected override void OnConfiguring(DbContextOptionsBuilder
    opBuilder)
    {
        opBuilder.UseSqlServer(@"Data Source=(LocalDB)\MSSQLLocalDB;Initial
        Catalog=CountryService;");
    }
```

```csharp
public DbSet<Country> Countries { get; set; }
public DbSet<Language> Languages { get; set; }
public DbSet<CountryLanguage> CountryLanguages { get; set; }

protected override void OnModelCreating(ModelBuilder modelBuilder)
{
    modelBuilder.Entity<CountryLanguage>()
            .HasKey(t => new { t.CountryId, t.LanguageId });

    modelBuilder.Entity<CountryLanguage>()
            .HasOne(cl => cl.Country)
            .WithMany(c => c.CountryLanguages)
            .HasForeignKey(cl => cl.CountryId);

    modelBuilder.Entity<CountryLanguage>()
            .HasOne(cl => cl.Language)
            .WithMany(c => c.CountryLanguages)
            .HasForeignKey(cl => cl.LanguageId);

    modelBuilder.Entity<Language>()
                                .HasData(
                                    new Language { Id = 1,
                                    Name = "English" },
                                    new Language { Id = 2,
                                    Name = "French" },
                                    new Language { Id = 3,
                                    Name = "Spanish" }
                                );
}
}
```

From there, we have to create a new migration with the command we used before to create the database, but this time, we'll name the migration to make it more transparent: Add-Migration SeedInitialData.

This is the same operation in the previous section; a file suffixed by _SeedInitialData has been created, and we need now to apply it to the database as we did before with the Update-Database command.

After querying the database, we should see the Languages table fed as shown in
Figure 9-15.

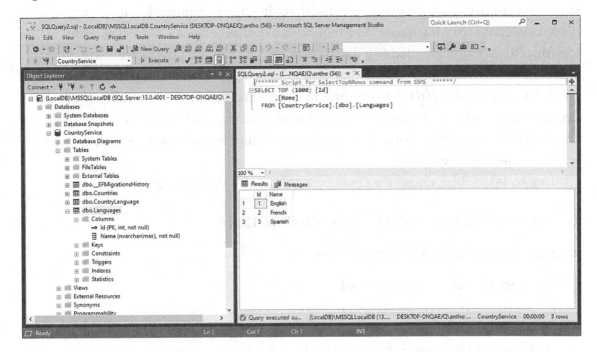

Figure 9-15. *The Languages table fed*

Query the Database with LINQ Queries

We have created our database, fed with reference data. Now we have to make the queries
using LINQ to carry out the following CRUD operations:

- Create a country

- Update a country

- Delete a country

- Retrieve a country

- Retrieve all countries

In the CountryService.DAL, let's create a folder named Repositories that will
contain only the concrete implementation of the data access layer. There, we will
create a class called CountryRepository that will consume the CountryContext class.
I suggest you start with the interface that the CountryRepository class will implement

in the CountryService.Domain layer. In this way, you'll form the habit of *defining the contract before its implementation.* Because good practice is to return domain objects from a repository, we need to create these domain objects required for our contract (CountryRepository interface). As a reminder, a domain object is not necessarily identical to an entity mapped to a database table. The domain objects will have minor differences with the entities of the data access layer and they are commonly called *Data Transfer Object (DTO).* In our example, we will only have one domain object, CountryModel, which will contain everything needed to define a country. This is why creating a domain object from one or more raw entities is good practice. Don't worry, it will become clearer very soon!

In a Models folder, create the CountryModel class as shown in Listing 9-4.

Listing 9-4. The CountryModel Domain Object

```
namespace CountryService.Domain.Models;

public record class CountryModel
{
    public int Id { get; init; }
    public string Name { get; init; }
    public string Description { get; init; }
    public string FlagUri { get; init; }
    public string CapitalCity { get; init; }
    public string Anthem { get; init; }
    public IEnumerable<string> Languages { get; init; }
}
```

As you can see, I'm using a record class instead of a regular class. I want to keep it immutable and a reference type; otherwise, we could have used a record struct. This is the first difference with the data access layer's Country entity, and the second difference is that we don't need in our business logic any dates and we don't need to send the client these dates either. Finally, we don't need to keep the language ID in my domain object. Keeping the language name (List<string> Languages) is sufficient.

Listing 9-5 shows the CreateCountryModel class, which we will use later to create a country. I'm building it here because I need to know its type to define the CountryRepository interface.

Listing 9-5. The CreateCountryModel Domain Object

```
namespace CountryService.Domain.Models;

public record class CreateCountryModel
{
    public string Name { get; set; }
    public string Description { get; set; }
    public string FlagUri { get; set; }
    public string CapitalCity { get; set; }
    public string Anthem { get; set; }
    public DateTime CreatedDate { get; set; }
    public IEnumerable<int> Languages { get; set; }
}
```

Listing 9-6 shows the UpdateCountryModel class that will be used later but needs to be defined now for the same reason as the CreateCountryModel.

Listing 9-6. The UpdateCountryModel Domain Object

```
namespace CountryService.Domain.Models;

public record class UpdateCountryModel
{
    public int Id { get; set; }
    public string Description { get; set; }
    public DateTime UpdateDate { get; set; }
}
```

It's time to create the contract that defines the Country repository. Listing 9-7 shows the ICountryRepository interface.

Listing 9-7. The ICountryRepository Interface

```
namespace CountryService.Domain.Repositories;

public interface ICountryRepository
{
    Task<int> CreateAsync(CreateCountryModel countryToCreate);
    Task<int> UpdateAsync(UpdateCountryModel countryToUpdate);
```

```
    Task<int> DeleteAsync(int id);
    Task<CountryModel> GetAsync(int id);
    Task<IEnumerable<CountryModel>> GetAllAsync();
}
```

In most cases, data access is done on external resources, and it is good practice that these accesses be asynchronous (*Task*) because we want to prevent thread blocking if this same resource takes time to respond.

If you have followed the previous instructions correctly, you should have the same elements in your CountryService.Domain project as shown in Figure 9-16.

Figure 9-16. *The CountryService.Domain layer with its content*

After following the instructions correctly, the GlobalUsings.cs file should look like Listing 9-8.

Listing 9-8. The CountryService.Domain GloblalUsings.cs File

```
global using CountryService.Domain.Models;
```

We can now create the concrete implementation of the `CountryRepository` class using LINQ, as shown in Listing 9-9.

Listing 9-9. The `CountryRepository` Concrete Implementation

```
namespace CountryService.DAL.Repositories;

public class CountryRepository : ICountryRepository
{
    private CountryContext _countryContext { get;set; }

    public CountryRepository(CountryContext countryContext)
    {
        _countryContext = countryContext;
    }

    public async Task<int> CreateAsync(CreateCountryModel countryToCreate)
    {
        var country = new Country
        {
            Name = countryToCreate.Name,
            Description = countryToCreate.Description,
            CapitalCity = countryToCreate.CapitalCity,
            Anthem = countryToCreate.Anthem,
            FlagUri = countryToCreate.FlagUri,
            CreateDate = countryToCreate.CreatedDate,
            CountryLanguages = countryToCreate.Languages.Select(x => new
            CountryLanguage { LanguageId = x }).ToList()
        };

        await _countryContext.Countries.AddAsync(country);
        await _countryContext.SaveChangesAsync();

        return country.Id;
    }
```

```csharp
public async Task<int> UpdateAsync(UpdateCountryModel countryToUpdate)
{
    var country = new Country
    {
        Id = countryToUpdate.Id,
        Description = countryToUpdate.Description,
        UpdateDate = countryToUpdate.UpdateDate
    };

    _countryContext.Entry(country).Property(p => p.Description).
    IsModified = true;
    _countryContext.Entry(country).Property(p => p.UpdateDate).
    IsModified = true;
    return await _countryContext.SaveChangesAsync();
}
public async Task<int> DeleteAsync(int id)
{
    var country = new Country
    {
        Id = id
    };

    _countryContext.Entry(country).State = EntityState.Deleted;
    return await _countryContext.SaveChangesAsync();
}
public async Task<CountryModel> GetAsync(int id) =>
    await _countryContext.Countries
                    .AsNoTracking()
                    .ToDomain()
                    .FirstOrDefaultAsync(x => x.Id == id);

public async Task<IEnumerable<CountryModel>> GetAllAsync()    =>
    await _countryContext.Countries
                    .AsNoTracking()
                    .ToDomain()
                    .ToListAsync();
}
```

Let's move onto the explanations of the previous code.

The `CreateAsync()` method is quite simple. It involves mapping between the domain object `CreateCountryModel` and the `Country` entity. However, thanks to the magic of Entity Framework Core, you can see that adding a `CountryLanguage` element is to say the association of a country and a language is done in the simplest way possible. I only needed to set the `LanguageId` property because I didn't know the `CountryId` value at this step. Entity Framework Core takes care of setting the `CountryId` when the `Country` entity is created in the database. Amazing, isn't it? Then I invoke the `AddAsync()` method, which is added to the Entity Framework Core context and allows synchronization with the database through the `SaveChangesAsync()` method. The return value is the `CountryId`.

The `UpdateAsync()` method is a bit special. Here, I needed to instantiate an entity `Country` with its Id. It was required to identify what country I needed to update and the properties I wanted to update: `Description` and `UpdateDate`. To tell Entity Framework Core that these fields need to be updated, I used the method `Property(p => p.{PropertyToUpdate}).IsModified = true` before invoking the `SaveChangesAsync()` method. The return value is the SQL affected rows.

The `DeleteAsync()` method principle is similar, but instead of updating some properties, we are deleting the whole entity from the Entity Framework Core context with the following instruction: `{EntityToDelete}.State = EntityState.Deleted`. The `SaveChangesAsync()` is again in charge of sending the instruction to the database. The return value is the SQL affected rows.

`GetAsync()` and `GetAllAsync()` are pretty similar. The first method returns a single `CountryModel` object using the `FirstOrDefault()` LINQ method, and the second one returns a collection of `CountryModel` using the `ToListAsync()` LINQ method. I applied, on both methods, the `AsNoTracking()` method, which is used to tell Entity Framework Core that it doesn't need to track the entity requested and saves performance because we are returning it to the client. It won't be updated further in the same HTTP request. If you want to learn more about *tracking*, you can read the following tutorial: `https://docs.microsoft.com/en-us/ef/core/change-tracking/`. I have also applied a custom method, an extension method, `ToDomain()`, to not repeat the mapping operation from a `Country` entity to a `CountryModel` domain object. Listing 9-10 shows the `CountryLanguageMapper` class.

Listing 9-10. The CountryLanguageMapper Class

```
namespace CountryService.DAL.Mappers;

public static class CountryLanguageMapper
{
    public static IQueryable<CountryModel> ToDomain(this
IQueryable<Country> countries) =>
        countries.Select(x => new CountryModel
        {
            Id = x.Id,
            Name = x.Name,
            Description = x.Description,
            CapitalCity = x.CapitalCity,
            Anthem = x.Anthem,
            FlagUri = x.FlagUri,
            Languages = x.CountryLanguages.Select(y => y.Language.Name)
        });
}
```

And there you go! Our repository is ready and implemented with the best practices. It was easy thanks to Entity Framework Core. We will move on to developing the service layer and the ASP.NET Core gRPC layer. If you have followed everything correctly (and I'm sure you did), the CountryService.DAL project should like Figure 9-17.

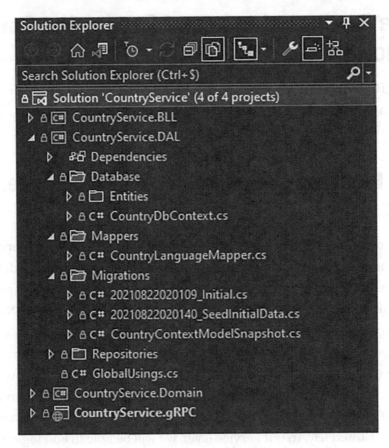

Figure 9-17. *The CountryService.DAL project and its content*

The GlobalUsings.cs file should look like Listing 9-11.

Listing 9-11. The CountryService.DAL GloblalUsings.cs File

```
global using Microsoft.EntityFrameworkCore;
global using CountryService.Domain.Repositories;
global using CountryService.DAL.Mappers;
global using CountryService.DAL.Database;
global using CountryService.Domain.Models;
global using CountryService.DAL.Database.Entities;
```

Write the Business Logic and Expose the Country gRPC Microservice

Our Country gRPC service is already well advanced. We will write the business logic of our application in the service layer, more precisely in the `CountryService.BLL` project, before writing the ASP.NET Core gRPC layer.

Write the Business Logic into the CountryService. BLL Layer

Now let's go to our service layer to write the `CountryServices` class. This service will expose CRUD actions through objects from domains that we have already defined. In addition to these CRUD operations, a particular business logic to be implemented here is the reason this layer exists: it provides an intermediary between the ASP.NET Core layer exposed to the client and the raw data received from a data source. By consuming the `CountryRepository` by dependency injection via its `ICountryRepository` interface, we will be able to abstract access to data at the service layer, which will allow greater flexibility. For example, when implementing unit tests, the service layer won't be aware of the existence of Entity Framework Core (and it doesn't need it), and the test will be more straightforward. Concretely, in our service layer, we will be able to add logic allowing us to handle the integers returned by the `DeleteAsync()` and `UpdateAsync()` operations; remember, these are the SQL affected rows, and the client does not need to know how many rows have been affected, but rather whether these operations were successful (affected rows > 0) or failed (affected rows <= 0). So, understand that the service layer for some of its operations returns a boolean value that will be used to condition the gRPC status in the ASP.NET Core gRPC layer. Easy, isn't it? Listing 9-12 shows the definition of the `ICountryServices` contract in the `CountryService.Domain` layer.

Listing 9-12. The `ICountryServices` Interface Definition

```
namespace CountryService.Domain.Services;

public interface ICountryServices
{
    Task<int> CreateAsync(CreateCountryModel countryToCreate);
    Task<bool> UpdateAsync(UpdateCountryModel countryToUpdate);
```

```
    Task<bool> DeleteAsync(int id);
    Task<CountryModel> GetAsync(int id);
    Task<IEnumerable<CountryModel>> GetAllAsync();
}
```

Listing 9-13 shows the concrete implementation of the CountryServices class.

Listing 9-13. The CountryServices Concrete Implementation

```
namespace CountryService.BLL.Services;

public class CountryServices : ICountryServices
{
    private readonly ICountryRepository _countryRepository;

    public CountryServices(ICountryRepository countryRepository)
    {
        _countryRepository = countryRepository;
    }

    public async Task<int> CreateAsync(CreateCountryModel
    countryToCreate) =>
        await _countryRepository.CreateAsync(countryToCreate);

    public async Task<bool> UpdateAsync(UpdateCountryModel
    countryToUpdate) =>
        await _countryRepository.UpdateAsync(countryToUpdate) > 0;

    public async Task<bool> DeleteAsync(int id) =>
        await _countryRepository.DeleteAsync(id) > 0;

    public async Task<CountryModel> GetAsync(int id) =>
        await _countryRepository.GetAsync(id);

    public async Task<IEnumerable<CountryModel>> GetAllAsync() =>
        await _countryRepository.GetAllAsync();
}
```

I wanted to keep the logic simple here, to show the principle of encapsulating business logic in a separate layer, but, if you wish, you can, for example, add logging with the ILogger interface, or add caching with the IMemoryCache interface. You can read the following tutorial if you are interested in further information about caching: https://docs.microsoft.com/en-us/aspnet/core/performance/caching/memory?view=aspnetcore-6.0.

At this point, your CountryService.BLL project should look like Figure 9-18.

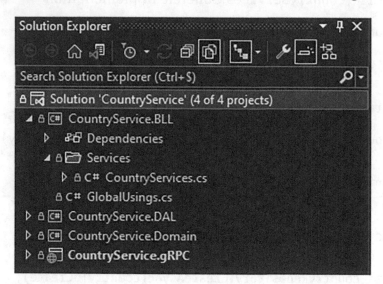

Figure 9-18. The CountryService.BLL and its content

The GlobalUsings.cs file should look like Listing 9-14.

Listing 9-14. The CountryService.BLL GloblalUsings.cs File

```
global using CountryService.Domain.Models;
global using CountryService.Domain.Services;
global using CountryService.Domain.Repositories;
```

Write the Country gRPC Service

We can now write our ASP.NET Core gRPC layer. To begin with, let's take our country. proto file and adapt it to our new reality. For example, I added Anthem, CapitalCity and changed the FlagUri so that it is no longer an array of bytes but a URL. I will remove any dates from the proto file. The service itself can manage them. They don't need to be sent in the payload. I renamed the package and csharp_namespace directives as well. Let's start with version 1 of the service by adding this proto file in the **v1** subdirectory of the Protos directory.

For purposes of this discussion, I'm assuming that you still remember how to perform the basic steps I taught you in previous chapters, such as adding a Protobuf file in the csproj file, generating gRPC stubs, configuring dependency injection, managing errors in gRPC services, etc., so I won't describe them again.

Listing 9-15 shows the adjusted country.proto file.

Listing 9-15. The country.proto File

```
syntax = "proto3";

option csharp_namespace = "CountryService.gRPC.v1";

package CountryService.v1;

import "google/protobuf/empty.proto";
import "google/protobuf/timestamp.proto";

service CountryService {
    rpc GetAll(google.protobuf.Empty) returns (stream CountryReply) {}
    rpc Get(CountryIdRequest) returns (CountryReply) {}
    rpc Update(CountryUpdateRequest) returns (google.protobuf.Empty) {}
    rpc Delete(CountryIdRequest) returns (google.protobuf.Empty) {}
    rpc Create(stream CountryCreationRequest) returns (stream
    CountryCreationReply) {}
}

message CountryReply {
    int32 Id = 1;
    string Name = 2;
    string Description = 3;
    string FlagUri = 4;
    string Anthem = 5;
    string CapitalCity = 6;
    repeated string Languages = 7;
}
```

```
message CountryIdRequest {
    int32 Id = 1;
}

message CountryUpdateRequest {
    int32 Id = 1;
    string Description = 2;
}

message CountryCreationRequest {
    string Name = 1;
    string Description = 2;
    string FlagUri = 3;
    string Anthem = 4;
    string CapitalCity = 5;
    repeated int32 Languages = 7;
}

message CountryCreationReply {
    int32 Id = 1;
    string Name = 2;
}
```

Listing 9-16 shows the implementation of the CountryGrpcService class. This class depends on the CountryReplyMapper static class, which is described after this listing.

Listing 9-16. The gRPC Service (CountryGrpcService Class) Implemented

```
namespace CountryService.gRPC.Services;

public class CountryGrpcService : CountryServiceBase
{
    private readonly ICountryServices _countryService;

    public CountryGrpcService(ICountryServices countryService)
    {
        _countryService = countryService;
    }
```

```csharp
public override async Task GetAll(Empty request, IServerStreamWriter
<CountryReply> responseStream, ServerCallContext context)
{
    var lst = await _countryService.GetAllAsync();

    foreach (var country in lst)
    {
        await responseStream.WriteAsync(country.ToReply());
        // CountryReplyMapper static class
    }
    await Task.CompletedTask;
}

public override async Task<CountryReply> Get(CountryIdRequest request,
ServerCallContext context)
{
    var country = await _countryService.GetAsync(request.Id);

    if (country == null)
        throw new RpcException(new Status(StatusCode.NotFound,
        $"Country with Id {request.Id} hasn't been found"));

    return (await _countryService.GetAsync(request.Id)).ToReply();
    // CountryReplyMapper static class
}

public override async Task<Empty> Update(CountryUpdateRequest request,
ServerCallContext context)
{
    var updateSucceed = await _countryService.UpdateAsync(new
    UpdateCountryModel {
        Id = request.Id,
        Description = request.Description,
        UpdateDate = DateTime.UtcNow
    });
```

```
    if (!updateSucceed)
        throw new RpcException(new Status(StatusCode.NotFound,
        $"Country with Id {request.Id} hasn't been updated, it have
        probably been deleted"));

    return new Empty();
}

public override async Task<Empty> Delete(CountryUpdateRequest request,
ServerCallContext context)
{
    var deleteSucceed = await _countryService.DeleteAsync(request.Id);

    if (!deleteSucceed)
        throw new RpcException(new Status(StatusCode.NotFound,
        $"Country with Id {request.Id} hasn't been updated, it have
        probable been deleted"));

    return new Empty();
}

public override async Task Create(IAsyncStreamReader<CountryCreation
Request> requestStream, IServerStreamWriter<CountryCreationReply>
responseStream, ServerCallContext context)
{
    await foreach (var countryToCreate in requestStream.ReadAllAsync())
    {
        var createdCountryId = await _countryService.CreateAsync(new
        CreateCountryModel
        {
            Name = countryToCreate.Name,
            Description = countryToCreate.Description,
            Anthem = countryToCreate.Anthem,
            CapitalCity = countryToCreate.CapitalCity,
            FlagUri = countryToCreate.FlagUri,
            Languages = countryToCreate.Languages
        });
```

```
        await responseStream.WriteAsync(new CountryCreationReply {
            Id = createdCountryId,
            Name = countryToCreate.Name,
        });
    };

    await Task.CompletedTask;
    }
}
```

To avoid redundant code in the Get() and GetAll() methods, I have created a mapper that maps the CountryModel type to the CountryReply type, as shown in Listing 9-17.

Listing 9-17. The CountryReplyMapper Static Class

```
namespace CountryService.gRPC.Mappers;

public static class CountryReplyMapper
{
    public static CountryReply ToReply(this CountryModel country)
    {
        if (country is null)
            return null;

        var countryReply = new CountryReply
        {
            Id = country.Id,
            Name = country.Name,
            Description = country.Description,
            Anthem = country.Anthem,
            CapitalCity = country.CapitalCity,
            FlagUri = country.FlagUri
        };
        countryReply.Languages.AddRange(country.Languages);

        return countryReply;
    }
}
```

If you wonder why I set the Languages property after setting the whole object, it's because, unfortunately, *Repeated<T>* properties are readonly. The only way to populate that kind of property is to use IEnumerable<T> Add() or AddRange() methods to add items into them.

Instead of using a hard-coded SQL connection string for our application, we will place it in the appsettings.json file, which is the best practice, as follow:

```
"ConnectionStrings": {
   "CountryService":  "Server=(LocalDB)\\MSSQLLocalDB;Database=Country
   Service;Integrated Security=True; MultipleActiveResultSets=True"
}
```

Then, to get the connection string within the Program.cs file, use the following line of code:

```
builder.Configuration.GetConnectionString("CountryService");
```

After configuring the SQL Server connection string in the appsettings.json file, completing services registration to run the app, and adding compression, gRPC reflection, the exception interceptor (introduced in Chapter 5), and REST endpoints to reveal Protobuf versions (Chapter 6), the Program.cs file should look like Listing 9-18.

Listing 9-18. The Final Program.cs File Implementation

```
var builder = WebApplication.CreateBuilder(args);

// Add services to the container.
builder.Services.AddGrpc(options => {
    options.EnableDetailedErrors = true;
    options.IgnoreUnknownServices = true;
    options.MaxReceiveMessageSize = 6291456; // 6 MB
    options.MaxSendMessageSize = 6291456; // 6 MB
    options.CompressionProviders = new List<ICompressionProvider>
    {
        new BrotliCompressionProvider() // br
    };
    options.ResponseCompressionAlgorithm = "br"; // grpc-accept-encoding
```

```
    options.ResponseCompressionLevel = CompressionLevel.Optimal;
    // compression level used if not set on the provider
    options.Interceptors.Add<ExceptionInterceptor>();
    // Register custom ExceptionInterceptor interceptor
});
builder.Services.AddGrpcReflection();
builder.Services.AddScoped<ICountryRepository, CountryRepository>();
builder.Services.AddScoped<ICountryServices, CountryServices>();
builder.Services.AddSingleton<ProtoService>();
builder.Services.AddDbContext<CountryContext>(options => options.
UseSqlServer(builder.Configuration.GetConnectionString("CountryService")));

var app = builder.Build();

app.MapGrpcReflectionService();
app.MapGrpcService<CountryGrpcService>();

app.MapGet("/protos", (ProtoService protoService) =>
{
    return Results.Ok(protoService.GetAll());
});
app.MapGet("/protos/v{version:int}/{protoName}", (ProtoService, int
version, string protoName) =>
{
    var filePath = protoService.Get(version, protoName);

    if (filePath != null)
        return Results.File(filePath);

    return Results.NotFound();
});
app.MapGet("/protos/v{version:int}/{protoName}/view", async (ProtoService
protoService, int version, string protoName) =>
{
    var text = await protoService.ViewAsync(version, protoName);

    if (!string.IsNullOrEmpty(text))
        return Results.Text(text);
```

```
    return Results.NotFound();
});
```

```
// Run the app
app.Run();
```

Figure 9-19 shows the CountryService.gRPC project after adding all the stuff discussed thus far.

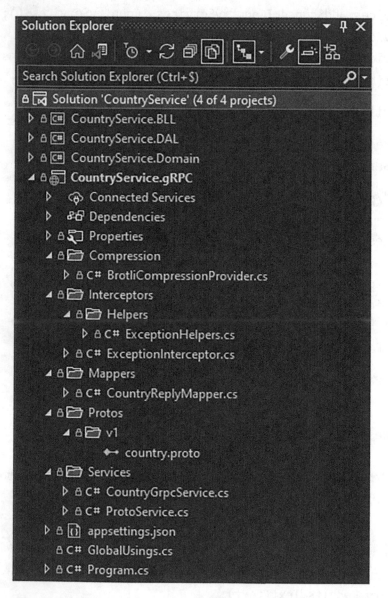

Figure 9-19. *The final* CountryService.gRPC *project and its content*

The CountryService.gRPC project GlobalUsings.cs file should look like the Listing 9-19.

Listing 9-19. The CountryService.gRPC GloblalUsings.cs File

```
global using System.IO;
global using System.IO.Compression;
global using Google.Protobuf.WellKnownTypes;
global using Grpc.Core;
global using Grpc.Core.Interceptors;
global using Grpc.Net.Compression;
global using Microsoft.Data.SqlClient;
global using Microsoft.EntityFrameworkCore;
global using CountryService.DAL.Database;
global using CountryService.DAL.Repositories;
global using CountryService.Domain.Repositories;
global using CountryService.gRPC.Services;
global using CountryService.BLL.Services;
global using CountryService.Domain.Models;
global using CountryService.gRPC.Interceptors.Helpers;
global using CountryService.gRPC.v1;
global using CountryService.gRPC.Mappers;
global using CountryService.Domain.Services;
global using CountryService.gRPC.Compression;
global using CountryService.gRPC.Interceptors;
global using static CountryService.gRPC.v1.CountryService;
```

Create and Layer the ASP.NET Core Razor Application

Now that our gRPC service is completed, we will create the web application allowing us to download the initial country file in the application, then display these countries to update and delete them. Let's start by creating the skeleton of our ASP.NET Core Razor Pages app.

Create the Application Skeleton

First, let's organize our solution. We are about to create a new web application in the same Visual Studio solution. I suggest creating two solution folders, one for everything related to gRPC and the other for everything related to the web application. Figure 9-20 shows the gRPC solution folder that welcomes all gRPC code and the Web solution folder for the Country Wiki web application.

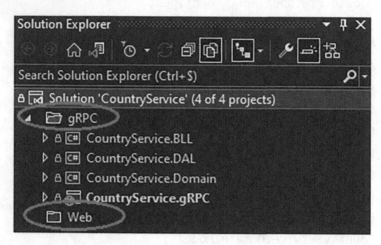

Figure 9-20. *gRPC and Web folders*

After creating the ASP.NET Core Razor Pages app, and layers similarly to the gRPC application, the solution should look like Figure 9-21.

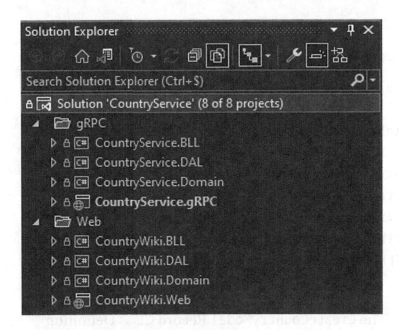

Figure 9-21. *The Country Wiki web application*

At this point, I will generate gRPC stubs (client stuff) into the CountryWiki.DAL layer, because my goal is to isolate gRPC as a data access technology into that layer as I did for Entity Framework Core in the gRPC application.

Define Contracts and Domain Objects

As we did for the ASP.NET Core gRPC project, we will define the contracts serving as interfaces between the data access layer and the service layer and the contracts serving as interfaces between the service layer and the Razor Pages.

Let's start with the contracts defining the interactions with the CountryWiki. DAL layer. Listings 9-20, 9-21, 9-22, and 9-23 show, respectively, the CountryModel, which is a projection (a DTO) of a country obtained from the data access layer, CreateCountryModel, which is the country definition that needs to be sent to the data access layer for purposes of syncing with the data source, CreatedCountryModel, which is a projection of the created country on the data source that contains only the country name and its id, and UpdateCountryModel, which represents the country metadata to be updated by the data access layer.

Listing 9-20. The CountryModel Record Class Definition

```
namespace CountryWiki.Domain.Models;

public record class CountryModel
{
    public int Id { get; init; }
    public string Name { get; init; }
    public string Description { get; init; }
    public string FlagUri { get; init; }
    public string CapitalCity { get; init; }
    public string Anthem { get; init; }
    public IEnumerable<string> Languages { get; init; }
}
```

Listing 9-21. The CreateCountryModel Record Class Definition

```
namespace CountryWiki.Domain.Models;

public record class CreateCountryModel
{
    public string Name { get; init; }
    public string Description { get; init; }
    public string FlagUri { get; init; }
    public string CapitalCity { get; init; }
    public string Anthem { get; init; }
    public IEnumerable<int> Languages { get; init; }
}
```

Listing 9-22. The CreatedCountryModel Record Class Definition

```
namespace CountryWiki.Domain.Models;

public record class CreatedCountryModel
{
    public int Id { get; init; }
    public string Name { get; init; }
}
```

Listing 9-23. The UpdateCountryModel Record Class Definition

```
namespace CountryWiki.Domain.Models;

public record class UpdateCountryModel
{
    public int Id { get; init; }
    public string Description { get; init; }
}
```

The data access layer (ICountryRepository) is defined as shown in Listing 9-24.

Listing 9-24. The ICountryRepository Interface

```
namespace CountryWiki.Domain.Repositories;

public interface ICountryRepository
{
    IAsyncEnumerable<CreatedCountryModel> CreateAsync(IEnumerable<Create
    CountryModel> countryToCreate);
    Task UpdateAsync(UpdateCountryModel countryToUpdate);
    Task DeleteAsync(int id);
    Task<CountryModel> GetAsync(int id);
    IAsyncEnumerable<CountryModel> GetAllAsync();
}
```

I chose to expose IAsyncEnumerable<T> for the CreateAsync() and GetAllAsync() methods instead of an IEnumerable<T> take advantage of the streaming feature offered by gRPC into my business logic layer (keeping the streaming feature). I will demonstrate a bit later the benefit of the IAsyncEnumerable collection type. Note that the CreateAllAsync() method input parameter is an IEnumerable<CreateCountryModel>, I prefer to keep a synchronous Enumerable source there. The data access layer will take the collection and could manage it synchronously or asynchronously. UpdateAsync() and DeleteAsync() methods don't return any value, except the *Task*. They don't need to return any value there. They only need to perform the specific action they are designed for. The business layer doesn't need to know if actions worked well or not by returning a value, like a boolean, as I did in the gRPC application. Instead, the data access layer will raise an exception if something wrong happens with the data source, which is gRPC there.

To end with the domain layer, we'll look at the contracts defining the interactions with the CountryWiki.BLL layer. Listing 9-25 represents the CountryUploadFileModel that contains the uploaded metadata file from the user. This file includes countries' data to be ingested into the data source to feed the wiki. I'll go into more detail about this further in this chapter.

Listing 9-25. The ICountryRepository Interface

```
namespace CountryWiki.Domain.Models;

public record class CountryUploadedFileModel
{
    public string FileName { get; init; }
    public string ContentType { get; init; }
}
```

Listings 9-26 and 9-27 show, respectively, the ICountryFileUploadValidatorService interface, which has the responsibility to validate the uploaded file (it's highly recommended to validate input files in terms of security and data consistency), and the ICountryServices interface, which defines business contracts for CRUD operations on countries.

Listing 9-26. The ICountryFileUploadValidatorService Interface

```
namespace CountryWiki.Domain.Services;

public interface ICountryFileUploadValidatorService
{
    bool ValidateFile(CountryUploadedFileModel countryUploadedFile);
    Task<IEnumerable<CreateCountryModel>> ParseFile(Stream content);
}
```

Listing 9-27. The ICountryServices Interface

```
namespace CountryWiki.Domain.Services;

public interface ICountryServices
{
    Task CreateAsync(IEnumerable<CreateCountryModel> countryToCreate);
    Task UpdateAsync(UpdateCountryModel countryToUpdate);
    Task DeleteAsync(int id);
    Task<CountryModel> GetAsync(int id);
    Task<IEnumerable<CountryModel>> GetAllAsync();
}
```

Since the business layer here has no idea (and should not) of how the data access layer will sync data with the data source, there is no need to use a IAsyncEnumerable collection. Using an IEnumerable<T> collection is a generic way to handle collections, and it's sufficient here. The CreatedAsync() method here, unlike the ICountryRepository, won't return any value. The concrete implementation of this interface will manage by itself created countries without impacting the front-end layer, which doesn't need to know this, and that's the goal of a business logic layer. The same reasoning applies to all others methods that return only a *Task* here. The front-end layer (CountryWiki.Web project) needs to display data requested only. If an error occurs, the front end will display an error page automatically (and the error will be logged), and that's it.

The GlobalUsing.cs file should look like Listing 9-28.

Listing 9-28. The CountryWiki.Domain Project GlobalUsings.cs File

```
global using CountryWiki.Domain.Models;
```

Figure 9-22 shows what the CountryWiki.Domain project should look like.

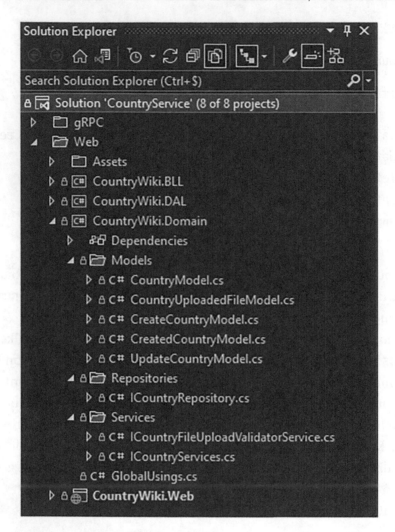

Figure 9-22. *The* CountryWiki.Domain *project*

Implement the Data Access Layer with the gRPC Client

According to the same principle mentioned earlier during the design of the gRPC application, we can, after defining the domain layer, write the implementation of our data access layer and business logic layer. Let's focus here on the data access layer. First, we will import the country.proto file here to generate the client stubs, as I showed you in Chapter 7, with the Visual Studio Connected Services window (refer to Figure 7-11); after compiling the CountryWiki.DAL project, the following class (the gRPC client) will be generated: CountryServiceClient. Don't forget to rename the charp_namepace in the Protobuf file to fit your project namespace (CountryWiki.DAL.v1). Continuing to gRPC client implementation, we will implement the concrete CountryRepository class from the ICountryRepository interface that we created in our domain layer. Listing 9-29 shows this implementation.

Listing 9-29. The CountryRepository Implementation

```
namespace CountryWiki.DAL.Repositories;

public class CountryRepository : ICountryRepository
{
    private readonly CountryServiceClient _countryServiceClient;

    public CountryRepository(CountryServiceClient countryServiceClient)
    {
        _countryServiceClient = countryServiceClient;
    }

    public async IAsyncEnumerable<CreatedCountryModel> CreateAsync(
    IEnumerable<CreateCountryModel> countriesToCreate)
    {
        using var bidirectionnalStreamingCall = _countryServiceClient.
        Create();
        foreach (var countryToCreate in countriesToCreate)
        {
            var countryToCreateRequest = new CountryCreationRequest
            {
                Name = countryToCreate.Name,
                Description = countryToCreate.Description,
                Anthem = countryToCreate.Anthem,
                CapitalCity = countryToCreate.CapitalCity,
                FlagUri = countryToCreate.FlagUri
            };
            countryToCreateRequest.Languages.AddRange(countryToCreate.
            Languages);

            await bidirectionnalStreamingCall.RequestStream.WriteAsync(
            countryToCreateRequest);
        }
```

```
        // Tells server that request streaming is done
        await bidirectionnalStreamingCall.RequestStream.CompleteAsync();

        // Read
        while (await bidirectionnalStreamingCall.ResponseStream.MoveNext())
        {
            var country = bidirectionnalStreamingCall.ResponseStream.
            Current;
            yield return new CreatedCountryModel
            {
                Id = country.Id,
                Name = country.Name
            };
        }
    }

    public async Task DeleteAsync(int id) =>
        await _countryServiceClient.DeleteAsync(new CountryIdRequest
        {
            Id = id
        });

    public async IAsyncEnumerable<CountryModel> GetAllAsync()
    {
        using var serverStreamingCall = _countryServiceClient.GetAll(new
        Empty());
        while (await serverStreamingCall.ResponseStream.MoveNext())
        {
            yield return serverStreamingCall.ResponseStream.Current.
            ToDomain();
        }
    }

    public async Task<CountryModel> GetAsync(int id) =>
        (await _countryServiceClient.GetAsync(new CountryIdRequest {
            Id = id
        })).ToDomain();
```

```
    public async Task UpdateAsync(UpdateCountryModel countryToUpdate) =>
        await _countryServiceClient.UpdateAsync(new CountryUpdateRequest
        {
            Id = countryToUpdate.Id,
            Description = countryToUpdate.Description
        });
}
```

Notice that I'm using `CountryServiceClient` as an injected dependency. I will show you how to configure it further when I show you how to configure the `Program.cs` file of the ASP.NET Core Razor Pages application.

As I mentioned earlier, because `CreateAsync()` and `GetAllAsync()` methods are talking to a streamed gRPC endpoint, I wanted to keep that opportunity to take advantage of the `IAsyncEnumerable<T>` collection by yielding results asynchronously. Why? Because I want to apply some logic (logging) in the business logic layer while iterating on the yielded result. I won't loop again on the result set while logging received content from the data access layer, unlike a regular collection such as an `Array` or a `List`. If you want to learn more about `IAsyncEnumerable<T>`, I strongly suggest you read this article: `https://anthonychu.ca/post/async-streams-dotnet-core-3-iasyncenumerable/`.

Listing 9-30 shows the `CountryModelMappers` class I designed not to repeat the same mapping logic several times.

Listing 9-30. The `CountryModelMappers` Class Implementation

```
namespace CountryWiki.DAL.Mappers;

public static class CountryModelMappers
{
    public static CountryModel ToDomain(this CountryReply countryReply) =>
        (countryReply == null) ? null :
        new CountryModel
        {
            Id = countryReply.Id,
            Name = countryReply.Name,
            Description = countryReply.Description,
            Anthem = countryReply.Anthem,
```

```
            FlagUri = countryReply.FlagUri,
            CapitalCity = countryReply.CapitalCity,
            Languages = countryReply.Languages
        };
}
```

The related GlobalUsings.cs file should look like Listing 9-31.

Listing 9-31. The CountryWiki.DAL Project GlobalUsings.cs File

```
global using CountryWiki.Domain.Models;
global using CountryWiki.Domain.Repositories;
global using Google.Protobuf.WellKnownTypes;
global using Grpc.Core;
global using static CountryWiki.DAL.v1.CountryService;
global using CountryWiki.DAL.v1;
global using CountryWiki.DAL.Mappers;
```

Figure 9-23 shows what the CoutryWiki.DAL project should look like.

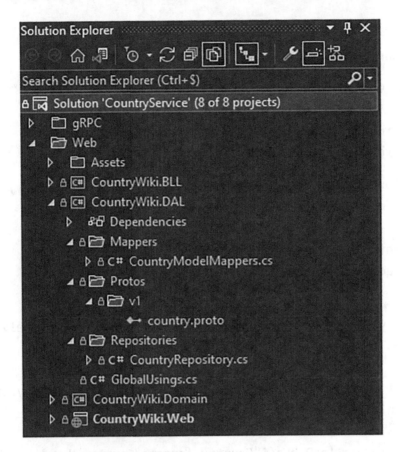

Figure 9-23. *The CountryWiki.DAL project*

Implement the Business Logic Layer

We have arrived at the layer for managing the business logic. I wanted to implement a business layer simply because I want to be able to trace (in my application logs) the result of the streamed data (I remind you that the business layer does not know if the data are streamed or not; it's just you and I that know). As I said in the previous section, I don't need to iterate a second time on the collection since the items are yielded each time an item is streamed using gRPC. After that, I no longer need IAsyncEnumerable. Indeed, I could, however, have returned to an IAsyncEnumerable<CountryModel>, but I did not want to expose it further than the business logic layer. We never know, its implementation may change and may never handle any IAsyncEnumerable content from the repository. Listing 9-32 shows the CountryServices class implementation.

Listing 9-32. The CountryServices Implementation

```
namespace CountryWiki.BLL.Services;

public class CountryServices : ICountryServices
{
    private readonly ICountryRepository _countryRepository;
    private readonly ILogger<CountryServices> _logger;

    public CountryServices(ICountryRepository countryRepository,
    ILogger<CountryServices> logger)
    {
        _countryRepository = countryRepository;
        _logger = logger;
    }

    public async Task CreateAsync(IEnumerable<CreateCountryModel>
    countriesToCreate)
    {
        await foreach (var createdCountry in _countryRepository.CreateAsync
        (countriesToCreate))
        {
            _logger.LogDebug($"Country {createdCountry.Name} has been
            created successfully with Id {createdCountry.Id}");
        }
    }

    public async Task DeleteAsync(int id)
    {
        await _countryRepository.DeleteAsync(id);
        _logger.LogDebug($"Country with Id {id} has been successfully
        deleted");
    }

    public async Task<IEnumerable<CountryModel>> GetAllAsync()
    {
        var countries = new List<CountryModel>();
        await foreach (var country in _countryRepository.GetAllAsync())
```

```
        {
            countries.Add(country);
        }
        return countries;
    }

    public async Task<CountryModel> GetAsync(int id)
    {
        return await _countryRepository.GetAsync(id);
    }

    public async Task UpdateAsync(UpdateCountryModel countryToUpdate)
    {
        await _countryRepository.UpdateAsync(countryToUpdate);
        _logger.LogDebug($"Country with Id {countryToUpdate.Id} has been
        successfully updated");
    }
}
```

Listing 9-33 shows the implementation of the CountryFileUploadValidatorService
class, which allows validating an uploaded file.

Listing 9-33. The CountryFileUploadValidatorService Implementation

```
namespace CountryWiki.BLL.Services;

public class CountryFileUploadValidatorService :
ICountryFileUploadValidatorService
{
    public CountryFileUploadValidatorService() { }

    public bool ValidateFile(CountryUploadedFileModel countryUploadedFile)
    {
        if (!countryUploadedFile.FileName.ToLower().EndsWith(".json") ||
        countryUploadedFile.ContentType != "application/json")
            return false;

        return true;
    }
```

```
public async Task<IEnumerable<CreateCountryModel>> ParseFile(Stream
content)
{
    try
    {
        var parsedCountries = await JsonSerializer.Deserialize
        Async<IEnumerable<CreateCountryModel>>(content, new
        JsonSerializerOptions {
            PropertyNameCaseInsensitive = true
        });

return parsedCountries.Any(x => string.IsNullOrEmpty(x.Name) ||
                                string.IsNullOrEmpty(x.Anthem) ||
                                string.IsNullOrEmpty(x.Description) ||
                                string.IsNullOrEmpty(x.FlagUri) ||
                                string.IsNullOrEmpty(x.CapitalCity) ||
                                x.Languages == null ||
                                !x.Languages.Any()) ? null :
                                parsedCountries;
    }
    catch
    {
        return null;
    }
}
}
```

The ValidateFile() method validates the file extension as well as its contentType. This implementation, therefore, expects to validate a JSON file, but the ICountryFileUploadValidatorService interface does not know the nature of the file to be validated, and this is the beauty of abstraction. It's generic!

The ParseFile() method ensures that the JSON data in the file respects the expected format defined by the CreateCountryModel domain object. If the format is not respected, the DeserializeAsync() method will throw an exception or an empty object, but here I prefer to catch it and return null instead. I don't want to make the application crash for this kind of error, but rather send back to the user a message telling him that the contents

356

of his file are not valid. Note here that I am using System.Text.Json to manipulate JSON. If you are familiar with NewtonSoft.Json, which does the same, please be aware that I highly recommend using System.Text.Json for its performance. To finish my explanation, the only tolerance (in the serialization/deserialization options with the JsonSerializerOptions class) that the names of the properties in the JSON file are not case-sensitive and thus can be either lowercase or uppercase. It doesn't matter, in my opinion, as long as the property's name is valid compared to what is expected, and I recommend that you do the same.

Listing 9-34 shows the GlobalUsings.cs file for the CountryWiki.BLL project.

Listing 9-34. The CountryWiki.BLL Project GlobalUsings.cs File

```
global using CountryWiki.Domain.Models;
global using CountryWiki.Domain.Repositories;
global using CountryWiki.Domain.Services;
global using Microsoft.Extensions.Logging;
global using System.Text.Json;
```

Figure 9-24 shows what the CountryWiki.BLL project should look like.

Figure 9-24. *The CountryWiki.BLL project*

Configure the ASP.NET Core Razor Pages Application

Before we develop the user web interface with ASP.NET Core Razor Pages, we need to do the following:

1. Create a background task (hosted service) that will handle uploaded file data and create a channel (it's different from a gRPC channel) that will make it possible to transfer data between the background task and the ASP.NET Core Razor Pages app (it's like two applications that are running in the same host). A global variable stored in an application options object will be used to display if a file is being synchronized or not.

2. Create and configure the gRPC client with the IHttpClientFactory and register all dependencies in the Program.cs file

Create a Background Task for Handling Uploaded File Data and Create a Channel to Store Data

ASP.NET Cores allows running background tasks as hosted services, which run as long as the ASP.NET Core application runs. It's useful because developers can handle long-running operations in the background without blocking the rest of the application. In our scenario, the uploaded file that contains countries' data will be synchronized to the remote data source, over gRPC, and it could be a long-running operation, so right after the upload is completed (and the file content is validated), the user can browse the application without waiting for the data synchronization to complete.

Listing 9-35 shows the SyncCountriesChannel class's implementation, representing a channel and its interface ISyncCountriesChannel. I created them in the ASP.NET Core Razor Pages application because they depend entirely on the background task (in terms of functionality, I won't reuse them in another service or another application). I put them in the same file. I don't need to separate them into other layers.

Listing 9-35. The `SyncCountriesChannel` Class and `ISyncCountriesChannel` Interface

```
namespace CountryWiki.Web.Channels;

public interface ISyncCountriesChannel
{
    IAsyncEnumerable<IEnumerable<CreateCountryModel>>
    ReadAllAsync(CancellationToken cancellationToken);
    Task<bool> SyncAsync(IEnumerable<CreateCountryModel> countriesToCreate,
    CancellationToken cancellationToken);
}

public class SyncCountriesChannel : ISyncCountriesChannel
{
    private readonly Channel<IEnumerable<CreateCountryModel>> _channel;
    private readonly ILogger<SyncCountriesChannel> _logger;

    public SyncCountriesChannel(ILogger<SyncCountriesChannel> logger)
    {
        var options = new UnboundedChannelOptions
        {
            SingleWriter = false,
            SingleReader = true
        };

        _channel = Channel.CreateUnbounded<IEnumerable<CreateCountryModel>>
        (options);
        _logger = logger;
    }

    public async Task<bool> SyncAsync(IEnumerable<CreateCountryModel>
    countriesToCreate, CancellationToken cancellationToken)
    {
        while (await _channel.Writer.WaitToWriteAsync(cancellationToken) &&
        !cancellationToken.IsCancellationRequested)
```

```
    {
        if (_channel.Writer.TryWrite(countriesToCreate))
        {
            _logger.LogDebug("Sending parsed countries to the
            background task");

            return true;
        }
    }

    return false;
}

public IAsyncEnumerable<IEnumerable<CreateCountryModel>>
ReadAllAsync(CancellationToken cancellationToken) => _channel.Reader.
ReadAllAsync(cancellationToken);
}
```

The class constructor instantiates a channel (which is not a gRPC *Channel*) that allows data to be stored for a consumer that needs these data. Synchronization between the "producer" and the consumer is synchronized safely. It's like a concurrent queue where only one item (the data) is passed to the *Channel* at a time and read (one at a time as well) on the other side. This channel is defined in the System.Thread.Channels assembly that has been introduced in .NET Core 3.

I used an unbounded *Channel* (a *Channel* that doesn't limit the number of items to be stored) with the method Channel.CreateUnbounded<T>() that takes as a parameter an UnboundedChannelOptions class. I don't need to set a limit there for the simple reason a file is rarely uploaded. It doesn't happen often. I set this UnboundedChannelOptions class with the property SingleWriter set to false. It means that many producers can write in the queue. Still, each producer has to wait for the preceding producer to complete the write operation in the *Channel*. The WaitToWriteAsync() method checks if the *Channel* is available and makes the producer wait if the *Channel* is not. Conversely, I set the SingleReader property to true because I want (and need) only one reader: the background task, which runs continuously. Once the *Channel* is created, I can implement the SyncAsync() method that verifies if the *Channel* is available and if the request has not been canceled with the CancellationToken passed as a parameter from the Razor Pages (I'll show it to you further in this chapter).

The ReadAllAsync() method returns an IAsyncEnumerable<IEnumerable<
CreateCountryModel>> where each item is of a set of countries (each set comes from
a single file). You may have already understood that several sets of countries coming
from their respective files can be handled, but one at a time in a queue, as I told you
before; if you want to learn more about the System.Threading.Channels, you can read
the great Microsoft blog post here: https://devblogs.microsoft.com/dotnet/an-
introduction-to-system-threading-channels/.

Now let's create a global variable that will handle the upload status of files. Listing 9-36
shows the GlobalOptions class that exposes the ProcessingUpload property.

Listing 9-36. The GlobalOptions Class

```
namespace CountryWiki.Web.Options;

public class GlobalOptions
{
    public bool ProcessingUpload { get; set; }
}
```

To make that object global—by that, I mean *Singleton*—I'll need to register it in the
Program.cs file with the *Singleton* lifetime in the dependency injection system.

This singleton object will switch state (ProcessingUpload = true *or* false) in the
background task. When data are being processed, the ProcessingUpload will be set to
true, then false when the process is done, or if an exception is raised.

To create this background task, I needed to create a class inherited from the abstract
class named BackgroundService and implement an ExecuteAsync() method. This
abstract class comes from the Microsoft.Extensions.Hosting assembly.

Listing 9-37 shows the SyncUploadedCountriesBackgroundService class that
represents the background task to be implemented.

Listing 9-37. The SyncUploadedCountriesBackgroundService Class

```
namespace CountryWiki.Web.Background;

public class SyncUploadedCountriesBackgroundService : BackgroundService
{
    private readonly ILogger<SyncUploadedCountriesBackgroundService>
    _logger;
    private readonly ISyncCountriesChannel _syncCountriesChannel;
```

361

```
private readonly IServiceProvider _serviceProvider;
private readonly GlobalOptions _globalOptions;

public SyncUploadedCountriesBackgroundService(ILogger<SyncUploadedCo
                                            untriesBackgroundService>
                                            logger,
                                            ISyncCountriesChannel
                                            syncCountriesChannel,
                                            IServiceProvider
                                            serviceProvider,
                                            GlobalOptions
                                            globalOptions)
{
    _logger = logger;
    _syncCountriesChannel = syncCountriesChannel;
    _serviceProvider = serviceProvider;
    _globalOptions = globalOptions;
}

protected override async Task ExecuteAsync(CancellationToken
cancellationToken)
{
    await foreach (var uploadedCountries in _syncCountriesChannel.Read
    AllAsync(cancellationToken))
    {
        try
        {
            _logger.LogInformation("Received uploaded countries from
            the channel for sync");

            using var scope = _serviceProvider.CreateScope();

            var countryServices = scope.ServiceProvider.GetRequired
            Service<ICountryServices>();
```

```
            try
            {
                // Processing sync
                _globalOptions.ProcessingUpload = true;
                await countryServices.CreateAsync(uploadedCountries);

            }
            catch (RpcException e)
            {
                var correlationId = e.Trailers.
                GetValue("correlationId");
                _logger.LogError(e, "Background synchronization has
                failed. CorrelationId {correlationId}", correlationId);
            }
            finally
            {
                _globalOptions.ProcessingUpload = false;
            }
        }
        catch (Exception e)
        {
            _logger.LogError(e, "Unable to manage uploaded countries");
        }
        finally
        {
            _globalOptions.ProcessingUpload = false;
        }
    }
  }
}
```

As you can see, I need to inject ISeriviceProvider by dependency to be
able to create any service instance when I need it, and concretely instantiate the
ICountryServices service to process a set of countries each time a file is uploaded with
the following lines:

```
await foreach (var uploadedCountries in _syncCountriesChannel.ReadAllAsync(
cancellationToken))
{
    try
    {
        ..... code .....

        using var scope = _serviceProvider.CreateScope();
        var countryServices = scope.ServiceProvider.GetRequiredService
        <ICountryServices>();

    ..... code .....
    }
    ..... code .....
}
```

Why am I'm doing this? The background service is *Singleton*, but I need scoped instances of ICountryServices (limited lifetime) not to share the same state of the ICountryServices service between each dataset process.

On the other hand, the other instances, such as GlobalOptions and ISyncCountriesChannel, must be *Singleton* to share the same instance through the application. ILogger<T> is by default *Singleton*, and I inject it to log each country's ingestion operation, logging the start of the process, and the end of the process when it succeeds. If the process fails, it is enriched with the CorrelationId coming from the exception of type RpcException.

Create and Configure the gRPC Client with the IHttpClientFactory and Register All Dependencies in the Program.cs File

Chapter 7 taught you how to create a gRPC client with a .NET 6 console application and import a proto file from the Visual Studio Connected Services window. This time, we are creating a gRPC client with the HttpClientFactory, which is a bit different, but still allows creating HttpClient instances and making HTTP calls. IHttpClientFactory is a .NET 6 built-in feature, and I'll show you how to use it properly.

After importing the `country.proto` file in the `CountryWiki.Web` project, let's go to the `Program.cs` file and configure the gRPC client, set up the compression, define the maximum messages size, and add the `TraceInterceptor` as introduced in Chapter 7.

ASP.NET Core exposes extension methods that return an `IHttpClientBuilder`, which allows configuring an `HttpClient` instance managed (reused or disposed) by the `IHttpClientFactory`. The suitable extension method for gRPC clients is `AddGrpcClient()`. Listing 9-38 shows the configuration of the `CountryServiceClient` (the gRPC client) with the base URL of the gRPC server, `AddInterceptor()` to configure interceptors (introduced in Chapter 7), `ConfigureChannel()` to configure channels c, and all the stuff required to make the application run (including the background task).

Listing 9-38. Configuring the `CountryGrpcServiceClient` with the gRPC Server Address, Logging, Interceptors, Compression, Messages Size Limit, and the Rest of the Stuff Required to Make the Web Application Run

```
var builder = WebApplication.CreateBuilder(args);

// Add services to the container.
builder.Services.AddRazorPages();
builder.Services.AddScoped<ICountryRepository, CountryRepository>();
builder.Services.AddScoped<ICountryServices, CountryServices>();
builder.Services.AddScoped<ICountryFileUploadValidatorService,
CountryFileUploadValidatorService>();
builder.Services.AddSingleton<ISyncCountriesChannel,
SyncCountriesChannel>();
builder.Services.AddHostedService<SyncUploadedCountriesBackgroundService>();
builder.Services.AddSingleton(new GlobalOptions
{
    ProcessingUpload = false
});

var loggerFactory = LoggerFactory.Create(logging =>
{
    logging.AddConsole();
    logging.SetMinimumLevel(LogLevel.Trace);
});
```

```
builder.Services.AddGrpcClient<CountryServiceClient>(o =>
    {
        o.Address = new Uri(builder.Configuration.
        GetSection("CountryServiceUri").Value);
    })
    .AddInterceptor(() => new TracerInterceptor(loggerFactory.CreateLogger
    <TracerInterceptor>()))
    .ConfigureChannel(o =>
    {
        o.CompressionProviders = new List<ICompressionProvider>
        {
            new BrotliCompressionProvider()
        };
        o.MaxReceiveMessageSize = 6291456; // 6 MB,
        o.MaxSendMessageSize = 6291456; // 6 MB

    });

var app = builder.Build();

// Configure the HTTP request pipeline.
if (app.Environment.IsDevelopment())
{
    app.UseDeveloperExceptionPage();
}
else
{
    app.UseExceptionHandler("/Error");
    // The default HSTS value is 30 days. You may want to change this for
        production scenarios, see https://aka.ms/aspnetcore-hsts.
    app.UseHsts();
}

app.UseHttpsRedirection();
app.UseStaticFiles();
```

```
app.UseRouting();

app.UseAuthorization();

app.MapRazorPages();

app.Run();
```

Note that I placed the CountryService server Uri in the `appsettings.json` file:

```
{
  ...
  "CountryServiceUri": https://localhost:5001
  ...
}
```

Upload a Data File with a Form, Display and Manage Data on Razor Pages

Let's move on to viewing country data and uploading country data.

Note   The primary purpose of this book is to show you how to use gRPC to develop an application with ASP.NET Core and .NET 6 only. So, I will omit some explanatory details about ASP.NET Core Razor Pages. If you want to learn about it in depth, you can read Microsoft's documentation here: `https://docs.microsoft.com/en-us/aspnet/core/razor-pages/?view=aspnet core-6.0`.

Let's start by going to the Razor `Index.cshtml` page to implement the file form upload and the HTML table displaying the list of countries.

Listing 9-39 shows a simple file upload form and a simple HTML table fed by the `Countries` property model.

Listing 9-39. `Index.cshtml` File Implements the File Upload Form and an HTML Table to Display the Countries List

```
@page
@model IndexModel
@{
    ViewData["Title"] = "Country Wiki main page";
}

<div class="text-center">
    <h1 class="display-5">Country Wiki main page</h1>
</div>

<form method="post" enctype="multipart/form-data">

    <div class="container mb-5 mt-5">
        <div>
            Upload countries (JSON only):
            <input type="file" asp-for="Upload" />
        </div>
        <div><input type="submit" value="Upload" asp-page-
        handler="upload"/></div>
        <div class="text-danger">@Model.UploadErrorMessage</div>

        @if (Model.GlobalOptions.ProcessingUpload) {
            <div class="text-center text-danger"><h2>A file upload is in
            progress...</h2></div>
        }
    </div>

    <table class="table">
        <thead>
            <tr>
                <th>ID</th>
                <th>Name</th>
                <th>Description</th>
                <th>Capital City</th>
                <th>Anthem</th>
```

```
                    <th>Spoken languages</th>
                    <th>Flag</th>
                    <th>Edit</th>
                    <th>Delete</th>
                </tr>
            </thead>
            <tbody>
                @foreach (var country in Model.Countries)
                {
                    <tr>
                        <td>@country.Id   </td>
                        <td>@country.Name</td>
                        <td>@country.Description</td>
                        <td>@country.CapitalCity</td>
                        <td>@country.Anthem</td>
                        <td>@string.Join(", ", country.Languages)</td>
                        <td><img src="@country.FlagUri" alt="@country.Name"
                        height="25" width="45" /></td>
                        <td><a asp-page="./Edit" asp-route-id="@country.
                        Id">Edit</a></td>
                        <td><input type="submit" asp-page-handler="delete"
                        asp-route-id="@country.Id" value="Delete" /></td>
                    </tr>
                }
            </tbody>
        </table>
</form>
```

Notice the usage of the `ProcessingUpload` property of the `GlobalOptions` object to display (or not) a message that a file upload is being processed.

I added a link to the Edit page and a button to delete a country in the HTML table. Both actions require the Id of the country.

The Index page's code behind (the C# code which handles the Index HTML page), the Index.cshtml.cs file implements the following actions:

- The Index page loading with the countries list, performed by the OnGetAsync() method, which executes the GetAllAsync() method from the ICountryServices service.

- The file upload, performed by the OnPostUploadAsync() method. This method validates the file using ICountryFileUploadValidatorService service methods, displays error validating in the Index file, or sends the data validated and parsed from the uploaded file to the ISyncCountriesChannel channel. If the file is correctly sent to the channel, a redirection is made to the Index page and refreshed with the latest data.

- The country deletion, performed by the OnPostDeleteAsync() method, executes the OnDeleteAsync() method from the ICountryServices service.

Listing 9-40 shows the Index.cshtml.cs file implementation.

Listing 9-40. The Index.cshtml.cs File Implementing Actions on the Index Page

```
namespace CountryWiki.Web.Pages;

public class IndexModel : PageModel
{
    private readonly ICountryServices _countryServices;
    private readonly ICountryFileUploadValidatorService _
    countryFileUploadValidatorService;
    private readonly ISyncCountriesChannel _syncCountriesChannel;

    public GlobalOptions;
    public IEnumerable<CountryModel> Countries { get; set; } = new
    List<CountryModel>();
    public string UploadErrorMessage { get; set; } = string.Empty;

    [BindProperty]
    public IFormFile Upload { get; set; }
```

```csharp
public IndexModel(ICountryServices countryServices,
                  ICountryFileUploadValidatorService
                  countryFileUploadValidatorService,
                  ISyncCountriesChannel syncCountriesChannel,
                  GlobalOptions globalOptions)
{
    _countryServices = countryServices;
    _countryFileUploadValidatorService =
    countryFileUploadValidatorService;
    _syncCountriesChannel = syncCountriesChannel;
    GlobalOptions = globalOptions;
}

public async Task OnGetAsync()
{
    Countries = await _countryServices.GetAllAsync();
}

public async Task<IActionResult> OnPostUploadAsync(CancellationToken
cancellationToken)
{
    if (Upload == null)
    {
        return await HandleFileValidation("File is missing");
    }

    var uploadedFile = new CountryUploadedFileModel
    {
        FileName = Upload.FileName,
        ContentType = Upload.ContentType
    };

    if (!_countryFileUploadValidatorService.ValidateFile(uploadedFile))
    {
        return await HandleFileValidation("Only JSON files are
        allowed");
    }
```

```
        var parsedCountries = await _countryFileUploadValidatorService.
        ParseFile(Upload.OpenReadStream());

        if (parsedCountries == null || !parsedCountries.Any())
        {
            return await HandleFileValidation("Cannot parse the file or the
            file is empty");
        }

        await _syncCountriesChannel.SyncAsync(parsedCountries,
        cancellationToken);

        return RedirectToPage("./Index");
    }

    public async Task<IActionResult> OnPostDeleteAsync(int id)
    {
        await _countryServices.DeleteAsync(id);
        return RedirectToPage("./Index");
    }

    private async Task<PageResult> HandleFileValidation(string
    errorMessage)
    {
        UploadErrorMessage = errorMessage;
        Countries = await _countryServices.GetAllAsync();
        return Page();
    }
}
```

Notice that the GlobalOptions object, injected by dependency as a *Singleton*, is assigned to the public GlobalOptions on the Razor Pages. In this way, I keep the reference of the same object, and I'm sure you understand, the value of the ProcessingUpload property is synchronized with the rest of the application.

Let's test the Index page and see what happens if the uploaded file is not a JSON file. Figure 9-25 shows the displayed error when a text file is uploaded instead of a JSON file.

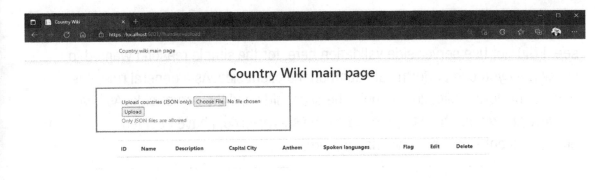

Figure 9-25. *A specific error message is displayed when the uploaded file is not a JSON file*

Figure 9-26 shows the error message when the data in the JSON file are not valid.

Figure 9-26. *A specific error message is displayed when data are not valid*

Note   Chapter 7 showed you how to validate server-side messages. As you can see, I did not use server-side validation here, for the simple reason I wanted to show how you can perform validation on the client side. As a general rule, it is good to perform validation on both the client side and the server side. As I have already shown you how to proceed on the server- side, I have decided to show you only the client -side of the validation here.

Let's consider now valid data on a valid JSON file, as shown in Listing 9-41.

Listing 9-41. Valid Data to Be Uploaded

```
[
    {
        "name": "Canada",
        "description": "Maple leaf country",
        "capitalCity": "Ottawa",
        "anthem": "O Canada !",
        "flagUri": "https://anthonygiretti.blob.core.windows.net/
        countryflags/ca.png",
        "languages": [1, 2]
    },
    {
        "name": "Canada",
        "description": "Maple leaf country. Imported twice from file,
        delete me",
        "capitalCity": "Ottawa",
        "anthem": "O Canada !",
        "flagUri": "https://anthonygiretti.blob.core.windows.net/
        countryflags/ca.png",
        "languages": [1, 2]
    },
    {
        "name": "USA",
        "description": "Uncle Sam country",
        "capitalCity": "Washington",
```

```
        "anthem": "The Star-Spangled Banner",
        "flagUri": "https://anthonygiretti.blob.core.windows.net/
        countryflags/us.png",
        "languages": [2, 3]
    },
    {
        "name": "United Kingdom",
        "description": "Sovereign country of North-western Europe",
        "capitalCity": "London",
        "anthem": "God save the Queen",
        "flagUri": "https://anthonygiretti.blob.core.windows.net/
        countryflags/uk.png",
        "languages": [1]
    },
    {
        "name": "France",
        "description": "Human rights country",
        "capitalCity": "Paris",
        "anthem": "La marseillaise",
        "flagUri": "https://anthonygiretti.blob.core.windows.net/
        countryflags/fr.png",
        "languages": [2]
    },
    {
        "name": "Mexico",
        "description": "Cradle of civilization country",
        "capitalCity": "Mexico City",
        "anthem": "Himno Nacional Mexicano",
        "flagUri": "https://anthonygiretti.blob.core.windows.net/
        countryflags/mx.png",
        "languages": [3]
    }
]
```

If we try to upload these data, the magic now happens! After the completed file upload, the Index page is reloaded with the message that notifies the user a file is being processed as expected, and after reloading the page, we can, at last, see our countries. Figure 9-27 shows the message "A file upload is in progress..."

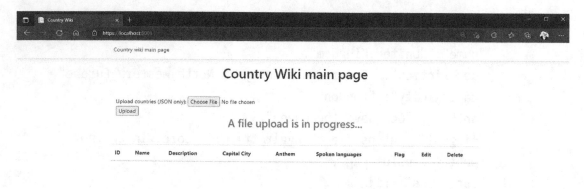

Figure 9-27. *The message "A file upload is in progress..." displayed after the completed file upload*

Figure 9-28 shows the Index page displaying countries.

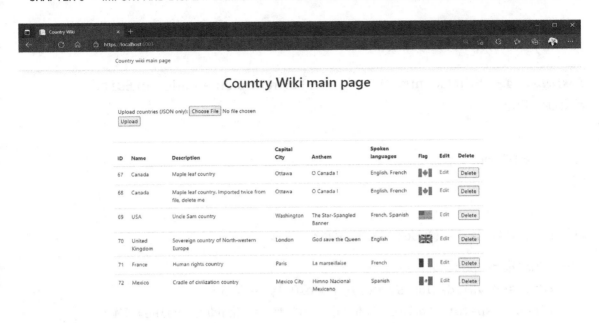

Figure 9-28. *Displaying countries*

If we delete the second row, which is a duplicate of the first row, the Index page should be appropriately refreshed as expected, as shown in Figure 9-29.

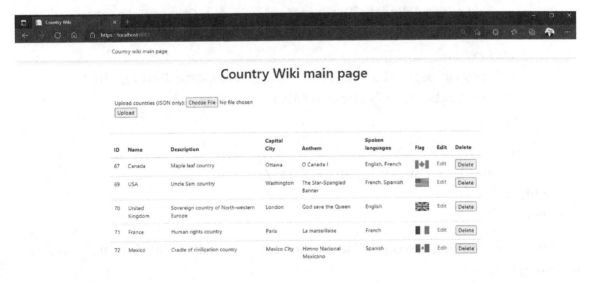

Figure 9-29. *Index page refreshed after deleting a country*

Moving to the Edit page, Listing 9-42 shows the form implementation allowing a country description to be edited.

Listing 9-42. Edit Country Description Form Implementation in Edit. cshtml File

```
@page
@model EditModel
@{
}

<h1>Edit Country - @Model.CountryName</h1>

<form method="post">
    <div asp-validation-summary="ModelOnly"></div>
    <input asp-for="CountryToUpdate.Id" type="hidden" value="@Model.
    CountryToUpdate.Id" />
    <div>
        <label asp-for="CountryToUpdate.Description"></label>
        <div>
            <textarea rows="4" cols="50" name="@Html.NameFor(m =>
            m.CountryToUpdate.Description)">@Model.CountryToUpdate.
            Description</textarea>
        </div>
        <div><span asp-validation-for="CountryToUpdate.Description"
        class="text-danger"></span></div>
    </div>

    <div>
        <input type="submit" value="Save"/>
    </div>
</form>
```

The code handling the country description edit in the Edit.cshtml.cs file is shown in Listing 9-43.

Listing 9-43. The Edit.cshtml.cs Implementation

```
namespace CountryWiki.Web.Pages;

public class EditModel : PageModel
{
    private readonly ICountryServices _countryServices;

    public string CountryName {  get; set; }

    [BindProperty]
    public UpdateCountry CountryToUpdate { get; set; }

    public EditModel(ICountryServices countryServices)
    {
        _countryServices = countryServices;
    }

    public async Task OnGetAsync(int id)
    {
        await RetrieveCountry(id);
    }

    public async Task<IActionResult> OnPostAsync()
    {
        if (!ModelState.IsValid)
        {
            await RetrieveCountry(CountryToUpdate.Id);

            return Page();
        }

        await _countryServices.UpdateAsync(new UpdateCountryModel {
            Id = CountryToUpdate.Id,
            Description = CountryToUpdate.Description
        });

        return RedirectToPage("./Index");
    }
```

```
    private async Task RetrieveCountry(int id)
    {
        var country = await _countryServices.GetAsync(id);
        CountryName = country.Name;
        CountryToUpdate = new UpdateCountry
        {
            Id = country.Id,
            Description = country.Description
        };
    }
}
```

Listing 9-44 shows the UpdateCountry class with the validation requirements on the Description property (required max length of 200 characters and a minimum length of 10 characters).

Listing 9-44. UpdateCountry Class Definition

```
namespace CountryWiki.Web.Models;

public class UpdateCountry
{
    public int Id { get; set; }

    [Required, StringLength(200, MinimumLength = 10)]
    public string Description { get; set; }
}
```

If we click an Edit link in the HTML table (on the Index page), we should be redirected to the Edit page, as shown in Figure 9-30.

Figure 9-30. *The* Edit *page*

An error message is displayed if the Description field requirements are not met, as shown in Figure 9-31.

Figure 9-31. *The error message is displayed when the Description field requirements are not met*

If the requirements are met, the update should work, and redirection should be made to the Index page with the data appropriately updated, as shown in Figure 9-32.

Figure 9-32. *The Index page reloaded with the updated data*

To finish with coding, the GlobalUsings.cs file should look like Listing 9-45.

Listing 9-45. The CountryWiki.Web GlobalUsings.cs File

```
global using System.IO.Compression;
global using System.ComponentModel.DataAnnotations;
global using System.Threading.Channels;
global using Microsoft.AspNetCore.Mvc;
global using Microsoft.AspNetCore.Mvc.RazorPages;
global using Grpc.Net.Compression;
global using Grpc.Core;
global using Grpc.Core.Interceptors;
global using CountryWiki.Web.Compression;
global using CountryWiki.Web.Interceptors;
global using CountryWiki.BLL.Services;
global using CountryWiki.DAL.Repositories;
global using CountryWiki.Domain.Repositories;
global using CountryWiki.Domain.Services;
global using CountryWiki.Web.Options;
global using CountryWiki.Web.Channels;
global using CountryWiki.Web.Background;
global using CountryWiki.Web.Models;
global using CountryWiki.Domain.Models;
global using static CountryWiki.DAL.v1.CountryService;
```

And your CountryWiki.Web project should look like Figure 9-33.

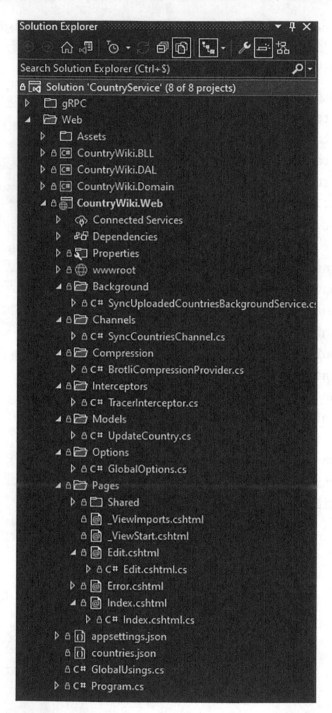

Figure 9-33. *The CountryWiki.Web project*

Et voila!

Summary

You have just finished an essential stage in this book. You were able to put into practice what you have learned in the previous chapters by developing a simple but complete web application, from the conception of the access to the data, to the exposure of this data with ASP.NET Core gRPC, and, finally, the consumption of this data in an ASP.NET Core web application, all while respecting current development best practices.

I did not introduce in this chapter all the functionalities that gRPC offers. It would have been too tedious. I focused on fundamental development with gRPC in .NET 6, which is enough for you to get started with your own applications. In any case, I hope I have instilled in you the desire to explore in more depth all that gRPC offers. The source code of this web application (the ASP.NET Core Razor Pages application and the ASP.NET Core gRPC application) is available for download on the Apress website at `www.apress.com/9781484280072`. You can have fun by developing new services, for example, by enriching protobufs with more complex messages. Note, however, that we are not done with gRPC and ASP.NET Core. You will discover in the following chapters an evolution of gRPC intended for browsers: gRPC-web.

PART IV

gRPC-web and ASP.NET Core

CHAPTER 10

The gRPC-web Specification

We have seen together a lot things that we can do with gRPC. However, as explained in Chapter 3, gRPC is not fully supported by browsers because it relies on HTTP/2. Fortunately, a browser-compatible version of gRPC has emerged: gRPC-web. In this chapter, you will learn

- The history and the specification of gRPC-web

- The gRPC-web JavaScript libraries

- gRPC-web versus REST APIs

History and Specification of gRPC-web

History of gRPC-web

As you already know, gRPC and Protobufs resulted from an open source project led by Google, initiated in the early 2000s and officially open-sourced in 2014. And then, Google began looking into the following problem: "How can we run gRPC in a browser?" Meanwhile, a UK simulation software development company, Improbable, had also been independently looking at the same problem. In the summer of 2016, the two companies joined forces to define a standard specification, which led to the development of the gRPC-web specification.

On the other hand, before 2016, there was a way to use gRPC with a browser, but it was neither very practical nor very efficient: use a REST API to convert RPC calls into REST endpoints. Figure 10-1 shows the flow from a gRPC server to a browser app using a REST API between them.

© Anthony Giretti 2022
A. Giretti, *Beginning gRPC with ASP.NET Core 6*, https://doi.org/10.1007/978-1-4842-8008-9_10

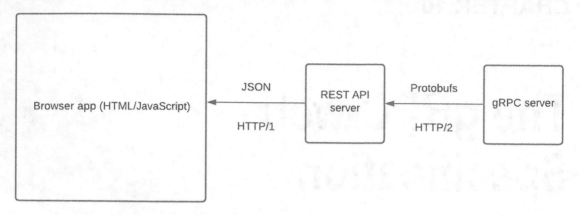

Figure 10-1. *The flow from a gRPC server to a browser app with a REST API between*

You surely understand why this solution is neither practical nor efficient and therefore not viable in the long term. Developing a REST API between the browser and the gRPC application poses a few problems:

- You have to build an additional application, which is tedious (and managing gRPC trailers and statuses which are not existing in the REST world, REST uses HTTP headers and HTTP statuses instead).

- It poses the risk of having a new application that may contain bugs and compromise the stability of the application, which is a potential single point of failure.

- It poses potential network problems (also a potential single point of failure to the application).

- Maintain this application if the application on the client side (browser) and/or server side (gRPC) evolves.

- You lose the performance benefit gained from HTTP/2 by going back to HTTP/1 and converting the binary payloads into JSON and vice versa, which slows down the application. Streaming data is not supported in REST APIs except streaming files such as video or sound files.

gRPC-web partially fixes these problems, and I will explain how in the following subsection.

The gRPC-web Specification

As previously mentioned, Google and Improbable joined forces to define the common standard gRPC-web, which supports the following:

- Unary calls and streaming server calls

- gRPC trailers present in the body of the response, unlike in gRPC

- HTTP/2 (yes, gRPC-web supports HTTP/2!) and will be ready when browsers are

- Two different `Content-type` header values:

  - `application/grpc-web+proto`, which handles binary payloads, but *only* unary calls are supported

  - `application/grpc-web-text`, which handles text payload encoded in Base64.

The principle remains similar to using a REST API. Still, a mandatory proxy converts HTTP/2 requests to HTTP/1 and vice versa and converts binary payload to text if `application/grpc-web-test` transport is used. But above all, the proxy removes the REST API potential single point of failure because it's not an app that you have developed, so no maintenance is required and no regression may occur. An example of a proxy that could be used is *Envoy*, a very efficient and reliable proxy that can take the gRPC-web flow. To learn more about Envoy and how to configure it for using gRPC-web, read the following documentation: `https://grpc.io/docs/platforms/web/basics/`. Anyway, gRPC-web with ASP.NET Core doesn't require a proxy, and I'll explain why in Chapter 11. Figure 10-2 shows the flow from a gRPC server to a browser app using a gRPC-web proxy between.

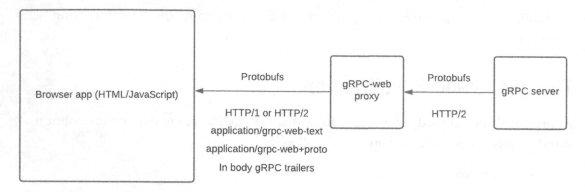

Figure 10-2. *The flow from a gRPC server to a browser app with a gRPC-web proxy between*

However, the collaboration between Google and Improbable stops at this common standard, because each develops its own JavaScript library, which I will present to you in the next section.

The gRPC-web JavaScript Libraries

Improbable and Google have each developed their own gRPC-web JavaScript library, and although they are similar, they still have two main differences, which is why I prefer one over the other.

The first difference is that, unlike the Google library, the Improbable library supports `XmlHttpRequest` (XHR) and the *Fetch* API to process *Asynchronous JavaScript and XML (AJAX)* calls. If you are not sure about the difference between using AJAX calls with XHR or the Fetch API, the following explains it very well: `https://www.sitepoint.com/xmlhttprequest-vs-the-fetch-api-whats-best-for-ajax-in-2019/`.

The second difference is that only the Improbable library manages itself (based on browser capability), the transport type to use (XHR or Fetch), and what gRPC-web mode to use (base-64 encoded or binary). This feature is good because binary is not supported on server-streaming calls, so if you let Improbable manage it for you, you will never get it wrong.

Based on that explanation, my preference obviously is the Improbable library, and thus this is the library I will use to show you how to use gRPC-web with Angular 12 in Chapter 12. If you are interested in the Google library, you can read the tutorial on the GitHub page at `https://github.com/grpc/grpc-web`. As for the Improbable library, it is available here: `https://github.com/improbable-eng/grpc-web`.

Although Improbable's implementation doesn't support deadlines (but does support cancellation) and interceptors, I still find it more convenient than Google's implementation (which has itself two differents behaviors like text or binary data transport). If you need to implement interceptors in JavaScript, you should use Google's implementation and follow its tutorial to implement Interceptors here: `https://grpc.io/blog/grpc-web-interceptor/`. Personally, I don't use those features very often, so the fact that Improbable's implementation doesn't support them isn't a big deal.

I haven't forgotten Protoc and the stubs generation in JavaScript/TypeScript either. We will also see that in Chapter 12.

To finish, Table 10-1 recapitulates the similarities and differences between the Improbable and Google implementations of gRPC-web in terms of features support.

Table 10-1. Similarities and Differences Between Improbable and Google Implementations of gRPC-web in Terms of Features Support

Library	XHR	Fetch	Unary	Server Streaming	Client and Bidirectional Streaming
Improbable	Yes	Yes	Yes	Yes	No
Google text	Yes	No	Yes	Yes	No
Google binary	Yes	No	Yes	No	No

With all this information about gRPC-web, you must be wondering, as I did initially, if you can replace the REST APIs and JSON with gRPC-web. I will answer that question in the next section.

gRPC-web vs. REST APIs

Since gRPC is not compatible with a browser, it's not easy to compare gRPC with REST APIs in applications running on a browser. gRPC-web fixes the compatibility issue, but is that a reason to replace REST? There is no right or wrong answer, but it's legitimate to wonder if gRPC-web can be an excellent alternative to REST APIs or replace them. Chapter 12 may give you the answers you are looking for with the example of the gRPC-web/Angular couple. For example, would you like to generate your gRPC stubs in JavaScript/TypeScript?

At this stage, however, I can tell you that gRPC-web, in terms of performance, is superior to JSON (whether binary or base-64 is used for transport). James Newton-King, Principal Software Engineer at Microsoft, affirms that the reduction in the payload is of the order of 50%, and the serialization/deserialization is, therefore, faster, so you will understand that the overall performance is excellent, even with HTTP/1, since browsers do not yet support HTTP/2 fully. If you are interested in James Newton-King's exciting post, you can read it here: `https://devblogs.microsoft.com/dotnet/grpc-web-for-net-now-available/`.

Finally, the following are the key takeaways from the gRPC-web versus REST APIs comparison:

- gRPC-web provided higher performance.

- gRPC-web web stubs are strongly typed (like gRPC).

- Swagger-type documentation no longer is needed. The Protobufs are there for that.

- REST APIs are widely adopted by the industry. It is a standard that will be difficult to compete with for a long time to come.

Note   Modern browsers support HTTP/2, but not entirely. That's why it's recommended to use HTTP/1 for gRPC-web in HTML/JavaScript apps. If you want to follow HTTP/2 evolution on browsers, check out the following website: `https://caniuse.com/http2`.

Summary

You have learned in this short chapter what gRPC-web is, its history, and how it works. I did not go into too much detail here because Chapter 12 explains the client part (JavaScript/TypeScript) and provides clear examples. Regarding replacing REST APIs with gRPC-web, the choice is up to you. There is no best choice. For performance concerns, you might choose gRPC-web but still want to use REST for its approved and proven technology. I also did not detail how to configure a proxy for gRPC-web because, with ASP.NET Core, we won't need it: ASP.NET Core supports it natively. In the next chapter, I will show you how to configure gRPC in ASP.NET Core to support gRPC-web and rework our gRPC services to overcome the incompatibility of browsers with the client streaming and bidirectional streaming...and much more!

CHAPTER 11

Create a gRPC-web service from a gRPC-service with ASP.NET Core

ASP.NET Core offers a particular implementation of the gRPC-web specification. First, it is straightforward to create a gRPC-web application from a gRPC application without altering the operation of the application and without using any proxy. Also, the implementation of gRPC-web in ASP.NET Core supports both client streaming and bidirectional streaming, but only for applications that do not use a browser to operate. Therefore, it will be necessary to create another version of the Protobufs for applications running in a browser (apps based on HTML/JavaScript only). Finally, compared to gRPC, gRPC-web is supported on Microsoft Azure.

In this chapter, you will explore the following:

- Working with gRPC-web and the .NET ecosystem

- Reworking the CountryService gRPC service to make it work with browser apps

- Support of ASP.NET Core gRPC-web on Microsoft Azure

© Anthony Giretti 2022
A. Giretti, *Beginning gRPC with ASP.NET Core 6*, https://doi.org/10.1007/978-1-4842-8008-9_11

Working with gRPC-web and the .NET Ecosystem

This section is not dedicated to .NET 6 only because it also discusses ASP.NET Core 6 server applications and all other .NET clients (not only .NET 6).

Note   This chapter takes code from Chapter 9 and adds some stuff to make it compatible with gRPC-web. So, it's important to read Chapter 9 before reading this chapter.

---

gRPC-web and ASP.NET Core 6

Implementing gRPC-web in ASP.NET Core 6 is surprisingly easy if you already know gRPC with ASP.NET Core 6. Why? Because ASP.NET Core 6 supports the *same features as gRPC*, so no implementation needs to be changed if (and only if) your client is not a browser. Remember, browsers *do not support* the client and bidirectional streaming services. To use your ASP.NET Core gRPC application in a gRPC-web version for the browser, you will have to rework the protobufs to only implement server streaming or unary services. This will be the subject of the next major section, "Reworking the Country gRPC-web Service for Browsers Apps."

Back to ASP.NET Core 6, what is the point of using gRPC-web if the client applications are not web applications running in a browser? Well, because there are a bunch of client applications in the .NET ecosystem that do not support gRPC over HTTP/2. Therefore, an HTTP/1 alternative to gRPC (gRPC-web) is necessary for the following types of clients:

- .NET Core 2

- .NET Framework

- Blazor WebAssembly

- Mono

- Xamarin.IOS and Android

- UWP

- Unity

Remember that gRPC-web could be a natural alternative to gRPC because hosting, for example, Microsoft Azure could be a challenge due to its limited support of HTTP/2.

Any application running at least .NET Core 3 can consume both gRPC and gRPC-web services.

So, I repeat, because this is very important: if your client is not an HTML/JavaScript app running in a browser (I also include JavaScript desktop applications such as ElectronJS), you can configure the previous CountryService gRPC service to run in gRPC-web mode.

Note   HTML/JavaScript apps running in a browser, or ElectronJS, are web apps like the CountryWiki we developed in Chapter 9. The CountryWiki is a monolithic server-side application that works differently from HTML/JavaScript apps. This chapter will describe browser-based or HTML/JavaScript apps (commonly named Single Page Applications) unlike monolithic apps like ASP.NET Core Razor Pages where rendering is computed server side.

First of all, you need to install the required NuGet `Grpc.Asp.NetCore.Web` package from the Visual Studio Package Manager with the following command:

```
Install-Package Grpc.AspNetCore.Web
```

Next, add the following middleware, which enables gRPC-web, to the ASP.NET Core pipeline:

```
app.UseGrpcWeb(new GrpcWebOptions { DefaultEnabled = true });
```

The `GrpcWebOptions` setting enables gRPC-web by default on any gRPC service that is already set up. If you don't want to enable gRPC-web by default to gRPC services, you can proceed as follow:

```
app.UseGrpcWeb();
app.MapGrpcService<CountryGrpcService>().EnableGrpcWeb();
```

I prefer to use the first way to proceed. I like to enable gRPC-web by default, because I think it is much more straightforward.

That's it! Listing 11-1 shows the Country gRPC service ready for gRPC-web usage with apps that are not brower based.

Listing 11-1. Configure gRPC-web for Non-Browser-Based Apps

```
var builder = WebApplication.CreateBuilder(args);

// Add services to the container.
builder.Services.AddGrpc(options => {
    options.EnableDetailedErrors = true;
    options.IgnoreUnknownServices = true;
    options.MaxReceiveMessageSize = 6291456; // 6 MB
    options.MaxSendMessageSize = 6291456; // 6 MB
    options.CompressionProviders = new List<ICompressionProvider>
    {
        new BrotliCompressionProvider() // br
    };
    options.ResponseCompressionAlgorithm = "br"; // grpc-accept-encoding
    options.ResponseCompressionLevel = CompressionLevel.Optimal;
    // compression level used if not set on the provider
    options.Interceptors.Add<ExceptionInterceptor>();
    // Register custom ExceptionInterceptor interceptor
});
builder.Services.AddGrpcReflection();
builder.Services.AddScoped<ICountryRepository, CountryRepository>();
builder.Services.AddScoped<ICountryServices, CountryServices>();
builder.Services.AddSingleton<ProtoService>();
builder.Services.AddDbContext<CountryContext>(options => options.
UseSqlServer(builder.Configuration.GetConnectionString("CountryService")));

var app = builder.Build();

app.UseGrpcWeb(new GrpcWebOptions { DefaultEnabled = true });
app.MapGrpcReflectionService();
app.MapGrpcService<CountryGrpcService>();

app.MapGet("/protos", (ProtoService protoService) =>
{
    return Results.Ok(protoService.GetAll());
});
```

```
app.MapGet("/protos/v{version:int}/{protoName}", (ProtoService
protoService, int version, string protoName) =>
{
    var filePath = protoService.Get(version, protoName);

    if (filePath != null)
        return Results.File(filePath);

    return Results.NotFound();
});
app.MapGet("/protos/v{version:int}/{protoName}/view", async (ProtoService
protoService, int version, string protoName) =>
{
    var text = await protoService.ViewAsync(version, protoName);

    if (!string.IsNullOrEmpty(text))
        return Results.Text(text);

    return Results.NotFound();
});

// Run the app
app.Run();
```

gRPC-web and All .NET Clients

This section aims to show how does look like a non-ASP.NET Core or a lower version of ASP.NET Core 3.0 client (because it is better to use the integration with the gRPC client factory that we developed in Chapter 9). These .NET clients use the same client without distinction by downloading the following Nuget package: Grpc.Net.Client. The latter targets .NET standard 2.0, .NET standard 2.1, .NET 5, and .NET 6. The implementation of a gRPC-web client is therefore identical to the implementation of all .NET clients. Listing 11-2 shows an example of this implementation on a .NET Core 3.1 gRPC-web client.

Listing 11-2. A .NET Core 3.1 gRPC-web Client

```
using Grpc.Net.Client;
using Microsoft.Extensions.Logging;
using System;
using System.Collections.Generic;
using System.Net.Http;
using CountryService.Client.Compression;
using Grpc.Net.Compression;
using static Apress.Sample.gRPC.v1.CountryService;
using Grpc.Net.Client.Web;

var loggerFactory = LoggerFactory.Create(logging =>
{
    logging.AddConsole();
    logging.SetMinimumLevel(LogLevel.Trace);
});

var channel = GrpcChannel.ForAddress("https://localhost:5001", new
GrpcChannelOptions {
    LoggerFactory = loggerFactory,
    CompressionProviders = new List<ICompressionProvider>
    {
        new BrotliCompressionProvider() // br
    },
    MaxReceiveMessageSize = 6291456, // 6 MB,
    MaxSendMessageSize = 6291456, // 6 MB,
    HttpHandler = new GrpcWebHandler(new HttpClientHandler())
});

// var countryClient = new CountryServiceClient(channel.Intercept(new
TracerInterceptor(loggerFactory.CreateLogger<TracerInterceptor>())));
var countryClient = new CountryServiceClient(channel);
```

Passing an instance of the HttpClientHandler class is necessary because it makes HTTP requests and handles HTTP responses.

Note that it is necessary to instantiate the GrpcWebHandler class because the latter offers a few options that are not provided by HttpClientHandler class, among them we find:

- InnerHandler, which is the previous HttpClientHandler passed in the constructor in the Listing 11-2.

- GrpcWebMode, which defines the Content-Type header. If you want to use server-streaming services, use the GrpcWebMode.GrpcWebText value. By default, if a value is not set, this latter value is used. If you use only unary calls, you can set it to the GrpcWebMode.GrpcWeb value.

- HttpVersion, which tells the client what HTTP version to use; by default, HTTP/1 is used. This object is typed as *version*, which takes as a parameter a string that defines the HTTP version: "1.1" for HTTP/1, "2.0" for HTTP/2. By default, the client capability, HTTP/2, will be used first, and if the client is not compatible, it will fall back to HTTP/1. For example, the Xamarin.Android HttpClient relies on AndroidClientHandler, which doesn't support HTTP/2. (An HTTP handler is the part of an HttpClient that makes the HTTP Request.)

Listing 11-3 shows the client previously shown in Listing 11-2 with GrpcWebHandler options set manually.

Listing 11-3. Set Up Manually GrpcWebHandler Options

```
var gRPCHandler = new GrpcWebHandler()
{
    HttpVersion = new Version("1.1"),
    GrpcWebMode = GrpcWebMode.GrpcWebText,
    InnerHandler = new HttpClientHandler()
};
var channel = GrpcChannel.ForAddress("https://localhost:5001", new
GrpcChannelOptions {
    LoggerFactory = loggerFactory,
    CompressionProviders = new List<ICompressionProvider>
    {
        new BrotliCompressionProvider() // br
    },
    MaxReceiveMessageSize = 6291456, // 6 MB,
    MaxSendMessageSize = 6291456, // 6 MB,
    HttpHandler = gRPCHandler
});
```

gRPC-web and ASP.NET Core 3+ Clients

Now let's move on to ASP.NET Core clients that are at least version 3. Configuration of these clients is also effortless. As in the previous section, you have to configure the client with an instance of GrpcWebHandler. The syntax is a little different here. We use the gRPC client factory. Don't forget to download the Nuget Grpc.Net.Client.Web package. Listing 11-4 shows the configuration of the gRPC-web client of the CountryWiki app, developed with ASP.NET Core Razor Pages.

Listing 11-4. The Country Wiki App Configured with a gRPC-web Client

```
var builder = WebApplication.CreateBuilder(args);

// Add services to the container.
builder.Services.AddRazorPages();
builder.Services.AddScoped<ICountryRepository, CountryRepository>();
builder.Services.AddScoped<ICountryServices, CountryServices>();
builder.Services.AddScoped<ICountryFileUploadValidatorService,
CountryFileUploadValidatorService>();
builder.Services.AddSingleton<ISyncCountriesChannel,
SyncCountriesChannel>();
builder.Services.AddHostedService<SyncUploadedCountriesBackgroundService>();
builder.Services.AddSingleton(new GlobalOptions
{
    ProcessingUpload = false
});

var loggerFactory = LoggerFactory.Create(logging =>
{
    logging.AddConsole();
    logging.SetMinimumLevel(LogLevel.Trace);
});

builder.Services.AddGrpcClient<CountryServiceClient>(o =>
    {
        o.Address = new Uri("https://localhost:5001");
    })
```

```csharp
    .ConfigurePrimaryHttpMessageHandler(() => new GrpcWebHandler(new
    HttpClientHandler()))
    .AddInterceptor(() => new TracerInterceptor(loggerFactory.CreateLogger
    <TracerInterceptor>()))
    .ConfigureChannel(o =>
    {
        o.CompressionProviders = new List<ICompressionProvider>
        {
            new BrotliCompressionProvider()
        };
        o.MaxReceiveMessageSize = 6291456; // 6 MB,
        o.MaxSendMessageSize = 6291456; // 6 MB

    });

var app = builder.Build();

// Configure the HTTP request pipeline.
if (app.Environment.IsDevelopment())
{
    app.UseDeveloperExceptionPage();
}
else
{
    app.UseExceptionHandler("/Error");
    // The default HSTS value is 30 days. You may want to change this for
        production scenarios, see https://aka.ms/aspnetcore-hsts.
    app.UseHsts();
}

app.UseHttpsRedirection();
app.UseStaticFiles();
app.UseRouting();
app.UseAuthorization();
app.MapRazorPages();
app.Run();
```

As you can see, the syntax is different here. We must use the
ConfigurePrimaryHttpMessageHandler() extension method to achieve our ends.
The latter returns an IHttpClientBuilder that allows us to chain the other extension
methods AddInterceptor() and ConfigureChannel().

This Country gRPC and gRPC-web service is now ready to serve non-browser-
based apps!

Reworking the CountryService gRPC service for Browser Apps

As you already know, browsers do not support client and bidirectional streaming
services. Therefore, it will be necessary to serve the same data to clients regardless of
whether they are using gRPC-web in a browser or not. Let's first review our interaction
scenario between the client and the gRPC server. Figure 11-1 shows the architecture
diagram of the Countries Wiki application with the gRPC-web service.

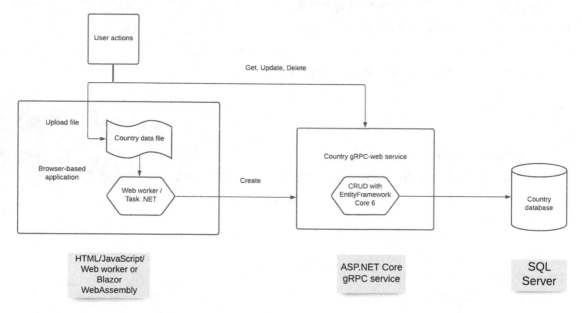

Figure 11-1. *The Countries Wiki architecture diagram with gRPC-web*

We can note two significant changes here:

- Uploading a file, which is parsed and validated on the front-end side, with JavaScript for HTML/JavaScript applications and with C # for Blazor WebAssembly applications.

- The absence of a background task allowed streaming the countries to be synchronized with the database. However, an alternative exists for HTML/JavaScript applications, whose operation is similar to background tasks: Web Workers. We will see this in detail in Chapter 12. As for Blazor WebAssembly, which does not support background tasks, will also have its alternative to background tasks, simply .NET Tasks.

I want to keep the responsibility of validating and parsing uploaded files client side instead of uploading the file to the gRPC server. The gRPC service will perform only CRUD operations from a strict contract given to clients, which is lightweight. In this way, the load is mainly on the client side instead of the server side, which helps keep performance stability.

Now let's rewrite our Protobufs, considering that we can no longer use a two-way streaming service. We are therefore going to have two very distinct Protobuf files:

- `country.proto`: A Protobuf file that we've already created that serves server applications or other non-browser-based clients.

- `country.browser.proto`: A new Protobuf file serving HTML/ JavaScript web applications. This name is pretty straightforward so that the consumer won't misunderstand the intention of the service generated from it.

We will use the same messages in each of these files. Therefore, we will create a Protobuf file containing the messages shared between the two files and then import them into each. (As mentioned in previous chapters, the Protobuf language supports reusability, so why deprive yourself of it?) Let's name the file `country.shared.proto`. It contains all the messages from the `country.proto` file that we created earlier and the `CountriesCreationRequest` message, a repeated list of the `CountryCreationRequest` message. We can no longer stream from the client, so we will send a list of `CountryCreationRequest` to the `Create()` RPC method. Listing 11-5 shows the `country.shared.proto` file.

Listing 11-5. The country.shared.proto File

```
syntax = "proto3";

option csharp_namespace = "CountryService.gRPC.Protos.v1";

message CountryReply {
      int32 Id = 1;
      string Name = 2;
      string Description = 3;
      string FlagUri = 4;
      string Anthem = 5;
      string CapitalCity = 6;
      repeated string Languages = 7;
}

message CountryIdRequest {
      int32 Id = 1;
}

message CountryUpdateRequest {
      int32 Id = 1;
      string Description = 2;
}

message CountriesCreationRequest {
      repeated CountryCreationRequest Countries = 1;
}

message CountryCreationRequest {
      string Name = 1;
      string Description = 2;
      string FlagUri = 3;
      string Anthem = 4;
      string CapitalCity = 5;
   repeated int32 Languages = 6;
}
```

```
message CountryCreationReply {
    int32 Id = 1;
    string Name = 2;
}
```

Now we can write the country.browser.proto file, describing the
CountryServiceBrowser service, as shown in Listing 11-6.

Listing 11-6. The country.browser.proto File

```
syntax = "proto3";

option csharp_namespace = "CountryService.gRPC.Browser.v1";

package CountryService.Browser.v1;

import "google/protobuf/empty.proto";
import "Protos/v1/country.shared.proto";

service CountryServiceBrowser {
    rpc GetAll(google.protobuf.Empty) returns (stream CountryReply) {}
    rpc Get(CountryIdRequest) returns (CountryReply) {}
    rpc Update(CountryUpdateRequest) returns (google.protobuf.Empty) {}
    rpc Delete(CountryIdRequest) returns (google.protobuf.Empty) {}
    rpc Create(CountriesCreationRequest) returns (stream
    CountryCreationReply) {}
}
```

The import directive requires specifying the full path of the Protobuf file from the
Protos directory, which contains all the Protobuf files. Otherwise, Visual Studio will
generate an error indicating that the file was not found.

The same applies for the country.proto file, as Listing 11-7 shows.

Listing 11-7. The country.proto File

```
syntax = "proto3";

option csharp_namespace = "CountryService.gRPC.v1";

package CountryService.v1;
```

```
import "google/protobuf/empty.proto";
import "Protos/v1/country.shared.proto";

service CountryService {
    rpc GetAll(google.protobuf.Empty) returns (stream CountryReply) {}
    rpc Get(CountryIdRequest) returns (CountryReply) {}
    rpc Update(CountryUpdateRequest) returns (google.protobuf.Empty) {}
    rpc Delete(CountryIdRequest) returns (google.protobuf.Empty) {}
    rpc Create(stream CountryCreationRequest) returns (stream
    CountryCreationReply) {}
}
```

You may be wondering why I re-created all the gRPC-web services for browsers in another Protobuf file when only the Create RPC method changes. Well, for two reasons:

- The CountryServiceBrowser service may evolve differently from the CountryService service (this happens more often than you might imagine).

- I don't want to tell the client that she needs to import two Protobuf files, the first country.proto, and a second exposing her only to the non-bidirectional version of the RPC Create() method.

There is still one step before designing and exposing the new version of the gRPC-web service dedicated to browsers: compile the Protobufs, as seen in the previous chapters but with a particular feature to allow Protobuf files to be imported.

Protoc allows declaring Protobuf files to import into others during compilation, thanks to a directive named proto_path that requires the path where the Protobuf files to import are located.

Executing the following command generates the stubs in C#; OUT_DIR is the directory where the stubs are generated, PROTO_DIR is the directory where the Protobuf file is to be compiled to produce the stubs, and IMPORT_PROTO_PATH is the path to the directory that contains all Protobufs that need to be resolved with the import directive.

```
protoc --plugin=protoc-gen-grpc=grpc_csharp_plugin \
       --csharp_out=OUT_DIR \
       --grpc_out=OUT_DIR \
       --grpc_opt=lite_client,no_server PROTO_DIR\country.proto \
       --proto_path=IMPORT_PROTO_PATH
```

As you can see, Visual Studio takes care of everything, you do not need to run this command yourself. However for the Protobufs to be imported with the import directive, you have to help Visual Studio to generate the right command. You have to modify in the .csproj files of your client and server application the Protobuf XML tag by adding the Link property to it. Its value is the name of the Protobuf file, whether it is imported or it imports another.

Listing 11-8 shows the .csproj file for the CountryService.gRPC project.

Listing 11-8. CountryService.gRPC File Updated to Import Protobuf File to Another

```
<Project Sdk="Microsoft.NET.Sdk.Web">

  <PropertyGroup>
    <TargetFramework>net6.0</TargetFramework>
    <Nullable>enable</Nullable>
  </PropertyGroup>

  <ItemGroup>
    <PackageReference Include="Grpc.AspNetCore" Version="2.39.0" />
    <PackageReference Include="Grpc.AspNetCore.Web" Version="2.39.0" />
    <PackageReference Include="Grpc.AspNetCore.Server.Reflection"
    Version="2.39.0" />
    <PackageReference Include="Microsoft.EntityFrameworkCore.Tools"
    Version="6.0.0">
      <PrivateAssets>all</PrivateAssets>
      <IncludeAssets>runtime; build; native; contentfiles; analyzers;
      buildtransitive</IncludeAssets>
    </PackageReference>
  </ItemGroup>

  <ItemGroup>
    <ProjectReference Include="..\CountryService.BLL\CountryService.BLL.
    csproj" />
    <ProjectReference Include="..\CountryService.DAL\CountryService.DAL.
    csproj" />
  </ItemGroup>
```

```xml
  <ItemGroup>
    <Protobuf Include="Protos\v1\country.proto" Link="country.proto"
    GrpcServices="Server" />
    <Protobuf Include="Protos\v1\country.browser.proto" Link="country.
    browser.proto" GrpcServices="Server" />
    <Protobuf Include="Protos\v1\country.shared.proto" Link="country.
    shared.proto" GrpcServices="Server" />
  </ItemGroup>

</Project>
```

The same updates are necessary for the Country.Wiki.DAL project, shown in
Listing 11-9.

Listing 11-9. CountryWiki.DAL File Updated to Import Protobuf File to Another

```xml
<Project Sdk="Microsoft.NET.Sdk">

  <PropertyGroup>
    <TargetFramework>net6.0</TargetFramework>
    <Nullable>enable</Nullable>
  </PropertyGroup>

  <ItemGroup>
    <PackageReference Include="Google.Protobuf" Version="3.13.0" />
    <PackageReference Include="Grpc.Net.ClientFactory" Version="2.32.0" />
    <PackageReference Include="Grpc.Tools" Version="2.32.0">
      <PrivateAssets>all</PrivateAssets>
      <IncludeAssets>runtime; build; native; contentfiles; analyzers;
      buildtransitive</IncludeAssets>
    </PackageReference>
  </ItemGroup>

  <ItemGroup>
    <ProjectReference Include="..\CountryWiki.Domain\CountryWiki.Domain.
    csproj" />
  </ItemGroup>
```

```
  <ItemGroup>
    <Protobuf Include="Protos\v1\country.proto" Link="country.proto"
    GrpcServices="Client" />
    <Protobuf Include="Protos\v1\country.shared.proto" Link="country.
    shared.proto" GrpcServices="Client" />
  </ItemGroup>
```

```
</Project>
```

We can now compile and write our gRPC-web service dedicated to the browser:
CountryGrpcServiceBrowser.

The only implementation that changes is the Create method. Due to the absence
of streaming from the client, we no longer work with an IAsyncEnumerable but rather a
classic IEnumerable.

The service has duplicate code, I admit, but again, the code may evolve
differently, so I'm not referring to encapsulating redundant code in functions.
However, if you wish to do so, go for it! Listing 11-10 shows the implementation of the
CountryGrpcServiceBrowser class.

Listing 11-10. Implementation of the CountryGrpcServiceBrowser Class

```
namespace CountryService.gRPC.Services;

public class CountryGrpcServiceBrowser : CountryServiceBrowserBase
{
    private readonly ICountryServices _countryService;

    public CountryGrpcServiceBrowser(ICountryServices countryService)
    {
        _countryService = countryService;
    }

    public override async Task GetAll(Empty request, IServerStreamWriter
    <CountryReply> responseStream, ServerCallContext context)
    {
        var lst = await _countryService.GetAllAsync();

        foreach (var country in lst)
        {
            await responseStream.WriteAsync(country.ToReply());
```

```csharp
    }
    await Task.CompletedTask;
}

public override async Task<CountryReply> Get(CountryIdRequest request,
ServerCallContext context)
{
    var country = await _countryService.GetAsync(request.Id);

    if (country == null)
        throw new RpcException(new Status(StatusCode.NotFound,
        $"Country with Id {request.Id} hasn't been found"));

    return (await _countryService.GetAsync(request.Id)).ToReply();
}

public override async Task<Empty> Update(CountryUpdateRequest request,
ServerCallContext context)
{
    var updateSucceed = await _countryService.UpdateAsync
    (new UpdateCountryModel
    {
        Id = request.Id,
        Description = request.Description,
        UpdateDate = DateTime.UtcNow
    });

    if (!updateSucceed)
        throw new RpcException(new Status(StatusCode.NotFound,
        $"Country with Id {request.Id} hasn't been updated, it has
        probably been deleted"));

    return new Empty();
}

public override async Task<Empty> Delete(CountryIdRequest request,
ServerCallContext context)
{
    var deleteSucceed = await _countryService.DeleteAsync(request.Id);
```

```
    if (!deleteSucceed)
        throw new RpcException(new Status(StatusCode.NotFound,
        $"Country with Id {request.Id} hasn't been updated, it have
        probably been deleted"));

    return new Empty();
}

public override async Task Create(CountriesCreationRequest
request, IServerStreamWriter<CountryCreationReply> responseStream,
ServerCallContext context)
{
    foreach (var countryToCreate in request.Countries)
    {
        var createdCountryId = await _countryService.CreateAsync(new
        CreateCountryModel
        {
            Name = countryToCreate.Name,
            Description = countryToCreate.Description,
            Anthem = countryToCreate.Anthem,
            CapitalCity = countryToCreate.CapitalCity,
            FlagUri = countryToCreate.FlagUri,
            Languages = countryToCreate.Languages
        });

        await responseStream.WriteAsync(new CountryCreationReply
        {
            Id = createdCountryId,
            Name = countryToCreate.Name,
        });
    };

    await Task.CompletedTask;
}
}
```

We are almost at the end! Just register the `CountryGrpcServiceBrowser` class as a gRPC service, like we did for the `CountryGrpcService` class, in the dependency injection system and one other thing: enable *cross-origin resource sharing (CORS)*. If you not familiar with CORS, it is a mechanism that allows a browser (or an ElectronJS app) to indicate to the server the origin of the HTTP request, for security reasons, to limit its access from various origins through various HTTP verbs and various headers. For gRPC-web to work with a browser, it will therefore be necessary to enable CORS. Here we are going to keep it simple. We will authorize all verbs, all the origins, and all the headers to facilitate application development. For gRPC-web to work correctly, the following additional headers are required:

- `Grpc-Status`
- `Grpc-Message`
- `Grpc-Encoding`
- `Grpc-Accept-Encoding`

To save the CORS configuration in the dependency injection system, you must use the `AddCors()` extension method to create the `AllowAll` policy with the `AddPolicy()` extension applied to the CORS options. The policy will be applied to the entire application endpoints (gRPC-web and any REST endpoints) with the `UseCors()` extensions, which take the `AllowAll` CORS policy parameter. To activate CORS properly, you must declare the `UseCors()` middleware *before* the `UseGrpcWeb()` middleware. Listing 11-11 shows the CORS configuration and activation in the `Program.cs` file.

Listing 11-11. Configuring and Activating CORS in the `Program.cs` File

```
var builder = WebApplication.CreateBuilder(args);

// Add services to the container.
builder.Services.AddGrpc(options => {
    options.EnableDetailedErrors = true;
    options.IgnoreUnknownServices = true;
    options.MaxReceiveMessageSize = 6291456; // 6 MB
    options.MaxSendMessageSize = 6291456; // 6 MB
    options.CompressionProviders = new List<ICompressionProvider>
    {
```

```
        new BrotliCompressionProvider() // br
    };
    options.ResponseCompressionAlgorithm = "br"; // grpc-accept-encoding
    options.ResponseCompressionLevel = CompressionLevel.Optimal;
    // compression level used if not set on the provider
    options.Interceptors.Add<ExceptionInterceptor>(); // Register custom
    ExceptionInterceptor interceptor
});
builder.Services.AddGrpcReflection();
builder.Services.AddScoped<ICountryRepository, CountryRepository>();
builder.Services.AddScoped<ICountryServices, CountryServices>();
builder.Services.AddSingleton<ProtoService>();
builder.Services.AddDbContext<CountryContext>(options => options.
UseSqlServer(builder.Configuration.GetConnectionString("CountryService")));
builder.Services.AddCors(o => o.AddPolicy("AllowAll", builder =>
{
    builder.AllowAnyOrigin()
            .AllowAnyMethod()
            .AllowAnyHeader()
            .WithExposedHeaders("Grpc-Status", "Grpc-Message",
            "Grpc-Encoding", "Grpc-Accept-Encoding");
}));

var app = builder.Build();

app.UseCors("AllowAll");
app.UseGrpcWeb(new GrpcWebOptions { DefaultEnabled = true });
app.MapGrpcReflectionService();
app.MapGrpcService<CountryGrpcService>();
app.MapGrpcService<CountryGrpcServiceBrowser>();

app.MapGet("/protos", (ProtoService protoService) =>
{
    return Results.Ok(protoService.GetAll());
});
```

```
app.MapGet("/protos/v{version:int}/{protoName}", (ProtoService
protoService, int version, string protoName) =>
{
    var filePath = protoService.Get(version, protoName);

    if (filePath != null)
        return Results.File(filePath);

    return Results.NotFound();
});
app.MapGet("/protos/v{version:int}/{protoName}/view", async (ProtoService
protoService, int version, string protoName) =>
{
    var text = await protoService.ViewAsync(version, protoName);

    if (!string.IsNullOrEmpty(text))
        return Results.Text(text);

    return Results.NotFound();
});

// Run the app
app.Run();
```

Our ASP.NET Core CountryService.gRPC app is now ready for any eventuality!

Support of ASP.NET Core gRPC-web on Microsoft Azure

Regarding Microsoft Azure support for ASP.NET Core gRPC-web, well, it's effortless. As long as HTTP/1 is enabled on Kestrel in appsettings.json, it will be possible to host on the following:

- A Windows virtual machine or Linux virtual machine

- A Windows AppServices or Linux App Services

- A Windows Docker container with Azure Container Instance (ACI)

- A Kubernetes cluster

A tiny thing about Azure App Services: Windows App Services work even if you don't configure Kestrel on HTTP/1, because App Services have a module named ASPNetCoreModuleV2 that will translate HTTP/2 requests into HTTP/1, unlike Linux App Services. So never to go wrong and use the same settings as either to use your service as a gRPC (the latter requires HTTP/2) or gRPC-web (the latter doesn't require HTTP/2) service, I suggest that you configure Kestrel with HTTP/1 and HTTP/2 as shown in Listing 11-12.

Listing 11-12. Configuring Kestrel to Run on HTTP/1 and HTTP/2

```
{
  "Logging": {
    "LogLevel": {
      "Default": "Information",
      "Microsoft": "Warning",
      "Microsoft.Hosting.Lifetime": "Information"
    }
  },
  "AllowedHosts": "*",
  "Kestrel": {
          "EndpointDefaults": {
              "Protocols": "Http1AndHttp2"
          }
      }
}
```

With fuller knowledge of of gRPC-web, you now understand the value of using gRPC-web in all types of clients, as we have seen previously, instead of gRPC, since the latter is not supported in most cases on Azure services.

Summary

You now understand the advantages and limitations of gRPC-web with ASP.NET Core 6 and how to expose gRPC-web services for any type of client, browser-based or not. In the latter case, you have seen that it was possible to use client and bidirectional streaming. Regarding the limits of gRPC-web compared to gRPC, this is not a big deal since we have adapted our services so that gRPC-web works almost the same as gRPC. This also allowed you to reuse Protobuf messages, thanks to the practicality of this language.

If you have followed everything so far, know that you have implemented clean code, learned how to reuse the existing code when necessary, I am thinking of the application layers (BLL, DAL) that have not been rewritten to support gRPC-web. Of course, it's possible to do more, such as encapsulating redundant code like code implemented in gRPC services, but I did not want to go this far for the reasons I have already mentioned.

You now have all the tools to create applications of all kinds with gRPC-web! In the next chapter, we will put this into practice by creating an application in HTML/JavaScript with Angular, a fun prospect!

CHAPTER 12

Import and Display Data with Angular 12 and gRPC-web

We continue with the practice of gRPC-web in this chapter but in a different way. Here we will get out of the ASP.NET Core context a bit to put ourselves on the side of the web browser: how to use gRPC-web in a purely HTML/JavaScript application. In the industry, these applications are called *single-page applications (SPAs)*. Their use has turned the web industry upside down. In this chapter, we will use Angular 12, an HTML/JavaScript development framework (TypeScript rather), with gRPC-web, and you will learn how to do the following:

- Recognize the advantages of using SPAs such as Angular

- Generate TypeScript stubs with Protoc

- Write data access with Improbable's gRPC-web client

- Upload a data file and display data with TypeScript, a Web Worker, and gRPC-web

- Manage data with TypeScript and gRPC-web

Introduction to SPAs

SPAs have revolutionized the web industry by competing with monolithic server applications. (However, monolithic applications are still widely used and still have a few good years ahead of them.) So, I felt compelled to write a chapter dedicated to SPAs with gRPC-web. Before going any further in this chapter, I would like to remind you how SPAs

419

© Anthony Giretti 2022
A. Giretti, *Beginning gRPC with ASP.NET Core 6*, https://doi.org/10.1007/978-1-4842-8008-9_12

work. A SPA is a web application that is accessible via a single HTML page. The goal is to avoid loading a new page for each user action, to streamline the user's experience. You might have understood that the relationship between the browser and server is somewhat different than the relationship between the browser and monolithic server app. A request is sent to the server to retrieve information to be displayed subsequently, and no other HTML page is downloaded from the server. A SPA has the following advantages:

- HTML/JavaScript/CSS content is loaded only once.

- The separation between the UI and the data to be displayed is clear and allows the developer to distribute better the tasks, which in addition greatly facilitates maintenance afterward.

- Performing actions on the HTML page avoids reloading the whole page from the server, which can be cumbersome if a lot of information is displayed. Responsibility for display is transferred to the client side, which is still rather enjoyable (server won't compute the rendering, and it saves time processing).

There are, however, downsides to a SPA:

- There are as many requests to the server as there are types of information to display (through AJAX requests), which can be heavy for the server when the page is loaded for the first time.

- The whole application is coded in JavaScript, which can sometimes be difficult to debug in the event of a problem.

- *Search engine optimization (SEO)* referencing is hard because, again, the whole application is written in JavaScript, which doesn't help SEO robots parse reference content from its HTML content.

As a front-end developer, you may or may not like using SPAs; my goal is to present all the options available with gRPC-web and let you decide which you like.!

There are quite a few SPA frameworks, but the most popular are the following:

- Angular

- ReactJS

- VueJS

I realize that I risk frustrating ReactJS and VueJS fans because I chose to use Angular, my favorite framework, for my gRPC-web demo, but I like Angular over other frameworks for a few reasons. First, its architecture is a *Model-View-ViewModel (MVVM)* model, which supports two-way data binding between the View and the ViewModel that provides change propagation between the View and the data. The second thing I like about Angular is that it supports the dependency injection principle, which, as previously introduced in the context of ASP.NET Core in Chapter 2, is a technique that weakly couples objects and service classes with each other and their dependencies. Dependency injection is really convenient and it makes testing your applications easy.

I won't go further into the details of why I love and chose Angular. That's not the goal of this book. However, I do hope this chapter will make you want to discover Angular if you are not already familiar with it, or at least apply to your own favorite SPA framework the principles that I will demonstrate with gRPC-web. Note that you will quickly understand this chapter if you already use Angular or another type of SPA framework. Otherwise, I strongly encourage you to learn the basics of Angular (version 12 precisely, the most recent version released) before you proceed further in this chapter so that you get the most benefit from it. The official Google tutorial at `https://angular.io/guide/what-is-angular` is well done and I think you will enjoy starting your first steps with Angular there.

Throughout this chapter, I will be using Visual Studio Code. Even though we can use Visual Studio 2022 to develop an Angular project, it is best to use Visual Studio Code for pure HTML/JavaScript/TypeScript applications. Visual Studio 2022 may be perfect for .NET applications, but it is, on the other hand, a bit heavy for simple HTML/JavaScript/TypeScript applications. If you are not familiar with Visual Studio Code, it is optimal for developing an HTML/JavaScript/TypeScript application because it does not contain any unnecessary functionality. I think in particular of all the menus of Visual Studio, which, for me, are unnecessary here. Visual Studio Code is also customizable. It allows you to install a whole bunch of plug-ins to enrich your development experience with a precise language.

Generate TypeScript Stubs with Protoc

Protoc is back! In Chapter 11, I told you that you don't need to learn commands with Protoc to generate your gRPC stubs. Well, that's true as long as you are using Visual Studio to generate your C# stubs. In this case, we will generate our stubs in TypeScript (Angular as a reminder uses TypeScript as programming language, so let's take advantage of it), and the only way to do so is to run the command manually in a command prompt.

Download the Correct Version of Protoc and Protobuf Well-Known Types

Download the latest version of Protoc here: `https://github.com/protocolbuffers/protobuf/releases`. As of this writing, the latest version is 3.19.3. Choose the appropriate download file for your operating system, Linux, Windows, or macOS. For my part, I am using 64-bit Windows, so I downloaded the win64.zip Protoc file. You also need to download the `protobufs-all` `.zip` or `.gz` file depending on your operating system. Then locate the folder `google/protobuf` and copy and paste it somewhere in your hard disk; I chose to paste directly at the root on the C: drive in a folder named itself `Protobufs`. This folder contains Protobuf *Well-Known Types* (previously introduced in Chapter 4). While compiling our Protobufs to TypeScript, we must notify Protoc of the location of these types, unlike with C# in Visual Studio; with the latter (with Protoc and the C# plug-in that is used), there is no need to specify where these files are. Protoc knows where to find them. As a reminder from Chapter 4, these files are

- `any.proto`

- `duration.proto`

- `empty.proto`

- `struct.proto`

- `timestamp.proto`

- `wrappers.proto`

Figure 12-1 shows `.zip` or `.gz` files to download, you won't need to download their JavaScript version pointed with the red arrow if you are using TypeScript, but needed if you want to use JavaScript.

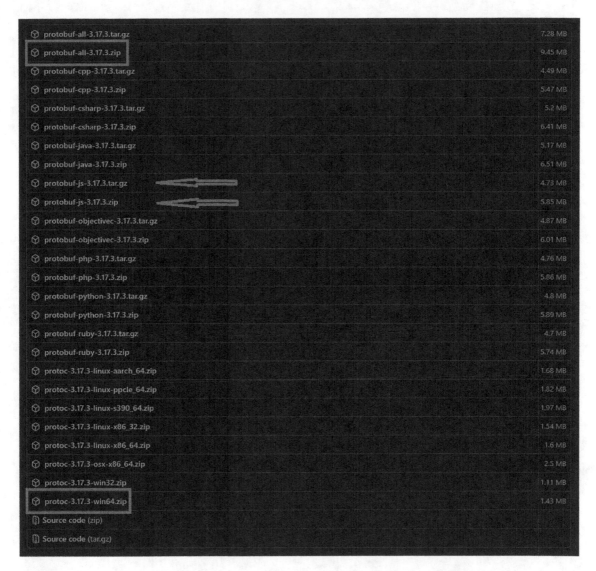

Figure 12-1. *Download the* win64 *version of Protoc if you are using 64-bit Windows*

Figure 12-2 shows, for example, the any.proto file stored in the C:\Protobufs\ google\protobuf folder.

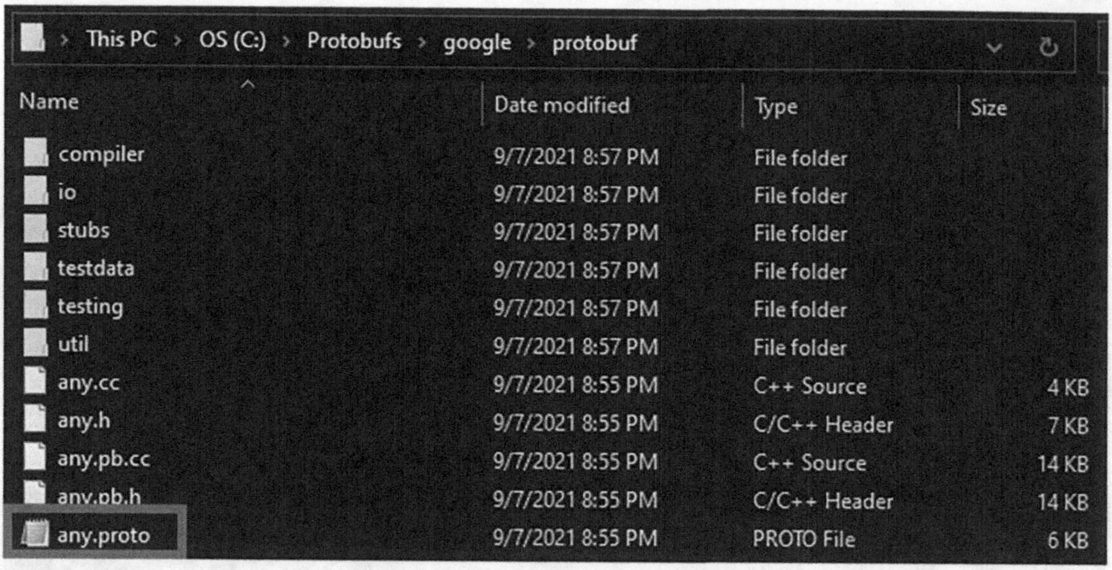

Name	Date modified	Type	Size
compiler	9/7/2021 8:57 PM	File folder	
io	9/7/2021 8:57 PM	File folder	
stubs	9/7/2021 8:57 PM	File folder	
testdata	9/7/2021 8:57 PM	File folder	
testing	9/7/2021 8:57 PM	File folder	
util	9/7/2021 8:57 PM	File folder	
any.cc	9/7/2021 8:55 PM	C++ Source	4 KB
any.h	9/7/2021 8:55 PM	C/C++ Header	7 KB
any.pb.cc	9/7/2021 8:55 PM	C++ Source	14 KB
any.pb.h	9/7/2021 8:55 PM	C/C++ Header	14 KB
any.proto	9/7/2021 8:55 PM	PROTO File	6 KB

This PC > OS (C:) > Protobufs > google > protobuf

Figure 12-2. *The any.proto file stored in C:\Protobufs\google\protobuf folder*

In Figure 12-1, you may have also have noticed the two arrows pointing to the Linux and Windows versions of Protoc (protobuf.js), allowing you to generate stubs in JavaScript. I suggest you download one of them if you plan to use JavaScript only in your projects; otherwise, download the generic version of Protoc for our Angular project, because the JavaScript version cannot generate stubs in TypeScript. To create the TypeScript stubs, we must use the generic version of Protoc, to which we will add a plug-in to achieve our ends. I suggest registering Protoc in the Windows Path variable (Environment Variables) to make your life easier. You'll be able to invoke Protoc from its name instead of from its absolute path. Figure 12-3 shows the flow from the System Properties panel to the Windows Path variable.

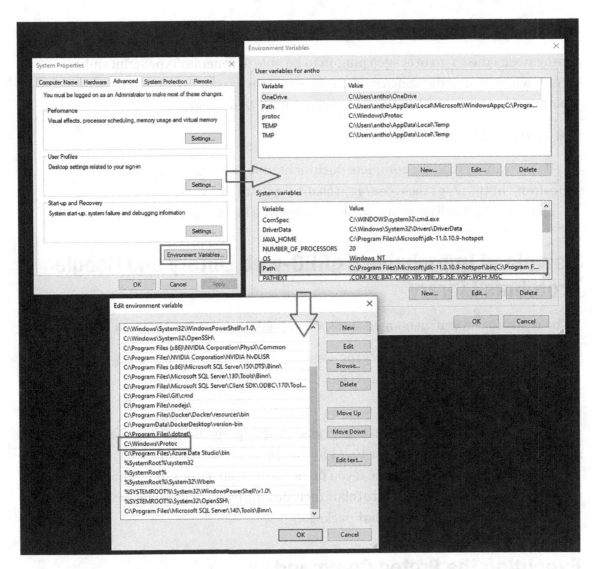

Figure 12-3. *Registering Protoc in the Windows Path variable*

Note   By registering Protoc like this, you will not interfere with the version of Protoc that Visual Studio uses when compiling a gRPC project. Visual Studio uses its version.

Download the ts-protoc-gen Plug-in

Protoc needs the `ts-protoc-gen` plug-in to be able to generate TypeScript stubs. After having created the skeleton of the Angular app by your own, named `CountryWiki.Angular`, download the following NPM package:

```
npm install ts-protoc-gen
```

If you want to read the complete documentation of this package, visit the GitHub repository: `https://github.com/improbable-eng/ts-protoc-gen`.

Don't worry, I will show you to use it correctly a bit later in this chapter.

Download Improbable's gRPC-web Library and Google Protobufs Library

To be ready to use your generated stubs, download the following NPM packages:

```
npm install @improbable-eng/grpc-web
npm install @types/google-protobuf
npm install google-protobuf
```

You guessed it, `@improbable-eng/grpc-web` is Improbable's gRPC-web client that I suggested you choose in Chapter 10. As for the `google-protobuf` package, it allows you to serialize/deserialize messages. If you do not download it, the gRPC-web client will not work. Finally, `@types/google-protobuf` includes the typed definitions for TypeScript of the classes in the `google-protobuf` package.

Executing the Protoc Command

For this project we will reuse the same Protobuf files for browsers as in Chapter 11 (i.e., the `country.browser.proto` and `country.shared.proto` files), which I advise you to put in a `protos` directory with the subdirectory `v1`; even though it's a simple Angular/TypeScript project, I like to structure my directories and files properly. Figure 12-4 shows the files arranged in the `protos/v1` folder.

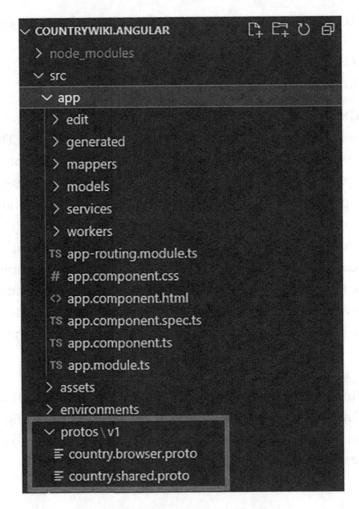

Figure 12-4. *Storing Protobuf files in* `protos/v1` *folder*

As you can see in Figure 12-4, I have also created other folders to store our code. I will explain them as we progress through the project.

Let's focus on the `generated` folder for now. This folder will contain all stubs generated by Protoc. To generate stubs in this folder, execute the following command in a terminal—for example, the Visual Studio Code Terminal—from the `src` project folder:

```
protoc --plugin=protoc-gen-ts="{ABSOLUTE_PATH}/node_modules/.bin/
protoc-gen-ts.cmd"
--js_out="import_style=commonjs,binary:./app/generated"
```

```
--ts_out="service=grpc-web:./app/generated" country.browser.proto country.
shared.proto
--proto_path="{ABSOLUTE_PATH}/src/protos/v1"
--proto_path="C:/Protobufs"
```

ABSOLUTE_PATH is the absolute path of the node_modules and the Protobuf files. This path must be absolute on Windows. On Linux, it could be relative. The path that contains the protoc-gen-ts file plug-in must include the .cmd extension on Windows because protoc-gen-ts on this operating system is a CMD file. On Linux, no extension is necessary. ./app/generated is the folder in which stubs will be generated. Make sure that before you execute the command, the generated folder *already exists*, because Protoc *won't create it* if it doesn't exist. Then separate by a space all your Protobuf files that you want to compile (even files to be included in others). For example, we need Protoc to compile the country.shared.proto file even though it's included in the country.browser.proto file. This is *mandatory* because if you don't add the country. shared.proto file into the compilation command, generated stubs *won't compile*. They require references to that file.

Finally, there are two --proto_path directives: the first one (src/protos/v1) tells Protoc where to find Protobufs to compile, and the second one (C:/Protobufs) tells Protoc where to find Well-Known Type Protobuf files. If you are not using any Well-Known Types, you don't need to add their path in the command. The command should properly generate stubs, as shown in Figure 12-5.

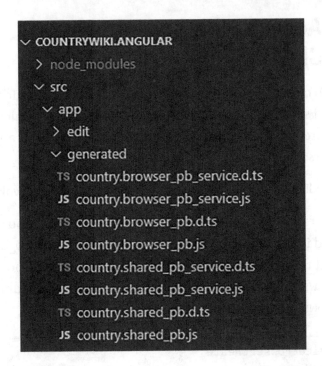

Figure 12-5. *Generated stubs*

Each Protobuf file added to the compilation will cause the generation of the following files:

- {ProtobufName}_pb_services.d.ts: The TypeScript definition of the {ProtobufName} client

- {ProtobufName}_pb_services.js: The JavaScript implementation of the {ProtobufName} client

- {ProtobufName}_pb.d.ts: The TypeScript definition of the {ProtobufName} messages

- {ProtobufName}_pb.js: The JavaScript implementation of the {ProtobufName} messages

In the case of the country.shared.proto file, which contains only messages, the country.shared_pb.d.ts and country.shared_pb_service.d.ts files will be empty.

Once the files have been generated, I can assure you the most complex task has been done. Consuming the generated clients will be straightforward with the Improbable library, and I will show you that in the next section.

Write Data Access with Improbable's gRPC-web Client

Writing a gRPC-web client is easy. Improbable offers a generic function for managing both unary calls and server streaming, the `grpc.invoke` method, which is called statically (it takes care of internally instantiating a gRPC-web client) and takes the following parameters:

`grpc.invoke(methodDescriptor: MethodDescriptor, props: InvokeRpcOptions)`

The `MethodDescriptor` is the TypeScript definition of the method you want to invoke. This method is defined in the generated `{ProtobufName}_pb_services.d.ts` file. It's a property of the gRPC-web service definition. Figure 12-6 shows the `CountryServiceBrowser`, its RPC function definitions, and, as an example, the `CountryServiceBrowserCreate` RPC definition highlighted.

```
type CountryServiceBrowserCreate = {
  readonly methodName: string;
  readonly service: typeof CountryServiceBrowser;
  readonly requestStream: false;
  readonly responseStream: true;
  readonly requestType: typeof country_shared_pb.CountriesCreationRequest;
  readonly responseType: typeof country_shared_pb.CountryCreationReply;
};

export class CountryServiceBrowser {
  static readonly serviceName: string;
  static readonly GetAll: CountryServiceBrowserGetAll;
  static readonly Get: CountryServiceBrowserGet;
  static readonly Update: CountryServiceBrowserUpdate;
  static readonly Delete: CountryServiceBrowserDelete;
  static readonly Create: CountryServiceBrowserCreate;
}
```

Figure 12-6. *The* `CountryServiceBrowser` *and its definition with the* `CountryServiceBrowserCreate` *RPC function definition example*

If you want to invoke the `CountryServiceBrowserCreate` RPC function, the `MethodDescriptor` parameter value will be `CountryServiceBrowser.Create`.

The second parameter, `InvokeRpcOptions`, has the following properties:

- `host`, which is a string representing the server URI; for example, `https://localhost:5001`.

- `request`, the Protobuf message to send to the server; for example, `new Empty()`.

- `metadata`, Trailers to be sent to the server; for example, `new grpc.Metadata({"TrailerKey": "TrailerValue"})`.

- `onHeaders`, a callback that handles Headers received from the server; for example, `(headers: grpc.Metadata) => { const headersValue = headers.get("HeaderKey"); }`.

- `onMessage`, a callback that handles messages received from the server; for example, `(countryReply: CountryReply) => { const country = countryReply.toObject(); }`. Note that any message received from the server needs to be deserialized with the `ToObject` method, which is defined in every message definition. This callback is invoked once in a unary call, and invoked each time a message is received in the case of a server-streaming call.

- `onEnd`, a callback that is invoked at the end of the call and allows to handle the response from the server like the gRPC status, Trailers, and any string message; for example, `(code: grpc.Code, msg: string | undefined, trailers: grpc.Metadata, endMessage: String) => { if (code !== grpc.Code.OK) { ... } else { ... } }`.

- `transport`, which is optional and allows to send browsers cookies to the server along with the cross-origin requests; for example, `grpc.CrossBrowserHttpTransport({ withCredentials: true });`. The `transport` property won't be used in this chapter, so if you want to learn more about it, you can read the following documentation: `https://github.com/improbable-eng/grpc-web/blob/master/client/grpc-web/docs/transport.md`.

- `debug`, which is optional and allows the client to print debug information in the browser's debug console.

Note that the grpc.invoke() method returns an object named Request that contains a method named close. Invoking that method, like the following, will *close* the connection to the server and *cancel* the request:

```
const request = grpc.invoke(…, …);
request.close()
```

Listing 12-1 shows the CountryService.ts file implementing the CountryService which is injectable, by dependency injection, in any Angular component.

Listing 12-1. The CountryService Implementation

```
import { grpc } from "@improbable-eng/grpc-web";
import { Empty } from "google-protobuf/google/protobuf/empty_pb";
import { CountryServiceBrowser } from "../generated/country.browser_pb_
service";
import { CountriesCreationRequest, CountryCreationReply, CountryIdRequest,
CountryReply, CountryUpdateRequest } from "../generated/country.shared_pb";
import { CountryCreationModelMapper } from "../mappers/
countryCreationModelMapper";
import { CountryReplyMapper } from "../mappers/countryReplyMapper";
import { CountryCreationModel } from "../models/countryCreationModel";
import { CountryModel } from "../models/countryModel";
import { environment } from '../../environments/environment';
import { Injectable } from "@angular/core";
import { CountryUpdateModel } from "../models/countryUpdateModel";
import { UploadResultModel } from "../models/uploadResultModel";

@Injectable()
export class CountryService {
  public GetAll(countries: CountryModel[]): void {
    grpc.invoke(CountryServiceBrowser.GetAll, {
      request: new Empty(),
      host: environment.host,
      onMessage: (countryReply: CountryReply) => {
        let country = new CountryModel();
        CountryReplyMapper.Map(country, countryReply.toObject())
```

```
      countries.push(country);
    },
    onEnd: (code: grpc.Code, msg: string | undefined, trailers:
    grpc.Metadata) => this.onEnd(code, msg, trailers, "All countries
    have been downloaded")
  });
}

public Create(countriesToCreate: CountryCreationModel[], uploadResult:
UploadResultModel, callback: Function): void {
    let countriesCreationRequest = new CountriesCreationRequest();
    CountryCreationModelMapper.Maps(countriesCreationRequest,
    countriesToCreate);
    grpc.invoke(CountryServiceBrowser.Create, {
      request: countriesCreationRequest,
      host: environment.host,
      onEnd: (code: grpc.Code, msg: string | undefined, trailers: grpc.
      Metadata) => {
        uploadResult.isProcessing = false;
        callback();
        this.onEnd(code, msg, trailers, "All countries have been
        created")
      }
    });
}

public Delete(id: number): void {
  let request = new CountryIdRequest();
  request.setId(id);
  grpc.invoke(CountryServiceBrowser.Delete, {
    request: request,
    host: environment.host,
    onEnd: (code: grpc.Code, msg: string | undefined, trailers: grpc.
    Metadata) => this.onEnd(code, msg, trailers, 'Country with Id ${id}
    has been deleted')
  });
}
```

```
public Get(id: number, country: CountryModel): void {
  let request = new CountryIdRequest();
  request.setId(id);
  grpc.invoke(CountryServiceBrowser.Get, {
    request: request,
    host: environment.host,
    onMessage: (countryReply: CountryReply) => {
      CountryReplyMapper.Map(country, countryReply.toObject());
    },
    onEnd: (code: grpc.Code, msg: string | undefined, trailers: grpc.
    Metadata) => this.onEnd(code, msg, trailers, 'Country with Id ${id}
    was successfully found')
  });
}

public Update(countryUpdateModel: CountryUpdateModel): void {
  let request = new CountryUpdateRequest();
  request.setId(countryUpdateModel.id);
  request.setDescription(countryUpdateModel.description);
  grpc.invoke(CountryServiceBrowser.Update, {
    request: request,
    host: environment.host,
    onEnd: (code: grpc.Code, msg: string | undefined, trailers: grpc.
    Metadata) => this.onEnd(code, msg, trailers, 'Country with Id
    ${countryUpdateModel.id} was successfully updated')
  });
}

private onEnd(code: grpc.Code, msg: string | undefined, trailers: grpc.
Metadata, endMessage: String): void  {
  if (code == grpc.Code.OK) {
    console.log(endMessage)
  } else {
    console.log('Hit an error status: ${grpc.Code[code]}');
    if (msg) {
      console.log('message: ${msg}');
    }
```

```
    trailers.forEach(trailer => {
      console.log('With the trailer ${trailer}: ${trailers.
      get(trailer)}');
    });
  }
}
```

The code is pretty straightforward, but I'll explain each function. First, I have implemented a generic onEnd method that performs logging and takes as a parameter a logging message and the gRPC status, Trailers, and a string message received from the server. This onEnd method does the same in every service method. That's the reason why I have created a generic one that is reused on every services below.

- GetAll() takes as a parameter an array of CountryModel. Because the grpc.invoke method doesn't return any message, we must pass an array by reference filled in the onMessage method. Remember, arrays are reference types. I used there a static mapper CountryReplyMapper.Map that maps the CountryReply message to a CountryModel. I'll show you a bit further its signature.

- Create() takes as a parameter an array of CountryCreationModel, which represents countries to be sent to the server. It also takes a UploadResultModel, filled by reference on the onEnd method, and will indicate that the upload is done. The third parameter, a Function, will be executed in the onEnd method and act as a callback once the upload is done. I'll give you more details further. The static method CountryCreationModelMapper.Maps will map the array of CountryCreationModel to an instance of CountriesCreationRequest.

- Delete() takes as a parameter an Id, a country Id that will be sent to the server. From this Id will be instantiated a CountryIdRequest object. As you have probably noticed, the latter is a Protobuf message and exposes set{property} methods for each property to be set in the message. Here setId allows setting the Id property of the CountryIdRequest.

- Get() takes as a parameter the country's Id to retrieve, and a CountryModel filled by reference. The same principle as before applies here to set the CountryIdRequest message. The static CountryReplyMapper.Map method maps the CountryReplyModel object to the CountryModel object passed by reference.

- Update() takes as a parameter a CountryUpdateModel object to be mapped to a CountryUpdateRequest message in the same manner as described previously.

Let's take a look at models used in this CountryService. Listing 12-2 shows the UploadResultModel class used by the Create() method. The latter inherits from the ActionResultModel, which contains data (the boolean success and the string errorMessage properties) necessary to report the state of an action performed by the user within the app. UploadResultModel is more specific by adding the payload property, which will contain the data uploaded (array of CountryCreationModel object) from a file, and the boolean isProcessing property that will indicate whether the data upload is ongoing or not. Note that dependencies like CountryCreationModel and ActionResultModel are described further following Listing 12-2.

Listing 12-2. The UploadResultModel Class

```
import { ActionResultModel } from "./actionResultModel";
import { CountryCreationModel } from "./countryCreationModel";

export class UploadResultModel extends ActionResultModel {
    payload: CountryCreationModel[];
    isProcessing: boolean;
}
```

Listing 12-3 shows the ActionResultModel class that the UploadResultModel class inherits from.

Listing 12-3. The ActionResultModel Class

```
export class ActionResultModel {
    success: boolean;
    errorMessage: String;
}
```

Listing 12-4 and Listing 12-5 show, respectively, the CountryModel class and the UpdateCountryModel class used by the CountryService class.

Listing 12-4. The CountryModel Class

```
export class CountryModel {
    id: number;
    name: String;
    description: String;
    capitalCity: String;
    anthem: String;
    languages: String[];
    flagUri: String;
}
```

Listing 12-5. The UpdateCountryModel Class

```
export class CountryUpdateModel {
    id: number;
    description: string
}
```

Now let's take a look at something really "hot." Remember, I have used in the CountryService class the CountryCreationService class that represents countries to be created from a JSON file. This class has a particular behavior. While writing this chapter, I discovered an excellent TypeScript library allowing data validation to fill the CountryCreationModel object. I decided to include that library in this chapter because I found it exciting to use (and very practical). This library is named ts-json-object and can be download with the following command:

```
npm install ts-json-object
```

This library in an effortless way. The ts-json-object library allows you to add annotations on the declaration of your property, such as, for example, indicate that your property is mandatory. Otherwise, the instantiation of the object you want to fill will fail. For all of this to work, the CountryCreationModel class must inherit from the JSONObject class. The latter creates a particular constructor of the CountryCreationModel class that takes as a parameter an anonymous object that will be mapped to the properties you want to fill. Listing 12-6 shows the CountryCreationModel class with required type annotations.

Listing 12-6. The CountryCreationModel Class and Its Annotations

```
import {JSONObject} from 'ts-json-object'

export class CountryCreationModel extends JSONObject {
    @JSONObject.required
    name: string;

    @JSONObject.required
    description: string;

    @JSONObject.required
    capitalCity: string;

    @JSONObject.required
    anthem: string;

    @JSONObject.required
    flagUri: string;

    @JSONObject.required
    languages: number[];
}
```

For example, if the description and/or any other property is missing, it will raise an exception. It means that the validation will be performed at the instantiation of the CountryCreationModel class. Listing 12-7 shows the missing properties while instantiating the CountryCreationMode class.

Listing 12-7. Instantiating a CountryCreationModel Object with Missing Properties

```
var countryCreationModel = new CountryCreationModel({"name":"Canada",
capitalCity:"Ottawa", "anthem":"Oh Canada !"}); // raises exception
```

To finish with the data access, Listing 12-8 and Listing 12-9 show, respectively, the static mapper classes CountryCreationMapper and CountryReplyMapper. They are pretty straightforward. That's why I haven't added more comments here.

Listing 12-8. The CountryCreationMapper Class

```
import { CountriesCreationRequest, CountryCreationRequest } from "../
generated/country.shared_pb";
import { CountryCreationModel } from "../models/countryCreationModel";

export class CountryCreationModelMapper {
    public static Map(countryCreationRequest: CountryCreationRequest,
    countryCreationModel: CountryCreationModel) {
        if(!countryCreationModel)
            return;

    countryCreationRequest.setName(countryCreationModel.name);
    countryCreationRequest.setDescription(countryCreationModel.
    description);
    countryCreationRequest.setAnthem(countryCreationModel.anthem);
    countryCreationRequest.setCapitalcity(countryCreationModel.
    capitalCity);
    countryCreationRequest.setFlaguri(countryCreationModel.flagUri);
    countryCreationRequest.setLanguagesList(countryCreationModel.
    languages);
    }

    public static Maps(countriesCreationRequest: CountriesCreationRequest,
    countriesCreationModel: CountryCreationModel[]) {
        if(!countriesCreationModel)
            return;

        countriesCreationModel.map(x => {
            let countryCreationRequest = new CountryCreationRequest();
            CountryCreationModelMapper.Map(countryCreationRequest, x)
            countriesCreationrequest.addCountries(countryCreation
            Request);
        });
    }
}
```

Listing 12-9. The CountryReplyMapper Class

```
import { CountryReply } from "../generated/country.shared_pb";
import { CountryModel } from "../models/countryModel";

export class CountryReplyMapper {
    public static Map(country: CountryModel, countryReply:
    CountryReply.AsObject) {
        if (country === null || countryReply === null)
        return;

        country.id = countryReply.id;
        country.name = countryReply.name;
        country.description = countryReply.description;
        country.capitalCity = countryReply.capitalcity;
        country.flagUri = countryReply.flaguri;
        country.anthem = countryReply.anthem;
        country.languages = countryReply.languagesList;
    }
}
```

We are now ready to manage data over a gRPC-web service and focus on the upload file form and the Web Worker to validate uploaded data.

Upload a Data File and Display Data with TypeScript, a Web Worker, and gRPC-web

Let's start by writing our HTML form and an HTML table to display the countries of our wiki. The *app* component (`app.component.html` and `app.component.ts`) is the app's entry point, and this is where we will write our HTML. Note that the code I present will remain basic, as this is not a book devoted to Angular. This way, even if you are not an experienced practitioner of Angular, you can easily understand the code.

The first part of the HTML component is a simple form allowing the user to upload a JSON type file. The validation of the latter will be done in the TypeScript code managing this HTML form. An `onChange()` method will detect the uploaded file that the `onUpload()` function of the TypeScript code will then handle the file upload when the user clicks the Upload button. We then have two types of messages to display to the user. The first indicates whether the upload was successful or not, and the second shows whether the uploaded file is still being uploaded.

The second part of the component displays the list of countries in a table with all their properties and two buttons, one to modify a country and another to delete it.

Listing 12-10 shows the HTML part of the app component used to display the countries and upload a file to feed this list.

Listing 12-10. The `app.component.html` File

```html
<div class="text-center">
    <h1>CountryWiki.Angular</h1>
</div>

<div class="container mb-5 mt-5 text-center w-25">
    <h2>Upload countries (JSON only): </h2>
    <div class="mb-1 mt-1">
        <input class="form-control" type="file"
        (change)="onChange($event)" />
    </div>
    <div class="mb-1 mt-1">
        <button (click)="onUpload()"
                class="btn btn-success">
                Upload
        </button>
    </div>
    <div *ngIf="uploadResult !== null && !uploadResult.success" class="mb-2
    mt-2 text-danger">
        {{uploadResult.errorMessage}}
    </div>
    <div *ngIf="(uploadResult !== null && uploadResult.isProcessing) ||
    isUploading" class="mb-2 mt-2 text-center text-danger">
        <h2>A file upload is in progress...</h2>
    </div>
</div>
```

```html
<div class="container text-center">
    <table class="table">
    <thead>
        <tr>
            <th>ID</th>
            <th>Name</th>
            <th>Description</th>
            <th>Capital City</th>
            <th>Anthem</th>
            <th>Spoken languages</th>
            <th>Flag</th>
            <th>Edit</th>
            <th>Delete</th>
        </tr>
    </thead>
    <tbody>
        <tr *ngFor="let country of countries">
            <td>{{country.id}}</td>
            <td>{{country.name}}</td>
            <td>{{country.description}}</td>
            <td>{{country.capitalCity}}</td>
            <td>{{country.anthem}}</td>
            <td>{{country.languages.join(', ')}}</td>
            <td><img src="{{country.flagUri}}" alt="{{country.name}}"
            height="25" width="45" /></td>
            <td><button (click)="onUpdate(country.id)" class="btn btn-
            secondary">Update</button></td>
            <td><button (click)="onDelete(country)" class="btn btn-
            danger">Delete</button></td>
        </tr>
    </tbody>
    </table>
</div>

<router-outlet></router-outlet>
```

TypeScript code in the app component is quite simple too.

The ngOnInit() method feeds the country list when the component loads (recall that the property countries is filled by reference) and the onChange() method gets the uploaded file. The onUpdate method redirects simply to the edit component, while the onDelete() method removes a country with an automatic refresh (thanks to Angular data binding). The country list is updated without recalling the RPC GetAll endpoint, and a call to the server is saved, so the performance gain is significant server side. The onUpload() method retrieves the uploaded file and sends it to a Web Worker with the postMessage() method, which will validate and parse the file (we will come back to it a little later) and then will receive in return the status (which is an instance of the UploadResultModel) of the validation with the onmessage event as well as the list of countries parsed from the file ready to be sent to the server with gRPC-web. If the upload is a success, the list of countries will be refreshed with the callback passed to the Create() method of the CountryService service (which I've told you about before). This callback is finally a simple invocation of the GetAll() method of the CountryService service. Finally, the isProcessing (sending to the server) and isUploading (uploading the file) action statuses are updated. Note that the CountryService service is injected by dependency as the Angular framework allows it. Listing 12-11 shows the app.component.ts file implementation. Note that the project structure at the end of the section will show you where to place files. I created a folder by class responsibility: services, models, etc.

Listing 12-11. The app.component.ts File Implementation

```typescript
import { Component, OnChanges, OnInit, SimpleChanges } from
'@angular/core';
import { UploadResultModel } from './models/uploadResultModel';
import { CountryModel } from './models/countryModel';
import { CountryService } from './services/countryService';
import { Router } from '@angular/router';

@Component({
  selector: 'app-root',
  templateUrl: './app.component.html',
  styleUrls: ['./app.component.css']
})
```

```
export class AppComponent implements OnInit {
  public title = 'CountryWiki.Angular';
  public countries: CountryModel[] = [];
  public errorMessage: string = null;
  public uploadResult: UploadResultModel = null;
  public isUploading: boolean = false;
  private _file: File = null;

  constructor(private _countryService: CountryService,
  private _router: Router) {

  }

  public ngOnInit() {
    this._countryService.GetAll(this.countries);
  }

  public onChange(event: Event): void {
    const target = event.target as HTMLInputElement;
    this._file = (target.files as FileList)[0];
  }

  public onUpload(): void {
    this.isUploading = this._file != null;
    const worker = new Worker(new URL('./workers/upload-file.worker',
    import.meta.url));
    worker.onmessage = ({ data }) => {
      this.uploadResult = data;
      if (this.uploadResult.success) {
        this._countryService.Create(this.uploadResult.payload,
        this.uploadResult, () => {
          this.countries = [];
          this._countryService.GetAll(this.countries);
        });
      } else {
        this.uploadResult.isProcessing = false;
      }
```

```
    this.isUploading = false;
    this._router.navigate(['']);
  };
  worker.postMessage(this._file);
}

public onUpdate(id: number): void {
    this._router.navigate(['edit', id]);
}

public onDelete(country: CountryModel): void {
  this._countryService.Delete(country.id);
  this.countries = this.countries.filter(c => c !== country);
  }
}
```

Now, let's implement the Web Worker. We'll name it upload-file.worker.

As a reminder, the Web Worker reads the uploaded file asynchronously (the onloadend event is triggered once the file is entirely read), validates its format, and parses its content to return, if successful, a list of CountryCreationModel objects. Because the task can be long depending on the size of the file, it is preferable to use a Web Worker for this kind of task, which runs in the background and does not block the UI. This Web Worker also returns the correct error message when validating the content and format of the file. As I indicated previously, using ts-json-object requires error handling, which is why I encapsulate in a try/catch block the instantiation of the CountryCreationModel object, which could generate an exception if validation fails. Finally, are you wondering why we do not invoke the gRPC-web client here? Unfortunately, the gRPC-web client uses the Windows object to function, and the latter is inaccessible from a Web Worker. It's a shame, but we already deported a large part of the task (reading and parsing of the file) in the Web Worker, that is not bad. Listing 12-12 shows the implementation of the Web Worker.

Listing 12-12. The upload-file.worker.ts Implementation

```
/// <reference lib="webworker" />

import { CountryCreationModel } from "../models/countryCreationModel";
import { UploadResultModel } from "../models/uploadResultModel";

addEventListener('message', ({ data }) => {

  const file = data as File;
  const reader = new FileReader();
  let result:UploadResultModel = {
    success:false,
    errorMessage: "",
    payload: null,
    isProcessing: true
  };

  let ext = file.name.substr(file.name.lastIndexOf('.') + 1);

  if (ext === "json" && file.type === "application/json") {
      // Read the file
      reader.onloadend = e => {
        try{
          let content = JSON.parse(reader.result.toString());
          result.success = true;
          result.payload = (content as any[]).map(x => new
          CountryCreationModel(x));
        }
        catch {
          result.errorMessage = "Cannot parse the file or the file
          is empty";
        }
        finally {
          postMessage(result);
        }
      };
      reader.readAsText(file);
  }
```

```
  else {
    result.errorMessage = "Only JSON files are allowed";
    postMessage(result);
  }
});
```

If we execute this code as is and we try to upload a non-JSON file, the appropriate error message appears, as shown in Figure 12-7.

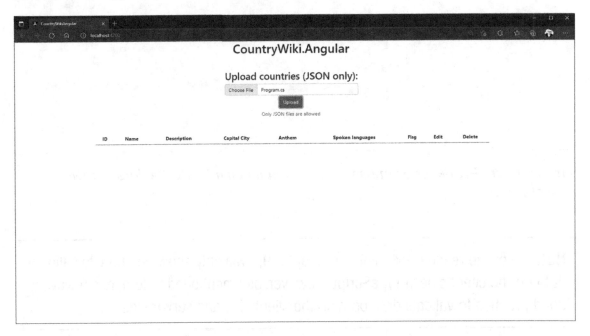

Figure 12-7. *Proper error message displayed when an attempt is made to upload a non-JSON file*

If a JSON file is uploaded but the JSON file schema is not as expected, the proper error message will appear, as shown in Figure 12-8.

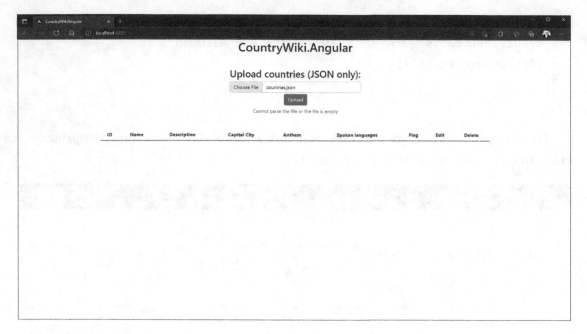

Figure 12-8. *Proper error message displayed when a JSON file doesn't meet expectations*

Note   For the reason I explained in Chapter 9, I will only show you how to validate data on the client side in TypeScript. However, as I mentioned before, it is always a good practice to validate data both on the client side and server side.

If the file meets the requirements, its data will be uploaded through gRPC-web, and the right message will be displayed, as shown in Figure 12-9.

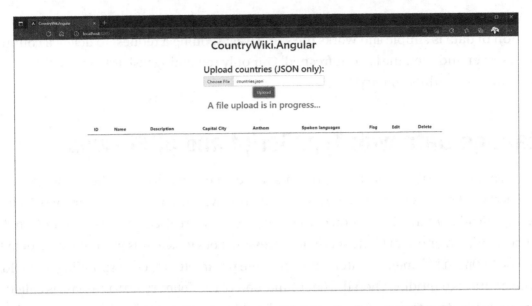

Figure 12-9. *Proper information message displayed when a JSON file is correctly being uploaded*

Then if no error occurs server side, the country list should appear as shown in Figure 12-10.

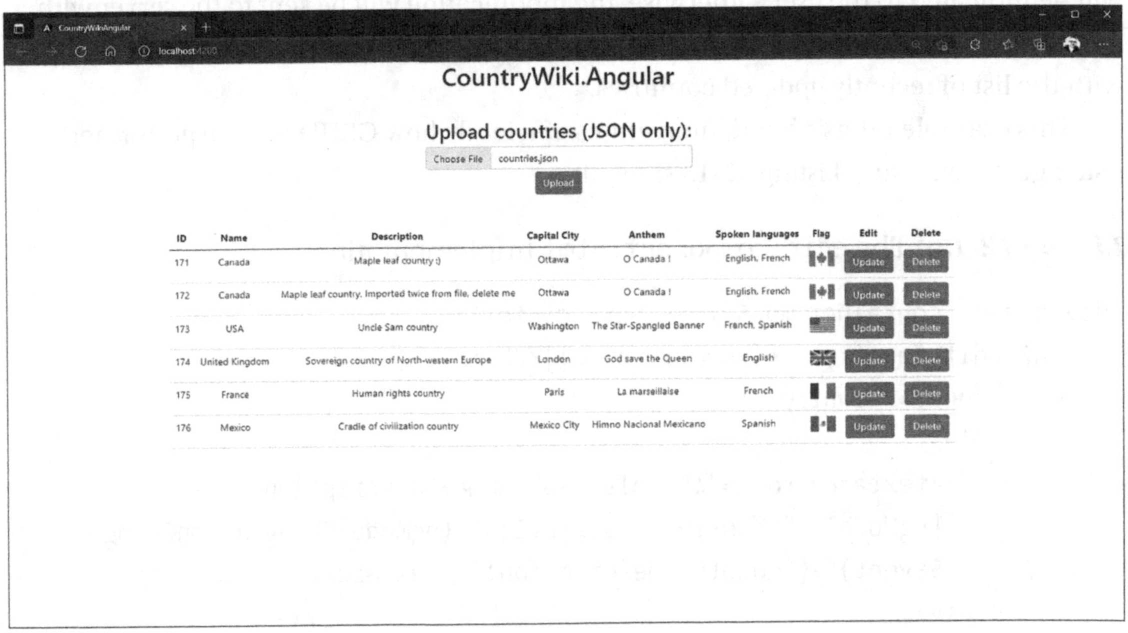

Figure 12-10. *Upload succeeds, and the country list is displayed correctly*

We managed with gRPC-web the sending and retrieval of data to the server. The deletion of data is simple and works the same way: sending a request to delete a country to the server and then the list is refreshed. Our only remaining task is to create the functionality to edit a country.

Manage Data with TypeScript and gRPC-web

Based on the same principle in the previous section, i.e., we will detect the elements modified on the edit component through JavaScript events. This edit component will allow the modification of the description of a country. Once the revised description is detected, it will be validated and sent to the server if successful. Let's look at this in a little more detail.

The ngOnInit() method intercepts the route parameter Id, corresponding to the Id of the country to modify. Then the Get() method of the CountryService class is called to retrieve the description of the country to be altered and is displayed in a text area in HTML. The onChange() method will detect the modifications made on the text area. The modification validation will be carried out with the onUpdate() method when the user clicks the Update button. This method validates if the description is a minimum of 20 characters and a maximum of 200 characters. If the validation fails, an error message will be indicated to the user. Otherwise, the modification will be sent to the server with the Update() method of the CountryService class. Finally, the page will be refreshed with the list of recently updated countries.

This example is basic but demonstrates efficiently how CRUD may be performed using gRPC-web, and Listing 12-13 shows it.

Listing 12-13. The edit.component.html Implementation

```html
<div class="container mb-5 mt-5 text-center">
    <h2>Edit Country - {{country.name}}</h2>
    <div *ngIf="country">
        <div>
            <textarea rows="4" cols="50" name="description"
            [ngModel]="country?.description" (ngModelChange)="onChange(
            $event)">{{country.description}}</textarea>
        </div>
        <div *ngIf="actionResult !== null && !actionResult.success"
        class="text-danger">
```

```
        {{actionResult.errorMessage}}
      </div>
      <div>
          <button (click)="onUpdate()">Update</button>
      </div>
    </div>
</div>
```

Listing 12-14 shows the TypeScript in the edit.component.ts file that manages the HTML code in Listing 12-13.

Listing 12-14. The edit.component.ts File Implementation

```typescript
import { Component, OnInit } from '@angular/core';
import { ActivatedRoute, Router } from "@angular/router";
import { ActionResultModel } from '../models/actionResultModel';
import { CountryModel } from '../models/countryModel';
import { CountryUpdateModel } from '../models/countryUpdateModel';
import { CountryService } from '../services/countryService';

@Component({
  selector: 'app-edit',
  templateUrl: './edit.component.html',
  styleUrls: ['./edit.component.css']
})
export class EditComponent implements OnInit {

  public country: CountryModel = new CountryModel();
  public actionResult: ActionResultModel = null;
  private static readonly _errorValidationMessage = "Description is must be
  between 20 and 200 characters";

  constructor(private _countryService: CountryService,
              private _route: ActivatedRoute,
              private _router: Router) {
  }
```

```
ngOnInit(): void {
  this._route.params.subscribe(p => {
    let id = p["id"] as number;
    this._countryService.Get(id, this.country);
  });
}

public onChange(event: Event): void {
  let description = event as unknown as string;
  this.country.description = description
}

public onUpdate(): void {
  if (this.country.description.length > 200 || this.country.description.
  length < 20) {
    this.actionResult = <ActionResultModel>({
      success: false,
      errorMessage: EditComponent._errorValidationMessage
    });
  }
  else {
    this.actionResult = <ActionResultModel>({
      success: true,
      errorMessage: ""
    });
    this._countryService.Update(<CountryUpdateModel>({
      id: this.country.id,
      description: this.country.description
    }));
    this._router.navigate(['']).then(() => {
      window.location.reload();
    });
  }
}
}
```

Pretty simple but efficient! I wanted to make it simple because, again, the goal here is not to teach you Angular but rather to give you more practice using gRPC-web with TypeScript and Angular and to demonstrate that it's not that complicated. Based on this project, you should be able to build a great application with Angular (or ReactJS or VueJS) and TypeScript.

Figure 12-11 shows the validation error message when updating the country description fails.

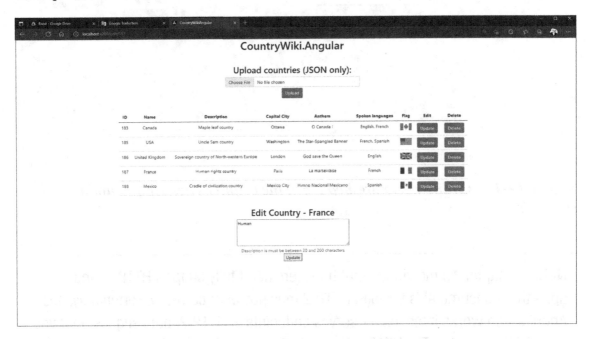

Figure 12-11. *Error message displayed when country's description validation fails*

When everything works as expected, the update request is sent to the server, and the country list is refreshed with updated data, as shown in Figure 12-12.

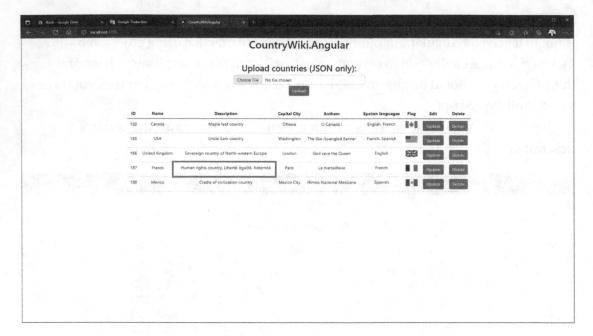

Figure 12-12. *Country list refreshed when the country's description update succeeds*

Note   Chapter 10 mentioned that browsers don't fully support HTTP/2, and apps that consume APIs through HTTP/2 may not work correctly. Fortunately, this Angular app works if the server serves endpoints in HTTP/2, but I suggest that you use HTTP/1 anyway. The HTTP/2 implementation in browsers is not complete. You might be faced with unintended behaviors.

If you have followed this tutorial correctly, the structure of your Country Wiki app will look like as shown in Figure 12-13.

Figure 12-13. Country Wiki app structure in an Angular project

It's up to you now to build a more extensive app based on these basic examples.

Summary

In this chapter I offered only basic CRUD operations to keep it simple so that everyone could understand gRPC-web and Angular. I tried to teach you here to generate the stubs in TypeScript and use the gRPC-web library. That was the main challenge here because, frankly, this chapter was the most complicated to write due to the lack of clear documentation for generating the TypeScript stubs with Protoc. However, I enjoyed writing this chapter a lot, and I hope you had the same pleasure reading it. Together we have gone off the beaten track, this chapter being a little different from the rest of this book, and I hope I made you want to use gRPC-web with TypeScript and SPA frameworks. I will meet you in the next chapter to talk about authentication management with OpenId Connect in ASP.NET Core gRPC.

PART V

Security

CHAPTER 13

Secure Your Application with OpenId Connect

I can't finish this book without talking to you about safety. Security is essential in an application, by which I mean that almost all applications need a mechanism to identify the user attempting to perform actions on your application. This is called authentication, which should not be confused with authorization, a mechanism allowing privileges to be given to an authenticated user—that is, allowing the user to perform specific actions that unauthorized users are not able to perform. In this chapter, you will learn how to do the following:

- Describe OpenId Connect

- Configure ASP.NET Core

- Use gRPCurl and gRPCui with a JWT

- Use a C# client with a JWT

- Use a gRPC-web client with a JWT

- Get user identity server side

Introduction to OpenId Connect

OpenId Connect is an identification standard that is layered on top of the OAuth 2.0 protocol, which is itself an authorization protocol. OpenId Connect works on the principle of delegating user authentication: with OpenId Connect, this responsibility is entrusted to a third-party service. The latter uses the protocol to ensure that the user is authenticated, so the application protected by OpenId Connect does not know how the authentication was performed.

© Anthony Giretti 2022
A. Giretti, *Beginning gRPC with ASP.NET Core 6*, https://doi.org/10.1007/978-1-4842-8008-9_13

Being completely independent of the application, this authentication system can be transverse and reused accross multiple applications to develop a single authentication. This is the very definition of the *single sign-on (SSO)* principle. We end up with an interaction between three actors:

1.   The client, which is a web app, for example

2.   The identity provider

3.   The protected resource

Figure 13-1 shows the relationship between the three actors.

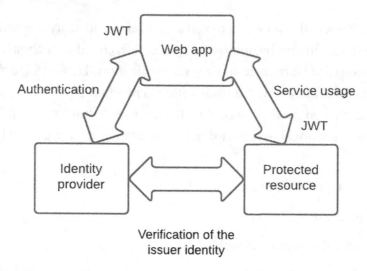

Figure 13-1. *The relationship between the three actors in OpenId Connect*

The client authenticates with the service provider, which issues a JSON Web Token (JWT) that is used to access the protected resource. This resource will validate the token received by retrieving the metadata from the identity provider to certify that the identify provider is the issuer of the JWT. Metadata is retrieved only once, and then the application can validate the JWT autonomously. A JWT is a JSON object accompanied by a signature and the reference to the key, which allows the signature to be verified. The whole is encoded in Base64, and dots separate the three parts. They are assembled as follows: the reference to the key, the JSON object, and then the signature. I will show you an example in the next section. An RFC standard describes JSON Web Token as an *Internet Engineering Task Force (IETF)* proposed standard (RFC 7519), and it can be found at this address: https://datatracker.ietf.org/doc/html/rfc7519.

This introduction is brief. The goal is not to teach you OpenId Connect in great detail but rather to help you understand the basic principle, the minimum, to allow you to use OpenId Connect as a means of authentication in ASP.NET Core. If you want to learn more about OpenId Connect, you can consult the official documentation for this protocol here: `https://openid.net/connect/`.

To configure ASP.NET Core with OpenId Connect, we must have an identity provider to achieve our ends. You may not know it, but a lot of applications use OpenId Connect, and I think you already know the most often used identity providers:

- Facebook

- Google

- Apple

- Microsoft (less frequently)

Figure 13-2 shows the `https://www.canva.com` website offering to authenticate with different providers.

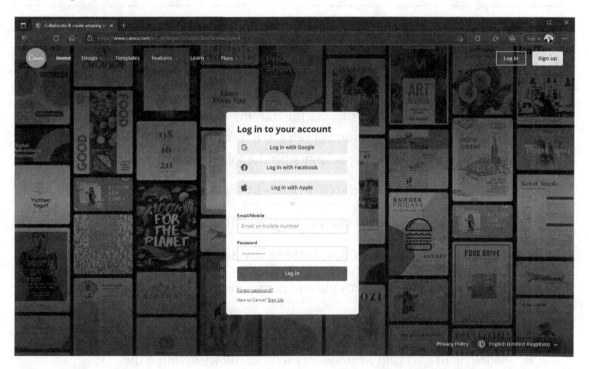

Figure 13-2. *Canva.com uses Google, Facebook, and Apple as OpenId Connect providers*

In the code samples in this chapter, I'll be using the Microsoft authentication platform based on Azure Active Directory. However, I will not go into details about its configuration. I will show you how to configure ASP.NET Core, and the authentication part will be up to you. Azure Active Directory and OpenId Connect are big pieces. To avoid losing the focus on the main subject, I invite you to learn more about the Microsoft identity platform here: `https://docs.microsoft.com/en-us/azure/active-directory/develop/active-directory-v2-protocols`. If you want to get things done quickly, you can follow my tutorial on setting up OpenId Connect on Microsoft Azure here: `https://anthonygiretti.com/2018/02/28/using-openidconnect-with-azure-ad-angular5-and-webapi-core-introduction/`.

Note   Along with this chapter, I will assume you could obtain the `access_token` JWT emitted from your provider, which is used as a bearer token. All my examples will show how to pass it to their respective client. I won't talk here about the `id_token` and the `refresh_token` either. These are explained in previous tutorials.

Configure ASP.NET Core

The configuration of a gRPC application in ASP.NET Core is strictly identical to any other ASP.NET Core configuration, regardless of the framework used concerning the validation of a token. The following configuration applies to a web API or other, for example. To get started, install the required NuGet package with the following command:

```
Install-Package Microsoft.AspNetCore.Authentication.JwtBearer
```

Then add the following `using` statement in your `GlobalUsings.cs` file:

```
global using Microsoft.AspNetCore.Authentication.JwtBearer;
```

Once done, go to the `Program.cs` file and configure and activate the authentication and authorization.

The configuration needs several lines of code:

- `AddAuthentication()` extension method: Allows defining the authentication based on a JWT by using the `JwtBearerDefaults.AuthenticationScheme` value.

- AddJwtBearer() extension method: Allows the setup of the *Authority*, which is the authentication server address, and *Audience*, which is the target application for which the JWT is emitted. Both of these values are supplied by the identity provider you have chosen. Then we will configure parameters used to validate the JWT: ValidateLifetime and ValidateIssuer, both of which are set to True, and Clockskew, which is used to manage the time gap between the JWT issuer and the application and will be set to 5 minutes. In other words, the latter allows a 5-minute gap between the JWT expiry Timestamp and the application, where the token lifetime is validated.

- AddAuthorization() extension method: Allows configuring authorization in ASP.NET Core by using the Authorize attribute.

The activation is only about adding two middlewares in the pipeline:

- UseAuthentication() extension method: Registers the *Authentication* middleware in the pipeline

- UseAuthorization() extension method: Activates the *Authorization* middleware in the pipeline

Both require being positioned after the UsersCors() and UseGrpcWeb() middlewares. Listing 13-1 shows the Program.cs file properly configured. *Authority* and *Audience* are partially hidden. They are specific to my Azure Active Directory tenant on Microsoft Azure. Note that I added the parameters in the code for demo purposes, but keep in mind the best practice is to add any configuration in the appsettings.json file as we did in Chapter 9 for the gRPC server Uri.

Listing 13-1. Configure and Activate OpenId Connect authentication and Authorization on ASP.NET Core

```
var builder = WebApplication.CreateBuilder(args);

// Add services to the container.
builder.Services.AddAuthentication(options =>
{
    options.DefaultAuthenticateScheme = JwtBearerDefaults.AuthenticationScheme;
    options.DefaultChallengeScheme = JwtBearerDefaults.AuthenticationScheme;
}).AddJwtBearer(options =>
```

```
{
    options.Authority = "https://login.microsoftonline.com/136544d9-xxxx-
    xxxx-xxxx-10accb370679/v2.0";
    options.Audience = "257b6c36-xxxx-xxxx-xxxx-6f2cd81cec43";
    options.TokenValidationParameters.ValidateLifetime = true;
    options.TokenValidationParameters.ValidateIssuer = true;
    options.TokenValidationParameters.ClockSkew = TimeSpan.FromMinutes(5);
});
builder.Services.AddAuthorization();

builder.Services.AddGrpc(options => {
    options.EnableDetailedErrors = true;
    options.MaxReceiveMessageSize = 6291456; // 6 MB
    options.MaxSendMessageSize = 6291456; // 6 MB
    options.CompressionProviders = new List<ICompressionProvider>
    {
        new BrotliCompressionProvider() // br
    };
    options.ResponseCompressionAlgorithm = "br"; // grpc-accept-encoding
    options.ResponseCompressionLevel = CompressionLevel.Optimal;
    // compression level used if not set on the provider
    options.Interceptors.Add<ExceptionInterceptor>();
    // Register custom ExceptionInterceptor interceptor
});
builder.Services.AddGrpcReflection();
builder.Services.AddScoped<ICountryRepository, CountryRepository>();
builder.Services.AddScoped<ICountryServices, CountryServices>();
builder.Services.AddSingleton<ProtoService>();
builder.Services.AddDbContext<CountryContext>(options => options.
UseSqlServer(builder.Configuration.GetConnectionString("CountryService")));
builder.Services.AddCors(o => o.AddPolicy("AllowAll", builder =>
{
    builder.AllowAnyOrigin()
            .AllowAnyMethod()
            .AllowAnyHeader()
            .WithExposedHeaders("Grpc-Status", "Grpc-Message",
            "Grpc-Encoding", "Grpc-Accept-Encoding");
```

```csharp
}));
builder.Services.AddHttpContextAccessor();

var app = builder.Build();

app.UseCors("AllowAll");
app.UseGrpcWeb(new GrpcWebOptions { DefaultEnabled = true });
app.MapGrpcReflectionService();
app.MapGrpcService<CountryGrpcService>();
app.MapGrpcService<CountryGrpcServiceBrowser>();

app.UseAuthentication();
app.UseAuthorization();

app.MapGet("/protos", (ProtoService protoService) =>
{
    return Results.Ok(protoService.GetAll());
});
app.MapGet("/protos/v{version:int}/{protoName}", (ProtoService
protoService, int version, string protoName) =>
{
    var filePath = protoService.Get(version, protoName);

    if (filePath != null)
        return Results.File(filePath);

    return Results.NotFound();
});
app.MapGet("/protos/v{version:int}/{protoName}/view", async (ProtoService
protoService, int version, string protoName) =>
{
    var text = await protoService.ViewAsync(version, protoName);

    if (!string.IsNullOrEmpty(text))
        return Results.Text(text);

    return Results.NotFound();
});

// Run the app
app.Run();
```

465

To apply authorization on your gRPC services, you'll need to add the Authorize attribute to your gRPC service class **OR** all/some methods. Using it on the class will enable authorization for all methods. Note that if you apply it on a class, you can still define methods as anonymous (no authentication required to access this code) by adding the AllowAnonymous attribute on it. If you intend to use the same authorization rule on each method, prefer adding the attribute to the class. It's possible to add the Authorize attribute to the class and one/several methods simultaneously. In this case, the method attribute will override the class attribute for this method. Listing 13-2 shows the Authorize attribute applied on the class, and specifically on the GetAll method, but with an extra parameter, Roles = "SuperAdmin", which tells ASP.NET Core to allow only authenticated users with the *SuperAdmin* role defined in the JWT. A nonauthenticated user will be denied any attempt to access these methods and will receive an UNAUTHENTICATED gRPC status. If the user is authenticated but doesn't have the SuperAdmin role with the token, the user will be denied and receive the PERMISSIONDENIED gRPC status.

Listing 13-2 shows the CountryGrpcService class protected from any nonauthenticated user, and its GetAll endpoint only allows authorized users with the SuperAdmin role.

Listing 13-2. The CountryGrpcService Protected with an Authorize Attribute

```
namespace CountryService.gRPC.Services;

[Authorize]
public class CountryGrpcService : CountryServiceBase
{
    private readonly ICountryServices _countryService;

    public CountryGrpcService(ICountryServices countryService)
    {
        _countryService = countryService;
    }

    [Authorize(Roles = "SuperAdmin")]
    public override async Task GetAll(Empty request, IServerStreamWriter
    <CountryReply> responseStream, ServerCallContext context)
```

```
{
    ...
}

public override async Task<CountryReply> Get(CountryIdRequest request,
ServerCallContext context)
{
    ...
}

public override async Task<Empty> Update(CountryUpdateRequest request,
ServerCallContext context)
{
    ...
}

public override async Task<Empty> Delete(CountryIdRequest request,
ServerCallContext context)
{
    ...
}

public override async Task Create(IAsyncStreamReader<CountryCreation
Request> requestStream, IServerStreamWriter<CountryCreationReply>
responseStream, ServerCallContext context)
{
    ...
}
}
```

This example is simple but allows you to do the necessary authentication and authorization in a gRPC application. More often, it is the write operations that require higher privileges with a particular role. I have shown you how to proceed. All you have to do is follow your organization's business rules to apply the proper criteria to protect your application. Before finishing with this introduction to OpenId Connect in ASP.NET Core, I would like to show you what a JWT looks like with a role assigned to user Anthony Giretti. First, generate a token, and then go to the https://jwt.io website to observe the content of your JWT. Figure 13-3 shows the JWT of my decoded provider.

Encoded PASTE A TOKEN HERE

Decoded EDIT THE PAYLOAD AND SECRET

eyJ0eXAiOiJKV1QiLCJhbGciOiJSUzI1NiIsIng
1dCI6Imwzc1EtNTBjQ0g0eEJWWkxIVEd3blNSNz
Y4MCIsImtpZCI6Imwzc1EtNTBjQ0g0eEJWWkxIV
Ed3blNSNzY4MCJ9.eyJhdWQiOiIyNTdiNmMzNi0
xMTY4LTRhYWMtYmU5My02ZjJjZDgxY2VjNDMiLC
Jpc3MiOiJodHRwczovL3N0cy53aW5kb3dzLm51d
C8xMzY1NDRkOS0wMzhlLTQ2NDYtYWZmZi0xMGFj
Y2IzNzA2NzkvIiwiaWF0IjoxNjMyNzQ3MTI3LCJ
uYmYiOjE2MzI3NDcxMjcsImV4cCI6MTYzMjc0OD
AyNywiYWlvIjoiQVZRQXEvOFRBQUFBZlZ0ZGM0K
0p6V2IrK1NFajJuVVFGSUduZEhWeW1pbW9UMkQ0
SDdwOEhiREZxN2JVMEhnQ1dTMFhKZFdpOGg0OWZ
JU090N0x2SEVHY21WdUxUY1piNmdQOFY3TDk0MG
JkclFRc0VqdkpLc1k9IiwiYW1yIjpbInB3ZCJdL
CJlbWFpbCI6ImFudGhvbnkuZ2lyZXR0aUBnbWFp
bC5jb20iLCJmYW1pbHlfbmFtZSI6IkdJUkVUVEk
iLCJnaXZlbl9uYW1lIjoiQW50aG9ueSIsImdyb3
VwcyI6WyI2Yzc4Y2Q2MC0xNmViLTQ2OTYtYWUyO
S04NGZlNzEzMzA1ZDQiLCI4MTE1ZTNiZS1hY2dh
LTQ4ODYtYTFlNi01YjZhYWY4MTBhOGYiLCJmYzE
5YTg2Mi02NDUyLTRlOTktOTlhMi04MjBhZmEzOW
NiZWUiLCIyYzM3MmQ5OC0xM2I2LTQwY2QtYjViM
i1mOTFmZTJlYzUxNjIiXSwiaWRwIjoibGl2ZS5j
b20iLCJpcGFkZHIiOiI3NC4xNS4yMjEuMzgiLCJ
uYW1lIjoiQW50aG9ueSBHSVJFVFRJIiwibm9uY2
UiOiIwZWY5NGI1NC1iY2MyLTQ0ZmYtYmJiZS05Z
jA2MTZhYmMwNWUiLCJvaWQiOiJmOTE3NWJjOC1i
N2VjLTRkOWYtOWI1My0yMGY2ODM2NmYyYzgiLCJ
yaCI6IjAuQVZnQTJVUmxFNDREUmthd194Q3N5em
NHZVRac2V5Vm9FYXhLdnBODkx0Z2M3RU5ZQUdrL
iIsInJvbGVzIjpbIlN1cnZleUNyZWF0b3IiXSwi
c3ViIjoiNDM3VmVqWnBzMVNqUnFaRXVHeWYtSEh
xQkZUMmdOdTRDS3p3OVllMGJHcyIsInRpZCI6Ij
EzNjU0NGQ5LTAzOGUtNDY0Ni1hZmZmLTEwYWNjY
jM3MDY3OSIsInVuaXF1ZV9uYW1lIjoibGl2ZS5j
b20jYW50aG9ueS5naXJldHRpQGdtYWlsLmNvbSI
sInV0aSI6InJBWFpFdmZaVxa2ZuMnpJRlk5QU
EiLCJ2ZXIiOiIxLjAifQ.Wg685GQEoPFdTk7ocP
iXkAfPQTFtqwwu7-

HEADER: ALGORITHM & TOKEN TYPE

{
  "typ": "JWT",
  "alg": "RS256",
  "x5t": "l3sQ-50cCH4xBVZLHTGwnSR7680",
  "kid": "l3sQ-50cCH4xBVZLHTGwnSR7680"
}

PAYLOAD: DATA

{
  "aud": "257b6c36-1168-4aac-be93-6f2cd81cec43",
  "iss": "https://sts.windows.net/136544d9-038e-4646-
afff-10accb370679/",
  "iat": 1632747127,
  "nbf": 1632747127,
  "exp": 1632748027,
  "aio":
"AVQAq/8TAAAAfVtdc4+JzWb++SEj2nUQFIGndHVymimoT2D4H7p8Hb
DFq7bU0HgCWS0XJdWi8h49fISOt7LvHEGcmVuLTcZb6gP8V7L940bdr
QQsEjvJKsY=",
  "amr": [
    "pwd"
  ],
  "email": "anthony.giretti@gmail.com",
  "family_name": "GIRETTI",
  "given_name": "Anthony",
  "groups": [
    "6c78cd60-16eb-4696-ae29-84fe713305d4",
    "8115e3be-ac7a-4886-a1e6-5b6aaf810a8f",
    "fc19a862-6452-4e99-99a2-820afa39cbee",
    "2c372d98-13b6-40cd-b5b2-f91fe2ec5162"
  ],
  "idp": "live.com",
  "ipaddr": "74.15.221.38",
  "name": "Anthony GIRETTI",
  "nonce": "0ef94b54-bcc2-44ff-bbbe-9f0616abc05e",
  "oid": "f9175bc8-b7ec-4d9f-9b53-20f68366f2c8",
  "rh":
"0.AVgA2URlE44DRkav_xCsyzcGeTZseyVoEaxKvpNvLNgc7ENYAGk.
",
  "roles": [
    "SurveyCreator"
  ],
  "sub": "437VejZps1SqRqZEuGyf-HHqBFT2gNu4CKzw9Ye0bGs",
  "tid": "136544d9-038e-4646-afff-10accb370679",
  "unique_name": "live.com#anthony.giretti@gmail.com",
  "uti": "rAXZEFvfZUqkfn2zIFY9AA",
  "ver": "1.0"
}

VERIFY SIGNATURE

Figure 13-3. *A JWT decoded on the* `https://jwt.io` *website*

As you can see, we find the information relating to the provider and the expiration date of the JWT in the first framed block, information on the user for whom the JWT was issued in the second framed block, and then follows the role(s) that the user has. So you might have understood, decoding your JWT will help you to debug your application if you have trouble with the expiration date of your JWT, if you are using the wrong audience, or if you are not using the roles correctly in your applications (or if you have improperly set up your JWTs with your identity provider).

In the next section, I'll show you how to pass the token into the header of the gRPC request with various clients.

Use gRPCurl and gRPCui with a JWT

If you recall from Chapter 5, I told you about two gRPC clients, gRPCui and gRPCurl, that enable you to run functions, but I only showed examples with anonymous calls. No authentication was required. In this section, I'll show you how to pass a JWT within requests.

gRPCurl

Let's start with gRPCurl. Figure 13-4 shows what happens if I execute the GetAll function without passing a token in the request.

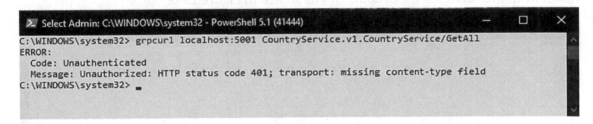

Figure 13-4. Invoke GetAll function without a JWT

As you can see, I do receive an UNAUTHENTICATED gRPC status. The ASP.NET Core framework warns me anyway that this is an Unauthorized (401) error. I guess that ASP. NET Core gRPC doesn't follow gRPC specs here because it should always return an HTTP 200 OK status no matter what.

Let's now add a JWT in the request to the same command as follows: -H "authorization: bearer {TOKEN}" It should produce an Unauthorized response because this JWT does not contain the expected role "SuperAdmin" as discussed in the previous section. Figure 13-5 shows the output of the command.

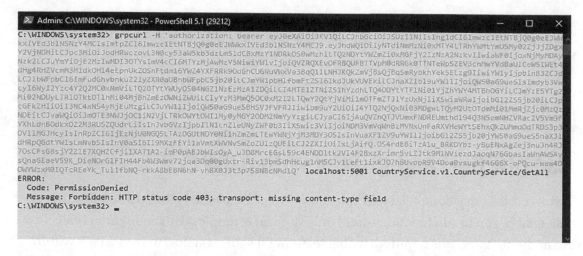

Figure 13-5. *Call GetAll endpoint with a JWT but missing the correct role "SuperAdmin"*

As expected, we received a PERMISSIONDENIED as grpc-status from the server, with an error message mentioning the access is Forbidden (403).

If now your JWT contains the correct role, the command should output the expected result from the service: a list of countries as shown in Figure 13-6.

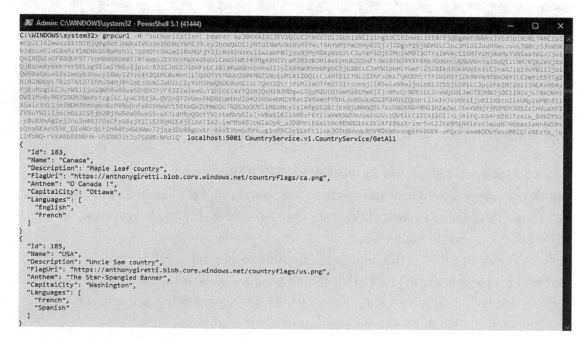

Figure 13-6. *Call GetAll endpoint with a JWT that contains the correct role*

By using this tutorial to add a JWT in the gRPCurl commands, you can do whatever you want now; you will no longer be limited in your actions if your gRPC service is protected with a JWT.

gRPCui

gRPCui is easier to use than gRPCurl because it's a GUI, and it also makes it easy to pass a JWT. But first, let's see what happens when the JWT is missing or when a JWT is passed in the request but without the proper role. Figures 13-7 and 13-8 show, respectively, those scenarios.

Figure 13-7. *Call* GetAll *endpoint without a JWT*

Figure 13-8. *Call* GetAll *endpoint with a JWT but without the proper role*

Logically, and it won't surprise you that we have the same errors we got using gRPCurl. Now let's see how to pass a JWT in the form provided for this purpose in the Request Metadata section. Figure 13-9 shows the first input used to define the name of the "authorization" metadata and its "bearer {TOKEN}" value.

Figure 13-9. *Fill Request Metadata form with the authorization header (metadata)*

If the JWT is valid and contains the correct role, no error should appear, and expected data should be displayed as shown in Figure 13-10.

Figure 13-10. *Call* GetAll *endpoint with a JWT with the proper role*

Use a C# Client with a JWT

Let's go back to C# and this time see how to pass a JWT into the request from a C# gRPC client.

First, I invite you to manage authentication errors; that is, manage UNAUTHENTICATED and PERMISSIONDENIED statuses. It is always valuable for correctly debugging authentication problems on the client side. Listing 13-3 shows how to use a token and pass it in the gRPC request by instantiating a Metadata object and adding the token with the "authorization" key and the "bearer {TOKEN}" value with the Add method. Listing 13-3 also shows how to handle errors with a try/catch block, using several catch statements, each involving a when statement allowing a particular filter to be applied on the exception. For example, we will discriminate according to the grpc-status; otherwise, handle the error more generically if it is not an authentication or authorization error.

Listing 13-3. Passing a JWT Through the Request and Managing Errors

```csharp
public async IAsyncEnumerable<CountryModel> GetAllAsync(string token)
{
    var list = new List<CountryModel>();
    try
    {
        var metadata = new Metadata();
        metadata.Add("authorization", $"bearer {token}");
        using var serverStreamingCall = _countryServiceClient.
        GetAll(new Empty(), metadata);
        while (await serverStreamingCall.ResponseStream.MoveNext())
        {
            list.Add(serverStreamingCall.ResponseStream.Current.
            ToDomain());
        }
    }
    catch (RpcException ex) when (ex.StatusCode == StatusCode.
    Unauthenticated)
            {
                    _logger.LogError(ex, "Token was missing or
                    invalid");
             }
            catch (RpcException ex) when (ex.StatusCode ==
            StatusCode.PermissionDenied)
            {
                    _logger.LogError(ex, "Token was valid but
                    missed particular role");
            }
    catch (RpcException ex)
            {
                    _logger.LogError(ex, "an error occurred");
            }
```

```
    foreach (var country in list)
    {
        yield return country;
    }
}
```

Figures 13-11 and 13-12 show, respectively, that an UNAUTHENTICATED error is issued when the token is missing and a PERMISSIONDENIED error is issued when the token misses a particular role.

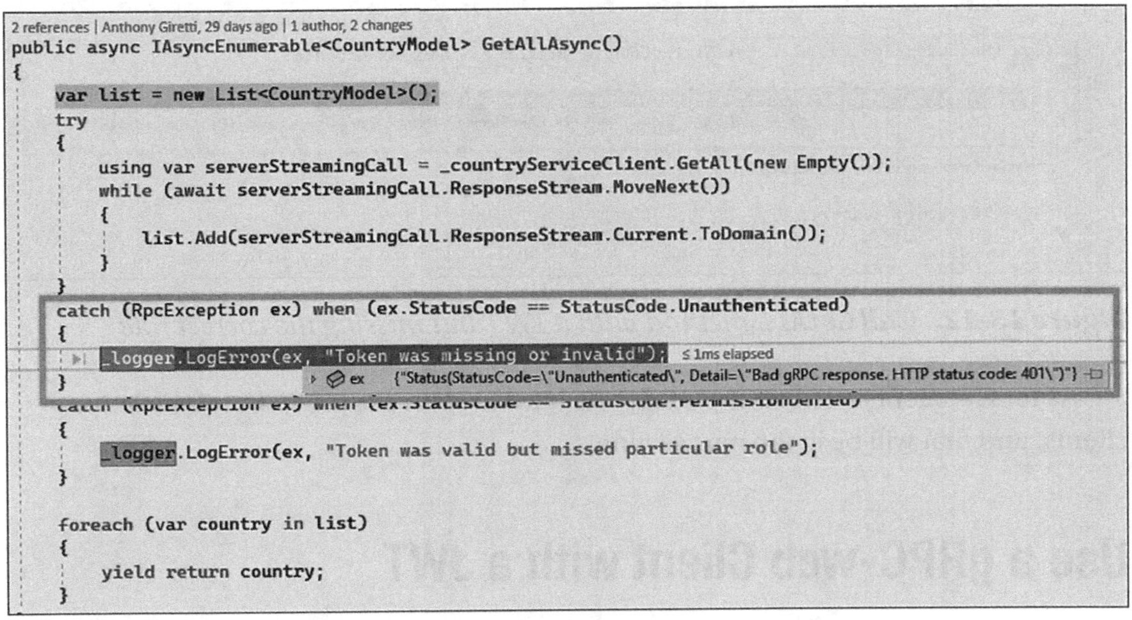

```
2 references | Anthony Giretti, 29 days ago | 1 author, 2 changes
public async IAsyncEnumerable<CountryModel> GetAllAsync()
{
    var list = new List<CountryModel>();
    try
    {
        using var serverStreamingCall = _countryServiceClient.GetAll(new Empty());
        while (await serverStreamingCall.ResponseStream.MoveNext())
        {
            list.Add(serverStreamingCall.ResponseStream.Current.ToDomain());
        }
    }
    catch (RpcException ex) when (ex.StatusCode == StatusCode.Unauthenticated)
    {
        _logger.LogError(ex, "Token was missing or invalid");  ≤1ms elapsed
    }                              ▸ ⊘ ex    {"Status(StatusCode=\"Unauthenticated\", Detail=\"Bad gRPC response. HTTP status code: 401\")"} ⊡
    catch (RpcException ex) when (ex.StatusCode == StatusCode.PermissionDenied)
    {
        _logger.LogError(ex, "Token was valid but missed particular role");
    }

    foreach (var country in list)
    {
        yield return country;
    }
}
```

Figure 13-11. *Call* GetAll() *method without a JWT*

```
0 references | 0 changes | 0 authors, 0 changes
public async IAsyncEnumerable<CountryModel> GetAllAsync(string token)
{
    var list = new List<CountryModel>();
    try
    {
        var metadata = new Metadata();
        metadata.Add("authorization", $"bearer {token}");
        using var serverStreamingCall = _countryServiceClient.GetAll(new Empty(), metadata);
        while (await serverStreamingCall.ResponseStream.MoveNext())
        {
            list.Add(serverStreamingCall.ResponseStream.Current.ToDomain());
        }
    }
    catch (RpcException ex) when (ex.StatusCode == StatusCode.Unauthenticated)
    {
        _logger.LogError(ex, "Token was missing or invalid");
    }
    catch (RpcException ex) when (ex.StatusCode == StatusCode.PermissionDenied)
    {
        _logger.LogError(ex, "Token was valid but missed particular role");    ≤ 1ms elapsed
    }                    ▶ ⊘ ex    {"Status(StatusCode=\"PermissionDenied\", Detail=\"Bad gRPC response. HTTP status code: 403\")"} ⊟

    foreach (var country in list)
    {
        yield return country;
    }
}
```

Figure 13-12. *Call* `GetAll` *method with a JWT but missing the correct role*

As for C # clients, you are also ready! We have to cover the gRPC-web TypeScript clients, and that will be in the next section!

Use a gRPC-web Client with a JWT

We've tried passing a token with almost any type of client. All that was missing was gRPC-web with TypeScript. So how does this work? Well, Improbable exposes a class of type grpc.Metadata that we will instantiate, then we will use its set method to create the same "authorization" header name, consistently with its value "bearer {TOKEN}" and, yes, it is always the same—fantastic, isn't it? Listing 13-4 shows how to create the header and pass it as a query parameter by setting up the metadata parameter.

Listing 13-4. Passing a JWT in a gRPC-web TypeScript Client

```
public GetAll(countries: CountryModel[], token: String): void {
    const metadata = new grpc.Metadata();
            metadata.set("authorization", 'bearer ${token}');
```

```
grpc.invoke(CountryServiceBrowser.GetAll, {
  request: new Empty(),
  host: environment.host,
  metadata: metadata,
  onMessage: (countryReply: CountryReply) => {
    let country = new CountryModel();
    CountryReplyMapper.Map(country, countryReply.toObject())
    countries.push(country);
  },
  onEnd: (code: grpc.Code, msg: string | undefined, trailers: grpc.
  Metadata) => this.onEnd(code, msg, trailers, "All countries have
  been downloaded")
});
}
```

Similar to the results shown in the previous sections, Figures 13-13 and 13-14 show, respectively, errors in the browser console when a JWT is missing or invalid or expired and when a valid JWT is passed but the required role is missing.

Figure 13-13. Call `GetAll` *method without a JWT*

Figure 13-14. Call GetAll *method with a JWT but missing the correct role*

There you go! We have used quite a few clients and played with the Authentication and Authorization with each one. We have one last point to cover: identifying the current user by accessing the HTTP context of the current gRPC request.

Get User Identity Server Side

To complete the loop, I will show you how to extract the HTTP context of a gRPC request (i.e., from its `ServerCallContext`, if you recall from Chapter 5). The HTTP context contains all the current request information, the headers, etc. but especially the authenticated user's information!

The line of code to extract the current user from the request is as follows:

```
var user = context.GetHttpContext().User;
```

Figure 13-15 shows the identity of the authenticating user through the `Identity` property of the `User` object.

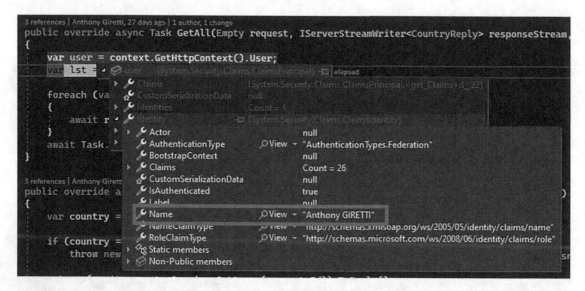

Figure 13-15. *Accessing the user identity*

The circle is finally closed!

Summary

We're done. This final chapter of the book has enabled us to revisit concepts that we have explored throughout this book, quickly and effectively. We have added a context of closer interaction with the user; that is, identifying users when they access the gRPC service. You have therefore learned everything you need to know about securing your application, and from here you can apply all the business rules as you wish to the application with an authenticated user. I am thinking in particular of the implementation of more refined logging when a user has higher privileges than others (the roles as we have seen); that is, log all the user actions on the application, even the critical ones with the elevated privilges that this user has. You can now put into practice what you have learned to build applications around gRPC! Thank you for reading this book until the end!

Index

A